Also by Paul Hendrickson

Seminary: A Search

*Looking for the Light: The Hidden Life and Art of
Marion Post Wolcott*

*The Living and the Dead: Robert McNamara and
Five Lives of a Lost War*

Sons of Mississippi

Sons of Mississippi

A Story of Race and Its Legacy

Paul Hendrickson

Alfred A. Knopf ◁▶ *New York 2003*

Copyright © 2003 by Paul Hendrickson
All rights reserved under International and Pan-American Copyright Conventions.
Published in the United States by Alfred A. Knopf, a division of Random House, Inc.,
New York, and simultaneously in Canada by Random House of Canada Limited, Toronto.
Distributed by Random House, Inc., New York.
www.aaknopf.com

Grateful acknowledgment is made to Ira Harkey for permission to reprint an excerpt from
The Smell of Burning Crosses by Ira Harkey. Reprinted by permission of the author.

Knopf, Borzoi Books, and the colophon are registered trademarks of Random House, Inc.

Library of Congress Cataloging-in-Publication Data
Hendrickson, Paul, 1944–
Sons of Mississippi : a story of race and its legacy / Paul Hendrickson.—1st ed.
p.   cm.
Includes bibliographical references and index.
ISBN 0-375-40461-9 (alk. paper)
1. Mississippi—Race relations.   2. Sheriffs—Mississippi—Attitudes—Case studies.
3. Sheriffs—Mississippi—Biography.   4. Sheriffs—Mississippi—Family relationships.
5. Whites—Mississippi—Attitudes—Case studies.   6. Whites—Mississippi—Biography.
7. Mississippi—Biography.   8. African Americans—Civil Rights—Mississippi—History.
9. Racism—Mississippi—Case studies.   10. Racism—United States—Case studies.   I. Title.
F350.A1 H46 2003
305.8'009762'09045—dc21   2002029857

Manufactured in the United States of America
First Edition

The author gratefully acknowledges the support of the John Simon Guggenheim
Memorial Foundation and the National Endowment for the Arts; both provided
writing fellowships for this work.

For Wil Haygood, who has shown me with his life

Make pictures from the very start, and you will feel what you need as you go along.

—Thomas Eakins, in a letter to Edmund C. Messer, July 3, 1906

Hopper's paintings are short, isolated moments of figuration that suggest the tone of what will follow just as they carry forward the tone of what preceded them. The tone but not the content. The implication but not the evidence. They are saturated with suggestion. . . . Our time with the painting must include— if we are self-aware—what the painting reveals about the nature of continuousness.

—Mark Strand on the work of Edward Hopper

1. Oxford, home of the University of Mississippi, integrated October 1, 1962, and where James Wesley Garrison was a deputy sheriff in 1962

2. Natchez, William T. Ferrell, sheriff, 1960–64, 1968–88

3. Greenwood, John Ed Cothran, sheriff, 1960–64

4. Money, site of Bryant's Grocery & Meat Market, entered by Emmett Till, August 24, 1955

5. Sumner, where Roy Bryant and J. W. Milam were acquitted for the Till murder

6. Pascagoula, James Ira Grimsley, sheriff, 1960–64

7. Hattiesburg, Bob Waller, sheriff, 1960–64

8. Port Gibson, Jim Middleton, sheriff, 1950–52, 1952–56, 1960–64

9. Pittsboro, John Henry Spencer, sheriff, 1960–64

10. Kosciusko, James Meredith's birthplace

11. Jackson, James Meredith's home

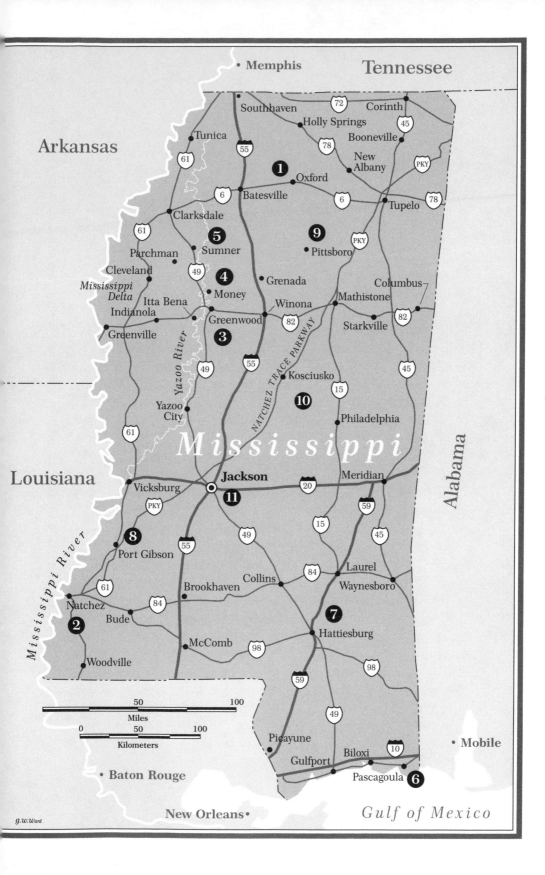

Contents

Sons of Mississippi

James Meredith leaned forward in his living room in Jackson, Mississippi, examining the photograph as if it were a document. He touched the face of the man tearing off the strips of gauze. Then the face of the one taking the tight practice chop with the two-foot-long hickory club. Then the face of the one in the Stetson, with the leering laugh, whose glasses are starting to slide down his alcoholic nose. He'd never seen the photograph before.

"They were Mississippi sheriffs?" he asked.

"Yes."

"And they were there at Oxford?"

"Yes, but they kind of disappeared when the rioting started."

"And you're writing a book about what happened to them?"

"Yes, but it's more about their descendants. If I can find them. If they'll talk to me."

He nodded. "You want to know what came down from these guys."

A semireclusive and famous and not-well man in his mid-sixties, trying to overcome prostate cancer and diabetes and maybe the demons in his mind, went back to looking. Meredith moved forward in his chair a few more inches, and just the slight moving made him look uncomfortable, old, in pain. His hand was still drifting across the glossy surface of a forty-year-old black-and-white photograph. It was as if his elegant fingertips were helping him to remember things.

"It wasn't this element that truly terrified me when I integrated Ole Miss," he said. "It was the element below this element. It was the element that wanted to be this element. First of all, every one of these men is what you'd call a leading citizen in Mississippi. My knowledge of this is what enabled me to defeat Mississippi in 1962. I knew these people better than they knew themselves."

At the door, he shook hands. There almost seemed new strength in him. "Well, keep reporting to me on your progress as you go around our state inquiring about these gentlemen," he said. Outside, in the Meredith backyard, a little dog with a black eye was still yipping and jumping behind the fence he couldn't get over. There was such determination in it.

September 27, 1962, Oxford, Mississippi

Prologue
Nothing Is Ever Escaped

It's made of wood and brick and cinder block, but from across the road it seems like something almost papery, as if from a dream. Once it was a Delta grocery store. Now it's a falling-down building in an all-but-deserted place called Money. But it is its own kind of American shrine. It holds the ghost of a little fat black kid from Chicago called "Bobo" Till, who is known to history as Emmett Till.

He was fourteen and never had a chance. They didn't just murder the cocky and supposedly fresh-mouthed Emmett Louis "Bobo" Till that Sunday morning in August 1955. They made him undress and caved in his face and shot him in the head with a .45 and barbwired his neck to a seventy-five-pound cotton-gin fan. Then they dumped him into the Tallahatchie River. His crime? He had reputedly wolf-whistled at a twenty-one-year-old married white woman named Carolyn Bryant, who was tending the counter of the grocery alone. He had supposedly called her "baby" and maybe popped his just-purchased two cents' worth of bubble gum in her direction and perhaps squeezed her hand and even asked her for a date. Maybe all of it was true, and maybe just shards of it. But something forbidden—or perceived to be forbidden—between a white woman and a black teenager in the rural Deep South of the 1950s seems clearly to have happened, and yet precisely what it was remains clouded in the historical mist. But there is no arguing the historical consequences for the course of civil rights in America, for America.

Nearly every Mississippi story sooner or later touches this one, ends up—

in some spiritual, homing way—right here, in absurdly misnamed and depopulated Money, along this ribbon of Illinois Central railroad track, on this backcountry asphalt, before this tottering and yet somehow beautiful and abandoned building where fatback and bamboo rakes and Lucky Strikes and lye soap and BC headache powder and so many other simple, needed goods and wares and staples were once sold to the locals. They were sold to black field hands of the Delta, primarily, who were living, as their forebears had lived, in tar-paper shacks stuck up on cinder blocks. On this spot, it seems more possible to imagine what some of it was like, the "it" being many things, but primarily the unpunished lynching of someone callow and roly-poly from the North who was visiting relatives in Mississippi and who didn't understand, not nearly enough, about the pridefulness and bigotries and paranoia and taboos and potentially lethal rages of the Jim Crow South.

There's no plaque from a state historical commission. It just is: a monument in ruin, forgotten, recalcitrant, collapsing in on itself, set against memory and the wind and these five decades of change—and nonchange—in American race relations.

Jet magazine, in showing the photographs of the battered corpse a little while after the killing, reported to its readers that when Till was pulled from the sludge-green river, a piece of skull three inches square fell loose from his head. Those pictures in *Jet* helped awaken a generation of future young black activists to what would soon, in the next decade, be called "the movement." That's the true legacy of the lynching of Emmett Till—it put so many eyes on the eventual prize. (Three months later, on December 1, 1955, in Montgomery, Alabama, a forty-two-year-old ascetic-looking seamstress named Rosa Parks would decline to give up her seat on a homebound suppertime city bus, and this, too, was to become one of the anchoring posts of twentieth-century American history.)

The beauty of the building has to do with its look of extreme fragility. A good cough would knock it over. Every five minutes or so, a car or pickup truck blows past on the two-lane, and then the structure seems to tremble and shudder a little more in its foundations. The wood looks thin as balsa. The double front door is padlocked. There's a peeling decal for Raleigh cigarettes by the doorknob. A crushed Sprite bottle is on the landing. Small creatures scurry about. Through the blades of broken plate glass in the door, you can see beams and rafters and other parts of ceiling and walls that have fallen to the foundation. You couldn't walk around in there. Just the randomness of the way things have crashed and settled themselves in against the flooring seems strangely purposeful.

Next door is an old wooden filling station with an overhanging slat-board roof. Someone lives in the back of the gas station, but nobody's answering the door. There are four signs in the two front windows: OUT OF BUSINESS; SORRY CLOSED; CLOSED; SORRY CLOSED. The windows are covered over with nailed-up blankets. On the other side of the grocery store, across a small side street, there's a mobile home. It's the town post office. But the clerk has left for the day.

Where there was once a window on the side of the building, there is now only a hole in a brick wall. On what was once the second floor of the grocery, a toilet is hanging on the far wall, and there is nothing below it. The toilet is bolted against the bare wall, with only air beneath, a ludicrous sight.

When Bobo Till walked up onto this porch and through these doors on August 24, 1955, the place was Bryant's Grocery & Meat Market. There were four Coca-Cola signs on the front. There were wooden benches outside, for checkers and idling. A chubby visitor, who knew how to dress smartly, entered about seven-thirty that evening. It was a Wednesday. He'd been in Mississippi about three days. The store was owned by a twenty-four-year-old former soldier named Roy Bryant and his pretty wife, Carolyn. They lived in the back and upstairs with their small children. She had coils of dark hair and had won beauty contests in high school. Till and his cousins and several friends—about eight young people in all—had come into town from the country in a 1946 Ford. The citified Northerner had a slight speech impediment caused by a childhood attack of polio. Perhaps this is where some of his known cockiness originated: in the need to overcompensate.

There were no real witnesses to what transpired. That's because the others who were with Till stayed outside and tried to watch through the plate-glass windows. The most commonly accepted version of what happened—although it has been subject to divergent accounts—is that Till, who'd been bragging to his country relations about his white Chicago girlfriend, maybe even showing off a photograph of her, was suddenly double-dared, egged on, to go in there and ask Carolyn Bryant for a date. She would later testify under oath that a Negro with a "northern brogue" had come in and made lewd advances—grabbed her, she said, jumped between her and the counter—and that he was still wolf-whistling as he sauntered out.

Roy Bryant was off trucking shrimp to Texas. He had a powerful and balding half brother named J. W. Milam. Big Milam, as he was known locally, was thirty-six and had a ninth-grade education and weighed 235 pounds. He had honored himself as a soldier in World War Two and you didn't want to make lengthy speeches when he was riled. Two days after whatever happened inside the store, an unaware husband came home to Money to his wife and two baby sons. Not immediately, but soon, he heard the story.

Two nights later, in the early hours of Sunday, August 28, two half brothers, bent on teaching a lesson about the customs of the Southern way of life, came for Emmett Till. They took him from his great-uncle's unpainted cabin, which was three miles from Money, off a gravel road, behind a cotton field. The great-uncle, Moses Wright, was a sharecropper and preacher. There were cedar and persimmon trees in his yard. Big Milam had a five-cell flashlight and a .45 Colt automatic.

There seems to have been a lot of driving around in the Delta night. There are stories of pistol whippings. There are stories about screams overheard, coming from a toolshed behind Big Milam's house. But there are also opposing stories—coming from Bryant and Milam themselves—about a victim's failure to whimper enough, to grovel satisfactorily for their mercy. Did he even boast to his abductors about the white girls he'd had in his life? After the half brothers had been indicted for murder, they would claim they had wished only to scare the boy. They'd claim they had set him loose. But later, in the pages of *Look* magazine and then in a 1959 book called *Wolf Whistle,* they'd tell it all. Why not? According to their own self-justifying accounts—the first published in *Look* three months after their acquittal, for which they were paid roughly $4,000 of journalistic blood money by a reporter named William Bradford Huie—the two, though especially J. W. Milam, taunted Till at the last with lines such as "You still good as I am?" and "You've still 'had' white women?" Out of the courtroom, protected by the provisions of double jeopardy, Milam could remember he'd said, "Chicago boy, I'm tired of 'em sending your kind down here to stir up trouble. Goddamn you—I'm gonna make an example of you—just so everybody can know how me and my folks stand." Once he was free, Milam could explain to Huie, a Southerner himself: "Well, what else could we do? He was hopeless. I'm no bully; I never hurt a nigger in my life. I like niggers in their place. I know how to work 'em. But I just decided it was time a few people got put on notice." So yes, it was acknowledged to the world, later, for the old lure of silver. They hadn't intended to kill him. He'd given them no choice. He'd refused to repent.

The body was found three days after the abduction. A young fisherman inspecting his trotlines in the river came on a partially submerged and nude thing hung in a drift with something heavy and very muddy tied to it. This was at Pecan Point, twelve to fifteen miles upriver from Money, in the neighboring county. It was August 31, 1955. The *Greenwood Commonwealth,* the only newspaper of size in that part of the Delta, ran a headline on page 1, opposite a story about comely Lucille Pillow getting crowned "Miss Teen Age Greenwood." At 3 P.M. on the day Emmett Till was found, Chi Omega alumnae honored the upcoming year's rushees with a swimming party at the home of Mrs. Charles S. Whittington of Greenwood, and on that day, too, the board of control of Leflore County met in the Confederate Memorial Building. And there was the gay Ladies' Day luncheon at the Greenwood Country Club.

Several days later, the body reached the IC railway terminal in Chicago, and thirty-three-year-old Mamie Bradley was awaiting it. Friends and family held her up. The casket sat on a Railway Express wagon. She studied the hairline and teeth and said she wanted an open-coffin funeral. She said she wanted the world to "see what they did to my boy."

Standing in front of the grocery, trying to conjure, it's hard not to feel disconsolate. What is there to do after a while but leave? Departing Money, to the north, there are railroad tracks on a high roadbed on the right; the river is moving imperceptibly on the left. Out in the stubbled fields of early winter, there are little snowy pieces of cotton leavings from this season's harvest. Those fields, impossibly fertile, are black and wet, waiting for spring and the first plowing. Spring in Mississippi is when the fields get "rowed up." That's how cotton men of the Delta say it, with such mellifluence: rowed up.

The five-day trial was held in an adjoining county in the town of Sumner. The verdict was rendered by an all-white jury of neighbors in one hour and eight minutes. If the name "Money" has powerful resonance to anyone who's ever attempted to understand the sins and racial sorrows of Mississippi, then "Sumner" will have resonance as well. It's the place where, if you squint, you can see straw-bottom chairs in a second-floor courtroom, the lone overhead fan, the widening moons of sweat beneath the rows of armpits.

During jury selection, Judge Curtis Swango, who was generally commended by observers for his sense of fairness in the trial, uncapped a Coca-Cola from the bench and sipped on it. Bailiffs passed pitchers of ice water and peddlers sold soft drinks to help wash down the box lunches folks had brought into the segregated courtroom. The small, restless children of the accused were allowed to sit now and then with their daddies at the defendants' table. One of these quite handsome children pointed a water pistol at people on the other side of the spindled railing and kept shouting, "Boom, boom, boom." Every morning the local head lawman—a fearsome three-hundred-pound sheriff in khakis and white short sleeves named Clarence Strider—came into court and acknowledged the black press table with a "Good morning, niggers."

Around the square, you can see Robin's Cleaners (IN BUSINESS SINCE 1932), Mid-Delta Home Health, a sad-sack video store, a barber in his single barber chair with his face hidden behind a magazine. He's holding up the magazine in both hands, his legs crossed, a shank of glossy shin showing. There are diagonal parking spaces in front of the Confederate monument next to the courthouse, most of them occupied by pickups.

Something like seventy reporters descended on this town in September

1955. Preachers in Harlem and on the South Side of Chicago and probably in Europe, too, by then had made Bobo Till the subject of their ringing sermons. The *Daily Worker* sent a representative. The *New York Times* and radio reporters and three TV networks came to Sumner.

In the circuit clerk's office, you ask, as you did earlier, on the phone: What has happened to the Till court records? The clerk pauses in her work, smiling agreeably, which is what nearly everyone always does in Mississippi. "Let me call over to Charleston, our other county seat, and just make sure for you," she says. A minute later: "Well, just like I thought. We just don't know. Either stolen or misplaced or done away with. People keep asking and we just can't find it." She adds, "You could look the case up in the docket book for 1955 if you care to."

And then some luck. Not twenty yards from the clerk's office, in a little redbrick building facing the western side of the square, is the law office of John W. Whitten, and sitting inside is John W. Whitten himself. From the circuit clerk's window you can see his shingle: BRELAND & WHITTEN, LAWYERS. He was one of the five attorneys in Sumner (there were only five practicing) who defended the accused. He's the one who warned the jury in the summation of the defense team's case that "there are people in the United States who want to destroy the customs of southern people. . . . They would not be above putting a rotting, stinking body in the river in the hope he would be identified as Emmett Till." He told the jurors he was "sure that every last Anglo-Saxon one of you has the courage to free these men in the face of that pressure."

He's eighty. He's in a little wood-paneled office with louvered shutters. An old black electric fan about the size of a skillet is above his head. A pressed white hanky, folded into a triangle, is sticking out of the vest pocket of his sport coat. His high-waisted pants are being held up by a pair of webbed suspenders. He still has his full head of wavy hair. He's a dapper and courtly man who's been a country lawyer since 1940—that's when he came out of Ole Miss Law, age twenty. Back then, you graduated, you were automatically in the bar, you didn't have to take a test to prove you knew the law.

He talks trip-hammer fast. He says he's had Parkinson's for the last twelve years. He doesn't do much legal work anymore, though just yesterday he wrote a will.

It's a Friday afternoon in December. He'll be going home soon. You want to know, of course, how he feels. You ease into it. "Did you ever regret it later, defending Milam and Bryant?"

"It didn't bother me at all," he answers. There is no hostility in it. Pause. "I felt like we didn't mistreat them in our own lives. Blacks, I mean." Did he have any idea at the time what kind of altering event of history this might be? "I guess I didn't." This comes out a little slowly. He reaches into a cup on the top of his desk. The cup is full of pecans. He takes two or three out and squeezes them in his palm.

In 1985, the thirtieth anniversary of the crime and the trial, a reporter for the *Jackson Clarion-Ledger,* the state's largest daily, looked up Whitten. The lawyer said he'd never confronted Milam or Bryant to try to learn whether or not they'd done it. "If I went to the moral heart of every case that came to me, I'd starve to death," he told the reporter.

He's remembering something. One day a while back, Roy Bryant came in the door. "I don't think I'd seen him since the trial. He had to identify himself. He looked terrible. 'I'm old,' he said. 'I'm sick. I can't work.' He said he was looking for some way to make some cash, and wondered if there was anything I could do for him. I told him, 'I don't know, only thing I can tell you, do what you did before: Trade with some of those who might want to write a book about you.' He left and then about six months later he was dead."

Immediately after the trial, Big Milam and Roy Bryant had lit up cigars, embraced their children, kissed their wives, and mugged for news photographers. But after the *Look* article was on newsstands in January 1956, the two men found themselves inexplicably shunned in their native Mississippi. It's as if the two didn't quite get what they'd just done to themselves. All those who'd defended them—an entire state, you could say—were appalled, though perhaps not entirely for the right reasons.

The shunned left the state and went to the Southwest for a number of years. The Bryants eventually divorced. So did the Milams. Big Milam died of cancer of the backbone on New Year's Eve 1981. Roy Bryant, who, after the trial, had taken work at seventy-five cents a day, lived for a long while in Orange, Texas. He got a job as a boilermaker. He lost a lot of his eyesight and complained he was legally blind. He came back to Mississippi and took over a store in a different county that belonged to family members and catered mostly to blacks. He seemed to have folded into the small print of history. At the Delta grocery where he was now the proprietor, he stood on stools and used a thick magnifying glass to read price tags. The *Clarion-Ledger* tracked him down there in the mid-eighties, and, while the acquitted man tried to deny the deed, he also said: "You mean do I wish I might wouldn't have done it? I'm just sorry that it happened." He said he feared retaliation. Bryant died of cancer in September 1994. The obituary in his local paper called him a "retired merchant." The obituary said, "He was an Army veteran and a Baptist."

To discern the afterlives of these two men, even epigrammatically, is to know what Faulkner meant about the killing of Joe Christmas in *Light in August.* That's the novel in which Joe is castrated and then Percy Grimm flings the bloody butcher knife behind him as one of his accomplices falls against a wall and begins to vomit. "Now you'll let white women alone, even in hell," Grimm says. But you can't get rid of sins like that, is Faulkner's point—even if you walk. Because the thing will just be there inside you, lodged between memory and forgetting, "musing, quiet, steadfast, not fading and not particularly threatful, but of itself alone serene, of itself alone triumphant." James Baldwin explained it lyrically, too, in *Notes of a Native Son.* He was talking about his father's tragic life, which had known so much bitterness of spirit against the white man, and how that bitterness seemed in such danger of passing to the son. At his father's funeral, Baldwin is moved to say: "All of my father's texts and songs, which I had decided were meaningless, were arranged before me at his death like empty bottles, waiting to hold the meaning which life would give them for me. This was his legacy: nothing is ever escaped."

They've horribly modernized the Sumner courtroom, where attorney Whitten orated. The shrine has been tampered with. Where are the green plastered walls and the yellowed pull shades with their little string loops? It was in this room, close to half a century ago, that an epiphany occurred for black America. A sixty-four-year-old unlettered Mississippian named Moses Wright, who was dressed up as though for church, rose from the witness stand and stuck out his trembling arm. Emmett Till's great-uncle pointed at J. W. Milam, and said: "Thar he." Columnist Murray Kempton described the moment the next morning for the readers of the *New York Post.* The witness "pointed his black, workworn finger straight at the huge and stormy head of J. W. Milam and swore that this was the man who dragged fourteen-year-old Emmett Louis Till out of his cottonfield cabin." When he was done, the old man, who'd soon get on a train and go up north and leave Mississippi forever, "sat down hard against the chair-back with a lurch which told better than anything else the cost in strength to him of the thing he had done. He was a field Negro who had dared try to send two white men to the gas chamber for murdering a Negro." Moses Wright, said Kempton, "had come to the end of the hardest half hour in the hardest life possible for a human being in these United States."

But the killers got off, of course. Except they didn't. Nothing is ever escaped.

As I said, nearly every Mississippi story sooner or later touches this one, including mine. Mine is about legacies—family legacies, essentially, and about a single photograph and about seven sheriffs in that photograph, sheriffs in the years of civil rights, and about the kinds of things they bequeathed. The photograph was taken in late September 1962, seven years after the killing of Emmett Till. The photograph, which isn't an icon image of the sixties—but should be—was recorded a few days before an all-night riot in Mississippi in which two died and hundreds were injured. It was made by an uncommonly brave and gifted white freelance photographer from Alabama named Charles Moore, on a Thursday afternoon, in a grove of elms and oaks and fine old catalpa trees, at Oxford, Mississippi, on the campus of a place known lovingly as Ole Miss. A week later, this document was published in a double-truck spread in *Life* magazine with this small headline down in the left-hand corner: "Local Lawmen, Getting Ready to Block the Law." There were a lot of other pictures in the story, but this was the one that stole your eyes. The caption that followed said: "The official upholders of law and order in Oxford, a group of Mississippi plain-clothesmen chortle as one of their number takes practice swings with a billy and another ties on an identifying armband. They are on the campus not to put down a riot but to take part in one of the incidents which led up to it. They mobilized earlier in the week to back up Lieut. Governor Paul Johnson when he turned [James] Meredith and U.S. marshals away from the enrolling office. But when the riot broke out, all local and state cops made themselves scarce."

That was more or less accurate.

They had gathered, these seven faces of Deep South apartheid, along with a swelling mob of others (who aren't visible but are everywhere about), along with their pridefulness and paranoia and potentially lethal rages, to do what they could to keep another American and fellow Mississippian, a black man, from forcibly integrating (with federal troops and marshals) the halls and grounds of their sacrosanct state university. That history has already been much chronicled. The saga of twenty-nine-year-old Meredith heroically and almost messianically bringing down the color barriers at the University of Mississippi is only a backdrop to the story I am going to tell, a kind of stage set and thematic clothesline for a different narrative to move against. I have been occupied with something else, and I suppose it could be termed—to borrow the poet Mark Strand's phrase in describing the paintings of Edward Hopper— "the nature of continuousness."

From the start, I wanted to know: How did these seven white Southerners get to be this way, and how did it all end, or how is it still going on, and was there no eventual shame here, and what happened to their progeny, *especially* their progeny, and was it all just ineluctable? To state it in another way: Where did the hatred and the sorrow go that flowed out of this moment—and out of a lot of other moments like it in seven particular lives that didn't get captured by a camera and reproduced on a photosensitive surface and then printed across two pages in a national magazine that, back then, possessed a kind of religious communicative power in America? How did a gene of intolerance and racial fear mutate as it passed sinuously through time and family bloodstreams?

How has that gene reshaped itself, and possibly for the better? The picture, which was in an anthology of Charles Moore's work entitled *Powerful Days,* triggered all these questions. There was something about the angles of cigarettes, and middle-aged men in white shirts and ties, and an armband that almost could have been a tourniquet. Something about a strange-looking priest (he had a club) and his profane deacons (they were laughing so nastily), semicircled around an altar or maybe it was the lid of a gleaming coffin (actually, it was the barely visible hood of a squad car), as they readied for their satanic rites.

Even now, after years of looking at it, examining it, carrying it, I can't precisely say what it was about the image that so took hold of me. It had an overwhelming storytelling clarity—and simultaneous confusion. It was only much later, with the research and reporting and interviews unfolding before me, that I found a certain corroboration for all I must have been imagining the first time I came across it. I stress the word "certain," as in provisional. I found it in old FBI records, in Department of Justice files, in declassified state governmental records in Mississippi, in numerous civil rights archives and repositories around the country. I found it in interviews with people who had known these men in their prime. I found it in lengthy talks with the two sheriffs in the photograph who were alive when I began the search for all of them. For at least one of the lawmen in this picture—he was more than a decade dead by the time I'd begun, and his name was Grimsley, which to me was an almost perfect name—I would obtain both an FBI record and a Justice Department file consisting of hundreds of partially blacked-out pages. In these pages, I would find suggestions and allegations and accusations of many dark things: attempted rape of female prisoners in the county jail, for instance, and the apparent intention to commit murder, or at least to sponsor it, on behalf of the thugs in his county to whom he was an inebriated local hero. There were memos in the file about this sheriff from J. Edgar Hoover to the assistant attorney general of the United States for civil rights, Burke Marshall. And for all of that, the documents were maddeningly inconclusive. No indictments were ever filed, not even for far lesser alleged offenses, such as taking payoffs from local whorehouses and illicit gambling joints. It was as if the powers that be in Washington decided to look the other way. Trying to fill in the words and phrases and sentences that had been "redacted" by the government censors chilled me. Reading through this file so many years later was like the journey itself back into the photograph: There was always something incomplete, hedgy, obscured, left to my imagination.

Which is why I need to say clearly that the book that follows isn't about the figures in this photograph, not finally, not ultimately. Instead, it's about what's deeply connected but is off the page, out of sight, past the borders. It's about what has *come down* from this photograph, from the moment of history that is its context. While there is much to tell about the seven men suspended here, my real interest is in the twenty-first century. Hidden in this glossy black-and-white rectangle are some modest surprises and small redemptions and blades of latter-day racial hope, however slender and promisory. The most important faces in this story are the ones you can't see—progeny, the inheritors—not within the margins of a documentary instant that was framed and clicked on September 27, 1962, at a signal event of the civil rights movement.

And yet even within these four borders, there is a face you cannot really see. It belongs to John Ed Cothran—the one over on the right, the sheriff with his back turned. He is very aged now, the last one alive. His mind is clear, or was until recently, although his hearing isn't good. I have spent many hours talking with him and Maudine, his third wife, whom he married several years ago on the spur, when he was two days shy of eighty-four, hopping over to Arkansas to find a JP who'd perform the ceremony for them on the Labor Day weekend. He has great-great-grandchildren. He gets up at 5 A.M. to make his coffee and then go to his La-Z-Boy to read that day's chapter of the Bible. One day several years ago, shortly after we'd met, when I knew very little about the full arc of his life, we were talking and he said, as if he'd just remembered, "Yeah, poor little Emmett. I helped fish him out."

"Emmett Till?" I said.

"Yeah, from the Tallahatchie," he said, as if it would have been obvious. "I wasn't sheriff yet. That was 'fifty-five. I was the deputy under George Smith. Me and Ed Weber, who was the other deputy, got Emmett's uncle in the car and carried him out to the scene and went down the bank and pulled in the body. The durn fan weighed about a hundred and forty pounds, it had so much silt and mud in it. When we got it cleaned up, I guess it weighed about half that. Couple days later, in the *Commercial Appeal* in Memphis, there was this big picture of me squattin' next to the gin fan. I caught hell for that from the sheriff, by the way. Said I had no business gettin' my picture took."

That night, at a library in Memphis, there he was, on a roll of newspaper microfilm, so much younger-looking, in his snap-brim fedora, in a white summer shirt with the sleeves rolled up his muscular upper arms, his Leflore County deputy's badge over his left breast. He was kneeling next to a gin fan still partially caked with mud. "USED IN SLAYING" were the first words of the caption. "Deputy Sheriff John Ed Cothran of Greenwood, Miss., yesterday examined a big cotton gin fan used to weight down a Negro boy whose body was found Wednesday in the Tallahatchie River." The Emmett Till case and his role in it—which wasn't critical to the outcome and was fairly minor in the scheme of things– provided the key to unlocking his essential character, which is all about keeping your back turned, about staying morally in the middle, while others around you do the more vile and naked work of racism. Just when I thought I understood his life, I didn't. Because some other muddying, silting fact had come unexpectedly into play, pulling everything down, throwing everything open to question once more. But John Ed's story, John Ed's life—and, far more redemptively, the story of his grandson and namesake, John Cothran, a native Mississippian who is nearing forty and works at the Home Depot—is not where the story begins. It starts with the declining moments in the life of Billy Ferrell. He's the figure in the center of Charles Moore's gelatin silver print, biting off the tip of his Lucky, pulsing the air with a stick that's tapered just like a baseball bat. "Headache sticks," cops in the South used to call them. Billy with his billy, up front and in the middle of the frame, laving himself in the light, just as always. When he died, at the end of winter in 1999, in his hometown of Natchez, at age seventy-five, you'd have thought the whole of Adams County was in mourning for him, at least if you were just skimming the surface of truth and reading tributes in the local paper. That's the way the erasure of the past tends to work, by selective memory and willed amnesia and the wearing away of time. And yet there are always some folks around who are willing to remember things whole.

Part One

Deeds of the Fathers

Where did they come from that day—cheesy and mean little cracker-box houses, or inviting spreads with cool green verandas? Some of both, actually. And why are seven men dressed so uncomfortably for this Indian summer heat? Because they're on a mission from God. They're confronting history, and they know it. Over their granddaddies' Confederate graves will the Kennedy brothers in Washington get away with sticking a black man into a Mississippi place that doesn't wish him. That was the two-note drumbeat of the White Citizens' Council when James Meredith was trying to register at Ole Miss, and you could hear the drumbeat all over the state: "nigger/Kennedy, nigger/Kennedy, nigger/Kennedy." In the mannered sixties South, if a man is being summoned to a moment of grave importance, he knows to look presentable, at least if he has any breeding in him. I'm not talking about peckerwoods and shrimp haulers and back-country trash, who'll snatch somebody from sleep with a five-cell flashlight and a .45 Colt automatic. Now, for a proper introduction. These sworn keepers of the Mississippi peace, these leading citizens of their respective communities, in order, going left to right, from the stub of cheap wet cigar on one end to that tourniquet-like armband on the other, are: Sheriff John Henry Spencer of Pittsboro. Sheriff James Ira Grimsley of Pascagoula. Sheriff Bob Waller of Hattiesburg. Sheriff Billy Ferrell of Natchez. Sheriff Jimmy Middleton of Port Gibson. Deputy Sheriff James Wesley Garrison of Oxford. Sheriff John Ed Cothran of Greenwood.

Dying Billy

In his retirement, which wasn't kingly but pretty sweet, Billy Ferrell loved sitting on the dock of his lake house, watching Taco, his Labrador–blue heeler mix, splash around for bream and shad and the occasional white perch. It didn't matter a doughnut that the dog seldom got anything. It was good just to be down at the pier by himself or with a crony, in a peeling metal chair on the moss-green unpainted wood, looking out over the shallow water of the skinny, torpid lake. Hazel Ferrell would be up at the house, fussing with something or other, and so he'd sneak a smoke, cupping it on the inside of his fist so his wife wouldn't know, saying to himself, Well, hell, what is life but a series of doing a bunch of little things you're not supposed to do? Sometimes she'd bring down coffee for him. Seeing his spouse coming, the high sheriff of Natchez—which is how everyone still thought of Billy Ferrell, even if he wasn't sheriff anymore, that was his boy Tommy's show now—would quickly stub the cigarette out on the backside of the deck and toss it in the water.

His arteries were clogging and the circulation in his legs wasn't good and there was a cancerous mass growing secretly in his lungs, but he was still a handsome man and he knew it. Vanity and pride had always been core Ferrell flaws. He wore gold-rimmed glasses now. The teeth were in trouble and his coal-black hair, which once had glistened in pictures and was parted forty-five degrees to the left, had thinned to long swipes of dirty white. He'd become ruddy-faced and gargly-voiced, and his breath seemed to emerge from him in hard little pants. And yet, this final Billy Ferrell—weakening, sedentary, semi-depressed, widened out—was still capable of coming at you with that old incisored, tough-guy, top-dog grin; with that noted, flat-lined, crow's-footed, predatory squint. The grin and the squint—didn't they explain everything about the Mississippi doctrine of Might Is Right?

Both had been there when he'd campaigned for sheriff the first time. That was in 'fifty-nine. He was a young man then, in his mid-thirties, good-looking as all get-out, albeit with a kind of blocky, sober, big-eared, straight-ahead earnestness in his speech and manner. He'd run ads for himself before the Democratic primary that summer, as all the candidates had, and there were a slew of them, candidates that is, something like eight or nine. He was already well known, since he'd been a sheriff's deputy for eight years, and since he'd lived in Adams County all his life, except for when he'd been to the war. "He has never been known to conduct himself in any manner that would bring discredit to his badge or the people he represented," the ads said. "We know Billy Ferrell and his Devotion to Duty, His Character, His Sincerity of Purpose, His Unrelenting Courage and his High Principles. Let's elect William T. 'Billy' Ferrell Our Sheriff and Tax Collector." And Natchez did. They elected him for the next twenty-eight years, with the exception of one four-year window of time, 1964–68, when he couldn't succeed himself because, back then, a sheriff in Mississippi could be sheriff for only four years at a stretch. In some counties (there are eighty-two in the state), sheriffs would get their wives elected as interim sheriffs, while they did the real thing behind the scenes. Billy Ferrell laid out a term (he sold Ford clunkers at Bluff City Cars and tried to run a Gulf station and hauled some gravel and worked for Premo Stallone's plumbing business and did a stint as a city policeman, but everybody knew he was just whiling his time), and then he came back in, and then the succession law was changed, and then Natchez and the county seemed willing to make him pope of the county for life. Well, white Natchez always seemed willing, and they had the majority. But after six terms, the high sheriff decided not to run anymore and handed the job over to Tommy in 1988. Tommy still had to get elected by the people, but he had the Ferrell name, and in Natchez, for most of the last half of the twentieth century, that name was almost synonymous with the word "badge." There'd been a sheriff in Natchez since 1798, and for one-fifth of that time the Ferrells had owned the title.

Billy had been number 32a on the ballot machines in that first race, and in the runoff campaign between himself and Morris Doughty, some unsavory elements had tried to buy him into withdrawing. There'd been a secret meeting on the levee, on the Louisiana side of the river, and somebody had produced a gob of hundreds, maybe $10,000 worth of hundreds, and stuck it at him. All Billy had to do was take his name off and let Doughty win. He'd never dreamed of so much money. But he wouldn't take his name off—not that he didn't think it over a heavy minute, walk around the back side of the pickup and discuss the situation with his old pal Premo Stallone, whom he'd known practically all his life. William T. Ferrell stayed on the ballot, and on election day, the lever with his name on it was the one that got pulled by enough Natchezeans for him to squeak it out. That contest marked the first time a county in Mississippi went modern with voting machines, but corruption being what corruption is, it didn't stop bribes or offers of bribes.

The lake house, to which Billy and Hazel had repaired after he'd hung up the gear, was on the Louisiana side of the Mississippi River, upstream a little bit from Natchez. To get there, you took the big bridge over to Vidalia, Louisiana, and then went to Ferriday, Louisiana, and then drove north to the lake and came on around to the back side of it and started looking for Ferrell Lane. When Billy and Hazel first got a weekend place up on Lake St. John— Billy was still sheriffing—all they could afford was a double-wide trailer. Now they had a three-bedroom brick house. If the garage door was open, and the retired couple was home, you'd spy a white Lincoln, never dirty. In the living room, the console TV with the fifty-two-inch screen would doubtless be going. Paw-Paw and Mimsy, as their grandkids called them, had an antenna that could pull in Moscow and Monterrey, Mexico, but they couldn't get good reception from a Natchez station, which was only across the river and about a half hour's drive away. Billy enjoyed tuning in Russia and Mexico on his giant wood-encased TV even if, as he said, he didn't know what the hell they were saying. He watched an awful lot of television in those last years at Lake St. John—not sex shows or Oprah, but news programs. He liked to say he knew what was going on, which is what he'd been content to say of himself when he was in office: He "had the rap from the ax," was his expression.

An example: Some collegians and two of their teachers got off a bus on July 5, 1961, in the semitropical antebellum river town of Natchez, which is in the southwestern corner of Mississippi, sitting on great bluffs, at a bend in the river. Billy had been sheriff of Adams County a year and a half then. The students and their two faculty chaperones were from Adelphi College in New York, and they were traveling on an interstate carrier out of New Orleans. From nearly the moment they stepped into the Trailways bus terminal at 5 P.M., they were watched. Even though Natchez was a tourist town, famous for its plantation "pilgrimages," site of the South's oldest slave-owning cotton aristocracy, they would have been watched: They were suspiciously young, traveling in a group, Northern accents. But even more so in this case, since right away they'd begun asking impertinent questions about the terminal's segregated waiting rooms. That evening, Sheriff Billy Ferrell sent a Teletype under his special teletypewriter number, NTZ-44. He sent it to General T. B. Birdsong, commander of the Mississippi Highway Patrol (he used to be a colonel, but now he was a general), and also to the director of the Mississippi State Sovereignty Commission, which was a state-sponsored and tax-supported agency whose charter was to spy on the civil rights movement. The

Sov-Com was based in Jackson, the capital city, two and a half hours away. THIS AFTERNOON ON A BUS FROM NEW ORLEANS LA SEVEN WHITE MALES AND FEMALES COMBINED ENTERED THIS CITY AND COUNTY. . . . THESE SUBJECTS HAVE BEEN CONSTANTLY UNDER SURVEILLANCE SINCE THEIR ARRIVAL BY OFFICERS THIS DEPARTMENT. THEY HAVE MAILED TWO LETTERS SINCE THEIR ARRIVAL. It was clear from the wire and from typed reports written in subsequent days by investigators of the Sov-Com that the desk clerk at the Eola Hotel had listened in on the group's phone calls and had reported to the sheriff. It was clear the postmaster was in on it, and so, too, the editor of the local newspaper, with whom the travelers naively thought they might arrange an appointment. SUBJECTS TOLD DESK CLERK AT LOCAL HOTEL THAT THEY WAS EXCHANGE STUDENTS TOURING THE COUNTRY TO FIND OUT ALL LOCAL CUSTOMS PRIOR TO THEIR SHIPMENT TO OVERSEAS COUNTRIES, the wire said. The authorities in Jackson wired back to Billy: OK WILL ADVISE ALL CONSERN. The collegians and their teachers left town on a bus the next morning. They were headed toward Little Rock, Arkansas, via Vicksburg, Mississippi. It was known they intended to stay at either the Albert Pike or the Marion Hotel in Little Rock. The constabularies up there would be alerted that a Barbara Wexler (W/F, ADDRESS 14 GRANGE LANE, LEVITTOWN, NEW YORK) and a Gail Yenkinson (W/FM, SAME ADD) and an Emilio Rivera (SAME ADD AND SUPPOSED TO BE A PROFFESSOR AT THIS COLLEGE), along with the others, were on their nosy way.

No one told this story at Billy Ferrell's wake and funeral; no one trotted out an old and semi-inconsequential document from the recently declassified files of the Mississippi State Sovereignty Commission. That would have been a rude and inexcusable thing. And yet such documents existed, by the fistful, available for anybody's reading by the time he expired. All an impertinent person in the post-totalitarian society of Mississippi would have had to do was drive over to Jackson, park his or her car, walk past the monument to the Confederate dead out front of the Department of Archives and History, near the State Capitol, across State Street from the big sign that says WELCOME TO DOWNTOWN JACKSON. BEST OF THE NEW SOUTH. All he or she would've needed to do was enter a room on the first floor and fill out a brief application and log on to a Hewlett-Packard Vectra XM2 computer. Soon as the nosy soul started punching up "William T. Ferrell" or "Ferrell, Billy," he or she would start to come on all sorts of interesting if essentially unsurprising items from thirty and forty years back—not evidence of murder or outright brutality, no; just greater or lesser little bigotries and incontestable evidences of a general mindset, such as this one, for instance: "Sheriff Billy Ferrell agreed to furnish the Chief of Police with the names of the negroes who had been participating in the afore mentioned activities, and also to begin a file at once in keeping records and names of any known agitators or any would-be agitators in his county and to keep us advised on current activities. The other Sheriffs likewise agreed to do the same."

In their retirement, the high sheriff and his wife had traveled some and generally enjoyed it. They had a motor home, until they sold it in 1996, and wondered afterward why they did. They'd gotten as far north as Edmonton, Alberta, gasping at the Canadian Rockies and the rest of the Lord's handiwork up there. Billy would do the driving, his only requirement being that Hazel and her sister—who'd be in the back, yakking—kept a pot of fresh coffee going for him at all times. One of their favorite destination spots was Branson, Missouri, where Las Vegas–like country music extravaganzas are based. Once they saw an eleven- or twelve-year-old kid in a spangled suit impersonating Elvis, damnedest thing you could imagine. Mickey Gilley, the big country star, had his own show and restaurant in Branson. He was from Ferriday, down near home, and he and Hazel were something like third cousins maybe a time or two removed. Gilley and Jerry Lee Lewis and the great TV preacher Jimmy Swaggart (you know: the one who'd taken illicit female flesh but wept for the nation's forgiveness) were all Louisiana boys and first cousins and performers who'd done well in the fame and loot department. More than once Billy and Hazel got to sit down with Gilley in his restaurant and have a drink with him and get some free show tickets. One time, Hazel carted up to Missouri a box of decorative golf balls from Gilley's old high school golf coach in Ferriday. He'd treated the two of them just like kin.

These years in semiexile on the Louisiana side of the river were comfortable and pleasant and full of respect, given what a man had accomplished in his life. But they were also flat and tedious years. Just not enough laving light. Billy was a man without hobbies. He'd always been the sheriff. Too often he'd just sit and remember, stare hard. In a more jovial mood, he'd tell cronies in town he'd gone to work for "Honey-Do." Honey, do this. Honey, do that.

In 1992, Natchez made him Santa for the annual Christmas parade, a coveted honor, and there was Billy, third car in the procession, red suit, riding through the neighborhoods in a top-down convertible, waving, tossing candies to black and white kiddies alike. Hazel framed the official parade invitation: "Santa and Mrs. William T. Ferrell Sr. . . . ."

Every Friday, he took his wife to town for her appointment at the hair garage. He'd drop her off and then tool the Lincoln over to the jail and get one of the better-behaved prisoners—a trusty—to wash it for a buck. Afterward, he'd meet Hazel and they'd sit at the Ramada Inn, which has a wonderful dining room with a wide, high-up view of the curling river. Folks always came up to the table to say, "Hello, Sheriff," and, "Hey, Sheriff, why don't you run again?" In these instances, they weren't addressing Tommy Ferrell, who was often sitting right there with his parents. "Sheriff" was reserved for William T.

Ferrell the elder, and would always be reserved, as long as he was above ground. William T. Ferrell the younger was head lawman of Adams County now, a man of immense pride and ego and accomplishment himself. He wore cowboy boots and a silver rodeo buckle and a blue blazer and a piece on one hip and a cell phone on the other. He liked to walk with his stomach out in front of him. He wore snappy ties and had two computers on his desk and thought of himself—and tried to run his department—as a kind of CEO of law and justice in southwestern Mississippi. His "agency," as Tommy called it, had something like fifty-seven on the payroll, twenty-seven of whom were uniformed officers and the rest of whom were support staff, including a doctor and a nurse for the jail. It was a $2.5 million budget he presided over. But for all his modernity, the son was a man with a severe attachment to the past, and the least benchmark of this were the photos he kept in his office. In between beautifully framed prints of Stonewall Jackson and Robert E. Lee was one of Nathan Bedford Forrest, a cofounder of the KKK and a brilliant Civil War tactician. Tommy had been his father's deputy for almost nineteen years, rising in the 1970s and 1980s above all the other deputies in the sheriff's department (not without their grumbling about nepotism) to become chief criminal deputy and chosen successor for the top job. And he'd gotten it. SHERIFF TOMMY FERRELL was now lettered in yellow-gold on the plate glass at the front door of the sheriff's department; lettered on the side of the county's twenty-four squad cars; lettered on the sheriff's helicopter; across the hull of a big white racing boat with twin outboards that sat parked and ready right out front of Tommy's office across from the courthouse, waiting—as if, need be, for the sheriff to morph into Dano on *Hawaii 5-0.* Tommy was the Ferrell family member moving rapidly through the various vice presidential seats of the National Sheriffs' Association, so that by June 2002, at age fifty-five, if nothing went sour, he'd become president of the whole shebang, headquartered in Washington, D.C., with its membership of something like 20,000. No Mississippi sheriff had ever striven so high, ever dared so high or public.

And yet somehow none of this mattered, not on Fridays, not to Natchez, when the once and ever high sheriff of the county brought his wife to town in the white Lincoln for her morning at the hair garage and then sat with her in the window at the Ramada with nearly the whole damn ville—the whole white ville, that is—coming up to say hello. Billy always protested to his family afterward that these homages were embarrassing, but you'd have to be a fool to believe that. One of the main reasons he and Hazel had moved to the lake house in the first place was so Tommy could have his own life. And yet it was so hard for Billy to stay out of town. In the family, whether they were at the lake house or visiting at Tommy's place in town, he refused to call his son "Sheriff." Couldn't bring himself to. And as far as his son's stature in the

National Sheriffs' Association, as far as Tommy getting his picture snapped in the halls of Congress with Senator Trent Lott of Mississippi and other important politicians up there, that was fine; and it's true that Billy often said aloud he hoped that the Lord would just let him live long enough to attend Tommy's "inauguration" in June 2002; but on the other hand the father seemed a little too eager to admonish his son: "Tommy, the people elected you sheriff of Adams County, not sheriff of the United States. You may think you're sheriff of the United States, but you belong down in Natchez." And that would rankle.

I met Billy Ferrell on October 1, 1997, the thirty-fifth anniversary of James Meredith's admission to Ole Miss. He had a year and a half left to him. He came out of the lake house and it was as if ink on a flat surface had come to life, sticking out its thickened paw. "Cut off your motor and come in a minute," he said. He was in a short-sleeve blue shirt and clean khakis and he smelled pleasantly of aftershave, possibly Old Spice. His wife was right behind him. She had red hair and was extremely well preserved and was putting a creamy lotion on her hands, a woman in a small dither, heading for the Lincoln, the trunk of which was open. "You can stay here tonight if you want to," she said, in her dither and generosity. "We've got to go. Those babies are about to be born." Paw-Paw and Mimsy were off to Baton Rouge, Louisiana, for the birth of their granddaughter's twins.

The day before, I had introduced myself to the paterfamilias on the phone from a hotel room in Jackson. There had been an intercessionary call on my behalf from the top cop in the state of Mississippi, an ex–FBI agent named Jim Ingram, who had offered to ask Billy to talk to me. Ingram was commissioner of the Department of Public Safety and knew almost every lawman in the state. He was particularly good friends with Billy. I had gone to see Ingram at his big office in the T. B. Birdsong Memorial Highway Patrol Building in the capital city in what by Mississippi standards could be called a skyscraper. I had brought the photograph with me and was worried that when I pulled it out and tried to speak in general terms about it, Ingram, whom I had not met before, might not approve of what I was attempting to do. But the opposite seemed true. He held it out in front of him at arm's length. "Oh, my. Billy was such a handsome guy then, wasn't he?" he said. Ingram is a huge, gregarious man with a booming voice. He's originally from Oklahoma. J. Edgar Hoover dispatched him to Mississippi during the civil rights years as part of a federal task force, and Mississippi eventually became Ingram's adopted home. "Would you like me to phone Natchez and speak to the Ferrells for you? Good friends of mine, the Ferrells, Billy and Tommy. You know, there's a third Ferrell, too, who's in law enforcement. They call him Ty. He's William T. Ferrell the Third. Young fella. Left the state for now. I think he's a border patrol agent somewhere out in Texas. He hunts illegal aliens. I'll be happy to make that call over to Natchez for you."

An hour later, the phone in my hotel room rang, and it was Billy. "Jim Ingram just called me," he said. I heard the wariness. "Well, the thing is this," he said. "Our granddaughter Candi down in Baton Rouge is about to have babies. Twins. Any minute. But if you want to, come over in the morning. Get here about ten-thirty. It'll take you about two hours' drive. We may have to go or we may already be gone. We're hanging by the phone. But come on in the meantime."

The next morning, as I drove toward Natchez on the Louisiana side of the Delta, yellow crop dusters were swooping and dipping above me, and behind them in the pale blue sky were their swaths of chemical smoke. Big cubes of baled cotton stood along both sides of the macadam, waiting to be trucked off. At a roadside stop in Waterproof, a portly man came out, inspected me, and said, "Boy, you sure are lost down here in the middle of the Loozyana delta with a shirt and tie on." I found Lake St. John and passed houses named Heaven and Emotional Rescue. I pulled into Ferrell Lane to witness the grandparental dither.

Billy led me inside. In the hall was the photograph from *Life*. It was laminated on a piece of plywood. The plywood had been heavily shellacked. The piece was sitting on the floor, propped against a doorjamb. "That's probably the one you're referring to, I guess," he said over his shoulder. I was pretty certain it had been brought out of the basement or a back closet and dusted off. Still, somebody had once cut the photo from a magazine and made it suitable for hanging.

The Ferrells were very cordial, if edgy. The imminent births must have accounted for a lot of the edginess, though not all. Hazel was sort of blurring in the background, her body language saying, *Hurry up, Billy.* Billy sat in a chair and breathed a little heavily. I tried not to break eye contact with him. I wasn't fool enough to take a notebook out, not then. When he used the expression "civil rights crap," he flashed his incisored grin, his predatory squint. He said that if I came back the next day he'd be glad to give me several hours of his time. "We'll be back from Baton Rouge late tonight," he said. "You'll probably want to stay over in Natchez. We'll have coffee on for you in the morning."

The next day, we sat talking on the dock for hours, just the two of us. Did anything startling fall out? Not really. Did he slip and use the word "nigger"? A couple of times, but less than I would have expected, frankly. Was he good company? Quite—if you could mentally block out what was constantly flowing under the conversation. He was being very careful. I was taking notes by then. It was so clear to me that a wily man was working overtime to control the memory of bad deeds. I didn't see the use in trying to nudge him much in another direction. Things would unfold eventually, I figured. He talked some about Oxford, and about what had happened up there in 1962 when James Meredith sought to enroll, trying always to put himself in the best justifying light. When the words "Robert F. Kennedy" arose, Billy said—and then the grin and the squint were back—"I couldn't stand that little snivelly-nosed sonofabitch." He didn't like either Kennedy, but the younger brother, the attorney general, had always ticked him off royal. Bobby was a pissant featherweight. And then he quickly apologized for saying these things. He apologized almost in a formally comic way. He didn't wish to be uncharitable about such a high and deceased officer of the United States government.

We didn't talk very much about the photograph itself, a copy of which I'd brought with me, and his copy of which was still sitting against the doorjamb in the hallway up in the house. I asked if it embarrassed him. "I resented hell out of it," he said. He said he wanted to sue Henry Luce at Time, Inc., didn't fear the Luces' money in the least. He told me he could still remember the spot on the Ole Miss campus where the thing was taken. He said he knew the tree he was standing under. He said, "Bob Waller, the sheriff standing right behind me, brought over this billy and said, 'Well, goddamn, Billy, look what I found in one of your patrol cars.' I was smoking a cigarette and I put it between my teeth and I took hold of the billy and I said, 'Goddamn, it's big as a baseball bat,' and that's when they snapped it. That's all there was to it." He said he heard afterward that the photographer made $1,500 for making a fool out of him that way in a national magazine, not that he could prove the guy made that much, but that's the amount he'd always heard. And get this: The guy was a Southerner himself, a white man. Billy said that if I really wanted to know, it was a very historic photograph in Mississippi law enforcement terms, because "in that one picture, you got the president of the Mississippi Sheriffs' Association—that's me—and then you got the various regional officers of the association standing around me."

Everything was so placid down on the pier that day—old fishing poles and drooping Spanish moss and green water lapping at the pilings. The dock was like a fishing camp. Taco splashed around, trying vainly to snare fish in his jaws. Billy said he'd been an altar boy as a kid, raised Catholic. His family had been poor and had moved around town a lot, and he didn't get to finish high school. He and Hazel had met on a blind date across the river in Ferriday. Her people were from other parts of Mississippi and Louisiana. The war came. Billy got drafted. He and Hazel were married on December 28, 1942—Billy had turned nineteen, his bride was seventeen—and two days afterward he was inducted into the army at Camp Shelby, Mississippi. Soon they'd promoted him to a line buck sergeant. He was in "ETO," he said: European Theater of Operations. He told how his daddy died horribly on a mail boat on the

Mississippi, down near New Orleans, when Billy was overseas in the war. (His father, who'd once been a part-time deputy sheriff himself, had gotten caught in the tug's rope rigging, and it sucked him in, suffocating and strangling him; he wasn't yet fifty.) These stories went on, engagingly. Billy had on speck-white Reeboks and a blue pinstripe shirt. He wasn't wearing socks, and I saw a little psoriasis sore on the inside of his left ankle. He kept plowing his meaty hand through the strings of his hair. He kept sneaking smokes from his pants pocket and watching out for Hazel, who was up in the house, fixing us dinner. In the South, "dinner" means lunch. He had told Hazel earlier that day he wanted me to experience one of her all-out, full-bore Southern dinners. His wife was in a terrific mood, he said. Those babies in Baton Rouge had come into the world safely.

He told a story about Big Julio May, the town bully. Billy was a deputy sheriff when he delivered a summons to a juke joint on State Street where Big Julio had a job. They got into an argument, but it was just shouting. Billy left the summons on the top of the bar and returned to his patrol car and suddenly there was Big Julio, leaning in over top of him, threatening to kill him. "I said, 'Julio, they didn't put me in this uniform to be a goddamn prizefighter on State Street. Now, you got your hand on the door handle. And I got my hand on this thirty-eight.' See, I'd taken off the safety. I had my hand resting on top of it. I said, 'Julio, you open this door and I'm going to show you what a goddamn stupid dago you are. I'm gonna blow your goddamn dago head off.' " Then the odd, comic formalism was back: "I guess in my heart I couldn't see myself being a street ruffian and a sworn officer of the law." He did not end up blowing Big Julio's dago head off (apparently Big Julio walked away), although later that night, out of uniform, Billy said he went looking for the town bully with a little snub-nosed .25-caliber.

It was clear he wanted to stay away from the subject of "civil rights crap." At one point, speaking of protest marches, he said, "You got a town full of half-drunk wild blacks and you're trying to control things with fifteen officers."

I shifted directions and asked about the comforts of his retirement. "All through the providence of God," he answered.

Hazel called us for dinner. I washed my hands in the bathroom and saw big, fluffy, nappy hand towels with "WTF" scripted on them. The three of us ate on pewter plates with pressed napkins, sitting at an elongated table in the kitchen by a window. The big TV in the other room was tuned to CNN. Hazel had set out the dishes on the countertop and we helped ourselves, buffet-style. She'd prepared sweet corn, black-eyed peas, steak and gravy, mashed potatoes. We drank sweetened iced tea. As we were finishing up, Billy pulled out something from his pocket. It was in a flat blue case. He slid it across. I opened the case and saw a gold honorary sheriff's badge. There was a card inside that described him as an "emeritus" lawman of Adams County. It was signed by Tommy Ferrell. "You can't stay away from it, I guess," Tommy's father said, and this time the grin was almost sheepish.

Almost fourteen months went by before I saw Billy again, and by then there were drastic changes. I had waited much too long. I had come to know a lot, not just about the sheriff in the middle of Charles Moore's frame, but about his six fellow lawmen as well. By then, I knew more of the crucial parts of the story.

By late November 1998, however, death had dropped broad hints on Billy. He was now staring aimlessly at a TV in Natchez. The Ferrells had forsaken the lake house so they could be close to family and hospitals.

First, there'd been open-heart surgery, a triple bypass. Paw-Paw and Mimsy had been out for the weekend to Tommy's hunting lodge. They were couch-potatoing, to use Hazel's expression. It was just the four of them: Tommy and his wife, Carole; Billy and Hazel. In the middle of the night, Billy started feeling sick. It was a tingling in his left arm. He tried to shake it, but the sensation wouldn't go away. Early that next week, he went to see his doctor, who knew right away what it was and ordered him into a hospital in Jackson. He was sixteen days in a bed in Jackson and there'd been artery splicings in three places. The mass on his lung, undetected for months, had been doing its killing work even while he was under the knife. So they'd come back from Jackson, put the lake house up for sale, found a town house in town on Martin Luther King, Jr. Street (which for decades had been Pine Street, the name change being a sore subject for white Natchezeans, the more so if they lived on Pine). In the summer, a month before the tumor was found, Billy and his lifelong friend Premo Stallone had driven to their Army reunion in Oxford. They'd been going to these reunions of the 219th Signal Depot for decades. Billy seemed almost to be slipping into early Alzheimer's. They went to a Shoney's restaurant, and he kept calling back the waitress to place his order. He tried to leave three or four tips. In the fall, he underwent radiation treatments. He was put on the prayer list at St. Mary's Basilica.

When I saw him, late in the month, he was fogged, depressed, shockingly thin. He had on house slippers, slacks, a sport shirt, a bathrobe. He was sitting in a maroon chair. There was a daybed behind him. I got him talking a little. He told me how he found out about his father's death. He was in Wem, England, with his Army outfit. This was 1944 and they'd just gotten there. He read the letter from home—no one had sent a wire—and fell back on his cot in the barracks and cried. He decided not to go home for the funeral, even though his superior officer had urged him to go. From his maroon rocker, Billy sort of acted it out for me. He held out his arm and then draped it over a chair. His fingers held an invisible letter. I thought in that instant he was going to cry. He nearly did. And yet what I remember most about that visit—which was the last time I saw him alive—was the way he talked of "raising those kids." He said it about half a dozen times. He was referring to his son, Tommy, and his daughter, Sherry, who lives in Baton Rouge. "We worked so hard raising those kids," he said. He mentioned "the hope of the flock." He was referring to grandkids and spoke specifically of Tommy's kids—Cricket Ferrell, who was finishing her law degree at Ole Miss, and Ty Ferrell, who was out in New Mexico as a U.S. Border Patrol agent, carrying on the family business. "So you can see, we've had this kind of pretty ordinary life," he said, "just the usual family dreams."

He held on through Christmas and into the first two months of the new year and then came the five-column headline on page one of the *Natchez Democrat* on March 1, 1999: "Adams County Mourns Loss of 'Greatest' Sheriff." There was a photo. "He had so many friends that there's no way to count them," someone was quoted as saying. "He was very good to the youth," someone else said. "We had our ups and downs about how things should be done, but I found him to be fair," the former mayor of Natchez said.

One of the stories told at the obsequies concerned the Great Shootout at Lake Mary. Billy had crawled under the floorboards of a shack out in the woods by a lake near the Homochitto River. He was lying on his back, firing up through cracks at a crazed person. The crazed person was black and his name was DeWayne Sampson Russell. According to the newspaper accounts afterward, Russell was an ex-inmate of the state insane asylum at Whitfield. This was in the summer of 1969. "Billy was hit several times and he still carried that lead," one of Billy's old deputies told a reporter at the *Democrat* when the paper wrote up the news of the high sheriff's death.

The case files of the DeWayne Sampson Russell incident reveal that two sheriffs from two counties, plus their respective deputies, were involved in the gun battle. Burnell McGraw, sheriff of Wilkinson County, which sits just below Adams County, had called Billy to ask for help. He said there was a hermit in an old house on the north side of Lake Mary, which spreads into both counties, and the hermit was threatening to kill anyone who came near him. Billy said he'd come. Before getting into his squad car with his deputies, he wrote out on a yellow legal pad an account of the phone conversation he'd had with his counterpart in Wilkinson County. He wrote the synopsis in longhand, in the remarkably neat and almost feminine script he'd learned from nuns in Catholic grammar school. The document is four pages long and it's in the case files in the Adams County sheriff's office. He wrote:

> After hearing this resume from Sheriff McGraw and being advised that he did not know if the subject would be in Wilkinson County or Adams County, I advised him that I would come myself with two of

my deputies and meet him and his deputy at the Court House in Woodville at 2:30 P.M. this afternoon. After talking to McGraw I issued the necessary orders to my department, naming Deputies Jim Logan and Fred Smith as the two to accompany me to Lake Mary. I advised them to have ready 1 M-15 high-powered .233 rifle w/scope and four clips of ammunition, 1 .45 cal machine-gun with two clips, the large gas gun for house barrage, 2 walkie-talkie radios, a bullhorn and Deputy Logan requested that he be allowed to carry his own 30-06 rifle with scope and this permission was granted. We had our standard handguns & belts, etc., so then we proceeded to Woodville, Miss.

In the back of the file there's an envelope with about fifty color snapshots, every one a picture of a dead man at the bottom of some wooden steps, arms akimbo, a leg stretched wide, the other leg behind him, a hat a few feet away, blood everywhere. The snapshots, taken from many angles, document a man stopped in a running motion. Also in the case file is an order for immediate closure, written and signed three days after the incident by an Adams County superior court judge. It's one page long: "State of Miss. vs. DeWayne Sampson Russell. This matter having come on for hearing on this day, and the Court having determined that the Defendant, DeWayne Sampson Russell, is now deceased and that it is to the best interests of the State of Mississippi that said matter be retired to the files and no further action taken with the cost of retiring this matter to be borne by the State of Mississippi. It is therefore hereby ordered and adjudged that this case be retired to the files."

What isn't in Case Report Number 7074—you'd have to look in other repositories in Mississippi—is an FBI roster of old Adams County lawmen (sheriffs, deputies, constables, police chiefs, city patrolmen) alleged to have once been active members of the Ku Klux Klan. Burnell McGraw's name is on one of those FBI lists. And on another lengthy FBI list (undated) of alleged members of the Adams County Klavern of the White Knights of the KKK, there's this: "Ferrell FNU." FNU means "First Name Unknown." There are other lists, too, in other repositories, where the name Ferrell can be found, without particular documentation, linked to the KKK. In the archives of the special collections at the University of Mississippi, there's a multipage listing of "Natchez Individuals Suspected of Belonging to Klan." This list is broken into categories: "RNC—reported, not confirmed." "UK—United Klans." "KS—strong klan sympathizer." "WK—white knight." The names on this document seem to have been compiled privately in the mid-sixties by civil rights activists in Natchez, when Billy was out of office as sheriff. The titles and job descriptions include owners of cab companies, employees at Johns Manville, International Paper, and Armstrong Tire & Rubber, bus station workers, a logging contractor, service station employees, a justice of the peace, an electrical inspector, city firefighters, attorneys, a bartender at a local club. The fourth entry on the first page of the list: "Ferrell, William T., or ex sheriff, now city policeman (UK) said to handle propaganda and spread rumors." I cannot prove that Billy Ferrell was or was not a Klansman. A name on an old list, whether from the FBI or a civil rights group, doesn't prove anything. There's a mound of circumstantial evidence to suggest he was in the Klan—and there's just as much circumstantial evidence and personal testimony, if not more so, to suggest the opposite. (A former Mississippi Grand Dragon said recently that Billy was not a Klansman.) I've since had the family's denials and explanations.

The funeral at St. Mary's parish on Tuesday, March 2, 1999, was grand— flag on the coffin, uniformed lawmen from across the state, twenty-one-gun salutes, slow-moving line of police cars to the cemetery, wires of condolence from high officials in Jackson. Tommy arranged for most of it. The day of the wake, Monday, was the last day for filing for the upcoming sheriff's race, and it looked as if Tommy might go unopposed. But just in case that turned out not to be true, he posted a deputy outside the courthouse to keep him informed. On the afternoon of the wake, Billy Ferrell's son kept excusing himself from the line of mourners to step outside Laird Funeral Home so that he could get an update on his cell phone from the deputy stationed at the courthouse. Damned if an old known Kluxer from the sixties, with no prayer of winning but who hated the Ferrells, didn't come forward at about 4:30 P.M. to post his name for the race. This enraged Tommy. It was the Ferrell family flaw. His pride and spleen couldn't bear the thought that somebody could run against him, siphon off a few votes righteously his.

In the late nineties, a twin son of James Meredith was in graduate school at Ole Miss, at the same time a granddaughter of Billy Ferrell was a grad student there, walking under the same beautiful trees. She's Tommy's child, the brainy one everybody in the family calls Cricket. While the painfully shy Joe Meredith worked toward his Ph.D. in finance, the terribly confident Christina L. "Cricket" Ferrell, a few buildings away, studied for her law degree. Their lives overlapped in Oxford for more than two years. For a while, they lived in off-campus housing a few blocks from each other, neither aware the other existed. Surely, they passed each other on walks every week. In time, I met them both. I wanted to arrange an introduction, but that didn't work out. One, I knew, was too inward, the other too cognizant, savvy. No percentage in it, she'd have said about sitting down to chat with the son of the guy at whom her granddaddy was figuratively swinging.

Lost Boy

Second from the right—ripping the strip of gauze, bogarting his smoke, furrowing his brow, surveying the barrel end of Billy's bat—is Jim Garrison. He looks to be forty, easy, maybe even forty-five, right? He is twenty-seven. He'll be dead by fifty-one. In the summer of 1986, he'll be laid gently in the family plot, which is about a hundred yards from the Faulkner family plot, down a grassy bank. "I am older at twenty than a lot of people who have died," says Quentin Compson in *Absalom, Absalom.* That's the story in which Quentin is at Harvard and his Canadian roommate, Shreve McCannon, says: "Tell about the South. . . . Jesus, the South is fine, isn't it. It's better than theatre, isn't it. It's better than Ben Hur, isn't it. No wonder you have to come away now and then, isn't it."

Garrison has just another twenty-four years. Who could know he'd wind up the manager of a Long John Silver fast-food joint in Corinth, Mississippi? *Hey, fries are up! Pull around to the next window, please, ma'am.* The restaurant is out on the bypass, Highway 72, and the local cops are his buddies and they stop in for coffee during the day to sit with him on break in the second booth along the wall. It's always the second booth for Garrison, sometimes looking out the window toward the parking lot and cursing about how many slopeheads and Mexicans are getting into the country nowadays. To get to the job from his two-bedroom mobile home in the Woodlawn Trailer Park, he drives his Buick Regal through the town's historic district (Confederate commanders, wounded at Shiloh, once lay dying in these beautiful homes), past Chevrons and Billup stations, past the Grace Bible Baptist Temple, past the public library that keeps stacks of old *Life* magazines up on the second floor. He was christened James Wesley Garrison, the son of Webb Garrison and Grace Alvis Garrison, and was the younger brother of Marion Webster "Billy"

Garrison (another cop in the family with an oddly uncoppish name), and who, just like Marion, is destined to die early of the family curse: cancer. In both cases, and in other cases of the extended family, too, it eats them grindingly.

He looks a little like Timothy McVeigh, who blew up the Alfred P. Murrah Federal Building in Oklahoma City in 1995 and was executed for it six years later in a Faulknerlike grotesquerie of public attention. That's an ink pen or a ballpoint hooked in James Wesley's shirt pocket, next to his badge, which is bouncing light. It looks like there's a wire of some sort coming up from the back of his neck and alongside his scalp, but actually it's a police antenna on the hood of another squad car barely visible at the back of the frame. He went to Uncle Sam at age sixteen, served a long hitch, and has been out only a year or so, which possibly explains the G.I. flattop. He prevaricated about his age to get into the Army. He served in Germany and Korea, making sergeant, signing up for MP duty, busting heads of drunk soldiers on weekend liberty, writing an occasional postcard back to his hometown of Oxford to his kid sister, Pat, that went along the lines of "Hiya, Sis. Nothing to do over here. Army's OK. Don't get married till I get home. Hope to be a cop when I get back. We'll get some fishing in at Sardis Reservoir. Miss Mississippi bad. Your big brother, Jim."

When the tumors came—in the mid-eighties, after law enforcement, after the bad marriage—they lodged in his esophagus and in his stomach and then metastasized to both sides of his brain, one side at a time. He lived for about a year. His obituary was three paragraphs long, deep on an inside page. Attorney General Ed Meese's Commission on Pornography had just issued its big report after a year-long study. The Oxford High basketball cheerleaders had just been awarded the Spirit Stick at summer cheerleading camp. Almost everybody from the Corinth Long John's drove over for the funeral—they'd shut the restaurant down that day. Even some big shots from the corporate offices in Kentucky came to pay respects.

He has two markers in the family plot, and the first one is small and black and flat to the ground. It doesn't say anything about his once being a sheriff's deputy or a highway patrolman or running a Long John's or having been depicted hugely in *Life* in 1962. It says JAMES W. GARRISON. SGT. US ARMY. KOREA. FEB. 18, 1935. JULY 9, 1986. The first time I was there, standing on the late-spring spongy earth, somebody had placed plastic lilies at the base of his stone. Next to the flat marker was a larger upright stone and on it was a carving of two hands folded in prayer. Beside the monument was a small white plaster angel. From the corner of my eye, I could see a tour group of Faulkner shrinegoers, taking photographs, bending over to read the inscription on the master's stone, which has been darkened with moss and the years of dampness. They'd disgorged from a bus that was parked at the roadside, next to a green historical marker with gold lettering that said THE CREATOR OF YOKNAPATAWPHA

COUNTY, WHOSE STORIES ABOUT HIS PEOPLE WON HIM THE NOBEL PRIZE, IS BURIED TWENTY STEPS EAST OF THIS MARKER.

About two miles from the immortal grave and the nearly anonymous grave, I am sipping the Coke that Pat James, a sweet-mannered and round-faced middle-aged woman, has brought to me in a tumbler, with a paper napkin around its glass base. An hour ago, when I called Jim Garrison's kid sister out of the blue, she said, after a moment's hesitation, "Sure, you can come over." She said she was just folding laundry and watching a TV movie. It was a Saturday afternoon. I mentioned *Life*. "Yes, that would be my brother," she said. "Oh, I know my brother was involved in that riot, because he had that picture in *Life* magazine. I remember his face was blistered after the riot, from the tear gas. My husband—he wasn't my husband yet—was turning hamburgers at the university grill when James Meredith was trying to register. He won't talk to you about any of that, though. I was very young."

She's in a back room, searching for something. On a bookshelf in the living room, with other family portraits, there's a colorized and framed portrait of her brother in a state trooper's uniform. This was in the seventies, after he'd been a deputy sheriff. He has blue eyes, at least in the colorized version. Pat comes back. She has a man's old leather billfold in her hand. It's a three-fold wallet and she holds it out in front of her and lets it fall open, in the way a cop might do who's just knocked at the door and is flashing his identification at you. There he is, on the other side of a cracked and broken little plastic window: his driver's license with a thumbnail picture of him. The face photostatted on Mississippi license number 001-52-7167 looks anything but serene. A very ill man must have gotten his license renewed, aware that he'd not need to renew it again. "It's his," she says, pressing the billfold to her bosom. "I keep things like this." She seems close to crying.

When he got on with the highway patrol, it was such a life's dream realized, she says. But it didn't work out. He left early. "His wife would go to roadblocks, they'd fight right there while he was on the job, it was terrible. Now, whether he resigned or if he was asked to leave, I don't know. He's my brother. I just leave it at that." Afterward, he worked in the family bait shop. Then he found the restaurant job at Long John Silver's in Corinth.

"All our men are buried there," she says of her brother's grave. She follows me out to the car. "If you ever get another one of those *Life* magazines, I'd love to have it," she says. "You know, keepsake."

In Corinth, up near the Tennessee and Alabama borders, about a ninety-minute drive from Oxford, Susan Plunk is about ready to get off work at Long John Silver's. She's in her thirties, very pretty, a new mom. She took the four-month-old to Kmart last evening, she says. She's worked at the restaurant since she was sixteen. "Of course I knew him," she says. "He was my first manager. He helped me with the first down payment on my first car. I needed a thousand down. He gave me five hundred. He was always doing things like that. He said, 'Susan, you shouldn't be driving any old car. You need a car like mine.' He went to the lot and got the deal. He took care of his parents, too. I know that. Their names were on his checkbook."

She used to sit with him every morning in the second booth. She was a high school kid and he was in his mid-forties. He'd drink coffee, she'd have a slice of pecan pie. At ten-thirty, they'd open for the day. He was always a tough boss, but fair. There were eighteen employees and all were white. Well, there was one black kid working in the place for a while, but it didn't work out. "He took a knife away from the kid. He drew it on Jim. He was a strong guy, you know." After that, there were no more blacks working for him.

I ask about his friends. "Cops. He liked hanging around with the cops. They all knew him."

Once, she brought in her high school annual for him to sign. He signed the yearbook so beautifully, she thought. It was something like "Susan, you'll always be in remembrance of me." On holidays, he'd have the staff out to his trailer. He'd do all the cooking. He'd turn the music up and everybody would dance. It was as if he never wanted to be alone.

I show her the magazine. The picture was taken two years before she was born. She stares at it for an instant. Jumping up: "Yes! It *is* him." She sits down, studying it. There's a smile on her face. "He didn't tell me about this. He never told me about this. I didn't know anything about this." She is somewhere between amused and peeved.

I ask about the cancer. "When he came back from surgery in Memphis, he didn't talk about it much." She makes a circle with her thumb and index finger. "He was that big around." He took to walking with a cane. He couldn't eat right. He tried to keep on working. He stared out windows a lot. Finally, he called his baby sister: "Pat, come get me." Just before she drove him home to die, one of the other female workers at the restaurant tried to hug him. He shrank from the pain of the embrace, putting his hands up. "Please," he begged. Pat James carried him to Oxford in the car and he went into the hospital that night and two weeks later he was dead.

Susan Plunk is crying, looking out the window toward the parking lot. "I went over to the hospital in Oxford to see him. I don't even know if he knew me. He had so much painkiller in him." The picture is open before us. We're in the same booth he always sat in when he was taking a break, or before the restaurant opened for the day.

"Did he seem to regret things?"

She knows where this is going. "You mean like racism things?"

"Uh-huh."

"Well, it would be hard to know."

Later, at Susan's suggestion, I look up one of his old cop buddies. Like so many others, he holds the magazine out in front of him. "Well, bless his heart," says this cop, who is still a cop. Later, too, some others who used to work at Long John's recall him fondly. Audine Stutts Nix dated him for a while. "He proposed to me, matter of fact," she says. "We went a year. I think he had his cancer long before they diagnosed it. He'd wake up in the middle of the night and vomit." And Tanya Lambert, who, like Susan Plunk, was a teenager when she first worked for Jim Garrison, in answer to a question of why he kept on working until the end, says: "I'm pretty sure it's because he just didn't want to be alone. He knew he was going to die, and he just didn't want to be by himself."

A few months later, I visited Pat James again and also an older sister, Mary Katharine Hemphill. If anything, the family memories were dearer, more entrenched. The talking was pleasant. The sisters referred to each other as "the doctor" and "the banker." Pat James, an R.N., has always ministered to the sick of the family, while her big sister, Mary Katharine, so natural with figures and ledger books, and perhaps a little more suspicious of strangers who are writers, has always kept an eye on the business side of Garrison matters. On the phone, Pat said she had asked her husband, Harold James, if he'd sit and talk to me this time. "I told him there was this man with a magazine and he'd like to talk to you about the riots. But my husband said to tell you, 'No, that's past. That's dead.' "

I've been served a Coke again, with a napkin around the base of the sweating glass. "We lived on a farm for a while when Jim was young," Mary Katharine is saying. "He was the cream and the love of the neighborhood. All these people would come to the farm and Jim would just shine for them." Pat: "I remember an old maid schoolteacher. Edna Snipes. When Jim worked in our bait shop, before he got the job at Long John's, he used to sit and talk to her. He never knew a stranger, Jim didn't. He loved the elderly." She hesitates. "You know, he so wanted his own children. He would have been a wonderful father."

Several days before he died, barely able to speak but sometimes calling out a name when a family member came into the room, Jim passed to Mary Katharine a little ledger book he'd long been keeping. In neat entries, he'd recorded the various small loans he'd made to friends and employees. "You go collect this," he whispered to his sister. Well, she tried to get some, but then forgot about it.

A twelve-year-old grandson has come into the living room as these stories are being told. The boy suspends himself upside down on a Barcalounger. "Look here, Wesley, your relative," Pat says. The kid rights himself, springs to the floor, comes over to take a look at the magazine. He grunts and goes back to standing on his head.

Since the family has lived in town for decades, I ask if they knew Faulkner. "We knew him," says Pat. "We knew this man. Well, we didn't really know him. We'd see him downtown, smoking his pipe, looking at people. He'd have his foot corkscrewed up behind him against the wall of Blaylock's Drug Store. We thought he was odd."

As I Lay Dying is Faulkner's tragic-cum-hilarious story of the Bundren family's odyssey across Mississippi to bury wife and mother Annie Bundren. Each member of the family tells the story, including Annie's son Darl, a kind of lost boy, who says: "How often have I lain beneath rain on a strange roof, thinking of home."

*I*n Kosciusko, James Meredith's hometown, up near the middle of the state, where I was just passing through, the young and attractive black woman with TRAINER on her tag softly put the change in my hand, not in the least self-conscious about her skin touching mine. A few feet away, in the booths, six elderly black men were talking. One spoke loudly about how he'd not been a good father, and so why should he think his sons would have turned out any differently as parents. They slurped their coffee and sat with their bodies slack. Another man said he could remember having to stare at the floor and not look up the whole time some son-ofabitch white man—any white man—demanded it, not necessarily by anything the bastard said, just by his presence. "I've lived through all that," he said. "Never forget it." Opposite him, a third man in this group said, "You're still afraid of white men, ain't you?" There was a strained silence. The man who'd told about having to stare at floors ate his Egg McMuffin. But to think: a half dozen old black men, up from apartheid, talking of these matters, loudly as they pleased, in the clean and well-lit Friday morning plastic cheeriness of a McDonald's in James Meredith's hometown. Around them at other booths and tables were another twenty or so diners—blacks and whites and some Pakistanis and I think some Choctaw Indians. Nobody paid any particular mind to anybody else. The entire room was eating and chatting and commingling with its own dreams and anxieties and separate resentments. It was the illusion of racial heterogeneity, and the more I traveled in the lush, blistered paradise and place of sorrows called Mississippi, the more I deeply understood the fact.

Grimsley

Law enforcement was in the hands of bigots, and bigotry was respectable.

—C. Vann Woodward, *The Strange Career of Jim Crow*

His neck seems violently red against the tight white collar.

—James Agee, *Let Us Now Praise Famous Men*

He loved his lid. "Boys, I'm getting me a Stetson hat and you all are going to wear one, too," he told his dozen deputies on the first or second day he came into office. He's got it steamed and blocked and dented just so. The leather band on the inside must be a greasy and sweet-smelling black: congealed sweat and Vitalis gone so rancid it's turned the corner and become strangely fine. Did he go all the way to New Orleans, to a famous hatter on St. Charles Avenue, just to buy his beaver chapeau? Somebody who knew him pretty well back then remembered that. In any case, there must have been some large vanity in this hefty man, even though others have wondered in retrospect whether the gaudy strut and effusive greeting—"Hello, son!" he'd cry at you from across a Pascagoula street, if you were white—were just a reaction to how ugly he felt inside. So maybe the "colorfulness" people speak of was cloaking a fearsome lack of self-worth. His face was deeply pocked. His bulbous nose was deeply veined. The head law enforcer went around his county with breath generally stinking from liquor.

His name was James Ira Grimsley. He's second on the left. He's fifty. Let him go on guffawing a little bit more in this silvered September light, his hands stuck in his trouser pockets, his specs sliding downward. He'll be on earth for another twenty-five years, until his diseased liver and asbestosis carry him off. He may have gotten the first germs of it inside him decades ago, when he'd worked in the local shipyards. He's going to die alone, on a Monday, October 19, 1987, in a boxy little pine-board house at 2506 Grimsley Drive in the sweltering town at the bottom of the state, on the Gulf Coast, where he was born and reared and is head lawman now. His wife will have gone before. There will be no children. Apparently, there will be no money. Poise him in your imagination, undisturbed, even as he's held on this sheet of developing paper. "All photographs are abandonings," a cultural critic at the *Washington Post,* Henry Allen, once wrote. "Once there was a moment, the click of a shutter, and now it's gone, a framed ghost, abandoned by time and failing memory. This is the sentiment at the heart of photography's mechanical mystery." This framed, inebriated ghost isn't going to be abandoned. You'll hear about his life, and of the way his hypocritical and equally bigoted fellow Pascagoulians began to forsake him, after they'd allowed him to become their drunken hero, within several months of when this photograph was made. They forsook him not because they were morally ashamed, of either his or their own behavior, but because their livelihoods and financial well-being seemed suddenly in the balance: They'd grown terrified that the federal government, disgusted with Mississippi and in particular with some of their own actions, might cancel lucrative contracts at the big Pascagoula shipyard, on which their economy so depended. But first, a few pages in a broader vein about high sheriffs and Mississippi in the torn years of civil rights.

The word "sheriff" is said to derive from thirteenth-century England, when kings began the practice of appointing officers of the court known as the Shire Reeves, or Reeves of the Shire. They were personal representatives of the king, empowered to collect his revenue and to preserve his peace. The office of sheriff, thought to be the oldest law enforcement office within the common-law system, may go back—if not by name, then in function—as far as the ninth century. So in Great Britain a sheriff was an important figure even before the Magna Carta. Sometimes he entered the realm of legend—the sheriff of Nottingham, for instance, who pursued Robin Hood in Sherwood Forest in the twelfth century. In Mississippi, not any longer, but for a longer while than for most other states of the union—really, right into modern times—"sheriff" always stood for two things: the district's tax collector and its top cop, who possessed nearly unassailable authority. And that is how a candidate campaigned for the countywide job. If he got elected, he could expect to get his cut of every tax dime taken in. But the ways in which he became rich— not that all Mississippi sheriffs automatically did—didn't necessarily have to do with those fractions, which were normally about 5 percent. A corrupt sheriff in Mississippi in the 1950s and 1960s made most of his illicit loot from payoffs for allowing whiskey joints to remain open. He made it from skims on the prostitution and gambling he'd permit to go on within his borders. Depending on the level of his corruption and avarice, depending on the makeup of the county itself, he could get quite wealthy, or only happily fixed. There's an old saying in Mississippi: All you have to do is "get that thing once," the "thing" being the office of sheriff. That's not a truism anymore, or so almost everybody insists, including current holders of the office. Nowadays, there are checks and balances on the office—some.

There were dry counties and wet counties back then—but liquor was illegal in every county, and had been since 1908—except that the state legislature had passed something called "the black market tax," meaning that there was legal taxation on a product that didn't lawfully exist. In certain towns and counties, the prohibition law was completely ignored, and joints and package stores operated openly; if not with impunity, at least with no fear of being shut down, so long as they kept to their payoff schedules. The sheriff had to get his monthly bribe, but others did, too. The sheriff, after all, was keeping the place clean: no sales to minors. If the bar owners and package-store proprietors operated within a town's limits, they could expect to get arrested by the constabulary once a month—say, on a Monday morning—and then they'd more or less happily troop down to City Hall to pay their $100 fine, allowing them to stay open for the next thirty days. (The money theoretically went into the city kitty.)

In terms of what were called lawful earnings, the head lawman worked on a complicated fee and commission system. He got a percentage from selling license tags, for serving a summons or a subpoena, from taking bail bonds, for feeding prisoners, for making arrests. He paid his deputies out of these fees and commissions. His deputies, picked by him, were on a salary set by him. The deputies, like constables (these were low-level law enforcement officials, managing a "beat" within the county), made mileage money whenever a prisoner was brought to a justice of the peace. The constable, unlike the deputy, also got paid a percentage of every fine, along with the JP and others, so on this level of law enforcement there was a financial incentive to write tickets and to make arrests on trumped-up charges. Civil rights workers were the fattest targets in the sixties, it doesn't need explaining. You can go through old newspapers and find in the fine print, under court proceedings, entries like this one: "Milton Hancock fined $175 by Judge Orman Kimbrough. $50 for reckless driving, $25 for improper equipment on automobile, $10 for resisting arrest. Car had no muffler, no right headlight, and 'did not look in good operating order.' "

Theoretically, a sheriff could be removed from office—but it was mostly a theory. There was some sort of archaic provision on the books that the county coroner could arrest the sheriff in an emergency. The sheriff's police power, extending to the next county line, was absolute—which isn't to say that weak men didn't sometimes get into office and become victims of their own power. Or maybe victims of the racist mayor (who perhaps kept his white sheet folded in the top drawer of the dresser in his bedroom). Or maybe victims of the leaders of the local Ku Klux Klan (who, in some cases, had their offices downtown, with Klan insignia on the door). Or maybe victims of the heads of that county's chapter of the White Citizens' Council (who, in a way, were the most pernicious Mississippians of all, since they attempted to conduct their bigotry with a kind of Rotarian respectability).

Sheriffs in Mississippi during the years of civil rights were of a type, but they also ran the gamut of human nature. If virtually none could be said to be anywhere near benevolent in his treatment of blacks, it seems equally true that only the vilest hated with a pure white unrelenting hatred. More than a few had to have been sadists—there is plenty of testimony around to make you believe that. It was as if the legacy of slavery came with their office, and so they lived up to it. That is a kind of epitaph for white Mississippi itself. And yet nothing is monolithic. As a noted book critic, Benjamin Schwarz, has written of Southern law enforcers in general (in a 1998 review of an important work of scholarship titled *Trouble in Mind: Black Southerners in the Age of Jim Crow,* by Leon F. Litwack): "Because by current standards nearly all white Southerners were racist, it is easy to assume that there is no point in distinguishing among their 'racist' attitudes. But it is doubtful whether a black sharecropper visiting a strange town in rural Arkansas, for instance, wouldn't care whether its sheriff was a segregationist who opposed violence and favored a degree of protection to blacks (however inadequate to modern eyes) or whether he was a virulent racist who would deny blacks the most basic rights and indeed encourage threats to their lives and property. Although perhaps both figures are reprehensible, both sorts of white men lived throughout the South and the difference between them could, for a black man, mean life or death."

In some counties of Mississippi, as the movement began, blacks outnumbered whites four to one. In 1962, there were still whole counties where not a single black was registered to vote. In his landmark work *The Strange Career of Jim Crow,* C. Vann Woodward, perhaps the greatest of all Southern historians, a deep if ambivalent lover of the South, wrote: "The state with the largest Negro minority and the last state to have a black majority of population, Mississippi was also the poorest state in the Union, and the most profoundly isolated from national life and opinion. Professor James W. Silver described it as 'a closed society,' which 'comes as near to approximating a police state as anything we have yet seen in America.' Its Negroes lived in constant fear and its whites under rigid conformity to dogmas of white supremacy as interpreted by a state-subsidized Citizens' Council."

James Silver was a white history professor at Ole Miss during the Meredith crisis, and afterward he wrote a book entitled *Mississippi: The Closed Society.* It is probably the most famous condemnation of the state ever written. "In such a society," Silver said, "a never-ceasing propagation of the 'true faith' must go on relentlessly, with a constantly reiterated demand for loyalty to the united front, requiring that non-conformists and dissenters from the code be silenced, or, in a crisis, driven from the community." Silver himself left the state in the middle sixties, driven out by many forces. He went to Notre Dame University and then afterward the non-Mississippi native retired to Florida, where he died. As much as there is to be admired in his courageous book, it seems a little exaggerated. The book would have you think that the collective pressures were so unspeakable that no ordinary white Mississippian in any community or town ever spoke out. But, in truth, in almost every community and town back then, there were ordinary heroic white people doing ordinary jobs who tried to bear some kind of witness—quiet or otherwise—against what was going on, and who didn't leave, and who weren't murdered, and who, in some cases, are living today in the same houses on the same streets. These white Mississippians, local people, if piteously few in number, were present, in the fifties and sixties, during the wall of water, along with the far more numerous and even more heroic black Mississippians, local people, who were present, willing to give away everything, including their lives, toward the promise of eventual freedom.

In 1963, which is when portions of Silver's book were first published, which is also the year thirty-seven-year-old Medgar Evers was slain in his driveway in Jackson, Roy Wilkins, head of the National Association for the Advancement of Colored People, said: "There is no state with a record that approaches that of Mississippi in inhumanity, murder, brutality, and racial hatred. It is absolutely at the bottom of the list." That same year, the Judiciary Committee of the Eighty-eighth Congress held civil rights hearings in Washington. The committee produced a "Chronology of Violence and Intimidation in Mississippi Since 1961," gathered mainly from civil rights organizations. There was this entry, for instance, page 1073, in the many pages of dense, shrunken type:

August 1962, Greenwood, Leflore County: Welton McSwine, Jr., 14-year-old Negro, was arrested by police after a white woman's house had been broken into. When police got the youth to the station, an officer said: "All right, nigger, you know why you are here, and we want to know who broke into that white woman's house." McSwine told them he knew nothing of the incident, saying that he spent all his time in the cottonfield, and suggesting that his mother could corroborate this. McSwine said officers then took him to a cell and beat him, first hitting him in the head with a blackjack; then one of the policemen beat him in the face with his fist while another hit him in the stomach with his club; then the officers made him lie naked on the floor on his side while they beat him with a whip. McSwine was released after intercession of his father's white employer.

Nothing ever came of that brutality, even though the charges (along with photographs documenting the beating) went to the Justice Department and to the FBI. Some of the people who beat McSwine are still living. They were city cops, not sheriffs or sheriff's deputies, and there is an indirect and tangential relationship to one of the seven men in this photograph.

In 1964, the year following those Judiciary Committee hearings, in the middle of what is known to history as Freedom Summer, the Southern Regional Council, a civil rights organization based in Atlanta, put out a publication called *Law Enforcement in Mississippi*. It listed "instances of violence and open intimidation" by cops against blacks and voter registration workers. It was only a six-month list. "Even so," the report said, "the list is almost certainly incomplete. . . . But more than are listed below are hardly needed, in order to document the almost unrestrained lawlessness which is permitted within the state against one class of people." This was at the time of the murders of three civil rights workers in Philadelphia, a Mississippi hamlet named for brotherly love. The names of the murdered became a national chant that summer: *Schwerner, Chaney, Goodman*. Not long afterward, the umbrella civil rights organization known as COFO (Council of Federated Organizations) assembled a book of affidavits entitled *Mississippi Black Paper*. It contained fifty-seven personal testimonies of violence against blacks and civil rights workers. The foreword was written by renowned theologian Reinhold Niebuhr. He said: "The crimes described in the following pages, committed either by local officials or with their connivance, include the bombings of homes and churches, the arrests of Negroes on false charges for every type of fanciful law infraction, and—most frightening of all—a brutality by the police that approaches sadistic cruelty and on occasion has resulted in actual murder."

In February 1965, six months after the bodies of Mickey Schwerner, James Earl Chaney, and Andrew Goodman had been excavated from under an earthen dam, the United States Commission on Civil Rights came to Mississippi for a week of public hearings. They were held in Jackson. In advance of the hearings, the commissioners had its Washington staff people bone up on the role and power of the Mississippi sheriff, the iconic figure of oppression in the struggle for civil rights. In a later report called "Law Enforcement," published after the hearings were concluded, the commission said: "The office of sheriff in Mississippi, as in other Southern States, is closely linked in history and character to the early English sheriff. During the last thousand years the sheriff's duty to enforce the law has remained remarkably unchanged. In Mississippi today, as in medieval England, the sheriff is the principal 'conservator of peace in his county.' . . . Although a sheriff is required to maintain records pertaining to the jail, he is not required to keep any investigation records. . . . As a practical matter, the elective sheriff is not subject to any executive or administrative review or sanction." The investigators quoted an earlier Brookings Institution study: "Since the sheriff is elected by the people, he can be made responsible only in part or in a minor degree to any other authority." The investigators quoted a still earlier study called *The Government and Administration of Mississippi:* "There is generally no state authority to compel the enforcement of a law by local officers." The investigators concluded this report: "The failure of law enforcement officials to curb racial violence is largely attributable to the racially hostile attitudes of sheriffs, police chiefs, and prosecuting attorneys. . . . In addition, failure to make prompt arrests, to take a firm stand against violence, and to announce an intention to punish law violators undoubtedly encouraged vigilantes to feel they could operate with impunity." It was as if the decent men from the United States Commission on Civil Rights had discovered Mississippi's laws were rigged.

The general counsel of those 1965 hearings was William L. Taylor. He is upper-aged now and has had a long, distinguished career as a civil rights attorney based in Washington. He can still remember some vivid things about traveling to what seemed like the moonscape of Mississippi. He and several investigators went to the state in late 1964 to do advance work. He was in Natchez, staying at the Eola Hotel, the city's finest. He went down to breakfast. Some local intimidators came up to stand a few feet from his table. They didn't do anything, they just stood there and looked at him while he ate. One evening, Taylor was interviewing a local white Catholic parish priest, active in the movement. They were talking in the priest's parlor in the rectory, and Taylor heard this funny cracking sound beyond the window. They turned down the light and went to the window and looked out and saw a man standing under a lamppost at a filling station across the street. He was lazily working a bull whip in the direction of the rectory.

In the published record of the hearings, there are little novels within novels. This exchange, for instance, with the sheriff of Natchez and Adams

County—who wasn't Billy Ferrell. Billy was out of office; Natchez had a new head lawman. Billy would be back, for keeps, as soon as it was legal for him to run again, but in 1965 the sheriff was another local son, Odell Anders, whose name was already beginning to show up on certain FBI lists of Mississippi cops who reputedly belonged to the Klan. Anders had been subpoenaed to the hearings, and he was under oath, and some of the questioning concerned his predecessor and the keeping of records as they related to certain criminal investigations the committee was interested in.

> *Mr. Anders:* I didn't take office until January 6, 1964. So we don't
>   have anything whatsoever which was, you know, before we took
>   office in '64.
> *Mr. Taylor:* Are there no records in the sheriff's office pertaining on
>   that matter which may have been filed by one of your predecessors?
> *Mr. Anders:* If there are, I haven't found them, no, sir.

One of the commissioners asks Anders's attorney: "Are you saying that the sheriff's office maintains no records?" The attorney representing Anders says: "There are some records, but nothing pertaining to those incidents."

> *Mr. Anders:* If there were records in the sheriff's office, I didn't find
>   them. Now there might be; I don't know. But if there are any records
>   on these four things before January 6 of '64, I don't know where they
>   are.
> *Commissioner Griswold:* Mr. Sheriff, have you made a search for
>   these records?
> *Mr. Anders:* In the Adams County office, yes, sir.

Further down in the transcript:

> *Commissioner Griswold:* When you took office as sheriff, did it
>   appear that all or most of the papers and records had been removed
>   by your predecessor?
> *Mr. Anders:* Sir, I don't—I don't know how many had been removed
>   or, you know, that hadn't been removed in the sheriff's office. I don't
>   know what was there prior to January 6.

And none of this will "explain" seven figures in a rectangle, sentient beings and sons of Mississippi who lived and strutted and died, but who've come together from different parts of the state, standing fearless in these refracted slivers of sunshine, to make their unwitting picture, to enjoy their group joke, to bar a black man from trying to improve himself, to keep the damn federals and anybody else from forcing something down their sovereign throats. So back, back to the one laughing loudest today, enjoying it most, "chortling," as the *Life* caption writers in New York will shortly describe it, bellied in the fan-whoosh of Billy's bat, this ribald, uncouth, bloated, dangerous, childless figure: James Ira Grimsley. It's as if he wishes to be the ripe burlesque of what already exists in America's mind when the words "Mississippi sheriff" are uttered. *Grimsley,* with a name that's out of Faulkner, and Charles Dickens, too. Faulkner, both goad and god of Mississippi, has died less than three months ago in Wright's Sanitarium in nearby Byhalia, Mississippi.

In a sense, you know the particulars of his life story already. Mark Strand, who writes so acutely about the paintings of Edward Hopper, has said: "Hopper's paintings are not vacancies in a rich ongoingness. They are all that can be gleaned from a vacancy that is shaded not so much by the events of a life lived as by the time before life and the time after." And another sentiment, this one from John Szarkowski, former director of the department of photography at the Museum of Modern Art in New York. He was once looking at the photographs of Eudora Welty, whose stories and novels about her native Mississippi are second only to Faulkner's in their literary beauty and understanding of the state. In the thirties, she'd made pictures of Southerners as an amateur and gifted and itinerant government photographer, and Szarkowski wrote of this work: "It would be both false and wrong to say that we envy the people described in these pictures; people cursed by ignorance and poverty and bad diet and worn-out ideas, but there is something visible here that prompts in us inchoate feelings of longing for lives that have in them something of the beauty and elegance of good theater."

Is his tie made of imitation watered silk? Is there a yellow-brown scorch from an iron imprinted somewhere on his eighteen-and-a-half-inch shirt collar? If you were giving this lawman a made-up name, before you knew anything about him, wouldn't it be "Mr. Loving It All"?

James Ira Grimsley, the profaning pope of Pascagoula. He drove up to Ole Miss in the middle of last night with three of his deputies: Pete Pope, Tony Greer, and Leon Lambert. (They have to be close by.) They got here a little before dawn. It took about five hours, what with these poor roads, in this very vertical state with its great distances between north and south. Even to do it in five hours, they had to haul. Grimsley's a native of the Gulf Coast, where the sunsets are magnificent and the sand fleas large and the bathlike ocean waters extremely shallow. He runs Jackson County down there, with its strings of whorehouses and uncounted gambling joints and "shinny" business, which is a localism for bootlegging. (Don't confuse Jackson County, sitting on the Gulf of Mexico, with the capital city, Jackson, which is Mississippi's only real metropolis and is up toward the center of the state.) Pascagoula is the place known throughout the South for making ships. The Ingalls Shipbuilding Corporation is the largest industrial concern in all of Mississippi, employing thousands. In Pascagoula today, Pascagoula being the seat of Jackson County, and "today" being September 27, 1962, the banner headline in the local paper is "Sheriff Goes to Oxford." The subhead is "Shooting Possible at School Campus, Says Rep. Hester." The story starts: "Sheriff James Ira Grimsley and three Jackson County deputies left early today for Oxford. James Meredith was reportedly expected to make another attempt to integrate Ole Miss later today." The piece tells how Governor Ross Barnett is said to be on his way back to the tinderbox campus, and how, in the capital city the day before, a legislator took to the floor of the statehouse to declaim it was possible a gun battle could erupt between Mississippi lawmen and the federals. Pascagoulians could read this news in their local daily for five cents if they were buying the sheet on the newsstand, and for even less if they were getting the paper at home.

It's not known whether he's got raw onions in the side pockets of his suit coat, but down in Pascagoula, he almost always has them. He'll carry them in his coat and try to sneak *chawnks* when he thinks folks aren't looking, hoping thereby to mask the foulness of his breath. He shows up at circuit court with the hidden onions, sits in the pews and joshes with his neighbors while he waits to go on the stand against some black he's arrested without cause. Everybody in town knows the sheriff is washed, not least his wife, Betty, not least his deputies, who try to cover for him, not least the judge hearing the case, who has contempt for his drunkenness but who more or less puts up with it, not least the prisoner in question, who's about to be shanghaied to the county farm for something like having a taillight out.

He weighs approximately 220 pounds and he's a shade under five feet ten. (This is from FBI documents that were compiled on Grimsley in the several months following the Meredith crisis.) He's a charter member of First United Methodist. He belongs to the Freemasons and the Odd Fellows. In his youth, he was an amateur boxer, and apparently not half bad at it. He sleeps in an apartment on the top floor of the courthouse and jail—when Betty Roberts Grimsley allows him up there. If he's too drunk, his wife will make him sleep downstairs in the docket room with one of the deputies. For all his bloatedness, he's agile on his feet. Allegedly, he likes to "cut" black women, which is a Southernism for trying to attack them sexually. (Again, this is from Justice Department and FBI documents, but also several Pascagoulians were willing to say it, remember it, all these years later.) Within less than a month from the moment of the photograph, the sheriff's own former chief criminal deputy, Harold Jones, having earlier resigned from the sheriff's department and having left the state and gone into the Army, will allege in a statement before a lawyer that will then be forwarded to the DOJ in Washington: "Worst part about the sheriff is that he'll try to cut every woman he gets alone.

Women who come to visit their husbands in jail. . . . Wife of a guy we held on car theft charges. Everytime she came in sheriff would cut her." He'll also say in this sworn statement before a lawyer: "There was no bag man. Each guy paid off directly to the sheriff." Was the former chief deputy telling the truth? Jones was known to be a straight cop, albeit a typical Mississippian who apparently felt it was fine to use the word "nigger" throughout a statement charging his superior with evil things.

What else is known? He's very attentive to his mother. He's the owner of Grimsley Grocery Store on Canty Street, where he extends credit to folks who seldom have the cash. It's a mom-and-pop affair, one cash register, lone bulb in the ceiling, oiled floors, and he doesn't tend the place himself, now that he's sheriff.

What else? He's got a beautiful letterhead on his engraved stationery, with renderings of the courthouse. "James Ira Grimsley," it says on the top left-hand corner. "Sheriff and Tax Collector." Three months ago, June 29, 1962, this letter went out on his stationery, under his name, to the director of the State Sovereignty Commission regarding one Hansel C. Travillion, "colored male": "Dear Mr. Jones: The above subject is the Director of Civil Defense for the colored in this County, he also operates the colored funeral home in this county. To my knowledge this subject has always been an up standing citizen and has no dealings with the NAACP or any other subversive organization." Those kinds of letters get written all the time.

What else? He tried to go hoboing in his youth with his first cousin Jack Maples. They'd hopped an eastbound freight, but by the time they got to Alabama, they were homesick for Mississippi. "Jack, don't you think mama's biscuits would be tasting mighty good this morning?" he'd said to the cousin.

Something else you'd hardly imagine from the picture itself: The sheriff of Pascagoula, a crude and physically sloppy man in so many ways, was in a premed curriculum at Millsaps College in Jackson from September 1945 to August 1947. Millsaps is one of the best liberal arts institutions in the state. The premed studies are probably part of the reason why he was able to get elected to the post of Jackson County coroner. In Mississippi, in these years, a man doesn't need a medical license to serve as coroner, although any kind of expertise or knowledge in that direction wouldn't hurt your chances. Grimsley served as county coroner from 1957 to 1960. He always had his eye on making the bigger prize of sheriff, folks say. He would go around to hospitals and funeral homes, doing his work, sitting with the families, plying for the vote.

(At Millsaps, in the registrar's office, they had to dig around for a while, but sure enough, there it was, written in ink on an old yellowed eight-by-ten card: his name and dates and courses and grades. The woman who looked up his record declined to show his grades, but, from the other side of the counter, she reported that he did passably well. She read off some of the courses he took: anatomy, physics, physiology, trigonometry, history, psychology. There was a note on the bottom of the record saying he withdrew but offering no reason. On the back of the card was an intriguing note: In 1964, a man who'd just vacated the office of sheriff in some shame and had made a general fool of himself at Ole Miss had requested Millsaps College to send his transcript to Ole Miss.)

Something else that may surprise: The sheriff of the county has a black deputy on his staff. They call him Cap'n Dan. Dan Wells lives up in Three Rivers, which is a black community twelve miles north of Pascagoula. He wears two pearl-handled six-shooters and rides a motorcycle and is allowed to do police work only among blacks. There is a story locally that Cap'n Dan once forgot himself and stopped a white woman. Harold Jones—chief deputy—reputedly got all over him, pulled the badge right off his shirt, and said: "You goddamn nigger, you know better'n to stop a white woman." (Captain Dan Wells, still alive, was asked about this story. Wells was in his eighties, still riding motorcycles. He was still a part-time policeman, in another county. While he didn't deny the story, he didn't quite confirm it either. Surprisingly, he didn't talk in particularly bad ways about Grimsley—not that he spoke fondly of him.)

The childlessness. It's a heart sore. He and Betty have never been able to have children, except for that one who came out of her womb stillborn, years ago, maybe back around the time of the war—nobody seems to recall precisely when it was. There is a story around Pascagoula that the baby was three weeks dead when Betty delivered, and that the doctor thought it might have been Mongoloid. After that, they didn't try anymore, or this is the common tale. There is another story that the sheriff still has a trunk of baby clothes hidden somewhere in the grocery store or perhaps among his disheveled things at the jail. He never talks about that long-ago stillborn, nor for that matter does he talk much about those few years of college. Betty, trained as a nurse, used to work at Pascagoula Memorial Hospital, though now she cooks for the prisoners at the jail. Weekly, she goes through the courthouse hunting for her husband's whiskey bottles. She gets them out of bottom drawers, from the backs of closets, under mattresses. She's even found them hidden in the judge's chambers. She smashes them right over her knee. When the sheriff gets too drunk, they have to ship him over to a resort motel on Dauphin Island in Alabama. He dries out and rolls back to Mississippi. Sometimes late at night, he gets so desperate for a drink he'll go upstairs and unlock one of the prisoners—a trusty—and send him to the Friendly Café or to the Palace Bar to fetch a half-pint of Seagram's VO in a paper bag. Sometimes he'll have the prisoner sign the ticket for the bottle, and sometimes he'll give the trusty the cash. (Again, this is from a stack of Grimsley documents stored in the vaults of the Justice Department and the FBI; the files were obtained through the Freedom of Information/Privacy Acts.)

A lot of the deputies who serve him didn't make the long drive northward with their boss in the middle of the night to Ole Miss. "Son, aren't you going to go?" he said to a one-armed man with flaming red hair who tends the jail and sleeps in the docket room. His name's Donald Quave.

"No, sir, I'm not goin'."

"Why not, son?"

"Sheriff, you can't fight the fucking federal government, you know that."

"Yeah, well, as long as I'm sheriff of the county, there won't be a goddamn nigger at Ole Miss."

He didn't hold it against Quave for not going—or so Quave will remember four decades hence when a man with a notebook asks about it.

Try doing something for a minute. Place your forearms on top of the photograph with your hands vertical to his face and shoulders, so that you've got him shrouded, separated, blocked out from everyone and everything else. Isn't he now just some old harmless country coot having himself a time at, say, the backyard wedding of his favorite niece? Okay, maybe he's a little tipsy right now. That flushed-looking face and that spreading nose (it looks put on with a hammer) do suggest a certain alcoholic reproach all on their own.

A story about Grimsley and some of his deputies: They call it the Crowbar Effect. Some of the people who wore a badge for Grimsley back then reportedly had a habit of breaking open the back doors of local grocery stores before dawn and going in and getting what they wanted and stuffing it in the trunks of their patrol cars. Then they'd call the store manager and raise him out of bed. "Been a break-in. Came on it in our rounds. You better get down here." The store manager had no choice but to go along with the little ritualistic burglary. Bill Dillon, a retired highway patrolman, remembered this story, as did others. Some of Grimsley's old deputies were asked if it was true. They denied it.

Pascagoula—with its melodic Indian name—is about a hundred flat miles east of New Orleans, about forty marshy ones west of Mobile, Alabama. As long as anybody can remember, the place has been tied to ships and the sea. In World War II, this fishing town on the Pascagoula River and the Gulf, with its population of about 5,900, swelled to an around-the-clock military shipbuilding city of 36,000. After the war, Pascagoula began to sink back to what it was before, although shipbuilding remained crucial to its survival. At low tide on parts of the Mississippi Gulf Coast, you can walk far out over the muddy sand and the water will still only be up to your knees. There's no surf at Pascagoula. This has something to do with the string of islands off the coast and the sharp slope of the land to the sea. It's not a pretty town, compared to so many beautiful Mississippi towns, although the big fine homes down near the water are certainly beautiful. Longfellow once mentioned Pascagoula in a poem, "The Building of a Ship." He told of "The knarred and crooked cedar knees." He talked of timber that was "Brought from regions far away / From Pascagoula's sunny bay." The shipbuilding industry continues on in Pascagoula, but the remainder of the Mississippi Gulf Coast seems mainly about retirement condos and a few obscenely large casinos. The Redneck Riviera is what some people call this curving stretch of sand between New Orleans and Mobile. The condo builders haven't succeeded in despoiling all of the wide beaches yet. In a way, the Gulf Coast of Mississippi is Florida still on the make.

There are three counties lining Mississippi's wedge of coast, and back when James Ira Grimsley presided drunkenly over one of them, a sheriff could rake in $300,000 a year. People claim as much as half a million a year in a sheriff's pocket, which is a startling figure for such a historically impoverished state. (In 1960, dawn of the movement in Mississippi, median income was $4,209 for whites, $1,444 for blacks.) A visitor hears these figures concerning sheriffs from former Gulf Coast highway patrolmen, attorneys, newspapermen, local historians, other cops—not that any of them can produce a scrap of paper proving it. They'll shrug, and grin, and say something along the lines of "Thought you'd be getting it by now. There *were* no pieces of paper for anything those guys did, practically speaking." One of the lesser mysteries about Grimsley is that he died so apparently impecunious. To listen to some of his old deputies, who still wish to take up for him, Grimsley never cared about money in the first place, and what money he had, he tended to give away.

You're looking at one image, but here is another. It was taken two decades after the photograph in *Life*. This one was published in a Jackson County newspaper on November 5, 1986. In the picture, which accompanies a small article, a seventy-four-year-old man with his wet hair parted down the middle is eleven months from dying. He's wearing a ribbed cardigan sweater and an open-collared shirt. His nose is horribly veined, swollen, pitted. The glasses are starting their characteristic slide downward. The face is hollowed out and shrunken from the one that got captured in *Life*. He looks phlegmy, rheumy. But it's him, all right. It's clear what the asbestosis is doing to him, but the accompanying feature doesn't say anything of that. Apparently, the town knows he's going to die soon, and so a reporter and a photographer have come to do this modest-sized puffball piece. The story's headline: "Former Sheriff Forged New Paths in Law Enforcement." It's such a wonderful lie, in terms of the real facts of his life.

Grimsley was a widower then. His wife of forty-four years had died a few months previous, in April. In the north of the state, James Wesley Garrison had died of a brain tumor that July, although Grimsley probably knew nothing of that, and probably nothing of those other six he'd once shared a joke with in *Life*. (Billy Ferrell, that day down on the dock, said of Grimsley: "Haven't seen Ira in years. No idea about him. No idea what happened to him. He was only sheriff once, you know.")

In this 1986 newspaper photograph, Grimsley is holding up yet another picture: an eight-by-ten group photo of a bunch of cops. You can practically see his crooked and liver-spotted hands trembling. The group portrait in his hand is of his younger self and his deputies. There are eleven deputies and most are in uniforms and Stetsons: Pete Pope and Leon Lambert and Tony Greer and Donald Quave and Harold Jones and the others who'd served him from 1960 to 1964.

I̲t wasn't hard to find Pete Pope. He wasn't a deputy anymore; he was the head lawman himself. He'd been sheriff of Jackson County since 1988 and was in the middle of another electoral campaign: up for his fourth term and wanted it bad. (He'd end up losing, in the 1999 summer primary, to Mike Byrd, the son of the man who had succeeded Grimsley in 1964. In Mississippi, sooner or later, everything seems to come back around.) Pete Pope said that he was a pup, something like twenty-one, when he went to work for "Mr. Grimsley." Pope served him for a term, and then, when Grimsley was through, Pope got on with the highway patrol, where he did several decades of trooper work, rising in the ranks. Afterward, he retired from the patrol and ran for sheriff of his home county.

He was in his office on the ground floor of the gray stone courthouse in downtown Pascagoula. It's the same courthouse where Grimsley hid his bottles. The sheriff had a desk of piled papers before him. He was in a coat and tie. His white squad car was parked on the other side of a window. He was sitting in a burgundy leather swivel chair. On the wall in the hallway, there was a signed picture to the "high sheriff" from Senator Trent Lott, a Pascagoula boy who made good. (The then Senate majority leader helped Pete Pope get a helicopter for the sheriff's department.) The back of the burgundy leather executive's chair was covered with a black cotton doily. The word SHERIFF was written across the doily in huge bright yellow letters. Middle-aged, loud, sure, silver-maned, liquid-voiced, friendly as tap water: this was Pete Pope, in control of his jurisdiction. Phones were ringing, radios squawked their half-intelligible sentences. The sheriff of the county was uninterested in any unflattering pictures that he thought some outrider might be coming to draw of "Mr. Grimsley."

He looked at the *Life* photograph and also a copy of the local newspaper photograph from 1986. He set them aside. "Compassionate man, his intentions were well," he said. "Called everybody 'son.' Called his wife that one time, I believe. Tickled me. He was a leaderman at Ingalls Shipyards way back, maybe about the time of the war. My own daddy had worked for Mr. Grimsley. We had come down here from a little town called Electric Mills. Listen, this guy was the most benevolent man you ever met in your life." The sheriff went into a story about how it was nothing for Grimsley to take money from his own pocket just so a prisoner's wife could get bus fare back to her hometown in another part of the state. Then another story about his own first campaign for sheriff. "Summer of 1987, probably it was. Over to his house. All bent up and old and couldn't breathe. And he's sitting there in the darkened room and you know what he said? Now, remember it's my first campaign for sheriff, didn't have any campaign money, and I'm sittin' in this room with this man I have so much reverence and respect for, and he says, 'Son, there's three hundred dollars sitting in the top of that dresser drawer over yonder, you take it. You take it for your campaign.' Now, I couldn't do that—and I needed that three hundred dollars. That's just the kind of man Mr. Grimsley was. Why, he'd go up there in the jail on a Saturday night and buy ice cream for the prisoners."

"How did he treat black people?"

"Treated 'em like you or I would," the sheriff said.

At the end of the visit, Pope said: "You know, we've changed down here in Mississippi. We've changed. Things aren't like they used to be. I was on the highway patrol working Interstate 10 out here in the county as a trooper, and we'd pull somebody over with out-of-state plates. You'd go up to the car and the person sitting in there would roll the window all the way up, maybe just two or three inches from the top, afraid to talk to you, afraid to talk to you." The sheriff shook his head in wonderment. "Mississippi's not like that anymore. I don't think you'll find anyplace that's made as many changes as Mississippi has. We're not just a bunch of ignorant rednecks anymore."

At the outset of the conversation, Pope had said, eyeing his interviewer steadily, his voice even, no seeming warning in it, smiling: "Now, I didn't go up there to Oxford the second time with Mr. Grimsley that weekend, I want you to know that. Mr. Grimsley went up there twice that weekend, you know. I went with him the first time—me and Tony Greer and Leon Lambert. The second time was when the riot broke out. That's when the trouble was. He took a busload of folks from here up there that time. You may know something about that. I wasn't along then. I stayed home. I think this picture in the *Life* that you have here with you was from the first time, wasn't it? They were gettin' ready for the riot. It hadn't happened yet, it hadn't quite cracked open yet, it was the eve of the riot, you could say. Truth is, I can't remember very much about going up there with Mr. Grimsley to Oxford. We left in the middle of the night and just hurried up there. But what I do know is I didn't go up there the second time, when all the burning and destruction were happening. You'll get that part right in your book, won't you?"

He was assured of it.

A few months later, Pope was still running hard for reelection. He was in the burgundy swivel chair again. The phones and radios were still ringing and squawking. This time, there seemed more candor in the frame—some. "I wasn't going to bring it up before, but I wasn't going to lie to you, either, about his drinking," he said. "Truth is, he was so bloated, he could take one drink and be flat drunk. But he was a good man, a good man. I won't go back on that." Pope said he knew of no criminal thing Grimsley had done in his life, certainly not while he was sheriff. He was shown some government documents strongly suggesting otherwise. Documents alleging gambling, prostitution, payoffs. Documents alleging rape. Documents suggesting both direct and indirect links to planned murder, or at least talked-of murder, including the planned or talked-of murder of James H. Meredith. Pete Pope said he didn't care about such documents nor did he need to look at them—he knew what he knew about James Ira Grimsley. He brushed them off. He rose from his desk, shook hands. "Treat my man right, will you? Say what you want about me. But be fair to Mr. Grimsley. And here's another thing you got to remember. All the people in this town who elected him and then later forgot him knew he was a drunk. You got to think of that. And here's another thing: Was he ever charged with anything? Not that I know of."

Grimsley's sister, Bessie Randall, was ninety-three, sitting in her kitchen. She shooed a visitor in. "His wife, Betty, always wanted him to go be a doctor," she said. "He ended up a sheriff." She seemed to grow a little sad. She described how some men in the Grimsley family had died of drowning—almost a pattern of drowning, she said. The word "drowning" suggested the word "alcohol," but the conversation didn't go that way. She was too old, too nice, to have ill thoughts of the dead spoken in her presence. "I stayed with him three months before he died," she said. "When I would sit with him at night till it would get late, he'd say, 'If I just had me a granddaughter, Bessie.' "

Leon Lambert was still working as a cop, in another county, in a town called Lucedale. He had on a blue straw Stetson, black cowboy boots. "Guess you want to know about that brick," he said.

"Brick?"

"I guess it wasn't a brick, it was a piece of concrete or cement. It was up there at Oxford, the second time he went up. They caught him with that arm coming down with a brick just as he was about to smash it through a window. It was when the riot was going on. I had a copy of that picture for the longest time. It was in some other magazine or newspaper, I forget which."

"What did he think about the pictures of him in national magazines showing him doing these things?"

"He wouldn't talk about it. About all he'd say when somebody would bring it up was, 'Well, they say I done that. I guess I don't remember.' "

Tony Greer was still in the Jackson County sheriff's department—working at a desk for Pete Pope. He seemed an old soft man, exhausted by life and police work. "I won't say anything bad about Mr. Grimsley," he said, and turned back to some papers before him.

Donald Quave, the one-armed ex-jailer, lived way back in the county, far from town. It was a Saturday about eleven o'clock in the morning. The ex-deputy was in a cement-block house, in a narrow bed, a fly swatter resting on his stomach, his arm in a plaster cast. He was staring at the ceiling. "Come in," he said, his voice meshing through a rusty screen door. A cow had run him down a month earlier, Quave said, going right into conversation. He hadn't felt right since. He said he was seventy and had never married. His red hair was sticking up wild. There seemed such a disconnect in his words about Grimsley. "One of the finest people I ever knew. James'd pull off his shoes and give 'em to you. He was always broke—he'd give money away fast as he'd get it. We'd get to fussin'. We were always fussin' at each other. He said to me one time, 'You country sonofabitch, you get your goddamn rags and get out of here, you're fired.' And I said, 'Hell, no, I'm not gettin' outta here. Somebody's gotta cover for your sorry mistakes.' And he kinda thought about that and laughed that big ol' laugh of his and said, 'Goddamn, Quave, I guess you're right.' You know about Betty, his wife. She'd find that whiskey bottle and bust it right in the middle of the courthouse floor. She'd make him go sleep downstairs with me."

Regarding Oxford and the *Life* photograph, Quave shrugged. "He was gonna show them 'goddamn niggers'—those were his words—that they weren't going to take Mississippi. I guess that's just about the way it was in his mind." The deputy was asked about what happened to Grimsley's life after Oxford, the way it seemed to go quickly down. "He got to where he stayed drunk all the time. The town knew. His deputies supported him. But everybody knew he was washed. He just went down."

The Grimsley deputy unavailable for conversation was Harold Jones, who'd broken ranks with the other deputies and had left the state and had said in a signed statement (forwarded to Bobby Kennedy's Justice Department) that the town and the whole county were stinking corrupt, and that Grimsley was the leader of it all, and that he, Jones, would be willing to go before a grand jury and say what he knew. (He never did, it seems.) But Harold Jones, like the ghost on a page in a magazine, was long dead.

In the immediate aftermath of the events that unfolded at Oxford, Grimsley, back home, made a darker, more malevolent turn. And then he got turned on by his townsmen, though hardly for the right reasons.

A lot of this is detailed in a very brave and literate and long-out-of-print book called *The Smell of Burning Crosses* by Ira B. Harkey, Jr. He was the editor and publisher of the small daily called the *Chronicle* that served Pascagoula and Jackson County when Grimsley was the sheriff. Harkey's was one of the very few liberal journalistic voices raised in Mississippi in the early years of civil rights. The best-known and perhaps most heroic voice of those years belonged to Hodding Carter II, publisher of the *Greenville Delta Democrat-Times,* up in the Delta. And yet Harkey's editorial voice, along with a handful of others throughout the state, was nearly as heroic—even if it didn't last nearly as long as Carter's. You won't find the name Ira Harkey in many civil rights books. He's been forgotten altogether by the historians or else relegated to the back notes, and perhaps one reason for this is that he left the state early, before the war was won. But he should not be forgotten. His courage was great. In 1963, Harkey won the Pulitzer Prize for a series of editorials that he had written during—but especially after—the Meredith crisis. Really, he won the prize for standing up to James Ira Grimsley's bigotry and to a Jackson County hate group that Grimsley led in Pascagoula in the several months following the crisis at Ole Miss. To this day, Harkey feels that several contracts were put out on his life, and that most probably they originated from the office of the Jackson County sheriff, and there are several FBI documents to suggest he may be right. It's important to repeat that most of the declassified government documents are full of obfuscations and blotted-out passages and hot defenses by Grimsley protectors and deputies, whose names, like almost everybody else's in the documents, are not possible to know. The censors inked them out long ago. It is true, as Pete Pope said, that Grimsley was never indicted by the government for any charge. The investigations seem suddenly to have been dropped. It's as if the government lost interest. Really, the documents raise far more troubling questions than they ever get close to answering.

Ira Harkey and his newspaper were not destroyed in the aftermath of Oxford by Grimsley and his Klannish vigilantes, though he had to stand up almost entirely alone to threats on his life and to acts of terrorism toward his newspaper. Only one other public figure in the corrupt, racist town—the state president of the AFL-CIO, Claude Ramsay, who lived in Pascagoula—came publicly to his defense. But Ramsay's appeal to his townsmen went first to economic fear. As Harkey wrote in *The Smell of Burning Crosses,* which was published by a small Illinois publishing house four years after he left the state: "Pounding at the one single argument that is likely ever to force white Mississippians up the path to racial justice—dollars and cents—Ramsay pointed out that a racial explosion in Pascagoula could cost Ingalls its contracts, all of them dependent to one degree or another upon the federal government."

Ira Harkey is not a native Mississippian; he is from New Orleans. He came to Pascagoula and the Gulf Coast in 1949 as a still-idealistic thirty-one-year-old, not long out of the Navy and the war. He had just bought the town's struggling weekly. He was a graduate of Tulane University who'd grown up wealthy and privileged in the Garden District of New Orleans. Yet somehow he'd also grown up very sensitive to the plight of black people in the South. As he wrote in *Crosses,* which is both his autobiography and the story of what happened at Pascagoula after Oxford: "I was possessor of an un-Southern and radical opinion that Negroes were human beings. I held also a quaint belief that the white people of Mississippi, Arkansas and Louisiana—the old darkest South—needed to have this truth revealed to them." Two men of the Deep South, both named Ira, of roughly the same age, whose lives had intersected and proceeded in such opposite directions.

And there isn't time or space to tell the Harkey part in the detail it deserves. Let his own words sketch what happened. Grimsley's hate group was called the Jackson County Citizens Emergency Unit (JCCEU). This is how *The Smell of Burning Crosses* opens:

> For four months in 1962–1963 Pascagoula citizen leaders abdicated their duty and allowed their community to be ruled by fear imposed by an organized gang of white supremists. This was an aftermath of the entrance of Negro Mississippian James Meredith onto the campus of his state university. The Pascagoula gang was cloaked in a quasi-legality lent it by the office occupied by its leader, the Jackson County sheriff, a bloated hard-drinking semiliterate ruffian. The nucleus of the gang was a group of men who had gained local fame by taking part in the riots at Oxford after Meredith's admittance September 30. These, numbering about thirty, had been called out over the Pascagoula radio station to be led by their sheriff in cars and a chartered bus to the University of Mississippi campus, arriving in time to enjoy the bone cracking and property destruction. They returned to Pascagoula as heroes of the Southern cause, these hoodlums who would have been barred from entering the back door of Robert E. Lee's stables. . . . Encouraged by the widespread approval that surrounded them . . . they decided to make their association permanent. They organized under a charter. . . . Calling themselves the "Jackson County Citizens Emergency Unit," they began to meet several times weekly in the County Courthouse, of which the sheriff was the custodian. . . . [T]hey outlined their program of civic improvement: to eradicate local "niggerlovers," to boycott all businesses that employed or sold goods to Negroes, to "attend to" persons placed on a list by an "action committee," to train a strongarm squad at weekly maneuvers . . . and in the main and particular to put out of business the Pascagoula daily newspaper, the *Chronicle,* identified by them as "the leading niggerlover in the State." I know about these things and what the 600-member Jackson County Citizens Emergency Unit intended to do in Pascagoula because I was editor and publisher of the *Chronicle,* the despised "niggerlover" who "ridicules our great Governor Barnett," "calls niggers 'Mr.' and

'Mrs.,'" "writes news stories so you can't tell who's a nigger and who ain't." For four months—from October, 1962, to February, 1963—my newspaper was the target for a campaign of vilification, boycott, threats and actual violence. . . . In Pascagoula, there was no power to which I could turn for help. The President of the County Board of Supervisors remained mute. Pascagoula's mayor, when it was suggested to him that the *Chronicle* needed police protection, thrust out his middle chin and replied, "I am a segregationist." . . . City and county police authorities shrugged. The Unit, after all, was sponsored by the sheriff, the chief law enforcement officer of the county. . . . Not a teacher, not a politician, not an industrial leader; not a clergyman, a physician, an insuranceman; nor yet a lawyer, a fisherman, a welder, a pecan rower, a shrimper, a banker, a pogyman nor a shipfitter—not an idler, a sage nor a maniac said a word on my behalf.

Harkey bought a .38-caliber ranger pistol to try to protect himself. "I received a long-distance call with information that facts 'usable' against Grimsley would be given me if I went to a certain Eastern city and interviewed a certain person. I flew there and received a sworn-to pile of dirt that I did not ever use."

A few weeks after the state president of the AFL-CIO publicly denounced what was going on in Pascagoula, authorities at the Justice Department and the FBI announced in Washington that they were stepping in to investigate. The story appeared as a news item in papers in New Orleans and other large Southern cities. Suddenly, the shipbuilding town on the Gulf was quite willing to disown terrorists in its midst. As quickly as they had made Grimsley the hero of Oxford, Pascagoulians just as quickly began to shun their most visible and besotted bigot, who was also their sheriff. As Harkey later wrote in *Crosses:* "The sheriff's Unit, which I referred to editorially as 'goons,' steadily lost attendance at its meetings. Only twenty-two hard-core hateists were present at the last session at which the *Chronicle* was able to slip in an undercover observer. There was not enough of the Unit's influence left by August to allow the sheriff to be elected to the minor post of state representative for which he was a candidate, being ineligible to succeed himself. The great warrior of Oxford received only 1,226 votes from an electorate of more than 16,000, running fourth in a five-man race."

Shipyard contracts weren't canceled. Within a year, Ira Harkey sold his paper and moved away. His personal life had unraveled by then; he and his wife had separated and would eventually divorce. Again, let an old newspaper wordsmith tell some of this, from *Crosses,* in moving and eloquent words:

When it was all over, after we had welcomed back the defecting
advertisers and had increased circulation to 8500—fifteen percent
more than it ever had been—I found I could not remain in
Pascagoula, could not bear to exist in the vacuum of an ostracism
that remained in force even after victory, could not function in a
silence of total isolation as if I were underwater or in galactic space. I
was a pariah. I do not know whether this was because hate had
become a permanent attachment to my person and accompanied me
everywhere, repulsing all among whom I moved, or whether I had
become an ambulatory and ubiquitous monument to the shame of
my fellow townsmen, galling their late-blooming consciences.

The editor was told later that as he walked from the *Chronicle* office for the
last time, a reporter he had recently hired "wrung his hands and drooled, 'Boy,
I can't wait to start writing nigger again.' "

Grimsley, and the group he led, became pariahs, too, once agents from the
New Orleans office of the FBI began to investigate the sheriff and the JCCEU.
Word that the feds were in town asking questions spread quickly through the
county, even if no Pascagoulian was privy to the reports being compiled. A high
official of the Justice Department wrote a memo to a fellow DOJ attorney:
"There is also a lot of Citizens' Council activity in Jackson County, including
the Jackson County Citizens' Emergency Unit, whose main purpose, apparently, is to kill Meredith." From another page of the hundreds of pages of compiled documents: "Sheriff JAMES IRA GRIMSLEY, who took group of officers
to University of Mississippi campus 9/30–10/1/62 was reported leader of unit
being organized . . . the purpose of the Unit was to secretly go to the University of Mississippi, at Oxford, Mississippi, 'to get' or kidnap [blacked-out
name], recent Negro enrollee at the University." A few lines down in the same
document: "Also, that [blacked-out name] told him the aim of this emergency
unit was to go to Oxford, Mississippi, some night to get [blacked-out name].
He said from his conversation with [blacked-out name] he got the impression
the group would kidnap [blacked-out name]."

Another document refers to "the reputation of Sheriff GRIMSLEY being
what it was for non-intelligent action most of the time." Another document
refers to the Ingalls Corporation worrying about the "Unit and the possibility it
might get out of hand under the leadership of Sheriff GRIMSLEY, who has
lost the respect of a good many of the top people of the county, due to his alco-
holism and other general conduct." Another document mentions the "public-
ity Grimsley obtained both locally and as a result of his photograph being in
full spread pictures of LIFE Magazine." Another document talks of the
JCCEU and its plan "to do away with [blacked-out name] and/or the newspa-

pers the *Chronicle Star* and Moss Point *Advertiser,* of which [blacked-out name] is Editor. [Blacked-out name] has also written articles agreeing with the action taken by the Federal Government in the Oxford incident and has been very liberal in the past with his racial viewpoint."

The New Orleans agents also wrote documents in the weeks after Oxford that contained never-acted-on allegations such as this one: "According to the victim here, she was arrested along with a female friend. . . . Thereafter, the sheriff attempted to rape her but didn't succeed. . . . The sheriff denies molesting victim and there are not witnesses. Other witnesses state that victim was intoxicated on both occasions." J. Edgar Hoover himself looked into the many charges against Grimsley. Hoover and Burke Marshall—Bobby Kennedy's assistant attorney general for civil rights—exchanged several classified memoranda. On May 31, Marshall wrote to the U.S. attorney in Jackson: "We agree this matter lacks prosecutive merit. Accordingly, our file has been closed." On one of the documents, this handwritten note: "Discussed with . . . Criminal Division, who advised me that Division would not be interested in pursuing the allegations in this complaint."

When his term of office was up, the unindicted and mostly shunned Grimsley left his quarters in the courthouse—but not Pascagoula. For a time, he served as a deputy to his successor. The word "pathetic" had seemed to attach to his name. "Hello, son," he'd still cry at townsmen from across the street. He tried to put himself up for top dog again—the outcome was foregone. In the 1972 city directory, he is listed thusly: "Grimsley James I (Betty R) emp County Sheriff Dept." He did odd jobs around the county and the courthouse, and for a time he worked as a security guard in a firm owned by some of his old employees. He ran his grocery. He spent time in a little "camp" he had built outside Pascagoula. In 1986, the local paper—it was now called the *Mississippi Press*—came to do the small feature and published a photograph of a pathetic-looking man with a bulbous nose. Perhaps some late-blooming civic consciences had been galled into a minor shame. Within a year he died. The obituary, published the day after his death, on October 20, 1987, was six paragraphs on an inside page. Four years after that, in 1991, it was possible to look him up in a just-published reference tome entitled *The Ku Klux Klan: An Encyclopedia.* James Ira Grimsley would get his own separate entry—fourteen lines—as would his long-since-defunct JCCEU.

Forty years from the tumults of Oxford and the stand he took, newspaperman Ira Harkey was a spry old gent in his eighties in a red sweater with a thatch of chin beard and a white mustache. He had lived in Ohio and Alaska and Nevada but finally had settled in the Hill Country of Texas. He had gone back to college and gotten a doctorate in journalism and had taught journalism at universities and had written a couple of books—but you could sense that there has always been a part of him since Pascagoula that has been unresolved and restless and sad. I was in his home in Kerrville about five minutes when he brought up a brother who had killed himself years earlier. Then he said, "He was an alcoholic, and so was I." That sentence seemed to come from nowhere, because all I had been thinking of on the trip to Texas was the framed alcoholic ghost.

"How were you able to stand up to a guy like Grimsley?"

This is the way he answered: "Yeah, but here's what I think: If I'd continued drinking, I don't think I could have stood up. I think I might have just taken the easy way. Just shut up."

He talked about many things, including his own failures as a father and husband. He told of the Pascagoula lawyer who had helped arrange for the purchase of his newspaper in 1963. "He was like all of them, this attorney. He said to me one time, when I was running the paper and not identifying people by race: 'I want to know who's a nigger, and if it's a nigger, I don't want to read the damn story. And, dammit, Harkey, you're lousing it up.' "

"They were all cowards." Perhaps it was said a little too easily.

"Yes and no," Ira Harkey said. "Later on, there were two or three people who gave me encouragement, to the extent of a few words. One or two people, a banker, a music store guy. They passed it to me privately and said, 'For God's sake, don't tell my wife.' But only one public official, Claude Ramsay, said anything." And then Harkey said, "One of the great changes that came in people's minds after segregation was this great relief: 'It's gone. It's off our backs.' This huge relief. They couldn't have articulated it. They didn't understand it in that sense. They knew it was wrong, and they were obsessed with it, and after it was over, there was this huge relief."

He looked at the issue of *Life,* and he opened it to the picture, and he laid out the big double-truck spread on his lap. He moved his head slowly back and forth, studying it. He put his index finger on Grimsley's face. He laughed softly. "To think, this guy wanted me dead." And then he said, in response to a question, "No, I don't feel hate for him at all. If anything, pity."

"He was a bigot." Once again, it was said perhaps a little too easily.

Once again, Ira Harkey said, "He was lots of things. Like any life."

On the next trip to Pascagoula, I stopped in to see Ira Harkey's son. He was a circuit judge now, and his office was thirty yards across the walk from where Grimsley ran the sheriff's department. Dale Harkey, middle-aged, said, "A lot of people, who wanted to speak up back then and couldn't, realize it was wrong and maybe they look at me and want to repair that a little. Things are better in Mississippi now, and things aren't better. We've changed the law and you can't argue with that, but have we changed people's hearts?"

I left the courthouse and drove down near the shallow water of Mississippi Sound and knocked on the door of Kathleen and Julius C. McIlwain's house. I had no idea if Kathleen McIlwain would be alive, although she and her husband were listed in the phone book. I needed to find out. I knew her name because I had found it in an old declassified document from the State Sovereignty Commission. She used to be the town librarian. She was never a public official. In her own quiet way, she tried to do what was right—I'm sure more than once. On August 6, 1962, about two months before the events of Oxford, an investigator from the Sov-Com walked into her library and demanded to know why black children were using its facilities. To quote from the report that the investigator from Jackson filed a week later to his superiors: "Mrs. McIlwain expressed a disapproval of the purpose of my visit. . . . She stated that she has never had any trouble with whites or Negroes and that she hoped I was not down there to cause trouble. She stated that she thought that the Negroes had the same rights as the white people had because she said that the Negroes pay taxes the same as the white people and why wouldn't the Negroes have the same rights to the facilities of the library as the white people." The town librarian wasn't murdered for such insolence; she wasn't driven out. But she had to have paid prices.

It was early afternoon, midweek. She was eighty-three. She and her husband were watching television. She didn't know who I was, but she invited me in. I have experienced this all over the South: a stranger at the door, invited inside. She was in a yellow sweater blouse and pants. In the living room were fine old sideboard pieces, and china, and silver glassware. She said that she and Julius had lived in this house on Columbus Drive since 1940. Their children had been raised here. She sat in a wicker chair with her ankles and her arms crossed. There was a small lacy handkerchief tucked inside the band of her gold wristwatch.

"I guess I don't understand what it was that enabled someone like you to be able to speak against the day," I said.

"Well, it's just how I felt," she said.

"Were you scared?"

"A little. But I knew it was right."

She didn't put it this way, but I think Kathleen McIlwain was trying to say that in every dark there are particles of light.

Yes, in every dark there are particles of light. Mississippi of an early morning, before the heat is up, can lie proud on the mind, like linen on your arm. Driving through the deep summer green of the Natchez Trace, what you are struck by most of all is the beauty. Not all white Southerners are overweight bigots, and not all rural Mississippi blacks are ennobled by their poverty—that is ever the temptation in an outsider's eye. The great beauty seems to slip up on you unawares. In parts of lower and eastern and northeastern Mississippi, the earth turns to a deep orange, almost red, in vivid contrast to the dark alluvial riches of the Delta. On the Trace, one of America's oldest roads, which cuts a diagonal through the state, the cardinals and jays will be flitting out beyond your car hood, as if to guide you, enchant you. The light on this road today seems clear as gin. You've gone ten miles and have yet to see another car. Last night, outside your motel, the air felt so moist and heavy and mysterious. It was early dark, and you were speaking to your family. You stood at a pay phone bolted to a utility pole as the blackness netted down over you in a kind of softening cone. You looked down and saw the cover of your notebook starting to coat with wetness. The scent of something perfumed was coming up—jasmine? Down the street, porches glowed with lamps. Then this morning at dawn, cruising on a four-lane with the window open, the air so freshening on your face, you looked over and saw Holsteins in a pasture, stolid as boulders, mist curling around their ankles. In Mississippi, just the white-lettered names on blurring green road signs seem invested with something rich and musical and seductive: Bogue Chitto, Neshoba, Ofahoma. These are Choctaw names. There's supposed to be a spot somewhere in this state called Hot Coffee, although it doesn't seem to be on any maps. There's another spot called Panther Burn—you've been there. There's a place called Increase. (It never has.) It's so puzzling that a land of such charm and physical beauty, a people of such natural grace and disposition to kindness, could have so appalling a history. Standing once in the Old Capitol Museum in downtown Jackson, not hating this state but taken with it, at least for now, you saw this printed on a small sign card: "I can love Mississippi because of the beauty of the countryside and the old traditions of family affection, and for such small things as flowers bursting in spring, and the way you can see for miles from a ridge in winter. Why should a Negro be forced to leave such things? Because of fear? No. Not anymore." Know who said that? James Meredith.

John Henry, Jimmy, Bob

Of these three, a briefer look: First, John Henry Spencer, from Pittsboro, Mississippi, Calhoun County, on the far left, with his ash-heavy cigar guttering down to its last acidic inch, with his sleeveless undershirt showing gauzily through his short-sleeved and thin-fabric outer shirt, like pentimento. Second, the hanging-back Jimmy Middleton, three over from the right, framed in the wedge of space between Billy Ferrell's head and Jim Garrison's head. Sheriff Middleton of Port Gibson, Mississippi, could almost be a mortician, or a mafioso, or a Baptist preacher, or maybe even a haberdasher from the Midwest, with that grim black hat and poker face that may be having some faint second thought—or darker thought. And third, the snap-brimmed, press-lipped, and forward-tilted-just-a-slight Bob Waller, immediately behind Billy, whose chin appears to be resting on Billy's right shoulder, and who, if you look again, is the only one in this frame looking directly outside the frame, beyond the frame, past the moment—to the photographer, it would appear, and to the photographer's box. And why would Sheriff Waller of Hattiesburg be peering without a lot of happiness at a man who's peering through the lens of a camera, getting set to depress its shutter? Because the sheriff's a photographer himself. Not an amateur, but a professional, with his own studio and successful commercial business, which is in the hands of someone else presently. Waller isn't an artist, but on some level he has to understand the art of the shot. He took portraits for a living for years before becoming a law enforcement officer, and he'll take them for years afterward. So he must see, if only in his subconscious, the inherent storytelling power, the visual tension, the perfect composition of Mississippi bigotry, all of it being sealed, even as Waller registers it, inside a mechanical box on a strip of cellulose acetate. His squinty regard of the unseen Charles Moore seems to have about it a small wishful lethality, and a tincture of mirth, and maybe even some photographic envy. *We'll get you for this, you sucker, whoever you are. Dammit, son, I'd almost trade places with you for a picture like this.*

John Henry. Fifty-four years old, eldest of these seven. His wife's name is Annie Lois, his daughter is an Annie, too. He once had a son, but John Emmett Spencer died tragically, gothically, in childhood. Thirty-five years hence, Pryor Funeral Home will put into a file, along with John Henry's vital statistics, a list of survivors, and the cost of his coffin: "He was a Mason, and he loved to sing." It's true enough. The old lawman will have made eighty-nine, passing from this world on May 29, 1997. Cancer and congestive heart failure will take him off, and afterward they'll rest him in a hidden cemetery, with a path parted in the woods, in a community called Spring Hill outside of a village called Slate Springs. He and his spouse will have been wed for sixty-two years. In the Spencer plot at Spring Hill Cemetery at the time of the burial, they'll cut into the stone Annie Lois's name and date of birth, beside her husband's dates, with a space for her own final date. In the June 4, 1997, issue of the *Monitor-Herald,* a weekly serving all of Calhoun County, John Henry Spencer, lifelong native, once photographed in *Life* with a stogie in his mouth, will get a twenty-one-line obituary, his extremely long life reduced to three paragraphs, and several of those lines of type being taken up with the names of his pallbearers and the reverend who performed the obsequies, Jim Vance—he's related, as are some of the pallbearers, as is half the county, or so it seems.

John Henry—everybody calls him this—is head lawman of an iddy-biddy little place. The county seat of Calhoun County, Pittsboro, is something like a wide spot in the road. It's just down Highway 9W from Oxford, where this Meredith trouble is taking place. There aren't even 15,000 people in Calhoun County. The sheriff's a farmer by trade. Lots of folks say he ran for sheriff in the first place and was able to get elected because of all the people he knows from church singings. He has a fabulous voice and loves raising it to the Lord at his own Ellard Baptist Church or any other gospel church that he gets invited to on a Sunday. What he particularly loves is an all-day gospel picnic-sing, in the middle of summer, with dinner served family-style on the grounds, with the sweat condensing on the aluminum water pitchers, with the long rows of tables stapled down with butcher-wrap paper, with the Good Book shouted aloud by the preacher as the evening sun is disappearing, like an orange wafer on the flat horizon. You wouldn't arrive at these wholesome mental pictures from studying a stumpy lawman with jug ears and thinning hair and a guttering-down 'gar, with a sleeveless undershirt showing gauzily through an outer shirt, standing manfully ready in this grove of trees at Ole Miss for what shall come. It might be more reasonable, from the way the lawman is presenting himself pictorially, to wonder where his blackjack is.

Decades hence, when a visitor to the county shows up, Sheriff Spencer's undertaker, minister, pallbearer, and widow will look at the picture, nod, say it's him, then instantly start to talk about what a "friend of man" he was. Each has his own expression of the same sentiment, each his own memory. Sonny Clanton, his great-nephew, a local attorney and one of his pallbearers who, at the time of Meredith, was just a kid in high school with an important football game that week, will say, "Uncle John had this benevolent way about him."

"But what about the picture?"

"I heard him say once that he had no real idea why he was even called up there."

Speaking of blackjacks: The sheriff has a nephew one county over who's also a sheriff and who looks a lot like him, and who's pretty good in the black-jack department. *His* name is Spencer Leroy Davis, although everybody calls him Spec. Sometimes the two lawmen get confused, because of their blood relation and similar body mass. Spec Davis, sheriff of Grenada, controls a bigger town and more populous county. No telling how many insults to the brain he's delivered to drunk soldiers who come into Grenada on Friday nights from nearby Camp McCain. All of the Spencers and the Davises were born in and reared around these several counties of north-central Mississippi. The uncle and the nephew—who are only five years apart and are serving concurrently— have driven up to Oxford together, summoned to this riot. The nephew must be close by, if out of the range of the photographer's viewfinder.

Spencer is destined to be sheriff of Calhoun County for just one term before he goes back to a life of farming and singing in church. In a way, he's an accidental sheriff, as opposed to a professional lawman. He may be the least violent and most racially tolerant of the seven in this picture. Tolerance of and violence toward blacks in Jim Crow Mississippi are relative ideas. It's fair to say of him that he was intolerant, not murderous, happy to be part of the system, as they all were and are.

From a State Sovereignty Commission document dated March 4, 1960, in his third month in office: "I visited Sheriff John Henry Spencer, the new Sheriff of Calhoun County, at Pittsboro, Mississippi. I also talked with Deputy Sheriff Carter, Circuit Clerk H. L. Crew and the Supt. of Education, Mr. Billie B. Gray. I was informed by all of these individuals that there is no known NAACP operating in Calhoun County. They have no names of any potential negro agitators and they are not acquainted with any possible racial unrest or problem within the county. All have advised that they will inform the State Sovereignty Commission immediately should such a situation arise."

From another document, July 11, 1960: "The Supt. of Education stated that so far as he knew there were no teachers in Calhoun County who were members of the NAACP or any other left wing organization advocating the mixing of the races. The Sheriff made a similar statement concerning conditions in Calhoun County. . . . Spencer did express his appreciation in that he now had an organization on which he could call in case of any trouble which might arise relating to integration."

Black teachers in the segregated schools of Calhoun County must be closely watched, because teachers can harbor dangerous ideas. Investigators from the state capital make regular trips to the county to consult with civic officials on who is "agitative." A Sov-Com report: "On March 13, 1961, I journeyed to Calhoun County. I talked to John Spencer, the Sheriff and his two Chief Deputies. . . . Supt. of Education Gray said he felt his Negro teachers of Calhoun County were well pleased with their new school buildings and their salaries. He said he did not think any of the Negro teachers were members of the NAACP. He also said it was the policy of the school to make inquiry into the teachers' background before employing them, and if it is discovered they have a Negro teacher who is an agitator the board does not re-employ them."

The sheriff spies on any local black, when he is asked to do so by his fellow racists in Jackson. This work is "in unison with our purpose," as the Sov-Com investigators put it. In April 1961, the sheriff was asked to "check on car tag #167-055—owner Taylor Ford—address Slate Springs, Mississippi, 101 Booker Ave." Not a lot came of it. From the report that was filed after the sheriff and others had turned in their info: "Taylor Ford is a no good Negro who makes his living by inveigling mostly Negroes out of their money by various methods. . . . All of the white people who have known Taylor Ford for years said . . . he is a dead beat, sham, and panderer. . . . ANALYSIS. Taylor Ford is just another dead beat Negro who earns his living by fleecing both white people and Negroes out of money by any method he can conspire to do so." Unfortunately, Ford isn't around to speak for himself.

Forty years onward, Annie Lois Spencer, almost ninety-one, is around, in a nursing home, in a wheelchair. Instantly, she remembers the stogie. Her eyes are bad, and so she rests her finger on the page at the approximate spot where her husband is half turning toward Billy Ferrell's bat. Her nails are painted an elegant red. Her voice is wheezy. The collar of her red blouse is locked at her throat. "He didn't smoke them very often," she says. "I think somebody had just given him that cigar that day."

On her husband's girth: "I think he was about a twenty-eight waist when we married. That was in 'thirty-five. He got big around the middle and proceeded to widen out, as we all do."

On her little boy, John Emmett, who died in the late thirties at about age three: "He was out playing. He fell on a toy bugle. It was made of tin. He was running with it. It sliced open his jugular vein at the throat and the mouthpiece went up into his brain."

Maybe "throat" has brought another memory. "My husband lost his voice box. He got cancer of the vocal chords. Malignant. They gave him a vibrator box to put up to his throat, but he didn't like it much. It like to killed him, because he couldn't sing in church the way he wanted to. I think it just did something to him when he lost his voice box. I don't know how long he had that cancer in him. He used to say, 'Oh, why did God give me this cancer, Annie, and take my singing away?' "

Jimmy Middleton, sheriff of Port Gibson and Claiborne County, which is a tiny and handsome wedge of the state over near the Mississippi River. This hanging-back man in the black hat and sidelong wan expression, who's framed between Sheriff Ferrell and Deputy Sheriff Garrison, has never been known to identify himself—on the street, in a legal document, on the signature line of a check—as "James Middleton." Jimmy, or at least Jim, is the name his parents gave him, and that's what he goes by. Jim S. Middleton's the law in a triangular-shaped agricultural county, just below the Delta, about halfway between Vicksburg and Natchez. (To further locate it, Vicksburg is about thirty miles north of Port Gibson, Natchez is about forty-five miles south.) His is a town and a county that prefer to think of themselves as "genteel." Thus far in the years of civil rights, Port Gibson has been largely free of ugly racial incidents. The movement won't come to the county until the mid-sixties. Historically, there have been lynchings in the county—but relatively few. Port Gibson, the only real town, is a community where the burghers and local farmers prefer to avoid the so-called unpleasant exchange—as long as blacks stay in their place. Claiborne County is undulant and fertile Mississippi hill country, half open, half wooded, rolling to the bluffs of the great river.

From a recent Sov-Com document drafted by an investigator named Virgil Downing: "I reached Port Gibson, Mississippi in Claiborne County by automobile at noon January 23, 1961 and immediately began to contact all City, County and State Officials as ordered by Director Albert Jones of the State Sovereignty Commission to obtain all information from them regarding any subversive or NAACP activity in Claiborne County. I contacted Sheriff J. S. Middleton and he stated that he knew of no NAACP activity in the county and was not having any trouble at this time and everything was alright. He informed me if any trouble developed from any subversive or NAACP organizations he would contact the Sovereignty Commission at once. Sheriff Middleton was very cooperative and stated he appreciated very much what the Sovereignty Commission was doing to help keep Mississippi segregated."

From another Sov-Com document, following another visit by the same investigator: "The sheriff stated that he keeps a close watch throughout the county for any violations and when he sees things developing that he thinks will cause trouble he stops it before it can develop further. He stated that the Negro Voter School was not active in the county at this time. Sheriff Middleton was very cooperative and assured me that should the NAACP ever cause him any trouble in the county he would cooperate with the State Sovereignty Commission in every way to keep all of Mississippi segregated."

He's fifty-one. He'll live another thirty-one and a half years. His obit will appear on page 8 of the local weekly: back page, under a bar of type that says "Deaths." It won't be cancer that'll kill the ex-sheriff, it'll be his heart, and probably also his deeply embittered spirit. The banks will have closed on his notes and he'll have been forced to sell his land. This is going to happen during the farm crisis that first hits America in the mid-1980s. He'll depart this life not owing anybody, it's true, but not having possession of his land, except for just a little bit that he will have been able to hold on to for the decade that he lives beyond the sell-off. On February 16, 1994, he'll suffer a heart attack at home and die en route to Claiborne County Hospital.

He has two daughters and a boy. The boy is fifteen now. His name's Jim Scott. (He's never been a James, either.) Jim Scott, who's going to go to college and find an upper-middle-class life in another part of Mississippi, will see this photograph in *Life* on his own, not too long after it's published. (It might be in the cellar of the family home.) He and his father won't discuss it, which isn't unusual, because Jimmy Middleton is an uncommunicative father. Not at all a bad father, at least in the son's eyes, just one who can't say what he feels. What the father can say is things like, "Leta, you take care of these kids. I'm going out to make a living." Becoming sheriff would be part of making the living. Before he's done, Middleton will have served two and a half terms as Claiborne County sheriff. He'll get a total of ten years in the job. (He came in in 1950 to fill the unexpired term of E. L. McAnnis. He had his own term in the mid-fifties. He laid out for four years. In 1960, they elected him again.) Like almost everybody else who's ever had it once, he'll want that thing bad again. He'll campaign hard for it in the back half of the sixties. But by then Dan McCay, Jimmy's old deputy, is the man.

The sheriff's wife's name is pronounced LEE-ta. Every morning Leta Middleton gets up and bakes dog bread for her husband's Walker hunting hounds. The sheriff lives with his wife and children on a farm outside of Port Gibson—he refers to it always as the Place. At the Place, on Route 547, the sheriff keeps about twenty of the hunting hounds in pens and brings them out for the annual shoot at the Whitehall Hunting Club. The Place is a handsome spread: white-frame house, dressed in stone on the bottom, sitting on a circular drive off the macadam. This might suggest that Middleton is some kind of country squire. It isn't so. He's out of Baptist hardworking stock. He's self-made. Didn't get very far in school. He's part owner of a livestock auction barn and a trucking company. At his sale barn, he's known among local blacks for giving fair prices. He loans money out of pocket to the blacks who work for him on the Place. If it's more than he wishes to loan, he'll drive the man to town and sign his note. He's irascible when it comes to his cattle—whites and blacks alike seem to want to steer clear of him when he's messing with cattle.

(Hezekiah Ellis, who worked for him in the 1950s and 1960s, was under an old car that was up on blocks when a reporter with a picture pulled into his dirt drive, which was far out into the countryside. He stood under a shade tree. "It was in him, it was in him. He didn't show it much, but it was in him," Ellis said. The antecedent of "it" was bigotry, and the subject had come up surprisingly fast. Despite this, Ellis spoke with a certain fondness. "He was a peculiar guy, but he was a pretty good guy." And then Ellis said: "If he was in a crowd, he'd be a changed man. You could see it. You could just see that seg stuff start to come out." The black man looked at the picture again. Suddenly, he hooted. "That's him to a tee.")

Port Gibson is just off the Natchez Trace. You come in from the Trace and drive down wide, leafy Church Street—so many churches and tended lawns and beautiful antebellum homes. But go two streets to the east and you'll be in stark black Mississippi poverty. Port Gibson is one of the state's earliest settlements. Its plantation economy was established in 1790, when white Virginians brought slaves up the river from New Orleans. By the eve of the Civil War, there were more than 12,000 slaves in this county—four times the white population. That 20 percent minority owned and controlled everything. Same old story now. There's a black street of commerce in Port Gibson known as Nigger Street, even though on the sign it says Fair Street.

U. S. Grant came through in May 1863. "Too beautiful to burn," was his verdict. He didn't burn it. (The town has those words on its city limit signs.) After the war, during Reconstruction, the blacks of Claiborne County briefly ruled. Item from the *Port Gibson Standard,* November 17, 1871: "Negro barbers and bootblacks turned lawmakers, even though they cannot write their names, lord it over the intelligent and refined planters and merchants who were lately their masters." By August 1876, however, God was back in his universe. The whites had regained political control. In place of slavery came sharecropping and tenant farming, other names for ownership of people.

Item from the *Port Gibson Reveille,* August 20, 1953: "First cotton bale ginned Friday. Grown by George Solman, negro, on the Sheriff Middleton Place."

Item from the *Reveille,* November 15, 1951: "You're not forgetting, are you, that your church or synagogue is the friendliest place in town? A warmhearted welcome awaits you there. New interests, new friends, and most precious of all in these trying times, an opportunity to renew your faith, to restore your courage, to find peace of soul in the company of men and women of good will. Take someone to church this week. You'll be richer for it." This civic advertisement is signed and paid for by Patterson Furniture Company, Piggly Wiggly grocer, Abe's Betty Jean Shop, Claiborne Motor Company, Lum's Men's Store, Allen Motor Company, the Jitney-Jungle, Claiborne Hardware. Sheriff Jimmy S. Middleton signs his name to this, which appears in the local paper just as the Port Gibson chapter of the NAACP is forming an underground membership.

They don't pass around Klan "Hate Sheets" in Port Gibson. They don't need to. Port Gibson's bigotry wishes to mask itself as a kind of paternalism. You could imagine the paternalism of this place as a kind of thin-mesh netting draped over the very air of the county.

From another Sov-Com document, this one dated June 27, 1960, twenty-seven months to the day before the photograph at Oxford is taken: ". . . I proceeded to Claiborne County, Mississippi, accompanied by Investigator Tom Scarbrough, for the purpose of contacting state, county and city officials, as well as members of the Chambers of Commerce and Citizens' Councils and advising them that as investigators of the Sovereignty Commission we were available to assist them in any way possible. Before leaving Jackson, we contacted Representative Russell L. Fox, Claiborne County, who furnished us the names of the following negroes that he classed as race agitators in Claiborne County."

Three Negroes are named as agitators.

The investigators stop in at the office of the sheriff. "[Middleton] stated that Ernest Jones is an advisor for other negroes in this area. He advises them of their rights, how much to charge white people for their work, and the Sheriff states that he can definitely be classed as a race agitator. . . . Sheriff Middleton and Chief Doyle advised that Carl (Gold) Thompson, 48 to 50 years of age, who operates the Thompson Funeral Home, Port Gibson, is believed to be a member of the NAACP; that he is not a known race agitator, but he is believed to agitate under cover when the opportunity presents itself."

Moving around town, the investigators check with the tax assessor, the circuit clerk, the president of the chamber of commerce, the superintendent of education, the chairman of the Citizens' Council, the chief of police. Each of these is white, but probably that doesn't even need be said. "Sheriff Middleton furnished a list of all negro registered voters in Claiborne County which are as follows." On the sheriff's list are eight blacks who live in District 1A; three who are in District 1B; two in District 4; two in District 5. That makes fifteen registered black voters as of June 27, 1960. By 1964, when Middleton leaves office, there will be 150 registered black voters in the county—progress. And after this will come aggressive voter registration drives and an economic boycott against white merchants, launched on April 1, 1966. The number of registered blacks will have grown by 1966 to over 2,600, and this will ensure

the election of black officials for the first time in the county since Reconstruction. Some of the political changeover will be attended by violence. In 1969,
the highway patrol will come in with tear gas. But the grassroots uprising by
Port Gibson's theretofore quiescent blacks will proceed, and by the start of the
next decade, blacks will own the voting majority. In 1972, the first black circuit
clerk in twentieth-century Mississippi will get elected in Claiborne County.
However, the whites will still seem to own the very air, no matter who is in
office. They will always manage to have the money.

   Bob Waller, beady-eyed picture taker, resting his jaw on the shoulder of
Billy's suit jacket. Well, it only looks like it.

   Right now—not the "now" of autumn 1962 in this sun-splashed leafiness
but the now of real time, as you're reading this and gazing in—you could travel
to the Waller Photograph Collection at the University of Southern Mississippi,
which is in Hattiesburg, where Waller lived and died and served one term as
county sheriff, and find thousands and thousands of his negatives. The
shooter kept careful, precise entries in ledgers and daybooks: commercial
work, portraits, weddings, funerals, aerial photography, car wrecks. It's the
contents of a life's work. Hundreds of manila envelope jackets bear descriptive
titles of what's inside: Airport fire. American Legion Baseball Banquet. Courthouse Cigar Stand. Catholic Senior Play. Speedy Morrison's 1947 Birthday.
Hattiesburg Krewer of Zeus Ball. These archived negatives are arranged by
year, from 1948, when Waller set up his own studio at home (he'd taken a cor-
respondence course, following some work in a photographic lab during the
war), to 1977, the year he died. It was a heart attack in his darkroom in the
middle of the night. Rather than disturb his wife, Tina, he called the hospital
and drove himself over. And it was the next day, or maybe the day after that,
that he died in an ambulance as they were taking him up Highway 49 to the
state university medical center in Jackson. He cried out and then he was
dead. His death made page 1 of the local daily for which he himself had once
worked as a sportswriter and staff photographer: "Bob Waller, Photographer
and Former Sheriff, Dies" said the headline on the two-column story in the
Hattiesburg American. This was November 18, 1977. There was a picture. He
was dead at sixty-seven. He'd gone fifteen years past the picture in *Life,* of
which there was certainly no mention that day. Elsewhere on the page were
these headlines: "Police Chief Brings Controversy with Him." And "Ku Klux
Klan Turns to Slick Public Relations Strategy to Reach Goals." And "MSU
Officials Deny Discrimination Charges."

   He's fifty-two here: born April 17, 1910. He lives at 207 North 22nd
Avenue. It's a white-frame rancher in a good neighborhood, with a carport
and a darkroom off to the side. In the Hattiesburg city directories of the 1950s,
he has advertised himself thusly: "Waller's Photo Service. Commercial Por-

traits. Color Portraits. Aerial Photography. Photo Finishing. Albums and Frames. Air-Conditioned Studio." He's childless. What Waller has for immediate family is his good-natured fat-girl wife, Tina, who plays bridge once a week with seven other local fat girls—they call themselves the Big 8 Club. What the sheriff of Hattiesburg also has is two toy Mexican bulldogs. Waller loves these dang little pups, which is how he refers to them. They ride around with the boss on the front seat of the sheriff's car. Waller will tie sombreros on their heads. He'll stop to get them cups of water and watch them slurp it up. When he's not in the squad car with the dogs, he's riding with them in his 1962 Galaxie 500. It's white and has 409 under the hood and four on the floor. Tina has a matching '62 Galaxie 500, white, only hers has 390 horses under the hood and is an automatic. Tina doesn't like Bob's dogs very much, if you want to know.

How to describe Robert Benjamin Waller, who attended Tulane University in New Orleans for a few years and who had a brother who was a reporter for the *New Orleans Times-Picayune* and who, in the Lord's due time, will come to rest beneath a pink stone in a corner lot at Roseland Park Cemetery next to a loblolly pine with a green birdhouse nailed to it? Describe him as charming, ignorant, friendly, suspicious, blindly loyal to the lost Confederacy, appalled by the present, and frightened of the future.

Since he's a photographer who enjoys keeping his hand in, and has some sense of historical preservation, the sheriff of Hattiesburg will sometimes make an arrest and drive a cuffed criminal to the scene of the wrongdoing and ask the fellow to pose next to the crime—say, a robbed grocery, say, a dead man between sheets at the city morgue.

He has big blunt hands, which aren't visible. They're a farmer's hands, although he has never farmed. (The hat and weathered face might make you imagine him right off as a farmer. And isn't that a farm hat shading that unmistakable outdoor face? But it was a life lived largely in darkrooms, except for his four-year stint as sheriff. He was never even a deputy sheriff.) Waller hasn't been caught in an atypical pose here—he often has a kind of stump-shouldered, forward-tilted, beady-eyed look about him. You can see the stance in other pictures. The sheriff likes barbecuing in the backyard on Saturdays with his three deputies—Frenchy Garreau, Gene Walters, and Willie Oubre. Frenchy's a drunk, but he's good company and an old pal of Bob's. The sheriff keeps a weekly golf game with Harry Fridge, an M.D., and Joe K. McInniss, a local cutup. The three are fierce competitors and good friends. Joe K.—it's what everybody calls him—is about the biggest joker in town, and once, as Harry Fridge was at the top of his backswing on the tee, the cutup let fly with an enormous fart. The doctor hung at the top of his swing and said, "Joe K., I see you still got that low hacking cough." He came down and knocked Christ out of the ball. Bob Waller loves telling this story.

Forrest County is down in the southeast corner of the state, in what they call the Pinebelt region. Hattiesburg, qualifying as a city by Mississippi standards, is a post–World War II boomtown. It's home to one of the nastiest white registrars in the South. That man is the circuit clerk and his name is Theron Lynd. He's massive and crew-cut. (Waller's photo archive has pictures of him.) Lynd makes sure blacks don't get registered to vote. Since the 1940s, he has had each of the 285 sections of the Mississippi Constitution written on a note card. When a prospective black voter comes in, Lynd picks out one of the cards and asks the man to explain the section. The explanation is almost universally judged faulty and so gets a failing grade. In 1960—Waller's first year in office—there are something like 22,000 white residents of voting age in the county, and nearly all are registered. There are about 7,500 blacks, and about 25 are registered.

From a letter he'll write a couple of months hence (January 11, 1963) to the director of the Sov-Com on his sheriff's letterhead: "Dear Mr. Jones:— There is strong evidence that Paul Weston is a member of the NAACP and probably CORE and all the others. However he is too smart to be active enough for us to be able to point directly at him." (This information will go all the way to the governor.) From another Sov-Com document, written by one of the agency's investigators, dated November 22, 1961: "I personally contacted Robert Waller, Sheriff of Forrest County, Mississippi. I was informed by Sheriff Waller that neither the NAACP nor any other subversive organization has caused him any trouble in Forrest County at this time. . . . Sheriff Waller was very nice and cooperative, and he expressed his appreciation for my visit, and the good work that the State Sovereignty Commission was doing over the State of Mississippi. . . . Sheriff Waller further stated that he was not anticipating any trouble from any of the colored citizens of Forrest County who have made it their home for a long time. He stated that if any trouble developed, it would come from outside sources—possibly the NAACP or other subversive organizations—who would encourage the younger Negroes to create this disturbance in an effort to break down the laws of the State of Mississippi."

From a Klan Hate Sheet that will be distributed a few years hence in Forrest County, which some people in Mississippi think of as "progressive" in race relations: "The NAACP, The Communits, The COFO and other Jew backed subversive organizations now have a perfect system of infiltrators in your homes. . . . Without apparently realizing the grave dangers involved, many white citizens take the *nigger* maids into their homes, to care for their innocent children. . . . They are trained to undermine the christian morals of your children, while they pretend to be 'a good ole nigger mammy' to your face. . . . If you think that it just couldn't be your maid, Let us remind you of this: You are dealing with decendants of savage africa, who will, like a wild animal, turn against you at a moments notice. In Africa they eat each other. Once they have been subjected to the communist doctrine of the NAACP and COFO or CORE they will cast aside any loyalty that years of kindness on your part may have brought about, and seek to destroy the hand that has fed them for so long."

There is a book called *Southern Journey,* which was published a few years ago and never found enough readers. Tom Dent, its author, deceased now, was from New Orleans, with a deep love of jazz and the blues. He was a black activist in the movement, and nearly a generation after the battle was won, he went back to the site of some of the old struggles, such as the F. W. Woolworth five-and-dime in Greensboro, North Carolina, where the first sit-ins occurred. One of the places he traveled to was the Mississippi Delta. At the end of his book, Dent writes: "During the civil rights years blacks had achieved the miraculous by kicking open the doors—but once inside, well, there was hardly anything there. It was almost laughable, a kind of special blues truth." He is talking to Unita Blackwell, black mayor of Mayersville, Mississippi. It's a beautiful spot on the river. Mayor Blackwell suggests that they go look at the river. "What did it all mean?" Dent asks. Blackwell tries to answer. "Well, we didn't gain *much*. We changed positions. The river changes positions; it's constantly moving, you know, taking on new routes, cuttin' off old ones. It may not look like it, but it is. Any powerful force will make a change. I suppose what we really gained is the knowledge that we struggled to make this a decent society, because it wasn't. And maybe it still isn't now, but at least we tried. That's history."

On one of my first trips into the Delta, I stayed at a Hampton Inn in Green-wood. It was a comfortable and friendly place. On the morning I checked out, I went down to ask the desk clerk if I could see a copy of the bill before paying it, since I'd made a lot of long-distance calls and wanted to be sure the charges were correct. I looked at the sheet and saw the word "Foreign" written alongside amounts for $1.24, $2.47, and $8.51. "But this can't be right, sir," I said. "I didn't make any international calls." "Oh, that just means out-of-state calls," he said. That afternoon, I stopped for a grilled cheese sandwich and an RC Cola at a gas station–café on Highway 49W. A three-hundred-pound man was sitting at a table with a thermos cooler. Besides myself and the cook, he was the only other person in the place. While I waited for my takeout, he mopped himself with a blue bandanna and talked of how hot it was and of how Mr. Tackett has 2,000 catfish ponds in the Delta and how blacks hereabout just plumb won't work. "You got lot of 'em like that up there where you live?" he said. I paid for my order and tried to smile and kept moving past him toward the screened door. I may have nodded imperceptibly at his question, already hating myself for it but afraid to do otherwise. "July going to be a burner, buddy," he said, waving.

The Man with His Back Turned

T here was no way to know, before that first encounter, that form was following function in an uncanny way, that the man with his back turned in a photograph was the man with his back turned in life: a seg all right, but never exactly or precisely a true hating seg. Rather, a seg who'd gone along. Rather, a seg who'd been unable, and apparently unwilling, to step outside his and his state's history of inhumanity. Rather, a seg who'd sought to look the other way while others (some of whom worked for him) did the broadly vicious and violent stuff. Rather, a seg who was caught between his personal distaste for treating people like dogs, like chattel, and his personal need to keep a six-pointed sheriff's star pinned to the pocket of his shirt and thereby have the esteem of his intolerant community. The man with his back turned on the far right in Charles Moore's photograph at Oxford, it turned out, was the morally ambivalent man who'd been head lawman of one of the scariest and most hate-filled and race-contested sixties' Mississippi towns there was: Greenwood. And for that paradoxical reason, and for some others, too (not least of which was that he was *alive* these four decades later), John Ed Cothran became the most compelling figure of them all—of the seven in the photograph, that is. It took a long time to figure him out, but at length an indelible impression of him emerged: inescapably tragic, unavoidably culpable, then as now.

"I just got one thing to ask you, mister," he said. "You got anything to do with the federal government?" He was unloading a white pickup in his driveway, and a younger man was assisting him. He didn't really look up as he said it.

"Not one thing, sir."

He grunted. "Come on, then," he said. He motioned toward the door of the handsome brick house with bluish-gray wood trim. He started across his heat-scalded yard while the unannounced visitor followed behind and worked furiously at processing a thought: Amazing. From the front, exactly what you'd have said. Short-haired and blocky and thick-necked. Same kind of glasses. Not as tall as he seems in the picture, but him all right, unmistakably. Everything but a tourniquet on his sleeve.

He had pinkish, freckled skin. His work pants were held up by a pair of crossed yellow-green suspenders. He was in white socks and ankle-high work shoes, the leather looking soft as lanolin, and he seemed to shuffle them along the ground slowly rather than to take actual steps in them. He had thin white wispy hair and there was a ridge of deep tan across his forehead, where the brim of his perforated ball cap stopped. He had huge, freckled, liver-spotted hands. He had an open, meaty face, more angular than broad, and it didn't seem malevolent. It seemed benign, accepting of old age. He had on a watch with a silver expandable band. His wrist was so thick that the band appeared to have his skin in a death hold. But the most powerful first sensation was of an old man still physically strong, remarkably so. His arms hung down like fence posts.

He was just home from a fishing trip with a middle-aged stepson at an oxbow lake over near the Mississippi River. They'd been away two days. They'd done pretty well. With an oozing curve of smile, he pointed at a plastic bucket full of white perch, fat as hogs, a few of them still flopping and gasping for air. This same slightly disconcerting smile was going to show up often on John Ed's face in the conversations of the next weeks and months.

He was eighty-three then—early summer 1998. His second wife, Sybil, to whom he'd been wed twenty-five years, had died two months previous. She'd fallen down beside him, going into Sunday church, and then seemed to recover, and then vomited in the pews, and then had lapsed into a coma, not to wake up. But there wasn't any way of knowing any of that right then, nor that he would be married again, to Maudine McClellan, by summer's end, nor that there was a small blue faded tattoo on his left forearm that said "JEC" and that had been put on crudely some sixty-five years earlier, when he was a Delta farmboy, nor that he'd helped drag Emmett Till's body from the Tallahatchie in 1955, when he was a forty-year-old deputy, and that he'd been in on the arrest of the two killers.

The previous evening, the director of a funeral home in Greenwood had provided the first and best surprise: The figure on the far right in the photograph was alive. "Sorry, can't give you death information on him," he said. "He's over in Moorhead. It's in the next county. John Ed's a little hard of hearing, but otherwise he's fine. He goes to a lot of funerals and wakes. People around here do that. Be sure to talk loud if you call him up." John Ed didn't answer his phone that evening, nor again the next morning. Moorhead, the funeral home director had related, was only half an hour away. He said it was the little Delta town in Sunflower County, directly west of Greenwood, famous for being the place where "the Southern crosses the Yellow Dog." Those were train lines.

Now, in the spic-and-span house, an old lawman and retired farmer took off his cap to reveal a scalp that looked pink and fair and tender as a baby's. He smoked Camels and sat pitched back in his blue La-Z-Boy in the living room with his hands clasped on his stomach, his legs nearly on a level with his torso. His house felt almost unnaturally unlived in—as if the late Sybil Cothran had cleaned it just before she died on April 17 and he hadn't touched things since. He slapped a bug and pinched it and studied it and then flicked it off with a surprising quickness. He jerked down the lever on his La-Z-Boy with the same quickness. He said he'd been having trouble with his ankles swelling. "Old doctor man give me some fluid pills, don't believe it's done any good," he said, pulling on his pant legs to exhibit a pair of swollen and hairless and pale legs.

He said, with edge, "I haven't got any use for FBI people even today." He cupped his ear and peered at me and said, "What? What's that?" He said, "I liked it, I just liked all of it, 'cept toward the last, when there was all that civil rights crap." Those were the same words Billy Ferrell had used in the first encounter: "civil rights crap." What John Ed Cothran meant was that he'd liked being a Mississippi lawman, a career he'd never really aimed toward, especially the single term he'd served as sheriff of Greenwood and Leflore County, except for how fractious things had gotten toward the end because of outside agitation, and the bleeding ulcer that was tearing his stomach. He'd served as a Delta lawman from 1949 to 1964—the first eleven as a sheriff's deputy, the last four as the head man. He said he came into office "on January 4, 1960." He meant the office of sheriff. The date was sealed inside him.

He talked of how he'd been subpoenaed to testify for the state at the Emmett Till trial in Sumner, and how he didn't like a bit of it. "Four goddamn hours," he said, holding up four knobbed fingers and folding his thumb behind. He talked in and around the Emmett Till murder. It didn't come up until late in the conversation, and then some random details just dropped out.

He said he was lonely. He said he was spending a lot of time with his Bible. Several times he said "nigger," putting it into sentences as a seeming simple declarative and descriptive statement, without any self-consciousness or particular seeming meanness or fear of contradiction or recrimination from some man with a notebook who might have lily-livered sensibilities. It was as if there weren't another authentic word. Of Till, for instance, he said, "What happened, see, was little Emmett went in that store. And the little nigger, he said to her, 'Hey, baby, come on with me, I got all kinds of white women back home.' "

He didn't talk much about James Meredith and Oxford, nor was a photograph from a magazine produced in which a lawman, in the foreground, with an armband knotted to his left sleeve, has his back turned to the camera. You can't precisely tell whether this figure's eyes are trained on a swinging bat. You hold it one way, and he seems to be doing so, and you hold the picture another, and he seems to be looking slightly off from the bat, downward. Since you can't see his face, you have to try to imagine where he's looking, what he might be thinking.

The Delta of Mississippi isn't really shaped like a delta. It's closer to a diamond, or an oval. It's that legendary garden in the northwest corner of the state that stretches from just below Memphis at the Tennessee border southward to Vicksburg, and which encompasses all or parts of twelve counties, and which is framed roughly by the rolling loops of the Mississippi and Yazoo Rivers. It's two hundred miles in length and about seventy across at its greatest width. It's the richest soil west of the Nile. The total area within its alluvial boundaries is about 7,100 square miles. It's been called "the most Southern place on earth," and there is a good book with that title by a Southern historian named James C. Cobb, who points out that although it seems tabletop flat to the naked eye, the Delta's surface is actually rather uneven, due to centuries of flooding and sedimentation by the Mississippi River and its tributaries. That may be so, but it's the utter-seeming flatness people remember. East of Greenwood, in Carroll County, the earth is pastured, timbered, rolling, and you can see it out the window and feel it all beginning to change beneath you as you drive. Inside the Delta, beginning immediately west of Greenwood and extending west toward the Mississippi, the earth is so level as to make you almost imagine you're traveling on the ocean floor.

The summer air is sweet, vegetal, smoky. The gray-black fields, snowy with their cotton, stretch out on either side of the roadbeds, which are often just two-laners. The tree lines, if there are any trees, form a green filmy blur at the horizon. At night, coming across U.S. 82, from Greenville to Greenwood, a distance of about fifty miles, it's so black. "The Mississippi Delta is a glamorous, sweating land of long twilights and hot dawns," wrote James Street in his book *Look Away!* But the most lapidary line about the Delta was written by David Cohn in a book called *Where I Was Born and Raised.* The Delta of Mississippi, Cohn said, "begins in the lobby of the Peabody Hotel in Memphis and ends on Catfish Row in Vicksburg."

Historian Cobb points out that Mississippians from other parts of the state tend to speak of traveling "into the Delta"—not of going to Clarksdale or Ruleville or Indianola. It's almost as if they were talking of entering some heart of darkness and enchantment, the heart of the heart of what Mississippi has stood for in their own and in the country's imagination. The reason this region bleeds the blues is because of the kind of dawn-to-dark stoop work that has gone on in its fields over generations. Much of that is over now—both the music and the stoop work. Agribusiness and corporate catfish farming have come in, even as there's come a great emptying out of the place and the erection of casinos up in Tunica County, near Memphis. They, too, seem surreal.

During slavery, blacks were the basic "machinery" of Delta cotton production. The area was sparsely settled before 1880 because of flooding from the Mississippi and its tributaries. Development of this boggy place was speeded by the railroads and by levee construction, and by 1910 the great flat garden had been cleared, drained, and planted everywhere the eye could gaze. As late as 1960, every county in the Delta still had more blacks than whites—the proportions ranging from 52 percent to 79 percent. But if so much has changed in the generation after civil rights, so much seems to remain, not least the fertility of the earth. The Delta topsoil is still twenty-four feet deep in places (as compared to, say, seven feet deep in southern Minnesota), and even now you can see plantation manors and plantation fields and plantation cabins sticking up from some of those fields, as if the Civil War hasn't been fought yet. In the middle of the twentieth century the Delta was still producing a million bales of cotton a year—in some years that was a tenth of the American crop; bale after bale of pure Delta cotton, five hundred pounds apiece, wrapped in burlap and tied with jute cloth, with all that human sweat, before being shipped to market. James Meredith once said that you could almost hear the backs breaking and the vegetation growing as you drove down Delta back roads. Amzie Moore, who belonged to an earlier generation of twentieth-century Mississippi civil rights heroes, once said of Delta heat: "Some days in the summertime in Mississippi, the weather is so hot you can almost see it." He was from Cleveland, another Delta town of civil rights legend.

B ut nothing like Greenwood's legend. For some in the movement, saying "Greenwood" is almost like saying "Selma." For a time, in early 1963, the Student Nonviolent Coordinating Committee (SNCC) transferred its headquarters to Greenwood from Atlanta and made the town the focus of its drive for civil rights in Mississippi. Bob Dylan and Sidney Poitier and Harry Belafonte and Dick Gregory and Pete Seeger turned up in Greenwood in the early sixties. (Dylan sang "Blowin' in the Wind," which was a hit record just then, not his own version, but Peter, Paul, and Mary's.) James Forman, head of SNCC, wrote an eloquent piece of protest and journal literature in Greenwood on scrap paper called "Some Random Notes from the Leflore County Jail." (It was John Ed's jail.) Forman and eight others were being held in that jail, and one of them was Bob Moses, the Jesus figure of the movement in Mississippi.

SNCC workers tried to tally some of the violence against blacks that went on in Greenwood within a few weeks in that late winter and early spring of '63, which would have been the fourth year of John Ed's tenure as sheriff of Leflore County. This was the year in Mississippi, after James Meredith's forced integration of Ole Miss, when whites seemed to be frothing in their collective fury and humiliation. The sheet compiled by SNCC workers in Greenwood reads like a war diary.

> On February 28, 1963, SNCC worker James Travis was machine-gunned by three white men seven miles from Greenwood. On March 6, 1963, three SNCC workers were shot at while sitting in a car outside the SNCC office. No one was hurt. On March 24, 1963, the SNCC office was burned down. On March 26, 1963, two shotgun blasts were fired into the home of SNCC worker George Greene. No one was hurt. On March 27, 1963, ten SNCC workers—including SNCC Executive Secretary James Forman—were arrested for "inciting to riot" while they escorted 100 Negroes to the courthouse to register. On April 2, 1963, Greenwood police arrested a SNCC worker and forcibly ejected comedian Dick Gregory from the courthouse lawn.

The brown Yazoo River still curls through the middle of it. Now as then, the town still proclaims itself "Long-Staple Cotton Capital of the World." Now as then, the county jail occupies the top two floors of the neoclassical stone courthouse at 310 West Market, and prisoners still stand behind its barred windows, looking down on slow-moving pedestrians and cars. You can drive by the courthouse and jail at midnight, the town asnore, and the prisoners are there, against their bars, the light shining from behind their backs the color of weak tea. In the sixties, the Leflore County Courthouse was the first place in the Delta where great numbers of blacks turned up on the steps in an attempt to register to vote. The afternoon daily, the *Commonwealth,* used to publish the names of those who'd tried to register—so that they might likely lose their jobs as domestics or yardmen when they went to work the following Monday. In 1962, the nonwhite median annual family income of Leflore County was $595. In 1962, the sheriff of Leflore County had an ornate wooden rolltop desk in the sheriff's department on the main floor of the courthouse, and next to the desk, hanging vertically from a cradle, was a phone with a receiver that weighed about four pounds. Until just a few years ago, there was a newsstand and a candy counter in the lobby of the courthouse, and on the greasy glass of the candy counter was a hand-lettered sign. It was adhered to the glass with gray electrical tape and said FULLER BRUSH PRODUCTS SOLD HERE.

Now as then, the gray steel girderwork of the bridge at Front Street, right behind the courthouse, carries you over to the white residential side. "The other side," Greenwood blacks still call it. There, on Grand Boulevard, are some of the finest homes and tended yards in Mississippi. You come the other way on the bridge, to the south bank, and in no more than half a dozen blocks you're in the middle of hard Delta poverty. Two Americas, then as now, side by side, in a town of less than 20,000, split by a swollen stream. Greenwood is 100 miles north of Jackson, 134 south of Memphis, the largest town between the two.

In 1963, Leflore County had 13,657 blacks of voting age; about 2 percent, or 268, were registered. Of eligible white voters in the county, 95 percent were registered. The total population of the county was just under 50,000. Whites owned 90 percent of the land and had a median income three times that of blacks. This paragraph from a report on Greenwood in 1963 House hearings of the Eighty-eighth Congress roughly summed it up: "There is no Negro clerk, bailiff, or prosecutor in any court in Leflore County. No Negro judge sits on any bench and there is no local Negro attorney. There has never been a Negro juror in Leflore. No Negro holds a job in any portion of the law enforcement agency, and the quarters in the Negro parts of the jails are inferior. The post office has employed Negroes as letter carriers restricted to delivering in Negro neighborhoods." And yet, within three years, by 1966, some kind of freedom would come: 7,000 of those nearly 14,000 eligible blacks of voting age would be registered.

The town had a rifle range, an archery club, a hunting and fishing club, a horseback club, a square dancing club, a community concert association, a little theater, five tennis courts, a country club with an eighteen-hole golf course, a public golf course with eighteen holes, a municipal swimming pool, and a small football stadium. None of the above was open to blacks. The library had air-conditioning and 41,000 volumes and six branches throughout Leflore County. Blacks were not allowed in any library facility except for one small branch in a black school. The town had five banks, more than Jackson had, and that only testified to the great concentration of cotton wealth.

Then, if not nearly so much now, East Johnson Avenue, along the railroad tracks, was the heart of a black Greenwood Saturday night. As far back as the forties, East Johnson jumped, like Beale Street in Memphis. It was barbershops and Kut-n-Kurl shops and fish stands and pool parlors and outdoor shoeshine stands. It was a juke joint called the Silver Moon where Sonny Boy Williamson or Big Bill Broonzy could show up unannounced and play the blues till dawn. It was a tailor shop called Tom Walker's that made the best suits in the Delta. There were Jewish and Lebanese merchants along East Johnson. Greenwood blacks, who'd spent the past six days chopping cotton on a plantation, would come to town on the backs of flatbed trucks, wearing

Saturday-night Tom Walker suits. The trucks had long benches in them, and canvas tops, and—momentarily—some lightened hearts. Aven Whittington's plantation outside of town encompassed 10,000 acres, and as late as 1955, Squire Whittington could proudly say at Delta soirées that he had 1,000 Leflore blacks living on his place.

The Greenwood Dodgers played Class D ball for the Cotton States League, and the *Commonwealth* always ran small display ads on the day of the game: "Baseball Tonight. Helena vs. Greenwood. Adm. 11c, 30c, 44c. Game called 8 o'clock." The ads didn't need to say that blacks could come but would have to sit in the bleachers. There'd be five hundred whites and blacks at a good Dodgers game, rooting for figures with fat mitts in their big spikes and full-cut flannels who were sweating through the uniforms to the skin, probably carrying around an extra ten pounds.

The mayor of this place was an unprincipled racist—Charlie Sampson, a chic dresser, with sweet fedoras and flowery neckties, a tall man, about six-feet-two. Nearly everybody figured him for Klan. He owned Leflore Dry Cleaning and worshiped at First Baptist. He once went to New York to be on the *Today* show, and all the way there—according to the legend—his bigot-cronies were coaching him not to say "nigger" on the air. It isn't known if he slipped. In any case, Mayor Sampson once blithely told the *New York Times,* "It's outsiders that's causing it. We give them everything. We're building them a new swimming pool. We work very close with the nigger civic league. They're very satisfied." This was spring 1963. James Forman of SNCC was writing his letter from the Greenwood jail. The town was suddenly in the national spotlight— "Greenwood was a crossover news flash," as Taylor Branch would put it years later in his majestic history, *Parting the Waters.* City police had just loosed a dog on marchers to the courthouse. The dog's name was Tiger. "Sic 'em, sic 'em," whites on the sidewalk screamed. "Greenwood had become a theater of war," *Newsweek* wrote in the lead piece in its national affairs report. The mayor released a statement: "What are these agitators and the Justice Department trying to accomplish with their present massing of colored mobs? . . . The only purpose of these agitators is to follow the Communist line of fomenting racial violence." For these several weeks, Greenwood existed at the epicenter of civil rights in America—and then the center abruptly moved, to Birmingham, to Bull Connor's fire hoses and attack dogs in Kelly Ingram Park.

But the hate ran on here. The city attorney, Hardy Lott, president of the local Citizens' Council, was a Greenwood firebrand, in partnership with the mayor, willing to do almost anything to keep down blacks. (He'd later defend Byron De La Beckwith, local fertilizer salesman and home-grown psychotic, against the charge of murdering Medgar Evers.) Lott and Sampson ran Greenwood and everybody knew it. Actually, Lott ran Sampson—he was the true power of Greenwood. Their police chief was Curtis Lary. In terms of law enforcement, he was the second-ranking uniformed officer behind the county sheriff. (In an oral history archive at Howard University in Washington, D.C., there's this 1968 exchange between an interviewer and a black Greenwood minister named William Wallace, who was active in the later years of the movement: "Is Chief Lary still head of the police?" "Yes, he's still head of the police." "What's his position?" "He has a job and he has to do what he is told.") The attorney for the LeFlore County board of supervisors, Aubrey Bell, was another prominent citizen-bigot who held a prized seat on the State Sovereignty Commission and threw grand parties and wore French cuffs and quoted Shakespeare before rural juries. Greenwood was the state headquarters of the Citizens' Council. From its offices at 115 Howard Street, the Council leafleted Mississippi with its racism, offering cash awards to high school students for essays on the moral necessity of segregation: "1,000 in Cash Given For Winning Essays."

Later, Martin Luther King, Jr., would come to the town without pity, prompting the authors of the local KKK Hate Sheets to write a special installment of their newsletter:

TO THOSE OF YOU *NIGGERS* WHO GAVE OR GIVE AID AND COMFORT TO THIS CIVIL RIGHTS SCUM, WE ADVISE YOU THAT YOUR IDENTITIES ARE IN THE PROPER HANDS AND *YOU WILL BE REMEMBERED.* WE KNOW THAT THE NIGGER OWNER OF COLLINS SHOE SHOP ON JOHNSON STREET "ENTERTAINED" MARTIN LUTHER KING WHEN THE "BIG NIG-GER" CAME TO GREENWOOD. WE KNOW OF OTHERS AND WE SAY TO YOU—AFTER THE SHOWING AND THE PLATE-PASSING AND STUPID STREET DEMONSTRATIONS ARE OVER AND THE IMPORTED AGITATORS HAVE ALL GONE, ONE THING IS SURE AND CERTAIN—YOU ARE STILL GOING TO BE *NIGGERS* AND WE ARE STILL GOING TO BE WHITE MEN. YOU HAVE CHOSEN YOUR BEDS AND NOW YOU MUST LIE IN THEM.

Greenwoodians, on both sides of the river, awoke to find mimeographed copies of these all-cap Hate Sheets rolled up on their morning lawns or shoved into the crevices of their front doors.

Sally Belfrage's *Freedom Summer,* published in 1965, poetically catches all that Greenwood and Leflore were—the strange allure mixed in with the astonishing hate of it. Belfrage, in her innocence and cheek and with her wonderful eye, had come south as a volunteer worker with hundreds of other idealistic collegians. "The early mornings were glassy and warm, with hardly a hint of the thick heat that would roll in later," she wrote. "The country was for-eign, resembling Spain or Syria or anywhere where heat and poverty combine to overwhelm attempts at the streamlined." Arriving in Greenwood for the first time, "We studied the faces of pedestrians and police for homicidal ten-dencies. Then we crossed the tracks, and for a block or two the wiry, cheesy commercial atmosphere remained but as a cheap exaggeration of itself; then the pavement bellied out and sidewalks disappeared or fell away in broken pieces: Niggertown."

The police were a law unto themselves. The worst ones were the ordinary officers—on both the city and county forces. Clarksdale, an hour or so away, was famous throughout Mississippi as a Delta town with a terrifying police chief, Ben Collins. But Greenwood had thugs in badges by the number. In 1964, a white civil rights worker named Paul Klein filed an affidavit against a city cop. This document has been published in several books: "Logan took a long knife out of his pocket and started to sharpen it, [directing] a running stream of threats at the three of us. He asked Johnson how he liked 'screwing that nigger' (indicating Miss Lane). Then he said, while sharpening the knife: 'sounds like rubbing up against nigger pussy.' He poked the knife up against my ribs a few times; then he held it out toward me, told me to put my hand on it and asked: 'Think it's sharp enough to cut your cock off?' "

In 1964, when "Delay" Beckwith came home to Greenwood following his two mistrials for the killing of Medgar Evers, the local cops embraced him as one of their own. They made him an auxiliary officer. They let him ride up front in the squad cars, with his own gun and club, as they cruised Niggertown.

Of all of the sixties cops whose names live on—Ben Branch and Ward Simpson and Ed Weber and so many others—the most feared and famous of the county may have been Big Smitty. Wilbur Wardine Smith. Mr. Big Smitty, as he preferred Greenwood blacks to address him, even the one or ones he was sleeping with over in Niggertown. (As Belfrage wrote in *Freedom Summer,* the real integration of the races in Greenwood "was always after dark, under the sheets.") A lot of the local cops kept girlfriends on the south side. Smitty, who loved beating up on blacks at the same time he was having them sexually, was known to keep his share, and, later, when one of these women tried to register at the courthouse in a group demonstration, he threatened to kill her, and so SNCC had to sneak her by darkness out of town, up north to Detroit.

Early and late in his career, Mr. Big Smitty was a town cop. But in the first half of the sixties, when the days were ugliest, he served as a sheriff's deputy. He fancied himself as the number-one criminal deputy of the sheriff's depart-ment. And Mr. Big Smitty, Deputy Sheriff Mr. Big Smitty, with that menacing coal-black mustache, with that 280-pound wide-body frame, with that shiny nightstick that seemed as long as a broom handle, with that big-barreled flash-light that came in handy for clubbing, worked for a quiet and spectacled man who had a blue tattoo on his muscular left forearm. The tattoo said "JEC." The blurry blue of the letters sat on a little patch of welted white skin.

I can't remember the first time I noticed the tattoo, but I recall clearly the day John Ed Cothran told me how he got it, and how he'd once tried to take it off. We were eating dinner. "You want to bless it?" his new wife asked, holding out a hand to him and a hand to me. The three of us held hands from our seats around the table, and John Ed bowed his head and said, "Heavenly Father, we thank you . . ." After we'd passed the corn on the cob and the pink-eyed peas and the fried green tomatoes and the mashed potatoes with garlic, the head of the house got to talking about something else and the tattoo just came up. He said he got it put on when he was seventeen or eighteen. He and two other Delta farm boys, Jim Venable and Herman Price, decided to get themselves a blue tattoo, and the tattooist, who was an amateur and didn't have the proper tools or know-how, hooked up a sewing-machine needle to a motor coil that got its juice from the battery of a Model T Ford. The thing ran at about the speed of a slow dental drill.

He extended his arm across the table to show it off, rubbing his knobby fingers over the raised surface. The smile was beginning to come up. The surface of his skin seemed like white scar tissue, healed over. He said, "I took me a knife once, or some other kind of sharp object, can't remember, and tried to dig the ink out. Didn't want it on my arm anymore. I dug at it, but I couldn't get the durn ink out so I just left it. I like to rotted my arm off doing that. My daddy had given me hell for gettin' that tattoo, by the way." What seemed to bring the curving smile was the recollection of trying to remove the blue initials with some forgotten sharp object and then suffering an infection. The smile came atop the words "dig the ink out" and "like to rotted my arm off." What did he use for the job—a dinner fork? A camp knife with a serrated edge?

Maudine, who'd been married to John Ed not quite a year by then, was in a yellow polo blouse. A small and perky woman, she'd recently turned eighty. Like her husband, she's religious, but she can't see the print of a Bible any longer. I'd called John Ed that morning—I always tried to keep things loose when I wanted to approach him for another talk—and Maudine had answered. "Come for dinner today," she said, meaning "Come for lunch." I'd been there for her meals before and remembered how wonderful the food was. I felt awkward about eating with people whom I was trying to plumb for secrets, but in the South it's so difficult to say no to those invitations. I'd been in John Ed's house five times by then, our talks lasting into long afternoons. Maudine had become a part of them. I'd learned by then to work in and around his poor hearing. "What? What's that?" he'd say, cupping his ear, and I'd look up from my notebook and repeat the question loudly.

In his third wife's presence, he'd continued to use "nigger," as if there were no other useful or accurate word. Maudine always said "colored." She didn't attempt to correct her husband. Sometimes, I'd try to look over to get her reaction when the word was being said several times in a story. This one, for instance: "Only time I got rough, really rough, I guess, when I was sheriff was with a drunk nigger from Schlater, Mississippi. I had him cuffed and he tried to jump out of my car coming back to Greenwood in the middle of the night. I'd gone up there to Schlater to get him out of some durn bar. And the durn nigger tries to jump out of the car as I'm bringin' him back and we ended up wrestlin' in a bar pit alongside of the road. Guy came down with his cuffs on the inside of my wrist and tore the artery and I was bleedin' all over the place. I caught him with the heel of my hand and broke his durn jaw. I put him in jail in the courthouse, and next day I'm taking the nigger to the county farm, and I took him without cuffs, 'cause I was just darin' him to try somethin'. When I get stirred up, I don't book no junk. I told that feller, 'I'd have blowed your brains out if you'd a tried somethin'.' " There seemed no particular reaction in Maudine, except admiration for his manliness.

John Ed and Maudine had gotten hitched on Labor Day weekend, 1998, right before his eighty-fourth birthday. He'd been widowed, second time, for not quite five months; she'd been a widow for twenty years. John Ed and Maudine and Maudine's former husband, Clyde McClellan, had all been friends for decades. After Clyde died, Maudine and John Ed and John Ed's wife, Sybil, kept visiting back and forth. They'd go to Delta reunions and auctions and church suppers. Maudine's from Leland, Mississippi, over closer to the Mississippi River. This is how John Ed described the sudden hitching to a woman he'd long known, though not in a carnal way: "I didn't want to be alone and I didn't want her to be alone. She's about two-thirds blind, I'm about two-thirds deaf, and so I said I'd see for her and she'll hear for me, and that's the way it's been, I guess. We just did it." They drove in his pickup to Eudora, Arkansas, because there weren't a lot of justices of the peace open in Mississippi on a holiday weekend, and anyway, they thought of the trip to another state as a sort of honeymoon, even though they drove right back. None of his family went to the wedding, although some of hers did. "I told the JP we wanted to be married, whole thing didn't take two minutes. We're just as married as if we'd done it in a church, and I told the JP, 'We're going to be the happiest teenagers you ever saw.' He said, 'You take this woman holding your right hand to be your wife?' And I said, 'I shore do.' He asked Maudine the same thing, and that was it." Whenever John Ed gets into his pickup, his bride climbs in on the other side and then scoots all the way over: a two-headed driver, with the two heads adding up to about 170 years in age.

His oozing curve of smile: I'm not quite sure when I began to think of it as a passageway to help decipher the hidden inner man, but—like with the tattoo—I can recall vividly the first time it got my attention. We were on the porch, sitting in white rockers. It was overcast and extremely humid. Little tears of perspiration kept gathering on his upper lip. He'd lick them off and go on with a story. He wasn't married to Maudine yet. This was my second time in his home. A cat named Sophie that had belonged to Sybil was meowing and curling at the base of our rockers. The cat kept him from rocking, which brought annoyance and more beads of perspiration. "Don't you need a cat?" he said. He spoke gruffly to the cat, but there didn't seem any teeth in the gruffness.

He started telling about a "little water head" grandchild, long dead. He'd been talking of his first wife, Maggie Myrt Cothran, who'd died young of stomach cancer. They'd had two children together, Billy and Betty. John Ed had outlived his first wife, Maggie, just as he'd recently outlived his second, Sybil. But anyway his mind was drifting back to this long-ago grandchild, Donna Kay, one of many Cothran offspring. Donna Kay had been born a Mongoloid. Betty Ellis, the child's mother, had been unable to care for her, so Donna Kay's grandparents took her in. The child had a red wagon with a little bed in it and she loved pulling her wagon up close to the television set in the living room. She'd turn on the set and lie down in the wagon. "She'd lay in it real close to that television and she'd start to laugh whenever blacks came on and then maybe that little water head would get a convulsion," John Ed said. This time there seemed something almost sheepish, something embarrassed, in the curving smile. He didn't use the n-word. It was unnerving to imagine a little girl with water on the brain lying in a red wagon in her grandparents' farmhouse, laughing at flickering images of blacks on TV—and her aged grandfather smiling so many years later at the memory of it. Donna Kay, John Ed said, had lived for six years.

He was wearing a diamond ring that day. It was set in the middle of a gold cluster, and eight starbursts were shooting from it like sunrays. The ring looked so incongruous on such large work-worn hands. He said he'd been given it by his first wife. He said he just decided to start wearing it again after his second had died.

In southern Mississippi, the former Imperial Wizard of the White Knights of the Ku Klux Klan, Sam Bowers, was set to go on trial for a 1966 civil rights arson-murder, and this was much in the news in the state. John Ed spoke of Bowers and of the Klan's attack on the family of Vernon Dahmer and of the prospect of justice at last. "Well, by damn, they ought to get him," John Ed said. "No call to go around hurting folks like that." He shook his head as he said it—sadly, genuinely.

He led a tour into the hall to look at some mounted pictures. There was a framed reproduction of a 1926 baptismal certificate. John Ed was twelve when he got doused in Christ. The certificate said he'd been "buried with the

Lord in baptism for the remission of sins." The baptism took place in the Quiver River near the town of Itta Bena, which is outside Greenwood and means "beautiful spot in the woods." After a while, we went out into the backyard and sat in peeling metal chairs. We looked at his garden: peas, butter beans, tomatoes, cukes, okra. He said he didn't even like to eat the stuff—he grew it to give it away to relatives and local widow women. The garden wasn't doing well—the heat was too intense, not enough rain. He showed some gourds he'd grown and had hollowed out and had strung high on poles, so the purple martins could nest in them. "They eat their weight in mosquitoes twice a day," he said. But the nesting martins weren't eating enough mosquitoes— the air was so thick with their high hum that he wanted to go back inside. We sat in the almost depressingly clean and rugless front room. There were long silences. He was smoking filtered cigarettes—he'd switched from his Camels.

"Don't you need a cat?" he said.

"I used to get on a tractor at daylight and go in the house and eat dinner and crawl back on that thing and go to dark," he said.

"My middle name used to have two d's on the end of it. Knocked one of 'em off. Got tired of having two on there. Now it's just Ed," he said.

"I'm lonely here," he said.

The next time I drove up to his home, the summer's heat had passed, and an old and seemingly nonmalevolent man opened the front door of 518 West Washington, and sitting in a middle distance behind him, her legs tucked beneath her, was a small white-haired woman. "I want you to meet my wife," he said.

R emember the parable of the wheel inside the wheel, and how one thing turns on another.

There was once a youthful SNCC voter registration worker assigned to Greenwood named Douglas MacArthur Cotton. Everybody who knows him from movement days calls him Mac Cotton. He's a native Mississippian and is past sixty now and lives far back in the woods, about an hour south of Greenwood, in a different county, closer to Jackson. He makes his living as a carpenter and odd-jobber. He wasn't the first SNCC worker in Leflore County in the early sixties, nor the last, nor is his story unique. But it's a story to remember nonetheless. On June 25, 1963, Mac Cotton brought two hundred people to the courthouse steps in an attempt to get some of them registered to vote. He got arrested. The *Commonwealth* ran a headline: "Ten Arrested at Noon Today for Loitering at Courthouse." The story said, "When they started sitting and gathering in a large group on the steps of the courthouse they were told by sheriff John Ed Cothran and his deputies, they would have to move." On another part of page 1 was an AP wire story about JFK telling millions in Berlin, *"Ich bin ein Berliner."*

The week before, on June 18, fifty-eight people had been arrested in Itta Bena. They, too, had been booked on charges of disturbance and breach of the peace, and they, too, had gotten their headline in the *Commonwealth* ("Sheriff Arrests 58 in Itta Bena"), and they, too, had suffered a rapid sentencing to the county farm. They'd been tried in groups of eleven or twelve, with no representation, and it had taken the sheriff's deputies (one of whom was the sheriff's son, Billy Cothran, home from a second tour in the Air Force and working again for his dad as a sheriff's deputy) a whole hour to herd all of them into and out of the courtroom. So, a week afterward, when Mac Cotton and nine others got carted off to Leflore County justice, it was one more headline in the local paper but nothing to call news. His trial took place about ninety minutes after the arrest. According to a later affidavit filed by Mac Cotton, the courtroom proceeding lasted five minutes and the sheriff refused to answer any of the defendant's relevant questions. By five o'clock, the prisoner had been moved to the county farm in a school bus with black grating on the window. He'd gotten four months and a $200 fine.

At the county work farm, the prisoners were put in striped uniforms and made to cut roadside grass with kaiser blades. If you wanted to go to the bathroom, you told the sarge, "Taking a leak here, Shot." One day out in the fields, the Shot cocked and pointed a pistol at Mac Cotton. He did this because the prisoner had asked the guard to call him by his name, and not by the word "nigger." Everybody stopped working. The moment defused, but afterward the prisoner and some of his fellow prisoners went on a hunger strike, and for this they were sent to the Mississippi State Penitentiary at Parchman. Things had notched themselves up now, for Parchman—it was all you ever had to say during the civil rights era, "Parchman"—was the prison hellhole of the South. Parchman Farms has been grieved into song and poetry by generations of Mississippi blues men. It sits on Highway 49W, in the middle of the Delta, about an hour's drive northwest of Greenwood. For most of the twentieth century, inmates at Parchman chiefly did one thing in daylight: work the farm's thousands of acres of crops, notably cotton, under the gun and bullwhip. The whip was known by some as Black Annie. The farm, as historians have written, provided a remembrance of slave times to blacks who'd thought they were free in a free world—although whites were incarcerated there, too. There's a book about Parchman called *Worse than Slavery*. Historically, both the penitentiary board and the parole board were controlled by Delta planters.

At Parchman, the sassy prisoner from Greenwood with a general's name began to suffer a drip from his penis, to get sores on his tongue, on his gums, and in his throat. Mac Cotton told a guard about this, and in answer to a question he made the mistake of saying "Yes" instead of "Yes, sir." For this, he got the hot box. "You goddamn niggers shut up that goddamn racket. I'll throw your ass in the sweat box," the guard said to the others, according to an affidavit later filed. Sometimes at Parchman, the guards would take you to the box naked, jerking you by your penis. In the box, the only air came from a crack under the door. Several days later, back in his cell, the prisoner, who'd supposedly gotten his mind right, ate with his fingers from a face bowl. At one point, there were fourteen men in one cell—one was trying to sleep against the commode. Mac Cotton had the unreasonableness to ask for someone else's food when that inmate said he had no appetite. The guards heard about this, and the next day they served Cotton three butter beans and a piece of crust about the size of a pair of dice. He told them to take these crumbs away, he didn't need them, and for this insolence he got put on the bars. Getting put on the bars meant that the guards made you stand on your toes while they roped you by your wrists to the top bar of your cell.

"I peed and shitted out all over myself," Cotton is saying. We are in his living room. We have not met before. I have brought with me a sheaf of declassified papers and affidavits and other things that I've obtained from civil rights archives and government files and from the declassified Sovereignty Commission files. I've come to his home to ask him about John Ed Cothran, who'd once arrested him on a courthouse step on a charge of loitering, with or without true malice in his heart, but in any case an action and an event that had put in motion a long string of dehumanizing moments and actions: You could think of it philosophically as the chain of moral consequence.

Cotton seems uninterested in looking at any of these papers, at least for now. He has placed them facedown on a coffee table, aligned their edges in a neat stack. "I think about this a lot," he says. He means Parchman penitentiary in 1963 and of his hanging on the bars and of the peeing and shitting out all over himself in front of his fellow freedom workers. "I think what God did for me. I was just kind of floating through the air after a time. After a while all of it was taken away. I imagine about after eight hours, I was removed from the pain of it."

His wife, Mamie, is typing on a computer and listening in. Grandchildren are playing in another room.

"Why aren't you riled up?"

"Why should I be riled up?" he answers.

"But they were invading your rights." (It feels ludicrous, phrasing it so weakly.)

"My whole existence was illegal in their eyes," he answers.

He has just come from Sunday church, which is a short walking distance from his home. At Pleasant Hill Missionary Baptist Church, the preacher had taken his text from Ezekiel, Chapter 1, Verse 16. The pastor had cried out,

"The big wheel turns, but the little wheel inside makes it turn." Mac Cotton and I had sat in the first pew. He held his Bible on his right knee. He was in a suit and tie. "Keep on rollin', keep on turnin'," the pastor had told the congregation. "You go all these miles in life and what you find is there's still a wheel in the middle of a wheel. The big wheel turns, but it's the little wheel inside the wheel that makes it turn." After the service, Mac Cotton had gone to the churchyard cemetery to look at his parents' grave site. His father, Emmitt Hezechia Cotton, was born in 1884. He died on December 3, 1960. He had gotten registered to vote in Mississippi somewhere around 1905—the rarest of accomplishments. His son said, "See, it's a continuity, it's a chain, that goes all the way back, it's all hooked together, just like the pastor said, is what I'm trying to tell you."

Back from church, back from the cemetery, in his living room, his tie pulled down, Mac Cotton is sipping clear moonshine from a fruit jar. And he is not riled.

He looks at the picture in *Life*. The name "John Ed Cothran" hasn't registered in him. He is shown a picture from the *Commonwealth,* in which you can clearly see the face of the sheriff of Greenwood.

"This is the man who arrested you on the steps—and then all that stuff happened."

"Yes!" he says. "Okay. Now I remember him. Now I remember this guy. Come to think of it, I think he was a kind of Southern gentleman. Law-and-order person. His kind or brand of Southern gentleman. Come to think, I can remember now that he was almost troubled. I remember him talking to me . . . before we were sent to the county farm. It was as if it was bothering him. He was saying, 'Well, what do you all want?' We said, 'Well, all the rights guaranteed to us under the Constitution.' He seemed at a kind of loss. It was almost as if he couldn't quite make himself come out and say to us, 'You're wrong.' At the same time, he sure wasn't going to say to us, 'You're right.' But you could see it was almost bothering him, that's the idea I had in my mind, as if he was sort of struggling with it himself."

Mac Cotton pauses. "I don't know what he did other times, of course. I'm telling you how it was right then between him and me. . . . This is what I think I remember." Mac Cotton pauses again. "Maybe he would have turned his back and let somebody else hang me, there's that, too."

David Jordan easily remembered John Ed Cothran—and even more so he remembered Wilbur Wardine Smith. Jordan is black. He is a lifelong Greenwoodian. He lives on the south side of the river and has had a long career in state and local politics. One morning in his home, he was looking at old government documents relating to incidents of police brutality by Greenwood cops during civil rights activities, with the names of the brutalizers blocked out, and before any questions could be asked, he flicked at the papers with his middle finger and said, "I'll bet this was Big Smitty." He had half a dozen Big Smitty stories to tell, including this one, which he said he personally witnessed one Saturday night in the Silver Moon: Big Smitty—who must have been a town cop at that point—walked in and saw a drunken man in a corner. The guy was sort of slobbering on the table and talking to himself. Big Smitty strolled over and the place came to a halt. The lawman put his billy under the drunk's throat, horizontally, clenching the stick at either end. Slowly he began sliding the man up the wall. "He had him wedged there by the throat, a couple feet off the ground, and his eyes started to pop and get glassy. The man was strangling to death, and then Big Smitty let him fall. The reason I remember this so well is because I was just a kid. I was a kid in the Silver Moon, and I saw this, against a defenseless man, and I'll never forget it," said Senator David Jordan, who represented the 24th District, which includes the three Delta counties of Holmes, Tallahatchie, and Leflore.

The legislator said he could remember when John Ed Cothran was campaigning for sheriff again, in the summer of 1967, after he'd been out a term. (He lost to the man who ran the county prison farm, John Arterbury, and after that he didn't run again.) Jordan and a committee from the Greenwood Voters League went out to the Cothran farm, south of town, on the Humphreys Highway. They were treated with much respect, Jordan said. There was something like apology in Cothran's voice. "You've got to think about this: for four black men to come up in the privacy of his living room, and for him to offer us refreshments, and to have him explain to us about the system. This is almost unheard of, is what I'm telling you. He said he couldn't do anything about it, the way the race thing was. He said it was the system. He said it had to be this way, and we told him we pretty much understood." Could the candidate have just been trying to get their vote? "I don't think so. I think a lot of these guys were caught in the system. These guys were afraid something was going to happen to them if they didn't go along with it."

Jimmy Green remembered him. He had recently retired from a combined forty-five years' public service on the school board, on the board of county supervisors, in the Mississippi statehouse. He is white and owns a big plantation farm west of town that he has lived on for seven decades. As a politician and Delta planter, he'd grown into a certain racial tolerance, earning the eventual respect of blacks, who'd turned him out of office for the board of supervisors. Early one morning, he stood under pecan trees in front of his farmhouse. For almost an hour, he'd been inside, drinking coffee, beating mainly around the bush of the key question: What was really in John Ed's heart? Jimmy Green said quietly: "John Ed didn't have malice. John Ed was afraid, and I've been knowing and liking him as long as I can remember. He didn't want to be too hard on them and at the same time he didn't want to lose the confidence of the people who ran the town." Green didn't quite look at me. "He was afraid of Big Smitty, really."

"Afraid in a physical sense?"

"Well, some of that, maybe. But afraid more of not getting elected again, afraid of Big Smitty's following." I said, "What would have made Big Smitty do all those nasty things in the first place?" Green shrugged. "To be a hero to that element. So he'd have that kind of following."

"Why would John Ed have Big Smitty working for him?"

Green shrugged and formulated his reply as a question. "So he didn't have to do it himself?"

Gray Evans remembered him. He is another upper-aged and extremely hospitable white Greenwoodian who's had a long public career, not without controversy and enemies on the south side of the river. He lives in a fine house on the north bank. He'd once had the bad form to work in Washington for the liberal Delta U.S. congressman Frank Smith. Smith, a friend of JFK, miraculously kept his House seat until 1962. Evans, who'd been a young aide to Smith, was a senior circuit judge in Mississippi when we spoke. In the early sixties, after working in Washington, he became Greenwood's prosecuting attorney and thus got pitched into the middle of things. It was as if Gray Evans's first name was a signal for where his mind was. He seemed to have regrets, although not by the cartful. "I knew things weren't right," he said. "We didn't do right by a lot of those folks back then. And yet I know in my heart I tried to stop some things that might have turned out deadly." Of John Ed Cothran, he said, "Putty. Just like putty in their hands." He said it with no pleasure. He made a squeezing motion with his fingers and moved his head from side to side. He was asked who the *they* were of "their hands." He said, "The Hardy Lotts, the Charlie Sampsons of the town." He said, with softness in his voice: "Weak man, weak man, really—that he ever was sheriff. He was always cut out to be a number-two." The senior circuit judge rubbed his fingers in his eyes and said he had the lingering but overriding impression that in a volatile situation John Ed would've slunk back and let another do it—not out of cowardice, no, but out of aversion to violence. "I suppose," he said, "he could be frightened into doing things he didn't want to do."

On the next trip to Mississippi, I asked George Greene about John Ed. The Greene family is one of the great families of the Greenwood movement. All the Greenes were heroic, not least the parents, who preceded the movement by decades. In the fifties, Dewey Greene, Sr., was president of the local NAACP. George Greene, one of the sons, hasn't lived in Greenwood for many years. He was in Jackson, where he worked at the Veterans Administration hospital in food service. He told old war stories about SNCC and COFO, and at length he was shown the picture of the man with his back turned. "Yeah, I remember him," he said. "Low-profile sorta guy. And I always thought those kind of guys were dangerous. Because you never knew what they were thinking."

Low profile. It's difficult to find John Ed Cothran's name in old civil rights suits brought by the federal government against Greenwood and Leflore County. He is seldom named as a defendant in these cases. When you search the record, it's easy to find the name Wardine Smith, along with other civic officials. Big Smitty, like his stomach, was right out there. But the head man, with guile or without it, was able to escape being named as a defendant. Most times.

There is also the parable of Thatcher Walt, a local editor who deviated from the norm, who chose at a crucial juncture not to go along. But you wouldn't have thought to call him liberal—not if you saw his signed editorials in the *Commonwealth,* which were often enough about the communist menace come to town. "In time these men will leave our midst. Behind them they will leave either the permanent wreckage of racial hostility (which they thrive on) or they will leave Greenwood much as it was before, a quiet town where Negroes and white people are living side by side in comparative harmony," he wrote. He went on in that same piece: "This pattern will not change in the foreseeable future. It is a tactic in the grand strategy of forces which seek to warp the social patterns of the South." When SNCC worker Jimmy Travis was shot in early 1963, Walt said (under a headline on the editorial page that proclaimed, "A Good Day to Get Shot"): "Travis is one of those self-styled saviors of the Negro race who is agitating for voters registration. What better way to mobilize on-the-fence opinion in Congress than to have a vote worker shot?"

And yet in the town without pity, newspaperman Thatcher Walt suddenly became suspect. When a cross was burned on the courthouse lawn, the editor—a native Mississippian—said that it was a stupid act. Even more important: After the out-of-town owners of the Leflore Theater decided to comply with the 1964 Civil Rights Act and to admit blacks, Walt and his wife, Thelma, and their small children crossed a picket line of hooting thugs. He'd already decided to get out of Greenwood and take a newspaper job in Laurel, Mississippi. The family emerged from the darkness of the movie and walked past the thugs and went home and immediately started receiving threatening phone calls, some of which they were certain came from the police. They were afraid to sleep in their bedroom and so four Walts slept on a Hide-A-Bed in the living room. Soon someone called the editor's wife and told her that her husband's body would be found in the Tallahatchie. Terrified, the family left for Clarksdale, where a relative lived. When they returned a few days later, someone fired a bullet through their front picture window. Mrs. Walt borrowed a shotgun and sat in the dark of her living room. The editor went back to his job at the *Commonwealth,* only to learn he'd been fired by the publisher and that the paper in Laurel didn't want him, either. There weren't going to be any more newspaper jobs in Mississippi for Walt. The family left the state and moved to Jacksonville, Florida, where he took a job at the *Jacksonville Journal,* before turning eventually to other work. He died in 1998. "I guess you could say this was my husband's attitude," Thelma Walt said on the phone when all this was suddenly brought up again. "Sort of 'Give a little, and you'll save a lot. Let's go on and comply and it'll be easier to live with them.' But in Greenwood, that was being the enemy."

In the movement, certain stories took on the power of instant myth. They were sustenance against the fear. You can find the following story in James Forman's beautifully written and righteously angry *The Making of Black Revolutionaries,* in a chapter called "Terror in the Delta." A SNCC voter registration worker named Sam Block is relating the incident. When the incident happened, Block wasn't yet a legendary figure in Mississippi and in the Greenwood campaign for civil rights. He was just an incalculably brave twenty-two-year-old: lean, deep-voiced, sinewy, 110 pounds dripping wet. This particular incident occurred when Block was canvassing the streets of south Greenwood almost entirely alone. He'd been the first SNCC worker to come to the county, in June 1962, delivered there by the charismatic Bob Moses in Amzie Moore's '49 Packard, all of them singing, "This land is your land / this land is my land." Over the next two years, Sam Block was going to come within an inch of losing his life more times than can be known. Some of his escapes seem to have been arranged by divine inspiration. This particular event occurred in mid-August of 1962, about six weeks before James Meredith integrated Ole Miss. The report of it burned through the movement like a grass fire.

> We went up to register and it was the first time visiting the court-house in Greenwood, Mississippi, and the sheriff came up to me and he asked me, he said, "Nigger, where you from?" I told him, "Well, I'm a native Mississippian." He said "Yeh, yeh, I know that, but where you from? I don't know where you from." I said, "Well, around, some counties." He said, "Well, I know that, I know you ain't from here, cause I know every nigger and his mammy." I said, "Well, you know all the niggers, do you know any colored people?" He got angry. He spat in my face and he walked away. So he came back and turned around and told me, "I don't want to see you in town any more. The best thing for you to do is pack your clothes and get out and don't

never come back no more." I said, "Well, sheriff, if you don't want to see me here, I think the best thing for you to do is pack your clothes and leave, get out of town, cause I'm here to stay, I came here to do a job and this is my intention, I'm going to do this job."

That didn't sound like John Ed Cothran, at least as John Ed could be discerned through the time-bends of an old man deep in his eighties, reading his Bible and tending his garden in the somnolent town where the Southern crosses the Yellow Dog.

But it's a fact that in the streets of 1962 Greenwood a lone black had faced down the county sheriff and lived to tell. Some called it the Wyatt Earp story. Later, Block would say he'd done the facing down deliberately—he knew nobody talked to a Mississippi sheriff that way, least of all a black man. As Block remembered a few years ago in California—about forty years after it had happened, and only a few months before he died—he'd been ready to give up his life that day on the slim chance that he might win, and for what that winning could do for the incipient Greenwood movement. That was always part of the story's myth—he'd gambled so large and won. "That he wasn't murdered on the spot is something of a miracle," Howard Zinn wrote two years after it happened in his 1964 book, *SNCC: The New Abolitionists,* one of the many valuable histories in which you can find a version of the incident. The story is in Clayborne Carson's 1981 *In Struggle.* It's in John Dittmer's 1994 *Local People.* It's in Charles M. Payne's 1995 *I've Got the Light of Freedom.* These are all important and closely documented books. In each it's "the sheriff."

Except it wasn't the sheriff of Greenwood—it was the bullying deputy. Sam Block himself is responsible for the years of mix-up. He confirmed that it was Smitty. Until he and I talked—and we'd first talked of it on the phone before I went to California expressly to ask him about it once again and show him photographs—Block said he never knew Big Smitty wasn't the county sheriff. He said, "That's what we called him, Sheriff Smitty. I didn't know he was the deputy sheriff. That distinction didn't even matter to me."

One can follow the telling and retelling of the Wyatt Earp story as it appears in books through the years. The primary source is almost always Block's own first-person account as published in Forman's 1972 book, *Black Revolutionaries.* Some authors drew details from an old *New York Post* piece—James Wechsler, a columnist, had interviewed Block in the summer of 1963 and had moved the story along with more color. In Seth Cagin and Philip Dray's 1998 book, *We Are Not Afraid,* the supposed villain is named: "On the courthouse steps, when Sheriff John Ed Cothron approached Block in a menacing fashion, Block stood his ground. Cothron asked where he was from. 'I'm a native Mississippian,' Block said." The account went on from there, with the misspelling of the surname of the man who'd been sheriff of Greenwood. (It should be said here, however, that sometimes even the *Commonwealth,* John Ed's hometown paper, would goof and spell his name "Cothron.")

The incident appears in Endesha Ida Mae Holland's lyrical book *From the Mississippi Delta,* published in 1997. She is a Greenwood native who worked in the movement and made it out of the Delta and earned her doctorate and became a theater professor at the University of Southern California—but, like almost everybody else, she got the story wrong in terms of who did the spitting and who said "I know you ain't from here, cause I know every nigger and his mammy." Ida Mae Holland named the spitter: "Leflore County sheriff John Ed Cothron."

(In at least one latter-day published source, Sam Block made it quite clear about whom he was talking. In a lengthy 1987 interview titled "Never Turn Back," published in the journal *Southern Exposure,* Block said: "We were standing in front of the courthouse, and Sheriff Smith came and spit in my face. He said, 'Nigger,' and he took his pistol out, and he shook his pistol in my face." A few lines down: " 'Sheriff, if you don't want to see me around here the next day, the next hour, the next minute, or the next second, the best thing for you to do is to pack your bags and leave because I am going to be here.' Big Smitty just dropped his hand and his gun in amazement.")

In Los Angeles several years ago, Sam Block, who had diabetes and other ailments, looked at a photograph of Big Smitty. "I'm three hundred percent sure," he said. The old SNCC worker, still lean as a string, looked at another picture of John Ed Cothran, taken from the front. Block said, "Truthfully, I can't even remember this guy's face." As he talked, he dabbed at his eye with a handkerchief folded into a small square. "I'm not looking for glory," he said. "I did it for what has been accomplished." He meant the work he'd done in the movement. His eye was watering and he dabbed almost daintily at it. He apologized and said it was the residue of an old beating. Two Mississippi high-way patrolmen had done it. They'd pulled their pistols on him in a jail cell in Columbus, Mississippi, and ordered him to run. Block said, "No, sir, I am not going to run." One of them said, "Yes, nigger, you are going to run." They hit him with the butt of a pistol and dislodged his eye. In California, Sam Block, Delta native, so far from home, with one good eye, kept telling stories. And then he shook hands and said goodbye. Five months later, he was dead. He was sixty. There was his obituary in a newspaper. He'd been trying to get a company going that would manufacture tire sealant.

On the day that he remembered about John Ed and Big Smitty and all the others, Block said that he longed to go back to the place that had been brutal to him. It was home. Simple as that, he said. "Loving all of it even while he had to hate some of it" is how Faulkner explained the strange pull of Missis-sippi. And Eudora Welty said: ". . . the home tie is the blood tie. And had it meant nothing to us, any other place thereafter would have meant less, and we would carry no compass inside ourselves to find home ever, anywhere at all. We would not even guess what we had missed." There were things he still wanted and needed to do in Mississippi, Sam Block had said on that day in Los Angeles, less than half a year before he died, dabbing at his watering eye.

A nd an old hard-to-know man—still strong, hearing-impaired, with a soft blurry blue tattoo—was in a little brick house with bluish-gray trim in the Delta town where the Southern crosses the Yellow Dog.

He had a bad cough that day. He seemed more agitated and distracted than in the previous visit. He pinched his fourth finger and thumb together and said, "Been takin' these durn pills, 'bout this big, but they're not doing any durn good. Delta crud. Got it in my throat. Went to the doctor man and he gave me a little white one and a big red one." He took a cigarette pack out of his pocket. "Cancer sticks," he said. "Aggin' my cough on. Stopped for a week but then started up again." That morning, at 5 A.M., he had read St. Paul's letter to the Colossians in the New Testament.

Maudine said, in a lowered voice, when he'd gone to another room: "Part of what's been giving him this sickness is worrying about all that brush to be cleared out back. Eats at him. He's been going out every morning. He'll work four hours and come in and tilt back in his rocker. But that's it."

It was unseasonably warm for February. After dinner, he went out into the yard in shirtsleeves. "How long is it after the scout comes before the rest comes, John Ed?" his wife said. She meant the purple martins. " 'Bout two days," he said.

"Where do they come from?"

"Central America," he said. It was plain they couldn't wait for spring.

He went into a story: "Only time I ever fired a piece at a body. Nigger raped a white woman. Cold, at night. He had her out in a cornfield. He raised up and started running. He made for a canebrake. After a while, he came out, hands up. He got sent to Parchman for life. Potts, Leroy Potts. Yep, that was his name, ol' Leroy Potts. Sent me a letter not long before I left office. He was trying to get out on parole. Asking me if I could help him in any way. It was the nicest letter you ever read, but I reckon I couldn't help him."

He talked of arresting fifty-eight blacks in Itta Bena—June 18, 1963. "One night there was this big upset out at Itta Bena, and my deputy, Ed Weber, called me, he was the town marshal out there, and he said, 'You'd better get out here,' and by the time I did they'd busted windows and been throwin' bricks and every damn thing. So I brought me a school bus out from town and loaded 'em up and took them into the courthouse, and there was this little Jewish lawyer from the Department of Justice and he said he wanted to talk to them. And I said, 'Now look here, you shore as hell are not gonna do that, not at this hour. Hell, no.' Hell, must've been midnight. I said, 'Mister, I don't care what you want to do and I'm not trying to be horsey with you, but it's goin' to have to wait till in the mornin'.'"

Maudine said, "Is that the ones went to Parchman, Jack?" Her husband said, "Some of 'em. A lot went to the county farm."

He went to his bedroom and brought out his old sheriff's star. It was tarnished and small. "Sheriff of Leflore County" it said. "Got my gun back there," he said. "Think I'll polish up my star and put on my gun and play sheriff."

Big Smitty came up in the conversation. "Big front on him," John Ed said. "Been dead a while."

And then, on his own, he brought up the spitting story, and how he'd come across it in a book, and how he'd seen his name staring at him right there in cold print. His niece, over in Sidon, Mississippi, had gotten the book first, he said. His sister Mary Nelle had showed him the same book and asked him if he'd done that. "Made me sick enough to go in there and vomit," he said. "And ain't true, ain't none of it true. I never did that to nobody. I never treated people like that." There was great distress in his voice.

"Isn't it the filthiest thing?" Maudine said.

"I don't like to be low-rated," her husband said.

"Filthy," Maudine said again.

"And it's a damned lie," John Ed said.

"But it *did* happen," I said. "Only it was your deputy, Big Smitty."

This is how he responded: "Never heard tell of it. Never knew anything about it. You sure Big Smitty done that? Wish old Big Smitty was here right in this livin' room so's I could ask him. But he's shore enough dead, ain't he?"

A couple of months later—the sixth visit to Moorhead in a year's time—I asked him directly: "Why did you allow a man like Big Smitty to work for you, knowing how he treated black people?" Everyone in Greenwood knew what Big Smitty was. John Ed said that he'd known Wardine Smith all through the fifties, when Smitty was a town cop, and that he, John Ed, had been responsible for bringing him into the sheriff's department and then getting him to stay on after John Ed had won the top job from the voters. "Didn't know about it. Woulda fired him in a minute if I knowed any of those things," he answered.

In California, the blurred picture had started to become clearer. It was as if the letters "JEC" weren't so faintly blue on a white background. Sam Block had clarified important things—and so had Wazir Peacock. In the movement, he was Willie Peacock. He was one of the earliest to work in Greenwood, arriving there not long after Block did. Willie Peacock, a Delta native like Sam, had graduated from Rust College in Holly Springs, Mississippi, in 1962, and had planned to enroll in a black medical school in Nashville. But the movement had intervened. On the phone, Peacock said he had converted to Islam in 1966. He said he'd left SNCC in disillusionment. Both he and Block had left in anger and disillusionment, he said. Too much of the movement, at least in Mississippi, was being lifted out of the hands of local people.

On the phone, Peacock said of John Ed Cothran, whom he remembered straightaway: "It's true you couldn't pick up hateful feelings from him necessarily. . . . His position was, 'I'm not going to step out and help you, but I'm not going to stand around calling you hateful names, either.' " Peacock said he could recall going out to the Cothran farm to get bail bonds signed. I tried to say something about how brave they were, and Peacock said: "Well, it's true the only protection we had was from a higher power. And if we didn't survive, then we had to believe that someone else would pick it up and take it along." He said, "We were born out of time almost. We just couldn't accept what we saw. We'd lived it growing up. But we just couldn't accept it anymore."

In Oakland a few weeks later, a thickset man in his late fifties, in a wool sweater, with a hoarse whisper, whose work was teaching the mentally disabled, sat at his kitchen table with photographs spread out before him. In a corner of his apartment, there was an altar. "Avenue F and—what is that, down from Taft?" Peacock said, trying to remember a Greenwood address. He, too, seemed so far from home and longing for it. "I tried to hate," he said. "It was never in me. That was the popular thing to do, hate them. . . . There was an acting out, that's for sure: 'If you don't want me in your life, okay, I don't want you in mine.' At some place way down, they knew we were human. They were fighting nature. It made them do inhuman things to other human beings. We used to say in the black community, 'In order to keep me in the ditch, you have to be in the ditch with me. You treat me ugly, you have to become ugly.' "

He looked at the photographs on the table. One was the picture from *Life* and another was of Emmett Till's unrecognizable face. The shot had been taken from Till's coffin and published in *Jet* magazine. Peacock had said on the phone that they were "all of the Emmett Till generation—Sam, myself, all of us, any of us, really, who grew up in Mississippi back then. That's why we went to work for freedom." Peacock, who's from Tallahatchie County, where the Till trial was held, was looking at a picture of a fourteen-year-old Chicagoan's mutilated face from *Jet* in 1955, and anger was rising. A religious man, a convert to Islam, seemed to be changing his mind about some things, taking a harder view, not least of the sheriff with his cohorts in *Life* who's got his back turned—maybe taking a harder view about any white person who'd had his back turned.

He said: "I do have a sympathy. . . . [But] he kept his hands clean. 'Hate' wouldn't be the word. My thing with people like him is this: There's a viciousness about this kind of person and you can never forget it. Smitty is all the way out there. He's easy to understand. This guy, you don't see everything. This man was not dumb. He was smart enough to know that one day the federal government was going to turn everything around. He had a healthy respect for us, me and Sam. He knew what time it was, that if something happened to us, somebody else would be coming. He didn't like us there. He didn't have to show his hand, either."

"So in a sense a guy like this is more dangerous?"

"Oh, my, yes."

He was told what his former SNCC colleague George Greene had said— that "you never knew what they were thinking." Peacock said: "That's it."

Leroy Potts, the black who was sent to Parchman for raping a white woman—or at least convicted of same—could he still be alive? Leroy Potts, at whose fleeing back Deputy Sheriff John Ed Cothran once fired.

Parchman had the record. The convicted man entered the penitentiary on May 20, 1955, and was paroled fourteen years later, on August 29, 1969. Three months later, he was back in. Got paroled a second time in 1972 and was out for good, until he died, three years afterward.

Ella Jean Lucas, his sister, is standing on her doorstep in the middle of black Greenwood. Her brother's been dead since 1975, she says. It was his heart, she says. He had obtained a factory job in Jackson after the second parole. He was going straight, she says. But his health declined and then he was gone by forty-six. Did his early death have anything to do with mistreatment at the prison? "I couldn't say about that," she says. She's got on a straw hat and it's pulled down over her head in folds. She stands on the top step of her asbestos-shingled and tidily kept house, holding open the screen door. Two green park benches are on either side of the steps. Roses climb a trellis behind her. Lucky to catch her at home this morning, she says, because she spends most of her time now sitting up with the sick and the dying. She goes to hospitals and nursing homes and hospices. "I have been told it is my gift." She's sixty-nine and her life has been hard. One night in the sixties, while she slept, her husband and another man were killed right out front of the house. Some kind of argument in the street and then the shots waking her up. None of this has ever wavered her in her faith in God. God has His reasons.

"I don't know whether he was falsely accused or what, Leroy," she says. "He told me he wasn't guilty. That's what he said. They convicted him. I was five years younger. I was always the one in the family to do the taking care. We lost our mother early, and the kids got farmed out. Something happened to my brother. I say it that way. I used to blame myself. He's sleeping out there in the clay." She says this, pointing toward a cemetery plot in another county, maybe thirty miles from here, where her brother and other family members are interred.

"He was at Camp Ten up there at Parchman. I'd all the time be taking cakes up there. They'd slice my cakes up, make sure no razor blades and knives were in them. The warden used to come by and get a piece. He said he loved my cakes. I got to know all them folks pretty good."

John Ed Cothran—does she remember that name? "I remember Mr. Cothran from the trial. He didn't seem like a vindictive man. I never knew Leroy wrote him a letter to try to get out."

How about the name Big Smitty? "I will tell you this about Mr. Wardine Smith," she says, nodding slowly. "When he was dying, they had him in a bed, and he had to be tied down, his arms and his legs, he was thrashing and fighting it so. He was just carrying on. I was a few doors down, visiting other sick folks. You could hear it all over the floor. He made a hard time of his outgoing."

A symbol is not an explanation. The naked eye is often faulty. The truth tends to live at the middle. It wasn't Leroy Potts's story or Sam Block's or Mac Cotton's or even Big Smitty's that permitted me to see John Ed Cothran whole in a grainy way. Rather, it was Emmett Till's. Rather, it was two things John Ed remembered all these years later that allowed me to begin to grasp an old man's interior. It was the Till kidnapping and murder and trial, taking place seven years before the photograph in *Life,* that helped unlock the once and ever morally ambivalent law enforcer.

To study the available record of John Ed's role in the Till case is to get the wrong picture—or at least not the whole picture. The man in the published record appears to be putting his conscience ahead of his predilections. That man comes across as nearly heroic in a bad time, willing to do his duty, to stand up. When you read the record, when you obsess on it, that is the conclusion. But it's a wrong conclusion. Parts of it are correct. But the "truth," if there can be any truth, is somewhere in the middle. It's ambivalent, a little blurry, perhaps unknowable in the end, something like a photograph itself that had once seemed so limpid in its messages.

I've already told how I drove to a library in Memphis on the night I first met John Ed. I sat at a newspaper microfilm reader and looked at a picture of the forty-year-old earlier self of the elderly figure I'd been with in Moorhead a few hours earlier. The man on the roll of microfilm was squatting next to a cleaned-up but still-silted gin fan.

In the days afterward, I read everything I could set my hands on about the case and his role. He'd been quoted in *Newsweek:* "The white people around here feel pretty mad about the way that poor little boy was treated. Northerners always think that we don't care what white folks do to the colored folks down here, but that's not true. The people around here are decent, and they won't stand for this." He'd been quoted in *Jet* magazine as "disagreeing" with those who were claiming that the decomposed thing pulled from the river wasn't Till. One of the chief proponents of the theory that it was a body planted by the NAACP was the massive sheriff of Tallahatchie County, Clarence Strider, who, in most newspaper photographs, is wearing sunglasses and a malicious grin. I would later find out that, besides being sheriff of the county that is north of Leflore, Strider was a big-time cotton farmer, with 6,000 Tallahatchie acres under cultivation. Going down the lane to his manor house was a string of cement-block plantation shacks, and on the roof of each, painted in white, were huge letters spelling out STRIDER.

From United Press International, September 4, 1955: "A deputy sheriff who witnessed the identification of the body said it was Till's. Deputy Ed Cothran said he 'completely disagreed' with Sheriff Strider. 'Emmett's uncle, Moses Wright, definitely identified the body as the boy,' Cothran said. 'I was with him when he did it.' " The deputy sheriff of Leflore had in his possession a ring taken off the body right after the fishing out. It bore the initials L.T. It had a date inscribed on it: May 25, 1943. The ring had belonged to Till's father, Louis Till. It had a flat crown. The boy had been wearing it when he left Chicago. The boy's uncle had identified it. These facts were told to the press in the hours and days after the body was located, and one of the principal tellers was the deputy sheriff of Leflore County. In some of the photographs of him, examining the ring, he looks almost sad. From the *Memphis Commercial Appeal,* September 5, 1955: "Deputy Sheriff John Ed Cothran of Greenwood showed a ring taken from the victim's finger to newsmen Sunday. It had the initials, 'L.T.' " From the *Jackson Clarion-Ledger,* September 4, 1955: "Cothran also said he had a small silver-looking ring pulled from the body by a Negro undertaker after it was fished from the river. . . . Cothran said relatives of the Negro boy told him the initials stood for Louis Till. Emmett's full name was Emmett Louis Till." From the *Commercial Appeal,* September 6, 1955: "Deputy Cothran said he didn't think 'there was any doubt about the identification at the river.' "

Again, to read accounts of what he said on the stand at the trial itself is to get a picture in your head of a lawman trying to uphold his duty. The trial transcripts themselves are lost, so the newspaper record takes on even more weight in forming that picture. Snippets of published trial testimony have shown up in at least one graduate school thesis, but they are inconclusive as regards John Ed. Sheriff George Smith of Leflore and his chief deputy both had testified under subpoena, for the prosecution's side. Both were in the witness chair on the opening day of trial, September 21. The deputy told the jury how he'd wheeled his car onto a dirt road near Pecan Point and had gone down the steep bank to stare at something that was "badly torn about the head."

H e gets his neck hugged by so many women," Maudine said.
"Maudine, your buddy's back," he said. He meant a hornet. He shuffled out to the kitchen and got a fly swatter and came back and then stalked it slowly around the living room. He was determined to get it. And he did, wedging and smashing it between the venetian blinds. Dinner had been fine again: macaroni and beef tips, boiled cabbage, turnip greens. As was his way, he talked of many things. And one of them this day was Emmett Till.

"I've read the record," I said, "everything I could find, and it makes you look pretty good."

"What? What's that?" he said, cupping his ear.

Loudly: "It must have come at some cost for you. Saying the things you said."

He turned the talk in another direction. He said the whole thing was a controversy made up by the press. They were trying to manufacture a split between the two sheriff's departments. "It's just the way they wrote it. Made me mad as hell. I wanted a retraction. I never said I knew the body was Emmett Till's for sure. I never saw Emmett Till alive. How would I know? All's I said was that I didn't know myself but that the boy's uncle was positive it was him. That's all I said. When I read that other junk in the paper, I wanted to sue that reporter. I told my boss I wanted to get a retraction. I think it was a durn reporter in Memphis that started it."

Now he remembered something else. There was a man from Tallahatchie County, whose name he could no longer remember, but who was there at the trial every day. After the acquittal, this man was waiting for him downstairs in the lobby of the Sumner courthouse. He was leaning against a pillar. He walked up and said, "You testified for the nigger-loving prosecution, Cothran. Didn't matter, though, did it? Up here in this county we never convict a white man for killing a nigger. That's why Tallahatchie's number one."

"Had to take his guff," an old man said.

He continued. Two months later, in Greenwood, a Leflore County grand jury was convened to consider whether a kidnapping charge should be brought against the two men who'd been let off from murder in the adjoining county. Once again, the head man of Leflore County and his chief deputy were called to testify. On November 9, 1955, the Leflore grand jury refused to indict Big Milam and Roy Bryant. They were free as air of all charges. As the deputy was leaving the courthouse, he saw the man who'd given him guff in Sumner.

"I went over to that feller. I said, 'Guess we don't indict them down here, do we? Now you tell me who's number one? Leflore's number one.' " John Ed Cothran said this, remembered this, and poked up a big pale index finger with the curving ooze of smile.

You never knew what they were thinking.

Several Januarys ago, on Martin Luther King, Jr.'s birthday, a non-Mississippian trying to understand Mississippi was in Greenwood and felt like going to church. It was a Sunday morning, and just as on any Greenwood Sunday morning, the whole town seemed to be at worship. It was unusually balmy. At the Episcopal Church of the Nativity, the rector preached on prophets and how they call into question things about ourselves we don't especially like. "They make us uncomfortable," the priest said, "and we drive them out." He told his flock they were self-evidently the brightest and best of their community—but it wasn't enough. He said it wasn't enough that they had done well professionally or financially. He said it wasn't enough that they were comfortable in life. No, the gospel demands that a Christian live in such a way that God's love will embrace everyone in a community. The priest spread his arms wide. There were no blacks in attendance and Martin Luther King, Jr., wasn't mentioned by name.

That afternoon, there was a memorial march through black Greenwood. It started at St. Francis of Assisi Catholic Church and ended a mile or so away at Friendship Missionary Baptist Church. Old ladies sat in metal lawn chairs out front of shotgun shacks and waved. Kids rode their bikes along the parade's periphery. The size of the parade kept swelling as people hopped off their porches and fell in alongside the marchers. People sang "We Shall Overcome" and "If I Had a Hammer." A man with a bullhorn kept the parade moving. "We are in the process, and we will make it," he cried. At Friendship Missionary Baptist, a woman played an aching piano. Light came through the amber windows and fell on wood paneling. Hand fans bladed holy air. Babies squalled. A robed choir in front of a maroon velvet curtain sang hymns. Someone in a beautiful falsetto voice sang the song that wonders, "Anybody here seen my old friend Martin?" Except for a couple of Franciscan priests and nuns and myself, the congregation was black. It could almost have been the early sixties, when a movement was in cry, when a sheriff with his back turned was trying to navigate in a gray middle zone of moral complicity. Only it wasn't the sixties. The hate here has gone mute, I thought. What remains, in Greenwood, in this arresting place called Mississippi, is a deep sense of separation. On the weekend commemorating Martin Luther King, Jr.'s birthday, Mississippi felt like a nation of strangers.

A picture is an action that must fill up its available space.

—Alfred Kazin, *An American Procession*

Every story is over before it begins. The novel lies bound in my hands, the actors know all their lines before the curtain rises, and the finished film has been threaded onto the projector when the houselights dim. . . . *All* stories, including history and biography, are past and therefore precluded. When we watch a documentary film years after it was shot, we know the outcome that the figures on the screen are trying to bring about or prevent. They have all aged or died, and what was present or future to them has become past.

—Michael Roemer, *Telling Stories*

Part Two

Filling Up the Frame

T*he picture's a double-reverse, the setup that wasn't. These guys sandbagged themselves. It's a posed-unposed shot that represents an uncanny documentary moment—far beyond what the photographer could have known or dreamed. In its magical, mechanical ways, the camera pinned truths of seven lives—not all the truths, no, yet some undeniable ones. Billy Ferrell, for instance, who always had to be the center of attention, being undone here by his ego. Or Grimsley, with his delicious and alcoholic malevolence. And of course John Ed, who didn't ever want to look but couldn't remove himself. The goal now is to document and contextualize the moment, the instant of the shot, the event that surrounds it, that day, that weekend.*

The goal is to put a slice of emulsion—one of billions of photographs in the universe—in its historical perspective. The place it needs to start is in James Meredith's living room. He is the first and last victim of a whooshing bat. That twenty-nine-year-old Air Force vet in the wan smile and dark business suit integrated the University of Mississippi in 1962 with such stoicism and courage, and then, a couple of decades later, when he'd already done so many bizarre things, went to work in Washington for race-baiting Jesse Helms, and after that endorsed ex–Imperial Wizard David Duke for governor of Louisiana and the presidency as well. I've wondered, as I've gazed and gazed again at this image, trying to see in it all that isn't here: Is the only real conclusion that Meredith's mad? I've thought a lot about what must be intolerable pressures of mind. For a long time, I didn't want to go back to try to talk to him. Besides, the story wasn't about Meredith anyway, although I knew in a deeper part of me that it was precisely about him. Because it's about what we're inflicted with, about what others do to us, about what we cannot escape—and about what we send down to others, our loved ones, in direct and oblique ways, wittingly and unwittingly.

American Haunting

The address is 929 Meadowbrook Road, Jackson, Mississippi.

In the midst of all that chaos—which came to its statewide frothing point in the last few days of September 1962—he kept a small white hanky folded into a square in his lapel pocket, and every now and then, pressed on all sides by federal marshals and reporters and Justice Department lawyers and faces contorted into hate, he'd take it out and dab with it at his beading upper lip. You can see this in the news film.

The last time in his house, three years ago, he'd gone on and on about his royal Choctaw blood. He was from the nation of Choctaws. His father had been a chosen leader of the former citizens of the Choctaw nation, whose forebears had been reclassified as blacks by the nineteenth-century bigots of Mississippi. "You see," he'd said, "the vast majority of blacks in this country who are successful have the same ancestry as mine—predominately Native American blood. Ruling-class families. Joe Louis was ninety percent Native American. At least. Same with Lena Horne. You understand what I mean?"

But how would that be proven? "Well, DNA would prove it, DNA would prove it," he'd said, his voice growing faint, as if already losing interest.

"Race is no longer a significant factor in politics in America," he'd said with perfect seriousness.

Pictures from a picture: a modest-sized gray house with gray shutters and closed blinds in an upper-middle-class integrated neighborhood a couple miles north of downtown. The listing in the Jackson phone directory: *James H. Meredith,* as if it were any old name. The blinds were drawn here three years ago, too. Plenty of times in the interim I have driven down this street without looking over. I've come to know pretty well one of Meredith's three sons, Joseph Meredith, who's up at Oxford, working on his doctorate at the school his father integrated before he was born. I have passed strained as well as fascinating hours in the company of this highly intelligent and extremely well-educated (Phillips Academy at Andover, Harvard) and very likable and yet so painfully reticent and cautious son, who's a twin, in his mid-thirties, and who's a father himself, divorced, and who has struggled for more than a decade with a life-threatening illness (lupus), and who—most important here—seems locked into father-son inheritances he cannot begin to understand.

But not until today has there been another try at conversation with Joe Meredith's dad, who once told an interviewer: "God's role for me is similar to his role for Moses and Christ." Who told another interviewer (and this, too, was long after America had mostly forgotten about him, or else was making a not-so-faint joke of him): "James Meredith is as foreign to me as he is to any-body else. You see, I created James Meredith to do certain things, so it was not a personal thing at all. I was never personally involved with him." Who had told *me,* one time before, with much derision: "I was never one of those folks—I had my own divine responsibility." By "those folks," he meant civil rights folks, movement folks.

He had said then that he'd been sick for several years. It was easy to believe. He was so frail-looking. His waist seemed narrow as a girl's. He said it was prostate cancer and diabetes and unspecified other ills he was trying to get over. He'd said, "Oh, man, I've gained ten, fifteen pounds, in the last month. As soon as I get my strength back . . ." He said he was trying to get well enough to go on with a biography of Cap Meredith, his father, "born in 1891, the same year the Constitution of Mississippi established white supremacy as the legal and official law of the land." Moses Cap Meredith—a prideful, reli-gious, autocratic scrub farmer and small landowner in the hills of Attala County, seventy miles north of Jackson—seems a huge part of the James Meredith riddle. Cap died in 1965. One of the things he taught his many chil-dren growing up—James was near the middle on the ladder of kids—was never to bow down to any white man.

He had picked up the phone on the first ring and had said to come straight over. It was a Tuesday morning in May; the whole state felt intoxicant with bloom. Fifteen minutes later, there was Meredith standing at his door, smiling, a ghost from the sixties, sixty-four years old, his hands so small and beautiful, his face so elegant and powerful and withered. Inside, he'd angled himself sideways in a straight-backed chair. It was primary day for municipal elections across the state, and he had put his name on the Republican ballot for mayor of Jackson. For the next two hours, the phone didn't ring once. "If I win, no one will be more surprised than I," he'd said, and it was about his only modest statement. (The next day, the *Clarion-Ledger* reported that he'd got-ten 478 votes.)

Big watery tears had started lining either side of his nose, and he'd excused himself and gone to another room and returned chewing a wad of gum. "Hope my chewing gum doesn't bother you," he'd said. "I find it helps my allergies." He'd begun working the gum in big smacks and pops. He'd left the room again and returned with a mimeographed pamphlet. On the cover it said, "James H. Meredith. Republican Candidate for Mayor. City of Jackson, Mississippi. MY PLATFORM AND POSITION." Some of the pages were stapled in upside down, and there was typed material running sideways in the margins. One of these sideways typed-in marginalia said: "WHO I AM. In order to understand my perspective on Higher Education, it will be necessary to know who I am and from where I come. Since the first article was written about me in 1961, I have never read an article about James H. Meredith more than 500 words long which did not make some reference to some mythical, strange, divine, or other such reference. Many writers have tried to unravel this mystery without success. I am here today going to give you a two minute summary of a 10,000 year history of who I am and why the mysticism."

He'd switched on a lamp at a cluttered table against a wall in the living room and moved aside a green vase of fresh-cut flowers, the better to look at the photograph. Those flowers had to be a woman's touch—Judy Alsobrooks's touch. Meredith's second wife works in local public television. (She's manager of a low-powered station at Jackson State University.) She wasn't home that day. Meredith's first wife, Mary June, died in 1979 at age forty of a massive coronary, leaving him with three sons who weren't yet on their own. Meredith's brother—who has worked as an auto mechanic at Kmart in Jackson, among other trades—once told an interviewer, "Losing his wife . . . I noticed the greatest change in James. He cried a lot, and I couldn't remember him ever doing that." Judy's touch must also have accounted for the sense of elegance in the room: the glossy piano, the two fine wing chairs, a striped sofa, the throw rugs on polished wooden floors. And yet there was a computer set up next to the piano, and on top of the printer an athletic trophy of some kind, precariously balanced. It was as if the living room, by itself, was trying to suggest a certain scatter amid the seeming calm. It was as if Judy's husband was getting lost in the confines of his own house, in the clicks and tumblers of his mind. The synapses would synapse, and then they wouldn't. He'd say something piercing, and then he'd say something cracked. Some of it felt calculated—as if he wished to mess with his visitor's mind, as if he enjoyed it. He once told a reporter: "I mean, I have been reading all my life that these people think I'm crazy. But you have to understand that I really thought they were crazy. I mean, they were out of their minds." That's behind him; today is another pained day in James Meredith's life.

He opens the door. There's a child in his arms. He hesitates for a split second, recollecting who this knocker is. Those large black-brown eyes—they'd darted and flitted and bored in so disconcertingly before.

"Mr. Meredith . . ."

But he's already turning away. "Come on in, I've got to feed this child."

His face is still powerful and withered-looking. There *is* a kind of regality there, Choctaw or otherwise. His skin still seems to have a light box under it. When he squints, five or six furrows, with a crook in each furrow, seem to ride up his head. There's a big vertical vein on his left temple. His tennis shoes are without laces, just as last time. Then he had on a pair of black socks that came barely to his ankles, and two outsized blue veins rode up his skinny shinbones. He's got on white sweat socks now. He's still got his wreath of gray-white beard. He's wearing a silver wedding ring. His glasses are in a case in the pocket of his pin-striped shirt. It looks like the same shirt. He's gained back a little weight—some.

"I'm the one writing a book about some Southern sheriffs—and their families. And I wanted to come back . . ."

"I know that," he says, pointing at a chair, seeming barely interested.

The child's name is Jenee. She is the child of his youngest child, Jessica. Jenee, very cute, looks about a year old and has pierced ears and a T-shirt that says SOMEONE WHO LOVES ME VERY MUCH WENT TO GULFPORT, MISSISSIPPI AND BOUGHT ME THIS SHIRT." He's got her on his lap and is spooning yellow puree into her mouth, catching the stuff at her chin in smooth swipes and putting it back in. "C'mon, child," he says. "Eat your dinner. You getting real sleepy, girl." He's tended babies in his time, bathed them, changed them—you can tell that. He seems both very tender and very firm. "Well, it's just me and her," he says. "Take care of her a lot."

A moment later: "Segregation was of no concern to me." He's catching the yellow goop before it falls.

"What was, then?"

"White supremacy. Segregation was like apartheid. There's only one thing that mattered—citizenship. C-I-T-I-Z-E-N."

Jenee is kicking at him.

"Where do you live?" he demands.

"Maryland."

"And where were you born?"

"California."

"And where did you grow up?"

"Illinois—although I also grew up . . ."

He waves it off. "Do you perceive there was a difference in bigotry between Illinois and Mississippi?" Before an answer can be given: "Maybe two degrees of bigotry in Illinois and ninety-nine in Mississippi. But it was all the same. No difference in what America was intended to be about."

To his grandchild: "All right, all right. I know you're sleepy, girl."

Then: "Listen, do you understand what the difference is between the civil rights movement and James Meredith?"

"Well, maybe not completely."

"All right. You got to understand that first. Did you read my book *Three Years in Mississippi*?" Before the answer can be given: "The civil rights movement was about the right to use public facilities and the right to the franchise. When Dr. King adopted nonviolence as a tactic, that acknowledged second-class citizenship. But what I was about was the right to use violence to defend your rights."

"You hold out for that?"

"I not only hold out for it. I assert it today. What do you think got me into Ole Miss? It was *violence*." He smacks his foot on the floor. His voice is loud. His granddaughter is really fussing now.

When he was seventeen, scrawny and predestined James Meredith, seventh of thirteen children, possessed of divine responsibility, was sent to live with an aunt in St. Petersburg, Florida, and there, at his new home and segregated black school, he realized that if he was going to establish himself quickly, he'd need to beat up two bullies who ruled. And so he did, in the first case using a stick with nails sticking out of it, in the second with his bare fists. After high school, in 1951, he went into the service—he chose the Air Force, believing it to be the most integrated—and it was there that a military psychiatrist examined him for his chronic anxieties about race. From a psychiatry report, dated April 29, 1960, when he was close to being discharged: "This is a 26 year old Negro S Sgt who complains of tension, nervousness and occasional nervous stomach. . . . Patient feels he has a strong need to fight and defy authority and this he does in usually a passive procrastinating way. . . . He loses his temper at times over minor incidents both at home and elsewhere. No evidence of a thinking disorder. Diagnosis: Passive aggressive reaction, chronic, moderate." Meredith quoted from his own diagnostic report in *Three Years in Mississippi*, which is the story of his entry into Ole Miss. It was published in 1966 by the Indiana University Press and is a moving and literate read, even as it's an often absurd one, with statements like this: "My most stabilizing belief is that I have never made a mistake in my life."

He took college extension courses in the Air Force. He met his first wife, who was from Indiana. He served in Japan, where he instantly felt "that air of difference about being a Negro that you can never quite touch." He got a reputation for being intensely thrifty—"nursing the dollar," said those who knew him. A rating officer wrote that he was the most financially scrupulous individual he'd ever known.

But now he's taking care of a grandchild and getting balled up in the story of one of his great-grandfathers, Mississippi Supreme Court Justice J. A. P.

Campbell. "My father's mother's father," he says. He was white but spent the last twenty-seven years of his life with his black family. He was eighteen years on the state Supreme Court. The jurist inspired him to "bring about the dismantling of everything he had set up." He says that his own destiny and divine responsibility derive partly from the racist, and then unracist, meanings of this forebear's life. But there are too many loops and turns to follow it completely. The child is going at serious decibel levels. "You real sleepy, girl, you real sleepy, girl, ain't you? I'm gonna let you cry yourself to sleep. I *will* give you your bottle." He takes her to another room. When he comes back, he looks at the photograph.

"Oh, I remember this picture," he says. He's standing in the middle of the room. He brushes the back of his hand across the width of the picture. "My goal was to convert them—*and* their descendants. All the ones who weren't born yet." He hands the magazine back. His interest has already died.

This tack is tried: "You're not a liberal, are you?"

He seems flummoxed—ambushed on a quiz show with a trick question. He's swallowing hard, squinting. A look of fear has passed over his face—which he's trying to mask. "Well, I had a point," he says. Then, "I have to agree with your last point. I am not a liberal. I'm not a conservative, either, at least as you go down one side or the other. Citizenship is my thing. You understand?"

He's on the Choctaws again. His line goes back 2,000 years, minimum, he says. "Choctaw civilization was the highest form of civilization when the Europeans came. I've written twenty-five books and they're all about that, in one form or another. And now I'm going to write my autobiography. Which I hope will be my biggest book of all."

"Do you have a title?"

"No, but I've got the first sentence. Excuse me." He goes to the back room. When he returns, the phone is ringing. "Hel-lowww," he says deeply, sonorously. "No, it's still for rent," he says. "You want to go look at it?" It sounds as if someone is inquiring about an apartment rental. Does the person on the other end know he's talking to *that* James Meredith? He hangs up and reads from a piece of paper in his hand: "Most of my life happened before I was born." He looks over for a comment. "It took me four or five years to write that," he says. "I considered the book half written when I wrote that sentence."

He is asked how he spends the bulk of his day. Planning the writing, he says. Caring for Jenee. An occasional lecture or appearance. And lately, some part-time teaching at a Christian academy up in Yazoo City. It's fifty miles each way. He and Jenee left at seven-thirty this morning and were back at midday. He's been teaching them to read and write. Some are grown-ups. "Most satisfying work I've ever done," he says, a softness in his voice.

"Later this summer, I'm going to take a bus trip across America, just to clear my mind. And then I'm going to go to Brazil. Doesn't matter if I don't talk to another soul, just so I can get my mind clear, to think, so I can come back and write. In order to get my mind prepared, I have to isolate myself." He says he's hoping God will let him live for five or six years, to finish this project. Most of his previous books have been self-published, in uniform blue binding. Some have beautiful titles and all of them contain patches of lucid and uncompromising prose—such as his *Letters to My Unborn Grandchildren,* in which he wrote on page 82 to Jenee and all the other Meredith offspring not yet in the world: "I returned to Mississippi in 1960 [from nine years in the Air Force] with a conscious purpose in mind, to attack what was considered the apex of White Supremacy in America, to strike it and destroy it." Some of these hard-to-find books, in their uniform blue binding, contain highly erotic writing.

Asked if a copy of his biography of Cap Meredith is available for purchase, he nods and gets up and goes to the back room and a moment later returns with the book. Payment is rendered by check. "Won't have this check long," he says, weighing the piece of paper in his hand. "Right off to the bank."

Trying to get it going again, thinking this will be an indisputable sentence, you say: "Guess Ross Barnett will figure a lot in the new book." (Ross Barnett being the cowardly and face-saving and selling-out demagogue of a governor who presided over his state's legal resistance to the desegregation of Ole Miss even as he kept inspiring the lowest-common-denominator race hatred that accompanied Meredith's forced entry into the school. It was an entry that took almost two years to achieve, through lower courts and higher courts and some Mississippi kangaroo courts, before its culminating September weekend on the green lawns of Oxford, attended by canisters of tear gas and the stench of cordite and two deaths and hundreds of arrests and an occupying U.S. Army numbering in the thousands.)

"Say," he says, with a look something like contempt, "if there was one thing Barnett loved, it was black people. I don't think there were but two people who understood that whole game, and that's me and Ross Barnett. Every time I ever saw him after that, I shook his hand."

"So you don't hate Barnett?"

"Why would I hate Ross Barnett?"

"But he said such awful things about black people—about you."

"Listen here, Barnett would do whatever it took to get elected. My mother had fourteen brothers and sisters, and the last one alive, he knew Barnett like his own brother." (Meredith, it turns out, has taken to telling people around Jackson in the last few years that he and the late, lamented Ross Barnett, governor of the state from 1960 to 1964, were distantly related on his mother's side.)

Trying to get him interested in the photograph again: "All dead now, these sheriffs, except this one—his name is John Ed Cothran and he's up in the Delta, just been to see him."

Any discussion of the photograph is dead. There's a deeper knot of silence in the room, a deeper knot of defiance in his face.

"The pressures on you from all that. The pressures when you were getting in must have been nearly unbearable."

"None. Absolutely none."

"Okay, but what about after you got finally admitted? Those Ole Miss students froze you out, they banged their meal trays on the tables when you came into the cafeteria. They set off cherry bombs in your dorm, they pelted you with eggs, they threw water balloons at you out of windows, they referred to your wife as 'Spider'—you know, that she was going to end up a black widow. They bounced basketballs for hours on the floor over your head in the dorm. They'd see the marshals who were taking you to class and call out, 'KKK—Kennedy's Koon Keepers.' "

"None. Absolutely none." His arms are crossed.

A moment later, he says this: "My goal was to make them what they oughta be. It's like a baby. A baby can't insult me. Anything they did, I saw as my shortcomings. I hadn't reached them. Do you understand what I'm saying?"

He shakes hands goodbye. In the other room, Baby Jenee must be in far dreamland.

G o back to the late summer of 1959, almost exactly a year before a black noncom "with a mission and a nervous stomach" came out of the United States Air Force. Self-proclaimed bigots and defenders of their granddaddies' way of life were running hard that summer for county and state offices. Mississippi voted for its sheriffs and other high officials in all eighty-two counties, and the results of the August primaries made the big local headlines in the dailies of Natchez and Hattiesburg and Greenwood and Grenada and elsewhere. But the larger headlines in every town and county belonged to the governor's race, said to be the bitterest campaign in state history to that date. Winning the Democratic runoff primary on August 25 was tantamount to winning the November election in this one-party state. In the days preceding the second primary, it was a commonplace to see increasingly louder ads in almost any weekly or daily: "Ross Barnett Is the Strongest and Most Vigorous Segregationist in the Campaign for Governor. Roll with Ross!" And over on the facing page: "I, Carroll Gartin, Lieutenant Governor, Am a Total Segregationist. With the Record of the Past Four Years, We Have Every Reason to Believe We Are Winning This Segregation Battle." Gartin was really a racial moderate—he was just doing what he had to do in hopes of securing votes. His opponent,

Barnett, sixty-one, was from a hamlet called Standing Pine, in east-central Mississippi (not far from James Meredith's home ground). He might not have believed it so deeply himself, but it didn't matter, for he'd already run twice for governor, in 1951 and 1955, and had lost, and no one in his state was ever going to "out-nig" him again for public office. Barnett had grown up the youngest of ten on a farm. He'd worked his way through school as a barber, janitor, logger, and kitchenware salesman. City folks down in Jackson liked to say that the candidate was "about two bubbles off plumb" in the smarts department. Many regarded him as bone-stupid, less a political demagogue than a genial old country fool. They loved quoting his malapropisms. It was true that by his third run for governor he'd already earned a considerable fortune in the capital city as the state's leading damage-suit lawyer. It was also true he'd been willing to defend blacks in his practice and that blacks were happy to have him as their attorney: Barnett could get them off. There was a wily not-to-be-underestimated quality about Barnett—which Robert F. Kennedy, for one, was going to underestimate at Oxford. It was said around Jackson that Barnett had a $100,000-a-year law practice.

In the 1959 race for governor, Barnett had the all-out support of the White Citizens' Council, more commonly known as the Citizens' Council or just the Council. The Council had been founded five years earlier, in July 1954, up in the Delta, to draw lines in the earth against mixing and the mixers. The Council had been established less than two months after the United States Supreme Court, in that despised thing called *Brown v. Board of Education,* had struck down the half-century-old Jim Crow doctrine of "separate but equal," which was a lie and a sham in all of the South but most especially in Mississippi. Because of *Brown,* it was now federal law that every school in the nation be integrated, or open to all races, though certainly it wasn't any kind of recognized law in sovereign Mississippi. In 1959, the emerging power in the Citizens' Council—in the capital city and across the state and in other Southern states as well—was William J. Simmons. He and Barnett lived close to each other in the fine old Jackson college neighborhood of Belhaven. Simmons was a large and disturbing man with hooded eyes and a mustache and a big chunky head. He wore dark suits and talked in a deeply pleasant drawl about the idea of a "supine surrender on our part" to those who'd come in and wish to destroy Mississippi's way of life. *No way,* was his answer. Simmons was the "prime minister of racial integrity," as one Mississippi columnist described him. His Jackson council was in the process of building up a card file that held the racial views of almost every white person in the city—and also in the process of identifying organizations subversive to the Mississippi way of life: the Red Cross, the FBI, the Elks, the YWCA, the Jewish War Veterans, the National Lutheran Council.

So the folksy, wily, not-too-bright Christian fundamentalist Ross Robert

Barnett, with the Council and William Simmons standing at his elbow, had emerged as the leading candidate in the gubernatorial race almost in spite of himself. There was a great sense in that campaign that white backs were against the wall—a spirit not unlike what had prevailed a hundred years before, in the decade preceding the Civil War. At one point in the race, the candidate got out of a small plane in the town of Olive Branch and walked into a propeller blade that was still turning lazily—but he survived and grinned it off and went on to win his landslide victory. He came into office in January 1960 (along with the new sheriffs of Adams and Leflore and Grenada and Claiborne Counties and all the other counties in the state) as the bellowing champion of states' rights, which, as everyone understood, was a fig-leaf name for white supremacy. That's how historian James Silver, in his book *Mississippi: The Closed Society,* painted Barnett. He was, said Silver, "an inflexible racist with a mind relatively innocent of history, constitutional law, and the processes of government." The governor was a deacon and taught the men's Sunday school class at Jackson's First Baptist Church. First Baptist, an immense white stone thing in the center of town, right across the lawn from the State Capitol, occupied a city block. Inside was a stage like Radio City's. There were several levels of balconies and tiered rows of dark pews in the main chamber, in this carpeted amphitheater of prayer. Also in the first pews of First Baptist were Thomas and Robert Hederman, owners of the state's largest-circulation and most unashamedly racist dailies, the *Clarion-Ledger* and the *Jackson Daily News*. (After Meredith's integration of Ole Miss, a columnist for the *Daily News* would write: "Watch the peace-lovers come to the fore, grab a nigger-neck and start bellowing brotherly love. . . . For us we'll just go on being a bigot, a reactionary, a rebel and lick our wounds till the next fight starts and plan to win somehow. We are licked but not beaten.") The theology of the flock of First Baptist, not unlike the theology of Mississippi, not unlike the theology of the *Clarion-Ledger* and the *Daily News,* was an unparsable mix of stone-white piety and righteous racism.

Once in, Ross hadn't rolled so well. He spent much of his time putting off job seekers. "Just kick open the door and ask for Old Ross," he used to say on the campaign trail. Some mornings the line outside his office door in the state capitol was forty yards long. He was ineffectual with the legislature. Word got out that he and his wife had spent $312,000 of taxpayers' money on such renovations as gold-plated handles on the bathtub faucets in the governor's mansion. He took to posing for official portraits with his head cocked and his wire specs dangling from two manicured fingers that were held aloft—like some fey backbencher in the English Parliament. An old wire-service reporter, Lewis Lord, who'd covered the Barnett administration, remembers how relaxed things were. Back then, Lord said, if you wanted to see the governor, you just

walked into his office and said hello to Miss Jean. There wasn't any press secretary. Miss Jean would nod you in. Lew Lord remembered that the governor
would get up from behind his desk and take him over to a little anteroom
"where there was an old-fashioned Coke machine with pull handles. He'd fish
two nickels out of his pocket and get two six-and-a-half-inch Cokes and we'd
sit there and talk. I think he was relieved not to have to talk to some office
seeker he'd promised something to in one of his three campaigns. I think half
the time he forgot I was a reporter." When you hear stories like that, you
almost want to start smiling at the historical memory of a long-deceased politician and demagogue named Ross Barnett. Forget it. He was as opportunistic
and craven in his need to remain in power as the far-smaller-time James Ira
Grimsley—and he'd prove even more craven and opportunistic than Grimsley
in the events at Oxford, two and a half years up the macadam in his mocked
and troubled administration. By then, having found the saving cause of James
Meredith trying to despoil Ole Miss, the governor would be exhorting the
youth of his state: "If you and I and all Mississippians had the courage of our
old daddies and granddaddies, we could perpetuate our ideals and way of life
forever."

In the late summer of 1962, the eve of Meredith's moment in history, a
thirty-one-year-old photojournalist was living miserably in a fifth-floor walk-
up in New York City's East Village. Charles Moore's unhappiness, as that summer began to dwindle down, in what could be called the twilight of American
apartheid, had less to do with his living conditions (his flat's one window
looked out on the brick wall of another building), or with the suffocation of a
city he'd not dreamed could be so large and dirty and vertical, than with the
condescension and rejection he was encountering in trying to get a freelance
career off the ground.

He was two years and three months older than Meredith. Like Meredith,
he was a native of the poor and rural Deep South. He was soft-voiced and had
a gentle, open face—which belied the tensile toughness of a former Marine
who'd also done a lot of prizefighting in his teens as a welterweight Golden
Glover. Like Meredith, Moore was wiry and slight of build. He had four small
children—three of his own, one stepchild—who were back in Alabama with
his estranged spouse. He owned a metallic-silver Austin-Healey sports car.
Two months before, in June 1962, he had driven east in it with his stake of
$1,500. And the stake was fast disappearing.

His own piece of native South was the northwestern corner of Alabama—
a little community called Valdosta, on the edge of a somewhat better-known
place called Tuscumbia (Helen Keller was born there), hard by burgs called

Sheffield and Muscle Shoals and Florence. He had grown up in these culturally dunned environs thinking segregation was the way things were supposed
to be. "I didn't dwell on the problems of blacks," he'd say years later. "In my
naïveté and lack of knowledge of the world, I accepted this. . . ."

His father was a Baptist preacher, although not the hellfire-and-
brimstone variety commonly associated with Southern Baptists. The Reverend Charles Walker Moore was known in that country as a decent and quiet
man, a persuader and exhorter rather than a screamer, and sometimes he was
even invited to preach at Negro churches. "Big Mo," black folks called him.
Occasionally, he'd take along his two sons. This had made a deep impression—it was the communal fervor, the power of the singing, the depth of belief
spilling from those backwoods, pine-board sanctums. In his older son's memory—that was Charles—Reverend Moore never used racial epithets at home.
He typically referred to blacks as "colored folk," a term of dignity and respect.
Was he an integrationist? No. Segregation was what God and man had
designed, even if the races came into close contact with each other every day,
as they did all over the rural Deep South.

In the Marine Corps (he'd gone in at seventeen, in 1948, with a parental
signature, before finishing high school), Moore had trained to be a combat
photographer. Upon his discharge, back in Alabama, he'd quickly set his
dreams on fashion photography. He loved pretty women in sexy clothes. Soon
he was restless, something that would prove a lifelong trait. With very little
money, he'd departed Alabama again, for California, where he'd studied por-
traiture and composition at the Brooks Institute of Photography in Santa Barbara. A year later, family problems, especially the illness of his grandmother,
forced him back home to be with his father and brother. For a while, he'd
seemed without focus. He'd found a job taking pictures at a local Olan Mills
studio, where he became a first-rate hack, spending his day shooting squalling
babies and the dressed-up families who trooped in for their portrait packages
at various price levels. He'd gotten good at putting rubber balls on his head
and rolling them off, distracting the babies so he could jump behind the camera and knock off the shot. The lights and camera stand were on a large X that
was taped to the floor; his subjects were eight feet away, posing in front of
backdrops. He'd learned much about the quickness of the mind's eye and the
reflex of a finger, so that what was being glimpsed within the small frame of a
lens could be acted upon almost instantaneously.

One day—it was 1957 now, and he was twenty-six—Moore had heard
about a newspaper job down in Montgomery, the state capital. The "Cradle of
the Confederacy," as white Montgomery was proud to call itself, was a pleasant
and still almost entirely segregated little Southern metropolis at a sharp bend
in the left bank of the Alabama River. The city made syrup and brooms and

window sashes and boiler parts. License plates were festooned with the
Rebel flag. Lunchrooms still had "Colored Only" sides and "White Only"
sides. He got hired—by both the *Montgomery Advertiser* and its sister paper,
the *Alabama Journal*. These were important dailies, segregationist sheets,
although less virulent in their bigotries than some Southern papers. The
Montgomery bus boycott had occurred two years before, but the new hire from
the northwest corner of the state had barely heard of that nationally watched
event, which began in December 1955 and lasted a year. (He'd never heard
the name Rosa Parks when he started at the paper.) His was the usual photo
staff work on a city daily: politicians cutting ribbons, society shoots by the
swimming pool at the all-white country club, high school football games.
Within a year, he had become chief photographer of the *Advertiser*, and it
seems accurate to say, from the vantage point of a lot of years removed, that a
sympathy for black people and for the incipient revolution going on in America and in his own city was something seeping into him by circumstance of
employment rather than something being embraced for its own sake. In any
case, the photographer had begun to hear a lot about a Montgomery pastor, a
native of Atlanta named Martin Luther King, Jr., just a little older than he
was, who'd come to town in 1954 and had helped lead the bus boycott, and
who'd recently helped found the Southern Christian Leadership Conference
(SCLC). "Mike" King, as parishioners at Dexter Avenue Baptist Church
thought of him, was a fast-rising national figure, but he was still a Montgomery
pastor, too. The downtown church where King orated on Sundays was little
more than a rock throw from where Jefferson Davis once stood and took the
oath of the Confederacy.

On September 3, 1958, Moore made a photograph of King being shoved
against a booking desk at police headquarters. The arresting cop has the minister in an arm lock. Another city cop is nearby, ready to help. They're booking
the preacher for loitering and refusing to obey an officer, but the real reason
they're booking him is because he's an uppity nigger. (King had showed up in
City Recorder's Court to testify on behalf of a fellow black, and the cops didn't
want him there.) The photographer got the picture from behind the police
desk, shooting straight at the clergyman. During the confusion of the arrest,
Moore had slipped around behind the counter, understanding that that was
the only spot from which to capture the abusive weight of white people in the
world—not that he thought of the instant in those terms, exactly. He shot over
the blurry shoulder of the desk sergeant (who has his fist cocked), so that what
you see, in the middle of the frame, is a well-dressed man (fedora, silky tie,
nice watch), his torso bent toward the counter, his arm twisted behind him,
his frightened wife looking on. The shot went out on the AP wires and
appeared in papers across the country, and then *Life* picked it up. It was

his first time in the magazine. It would become one of the great civil rights photographs.

He kept seeing, kept shooting, kept finding himself involved with black people in ways he'd not previously known. Still, he didn't have to take moral sides. He was earning his living—covering news in the festering city where he lived. His press pass and the box being held up to his eye were protecting him from larger questions. The governor of Alabama, John Patterson, had taken to telling fellow bigots that the reason that photographer for the local paper was shooting so many racial scenes is because he wished "carnal knowledge of nigger gals." In early 1960, segregated lunch counters had begun falling throughout the South. (The sits-ins had begun at a Woolworth's in Greensboro, North Carolina, on February 1, and had spread to Nashville and even to northern climes such as Madison, Wisconsin. Within a year, black collegians and others had desegregated hundreds of lunch counters in Texas, Oklahoma, Florida, and the border states of the South—but not in Mississippi. Many of the new recruits to the movement enlisted with SNCC. Far more radical than King's Southern Christian Leadership Conference, SNCC originated at a collegiate conference sponsored by SCLC in April 1960.)

In late February of 1960, in Montgomery, thirty-five black students from Alabama State University had tried to enter the basement cafeteria in the State Capitol. They were denied. The local supremacists were aroused. Vigilantes went out looking for protesters on downtown streets. Some carried eighteen-inch clubs inside their jackets or in paper bags. On Saturday afternoon, February 27, reacting to a tip, the chief photographer and the city editor of the *Journal* ran from their offices to the corner of Perry Street and Dexter Avenue, where whites and blacks were shouting and shoving at each other. The ruckus was across the street from Green's and just down from Kress's— each a popular five-and-dime with a lunch counter. Just as he got there, Moore saw a man wearing a tam and a short jacket reach down and pull a piece of tapered wood from a bowling bag. It was a miniature baseball bat. According to the account in the next morning's paper, the assailant "darted in and struck the girl from behind with a baseball bat." The photographer didn't even have time to get the camera up to his eye, so he made the shot on the run—literally. He took it at a tilt, which only added to the power, the picture's sense of violent immediacy. He clicked the shutter as the man in the tam and jacket is cocking back with a flat baseball-like swing, and just as the victim—a black woman whose face also can't be seen—is putting up her hands to ward off the coming blow. Her purse is on the curb, and a stick of gum and maybe a tissue and a compact case have fallen from it. In a way, the cocked toy bat, halted at its backswing, was a prefiguring of another grab-shot two years later on a college campus under some trees in an adjoining state. Incidentally, the hater with his bat, Sonny Kyle Livingston, had a kid sister who was about six-teen, who lived just down the street from Moore, and she'd recently done babysitting at Moore's home. Moore had had no idea of the connection. It's the way the layered South works.

Life had begun to run more of Moore's civil rights work on a picked-up basis, and the chief photographer on the medium-sized Southern daily was feeling restless again. With his saved stake (he'd been slipping $20 bills into a top drawer in his bedroom whenever he was able), he resigned from the *Advertiser* and loaded up his Austin-Healey and headed for Manhattan in June 1962—where, in that steamy summer, separated from his wife, from his own people, missing his children and feeling guilty about having left them, encountering Eastern elitism and condescension, he quickly turned miser-able. He'd gone to New York with the idea of trying fashion photography and perhaps also the celebrity and corporate worlds of photography. One morning, he went down to get his car and found it smeared with raw eggs. He felt he knew why: the Alabama plates.

The discouraged freelance got in to see Howard Chapnick, founder of the Black Star Photo Agency. He had his portfolio with him. Instantly, Chapnick saw the loneliness and unhappiness—and the giftedness. "Look," he said, "this town's no place for you. You belong on your own ground. The civil rights story is getting bigger and bigger. I think there's going to be serious violence down there in the next year or two. You've already done some amazing stuff. I'll put you on a retainer and make you one of our photographers, and what you're going to do is go back home and document it all. What do you say?" The air seemed hardly dry on the offer before Moore was loading his car. He slipped the noose of his lease and of the Manhattan freelance fantasy in the middle of the night. He drove through the Lincoln Tunnel and he didn't slow down until he was at the Chesapeake Bay, about dawn. When he crossed into Virginia, Southern soil, he got out and almost kissed the ground. He got back in the sports car and barely stopped until he was in Montgomery. In less than two months, he was going to take some pictures in Mississippi that would splash themselves across the pages of *Life*. One, in particular, taken with a Nikon and a 100-millimeter lens, would be published in a double-truck spread. His career was about to find its turning point. A son of the white South was on the verge of becoming utterly disloyal: shooting photographs from the point of view of the oppressors and their evil. One of Moore's gifts over the next several years would be knowing where to stand: right behind the poi-soned power source of it all. In his glands, the returning native must have known he'd soon encounter implied death threats such as this: "Know what, boy? You're worse than a nigger. You're a white nigger. And worse than that, you're a white *Life* magazine nigger." It was never a visceral hatred of his subjects that was going to come through Moore's lens—not in his pictures at Oxford, not in the ones from Bull Connor's Birmingham in the following spring, not in the images recorded on Bloody Sunday at the Edmund Pettus Bridge in Selma in March 1965. He was just going to get his people as they were. It's what James Agee, another loving and utterly disloyal son of the oppressor South, in his lyric prose meditation on Alabama tenant farmers, *Let Us Now Praise Famous Men,* termed "the cruel radiance of what is." But here is a question: For an essentially gentle man to achieve such a magnificent documentary portrait of his own kind, wouldn't he almost have to break himself in half?

A t the point the photojournalist was ditching the East Coast and turning spy in his own country, a man he'd not yet heard of had already spent about a year and three-quarters trying to gain admission to Mississippi's premier public institution of higher learning. (Premier, yes, as far as it goes. But as Willie Morris, native Mississippian, deceased, a fine writer and a fine man, who, among other literary accomplishments, served as the youngest and best editor-in-chief in the history of *Harper's Magazine,* once wrote: "Ole Miss is an institutional symbol, a pseudo-genteel outpost of brainless young beauties, incipient drunks, and winning football teams. Faulkner was not allowed to speak there." *Time* magazine was only a little less kind when it wrote, during the Meredith crisis: "[It] has its attractions—a green and pleasant campus, a perennially powerful football team, and very pretty coeds, two of whom won the Miss America contest in successive years, 1958 and 1959. But it is a cheerfully unintellectual institution with nothing special to offer the mind of an earnest man of twenty-nine.")

Meredith had come back to his home state in August 1960, his will and imagination centered on one thing: entry into the university at Oxford. He'd come home with a wife and a young son. On January 21, 1961, five months after his discharge, and the day after John F. Kennedy's inauguration (the election of Kennedy had fueled the sense of messianic resolve), the ex-sergeant wrote to the admissions office at the university, requesting a catalog and application forms. He was already in school on the G.I. Bill, enrolled at all-black Jackson State College. He'd earned college credits in the service and had something like three semesters remaining—about a year and a half—to get a degree. At Jackson State, Meredith sometimes went to class in a military uniform and a black leather biker jacket and pea cap and carrying a cane. He later would say it was because he wanted to look like a "hood." Nothing hoody about those first correspondences with Ole Miss—the soul of politeness, he was.

It's important to stress that Meredith's decision to strike at the most visible bastion of segregation in the South was personal and not directly related to what others spoke of as the movement in an uppercase way. To Meredith, "movement" was a nearly irrelevant word, a crutch word, implying weakness on an individual's part. As crucial as the Meredith–Ole Miss story is to the story of civil rights in America, as powerfully symbolic as Meredith became for both blacks and whites, the events of Oxford in the fall of 1962 are essentially outside that history, aberrant, like the man himself. Indeed, as civil rights scholars like John Dittmer have made clear (Dittmer's 1994 book, *Local People: The Struggle for Civil Rights in Mississippi,* is an immensely helpful guide in studying Mississippi in the sixties), the immediate impact of the desegregation of Ole Miss was to turn things backward for blacks in the state. His admission merely intensified white Mississippi's wrath—in already wrathful places like Greenwood and Natchez and Pascagoula. They'd been so humiliated by the Kennedys and their kind.

The applicant heard from the school in less than a week—registrar Robert B. Ellis had assumed he was white. Meredith filled out the forms and mailed them back on January 31, 1961, slipping in a polite little stick of TNT: "I sincerely hope that your attitude toward me as a potential member of your student body reflects the attitude of the school and that it will not change upon learning that I am not a white applicant. I am an American-Mississippi-Negro citizen." He pinned a formal portrait of himself to the top of the application. This sentence, and the photo, put into gear—by the university administration and the state attorney general's office and the board of trustees and the governor's office—a series of diversions, obfuscations, deceptions, delays, and ad hoc rewrites of school policies. The legal history of this has been told in numerous places. The nut of the story is that for the next year and seven months—from the end of January 1961 until mid-September 1962—the courts and the university rejected appeal after appeal and try after try by Meredith to get into the school while Ross Barnett fanned the already inflamed mind of the populace. Early in the process, knowing he couldn't afford high court costs, Meredith sought the friendship and counsel of Medgar Evers, local field secretary of the NAACP. He also wrote to the NAACP Legal Defense Fund. (In later years, he'd hotly proclaim, "They joined *me*. They joined *me*. You understand that?") Thurgood Marshall, director of the defense fund, a future Supreme Court justice, replied, "I think it should go without saying that we are vitally interested in what you propose." The NAACP defense team was headed by Constance Baker Motley and Jack Greenberg.

After two formal rejections, Meredith and the fund filed suit in federal district court. A hearing was set for June 12, 1961, in Biloxi, Mississippi. It was rescheduled and moved to Jackson. It was put off again. More delays. After

118 days—December 1961 by then—the judge ruled against the plaintiff. The school's admissions policies, he said—"and I find as a fact"—were not designed "in any attempt direct or indirect to discriminate against anyone solely on the grounds of race and color." The Fifth Circuit Court of Appeals in New Orleans upheld the lower court but reversed the district judge on several key points. Accordingly, the Fifth Circuit sent the case back to the district court and demanded a full trial. That trial opened on January 16, 1962—but got delayed. A year had passed since Meredith had written for the forms. He'd endured abuse in the papers and in the streets. He'd missed three potential semesters. And he was undeterred.

At his trial, the state attorneys called him a troublemaker who was lacking in moral fiber—it was for these reasons, rather than race, that the university felt morally obliged to deny him admission. On February 3, Judge Sidney J. Mize ruled against him again. Another appeal to a higher court. It was five more months, June 25, 1962, before the Fifth Circuit overturned the district court. "We find that James Meredith's application for transfer to the University of Mississippi was turned down solely because he was a Negro," wrote U.S. Court of Appeals for the Fifth Circuit Justice John Minor Wisdom. Meanwhile, state officials had tried to prosecute Meredith on a charge that he'd violated state law in 1960 by listing Hinds County as place of residence on his voter registration while listing Attala County on his university application.

Now a federal judge in Meridian, Mississippi, Ben F. Cameron, a member of the Fifth Circuit Court of Appeals, began issuing stays. The judge issued three stays; the full court of the Fifth Circuit in New Orleans overturned them. The fourth stay, on August 6, 1962, was appealed by Meredith and his attorneys to the U.S. Supreme Court. The board of trustees of the school divested the university chancellor of any authority to act on Meredith's application. On September 10, Justice Hugo Black in Washington vacated all stays and any further legal objections and ordered the admission of the applicant. That might have seemed the end of the legal road—but this was Mississippi. Three days after the Supreme Court ruling, the governor went on statewide television to invoke the long-discredited doctrine of "interposition," demanding the resignation of any school official "who is not prepared to suffer imprisonment for this righteous cause. . . . We will not drink from the cup of genocide. . . . We must either submit to the unlawful dictates of the federal government, or stand like men and tell them NEVER!" This happened on Thursday evening, September 13, and in a sense everything up to here was but prologue. Over that weekend, unknown to anyone in Mississippi except several of his close advisers, and known to only a very few people in Washington, Ross Barnett began a series of telephone conversations with Attorney General Robert Kennedy. The secret conversations were all about finding a way out and saving face—on both sides. They were all about staging a show of defiance while arranging a surrender under the table. For nearly a fortnight, each side tried to manipulate and bargain wtih the other—and both sides spiraled toward a bloody center, and nearly all of it got recorded on audiotape. And some cops under some trees getting their picture snapped at the penultimate moment—no more than the rest of a frothing state in that final week of September 1962—didn't know, at least didn't know at the time: that, really, they were bit players, pawns, peons, in what, at bottom, was a charade and a lie and a rank hypocrisy between Barnett and the Kennedy brothers. A lie and a charade and hypocrisy with so many tragic consequences.

Here, it had to have been right about here, on the other side of these little guardrail posts with their drooping chains. The wooden posts, each about two feet high, spaced maybe ten feet apart and yoked to each other by the looping links of black chain, rim the outer edge of a large, oblong, parklike space known as the Grove. Anybody who's ever stepped inside the Ole Miss gates has seen the Grove. It's just past the stone railroad bridge on University Avenue, after you enter the central portal. The Grove spreads over something like six or seven acres; it dips and rolls and offers picnic tables and love benches under magnificent old trees. On fall football weekends, this space is jammed with elegantly dressed alumni, many of whom host lavish pregame picnics under tenting. The faithful start setting up the tables and tenting as early as 7 A.M.—even if the game won't be played till evening. Some of the tents feature waiters in tuxes circling among the guests with silver trays. Some of the tents have their own jazz combos. Alumni wander about, tent to tent, family to family, embracing, storytelling. The male grads will be in their red Ole Miss blazers, the women in cocktail dresses and heels. About two hours before kickoff, the team, not yet suited up, leaves Kinard Hall and comes across campus toward the Grove and the Walk of Champions. The faithful form a human corridor for the players to walk through—this is a more solemn than fevered moment. The ritual is known as "Rebel Walk." Afterward, these Ole Miss families, with their two and three generations of alums, exit the Grove and take their seats in the stadium and do the "Hoddy Toddy" cheer and watch the afternoon's tilt in the warming sun against the Vanderbilt Commodores or the LSU Tigers. Until a few years ago, it was a commonplace for Rebel fans in Vaught-Hemingway Stadium to wave their Confederate battle flags after great plays. You'd even see the little flags being waved during the playing of the National Anthem before the first whistle. Recalcitrants still do it.

But the photograph, and the taking of it: September 27, 1962. It must have been just to the right of this scarlet oak. Billy Ferrell remembered that it was snapped directly opposite the Alumni Center, on the edge of the street called Grove Loop. That would mean very close to this massive tree, which may be older than the university itself; which is almost 160 years. Moore himself can't remember the precise spot, and what does it really matter anyway? If you face this way, northeast, toward Grove Loop and the Alumni Center, the Lamar Law Center will be on your left. That's where Billy's granddaughter Cricket studied for her law degree, which she earned in the spring of 2000. The law school building wasn't up when the camera recorded her granddad making a proud, unwitting jerk of himself.

(Time out. Study it again. Have you focused yet on the blurry curve going down the left side? It's a Mississippi state trooper. There's the brim of his trooper's hat. And his chin strap. The suggestion of a cheek or maybe an ear. The slope of his uniformed right shoulder. I remember the first time I "saw" this trooper. I was in the Grove, with my beat-up copy of *Life,* pacing and talking out loud, no doubt making an unwitting Northern jerk of myself. I think I gave out with something like a little Rebel whoop when I realized that it was a trooper's shadow. I'd just sighted a fairly obvious thing in the picture.)

On the day it was taken—a Thursday in America—this space must have seemed any color but green. Red, maybe. Hysteria had seized Mississippi, hysteria accompanied by a weird holiday mood. The riot itself was still three nights off, but things had reached a killing pitch, and not only in this patch of park. The Grove was fairly overrun with lawmen and reporters, although many professors were still trying to hold classes. Freshmen sported blue and maroon beanies; there were signs everywhere promoting candidates for homecoming queen. Across the state, some radio stations had suspended programming in place of bulletins, and these alternated with the playing of "Dixie." In the capital city, roughnecks in slow-moving cars were blaring their horns through downtown streets. Inriders from other states, carting coolers and weapons, were headed to Oxford. (The FBI was filing a stream of reports to Hoover in Washington.)

In the northerly town of Grenada, the *Sentinel-Star* reported: "Roughly 400 sheriffs, highway patrolmen, and deputy sheriffs have put away their weapons and are now armed only with Billy Clubs, tear gas and steel helmets. All entrances to the campus are blocked. Six police dogs, one about the size of a small horse, have been added to the force." In the southerly town of Hattiesburg, where Bob Waller was sheriff, the *American* reported (it was a UPI wire story running on front pages all across the state): "A legislative leader for Gov. Ross Barnett said today it is 'highly possible' that a gunbattle could erupt on the University of Mississippi campus between federal authorities and state officers. Rep. Walter Hester of Adams County told United Press International he thought it 'likely' that state, county and local law officers would attempt to fight off marshals if they tried to forcibly take Negro James Meredith into the school. However, Hester said he did not foresee an all-out insurrection. 'We can't win a shooting war with the U.S. Army,' he said."

In Natchez, tucked down in the southwest corner of the state, on the big river, where Sheriff Billy Ferrell presided, the *Democrat* was telling its readers in a special edition (and the story would run again the next day, on Friday the twenty-eighth, with fill-ins): "At Oxford, Mississippi Thursday massed a citizen army of peace officers at the gates of the University of Mississippi. . . . From every corner of the Magnolia state came sheriffs and their deputies. . . . The exact role of county sheriffs and their deputies and the scattering of city police remained in official secrecy. Sheriff William T. Ferrell of Natchez, president of the sheriffs' association, said he began the telephone relay that got the word around the state. . . . Ferrell mentioned receiving orders before he made the call. He declined to elaborate."

In Pascagoula, on the Gulf, where James Ira Grimsley was sheriff, the *Chronicle* published a story with a banner headline, which I quoted earlier: "Sheriff Goes to Oxford." The sheriff had left for the campus in the middle of the night with three deputies. The paper's editor, Ira Harkey, was drafting on his beat-up black Remington typewriter another of his stand-alone editorials. He'd written and published some brave and literate ones already. On September 14, the morning after Ross Barnett's interposition address on TV, Harkey had written: "It is not 'the Kennedy administration' that is making demands upon Mississippi. It is the United States of America, it is democracy itself, it is the whole of humanity. These surely will not back down either." Five days later, on the nineteenth, the editor had said: "In a madhouse's din, Mississippi waits. God help Mississippi." Since then, the bead of hate had done nothing but swell.

Charles Moore is remembering the moment when he found the shot and clicked the shutter. It's early summer 2000, thirty-eight years from the din. He's sixty-nine. After decades of wandering, he has moved back to the corner of northwest Alabama where he grew up. He is thin, wiry, white-haired. He's in a blue shirt with epaulettes. He's got on New Balance sneakers. He looks pretty much as you might imagine an old photographer and Golden Glove welterweight. He seems modest, retiring, decent, lonely, likable, a bit unfocused and weary—yet oddly vital too. He says he has recently separated from his wife of four years. He says that until today, he's never known the names of any of the men in the photograph, much less anything of their stories. He just took it and moved on—like any shooter in a war zone.

He's down on his living-room rug, and the magazine is open in front of him. Lovely light is coming in. He bought this rug in India in 1965, when he was shooting an overseas assignment, after he was burned out with civil rights photojournalism. So many clicks since a click in the Grove.

"I focused only on that," he says. "I just saw this group of men, and I saw this guy holding this bat kind of thing. If you're any kind of halfway decent photojournalist, you just go toward that. They were huddled. When I saw the stick, that just drew me in. I came up behind the trooper. That wasn't right. So I came around behind him so I could get them over his shoulder. I wasn't trying to hide behind him. That didn't occur to me. It did to some later. I guess I made four or five shots. I knew the instant I'd made it."

He once told a reporter about his art: "I project myself into a person. I look at everything, the arms, the hands, the expression. I wait for the moment. . . . I shoot."

"That thing that looks like a shiny coffin lid—it's a patrol car, right?"

"Yeah, and it irritates me," he says.

"Why?"

"It's that thing that's just going out of the picture."

"This man's name is John Ed. He's alive. Last one."

"What's he like?"

"He never wanted to show his face."

He laughs at that. "Okay, see how he's holding in the picture here? He's keeping this white shirt on this other guy from going out of the picture." He means Jim Garrison. He is surprised to learn Garrison was only twenty-seven. He moves his hand across the right side of the print, from John Ed to Garrison, then across the other faces. "Same on the left side, in terms of the framing and composition. The shape of this trooper is holding in this side. He's holding in this man's white shirt. Course, this is the aesthetics of it. You're looking for something else."

"They called him John Henry, that one you've got your finger on."

"I love the cigar. They used to mash their cigars, guys like that."

"How far away were you from his back?"

"Maybe eight feet, right behind that trooper. Whenever I go in, I preset. I probably set it at eight to ten feet. I had the lens opening at maybe f-8. I'd say ten feet and f-8."

"Did they sort of seem like they were out of a movie?"

"You mean like Humphrey Bogart or something? Yeah, I guess part of it is the way they're smoking." He touches Billy. "These could be any thugs anywhere. I've known guys like this all my life. Lotta ego this one here, right?"

"Most died pretty miserable deaths. Cancer. They lingered with it. Billy Ferrell did, although others lingered even longer. Did they scare you that day?"

"Not especially." Then slowly: "I think we human beings have to pay a price for the things we do on earth."

"Can you remember what time of day you took it?"

"It just hits me it would be afternoon. Maybe early afternoon, one or two."

H ang on to "early afternoon," early afternoon of Thursday, September 27, 1962—at maybe one or two o'clock. Hang on to this approximate time and date while a documentary, in miniature, unfolds. It's going to proceed chronologically, from September 20 through September 30, the latter being the night of the riot itself. By far the best account of this chaotic period— almost a minute-by-minute re-creation—remains Walter Lord's 1965 book, *The Past That Would Not Die*. In Lord's novelistic and yet very factual story, the *Life* photograph didn't rate a mention, nor should it have, really: As I've said, Billy and Ira and John Henry and Bob and the two Jims and John Ed— along with almost everybody else involved, up to and including the enrollee himself—were peons in the larger frame, the larger expediency.

A ten-day box of famous Mississippi time:

On Thursday the twentieth, in Jackson (Charles Moore hadn't arrived in the state yet), the board of trustees of the university convened for its regular monthly meeting and voted to appoint the governor the emergency registrar of the university. The state legislature had already passed special Senate Bill 1501, making Meredith ineligible for entry because of the (trumped-up) criminal charge concerning his driver's license registration. As the board of trustees met, the governor himself was speeding to Oxford, three hours northward by car. As an extra measure, the newly appointed registrar was armed with an injunction from some local flunky justice of the peace prohibiting Meredith's enrollment. Throughout the day, Bobby Kennedy and Barnett's surrogates had been on the phone. RFK was pressing the governor for assurance that Meredith would be protected from violence and that he wouldn't be arrested at the last minute by a rogue sheriff or two. At 4:53 P.M., Washington time, the principals spoke. This meant it was 2:53 P.M. in Mississippi, although Kennedy and Barnett could never seem to get the time difference straight. (There was a two-hour time difference in those days.) "Hello, Governor, how are you?" Kennedy said. They discussed the situation as it now stood—which was that Meredith was going to make a try to get in, without being arrested or harmed, and that Barnett would formally and peaceably deny him, and that no one on the outside need know it was just a skit before the real thing. "Thank you, Governor," Kennedy said, ringing off. "Nice to talk to you," to which Barnett said, "Thank you, General."

At about 4:30 in Mississippi, Chief U.S. Marshal James McShane and

John Doar (of the civil rights division of the Justice Department, working under Burke Marshall), along with NAACP attorney Constance Baker Motley, accompanied Meredith onto the campus. They walked into the Alumni Center, through a mildly jeering crowd, to the adjoining Yerby Center. In a small auditorium, in the center of the room, two folding tables had been placed together with chairs on either side. Sitting there was the new registrar, a thin-lipped man in glasses with outward angling jaws and a good-looking suit. "Which of you is Mr. Meredith?" Barnett asked. This got laughs. The governor read a proclamation that interposed his authority between the U.S. Supreme Court and the sovereign state of Mississippi. After Meredith's departure (some Ole Miss students threw rocks at the car going off the grounds), the governor sat around with his advisers. He was feeling jovial and successful. One of these advisers said, "Ross, how far are you going to go with this thing?" Barnett said, "How far would you go?" The adviser said, "I'd make them point a gun at me and tell me to move over. Then I'd move over and say come on in." There was big laughter. The governor said, "That's exactly how far I'm going."

The Fifth Circuit ordered the university trustees to appear in federal court on Monday morning, the twenty-fourth, to show cause why they should not be cited for contempt. The chancellor of the school and his trustees were now facing the real prospect of jail time. On Monday, in New Orleans, the board took a vote outside the courtroom and agreed to Meredith's registration the next day. At 9:50 Monday evening Kennedy and Barnett talked. "Governor?" Kennedy said. Barnett: "General, how are you tonight?" Kennedy: "I expect that you probably heard the decision of the court and the agreement of the board of trustees . . ." Barnett: "Did they agree to that?" Kennedy: "Unanimously." Barnett: ". . . That's really shocking to me. I heard it a little while ago." Kennedy: "They agreed to do it by two o'clock tomorrow." Kennedy again pressed for assurances of protection. Barnett sounded almost incoherent: "I tell you now I won't tell you what I am going to do. I don't know yet." The two kept asking each other what time it was. Barnett: "It's nearly eight o'clock here. What time is it there?" Kennedy: "It's about ten o'clock." At the end, Barnett said: "I will let you know what our proceedings will be." Kennedy: "Thank you, Governor." Barnett: "It was nice to talk to you."

The next day, Tuesday the twenty-fifth, they were on the phone with each other throughout the day. In Kennedy's mind, or so one can certainly construe from the tapes and transcripts, the registration was now going to go through successfully, one way or the other, no more playacting. Barnett had had his ego-boosting. Chief Marshal McShane and John Doar picked Meredith up from a guest house at Dillard University in New Orleans. The trio flew to Mississippi in a green, twin-engine Cessna 220 owned by the U.S. Border Patrol—but not until Meredith had gone downstairs in the old airport lounge to use the colored bathroom and snack bar. They arrived in Jackson that afternoon. The government men accompanying the applicant had been informed that the registration was going to take place not at Oxford but at a federal building downtown in the capital city. At midday, Washington time, Kennedy and Barnett spoke. Once more, Kennedy kept asking for assurances from the governor that the crowds would be controlled and that there would be no violence. Kennedy: "Will there be anything done by the state officials or the city officials to interfere physically?" Barnett: "I couldn't promise you that. Not physically." As the conversation went on, Barnett sounded more and more evasive, as if he could pull a double cross. Kennedy: "Governor, you are a part of the United States." Barnett: "We have been a part of the United States but I don't know whether we are or not." Kennedy: "Are you getting out of the Union?" Barnett: "It looks like we're being kicked around—like we don't belong to it. General, this thing is serious." Kennedy: "It's serious here." Barnett: "Must it be over one little boy—backed by Communist front—backed by the NAACP, which is a Communist front?" A few exchanges later, Kennedy said: "Governor, I am only in it because there is an order of the court. . . . Could I give you a ring?" Barnett: "You do that. At F1-3-4938 and Fleetwood 3-1585 or if both lines are busy, just call the Governor's office." Things remained just as unsettled in subsequent conversations. It seemed as if Barnett would relent—and then not relent. "There will be no violence at all," the governor promised.

At 4:10 P.M. in Mississippi (6:10 in Washington), about twenty minutes before the arrival of the hopeful enrollee, Kennedy said to Barnett on the phone: "And I understand that there is a big crowd around the State House. . . . Can you clear the crowds so we don't make a big circus?" Barnett was on the phone in the Woolfolk State Office Building, which was across the street from the Capitol. The building was jammed with legislators, cops, media. Barnett, responding to Kennedy's question, said: "You would have a big space. They're not going to bother him." *Time* magazine—unaware of what was happening backstage—would write in its issue the following week: "The great gold eagle atop the State Capitol in Jackson, Miss., glistened nobly in the afternoon sun. Down below, a green automobile pulled up at a sidewalk packed with a rumbling crowd. Out stepped a dapper Negro." The dapper Negro and his escorts entered the Woolfolk building, past the crowds and TV lights. They rode the elevator to the tenth floor and walked down the hall toward room 1007. Barnett, in his undertaker's fedora and dark suit, appeared at the door and said again, for the cameras, "Which of you gentlemen is Mr. Meredith?" Again, the governor read his proclamation of interposition. Legislators were standing on chairs and tables and one cried, "Get going! Get going!" John Doar said, "Do you refuse to permit us to come in the door?" Barnett: "Yes, sir." Doar: "All right. Thank you." Barnett: "I do that politely." Doar:

"Thank you. We leave politely." Barnett shouted after them, through the hoots of the crowd: "Y'all come see me some time at the mansion." Down on the street, as the green sedan pulled away, a teenager shouted, "Goddamn dirty nigger bastard. Get out of here and stay out."

When Kennedy called Barnett at 7:25 P.M. (RFK's time), he was hot. Barnett described what he'd done not quite an hour earlier. "They were cheering our side and booing Meredith. Nobody tried to fight him," he said. Kennedy: "And he didn't get registered." Barnett: "No, I read the proclamation similar to the one I read the other day. . . ." Kennedy: "He is going to show up at classes tomorrow." Barnett: "At Ole Miss? How can you do that without registering?" Kennedy: ". . . He is going to show up for classes. . . . It is all understood. . . . He is going to go to classes. He is going to be there." Barnett: "Well, I don't know what will happen now. I don't know what we'll do. I didn't dream of a thing like that." A few exchanges later, Barnett said: "If you knew the feeling of about ninety-nine-and-a-half percent of the people in this thing you would have this boy withdraw and go somewhere else. . . ."

Kennedy: ". . . But he likes Ole Miss."

Barnett: "I don't believe you know the background of all this. . . . I think he's being paid by some left-wing organization to do all this. He has two great big Cadillacs, no income, riding around here. Who is giving him all this money? You see, General, the NAACP, I told you this morning, no doubt in my mind, it's a front organization for the Communists and they would do anything about bringing about hatred among the races. We never have trouble with our people, but the NAACP, they want to stir up trouble down here. I wish you could talk to them about the South."

Ten minutes later, Kennedy called Barnett back to advise him of the time that Meredith would arrive on campus in the morning. Kennedy: "Governor, this isn't a question of the boy going to the University of Mississippi. It's the federal government. If you were here as Attorney General you would have to do the same thing. I never knew the name up until a week ago and have no interest." Barnett, a few exchanges later: "We would argue all night about that. You can never convince me that the white and the Negro should go together." Kennedy: "That doesn't have anything to do with you or me." Barnett: "One of the questions here is moral turpitude." Kennedy: "Are you against him because he is a Negro?" Barnett: "Oh, no."

The next morning, Wednesday, September 26, McShane, Doar, and Meredith flew to Oxford for the third attempt in a week. This time, Lieutenant Governor Paul Johnson stood in for Barnett, whose plane was said to have been grounded in Jackson by low-hanging clouds. The governor was speeding to the campus by car with two carloads of Mississippi reporters in his wake. At Calhoun City, he had his driver pull over at a filling station so that he could get a Coke and take a leak. Dub Shoemaker, a reporter for the *Daily News* in Jackson, who was in one of the chase cars, remembered years later that he felt as if he had somehow stepped whole into Robert Penn Warren's book *All the King's Men,* which is a fictionalized portrayal of Huey Long of Louisiana. Barnett was full of greeting and hand-grabbing with all the locals.

The headline that morning in the *New York Times* (three Meredith-related stories made page 1) said: "U.S. Is Prepared to Send Troops as Mississippi Governor Defies Court and Bars Negro Student." At the university, McShane, Doar, and Meredith stepped forward alone to face a line of state troopers and sheriffs. Billy Ferrell was one of them. The lawmen were unarmed—they'd been ordered to form a line unarmed. To Meredith, this didn't mean that guns and clubs and ropes weren't in the vicinity. In *Three Years in Mississippi,* he wrote: "If I know Mississippi white folks there were not many unarmed people there. They had guns on the seats, in their boots, under their belts, in their pockets, and everywhere. We were led to the roadblock about a half mile off the campus where Lieutenant Governor Paul Johnson had set up his retinue, including the properly oriented TV cameramen and radio and news reporters."

Doar approached Johnson, who'd been a Marine on Iwo Jima in World War II and who was a former president of the Ole Miss student body. "We want to go in and get this boy registered," said Doar. The lieutenant governor, a Bible class teacher, shook his head in a no. McShane, a former New York City cop, an ex-prizefighter with a pug's classic face, said: "I think it's my duty to try to go through and get Mr. Meredith in there." Johnson answered, "You are not going in." McShane walked up and down the row. Suddenly, he tried to bust his way through the line with a shoulder block. The chief marshal had been instructed by Justice Department people to try to obtain visual proof of a physical resistance, and now he had it on film. McShane balled up his fist. The lieutenant governor balled up his fist. Toe-to-toe stood Mississippi and the U.S. government. But soon it was over. The trio left the campus and returned to Memphis and the Millington Naval Air Station.

This brought the crisis to Thursday, the twenty-seventh, when events reached their scariest boil and yet didn't boil over: the day Moore took the photograph. As Meredith wrote in *Three Years:* "Undoubtedly the most tension-filled attempt was the one that did not take place." The "greatest Federal-state clash since the Civil War" is how the *New York Times* described the situation in its lead paragraph on the following morning. There was no clash in physical terms—that was still a couple of days away. In his memoir, Meredith referred to the twenty-seventh as "lynching time." The word was uppermost in his consciousness during the ninety-minute drive from the naval air station in Tennessee to Oxford in the dying afternoon. Either he was going to be killed by mobs or he was going to get registered—there didn't seem a lot of room for anything in between. As Meredith and his guards drove out of the gates of the air station, toward Mississippi and "lynching time," he had begun humming W. C. Handy's "St. Louis Blues": "I hate to see that ev'nin sun go down."

In an earlier part of *Three Years,* Meredith defined "lynching time": "What are the essentials of a lynching ceremony? There must be a common victim for the lynching community and he must be guilty in the minds of the lynchers of threatening the virtue or purity of the white woman. It is important to understand that the whole community is always involved in a lynching, even though the actual violence itself may be done or even observed by only a small group from the community. If the community is not totally involved, it would not constitute a lynching."

In an oral history of the Kennedy presidency, published in 1993 and entitled *Let Us Begin Anew,* Meredith is quoted as saying: "In order to prevail, I had to get the federal government on my side. . . . I was well aware of the contact between Ross Barnett and the Kennedys. Between them I was always sure the U.S. government was going to win."

Early in the afternoon, Robert Kennedy and Ross Barnett were trying to fashion their most harebrained and self-serving scheme to date: make it seem as if the federal side was barging its way in with drawn guns. A skit right from the Old West. There would be the pulling of at least one (unloaded) gun by the chief marshal, accompanied by the slapping of holsters on the part of the other marshals—or at least this was Kennedy's sense of how the scene should be played. Taylor Branch, in his book *Parting the Waters,* in a lengthy and authoritative chapter called "The Fall of Ole Miss," wrote of this surreal conversation: "Drifting inexorably into public relations, they fashioned an agreement to stage a fake showdown at the gates of the campus. Two dozen armed U.S. marshals would support Meredith, and Barnett, yielding reluctantly to superior force, would retire to the new task of getting Meredith out of Ole Miss. Ironically, this solution faltered when Kennedy's desire to appear accommodating did not quite satisfy Barnett's desire to look as though he was being pushed around." Yes, that's basically what happened. But there would be another way to view the secret conversation of that day: as deeply revelatory of the character of a pair of moral opportunists who'd do almost anything for a favorable out. In this respect, Barnett and Kennedy were brothers under the skin. If Barnett was pathetic and weak and willing to take a whole state down with him, Kennedy, a smarter and braver and more guilt-ridden man, was all about ad hoc opportunity. To study September 27 through the prism of a single photograph, and through the seven lives in that photograph, and in what has traveled downward from those lives, is to see things convincingly in the context of a self-serving, whipped-up hatred—which the seven in the picture were only too glad to have whipped up. But the fact remains that they never knew—not even later, some of them—the extent to which they were dupes of expedient men. They were simple enough in their loyalties and loves to believe their governor when he cried, "Never!"

In the South, as has been observed, people who aren't victims of injustice often are victims of irony. It was the kind of coincidence the South seems to crave: the hour when RFK and Barnett were giving themselves away on tape to future generations of historians may have been the very same hour when seven ignorant cops ("ignorant" being invoked deliberately here) were getting their picture snapped. These Southern cops, seething, peacocking, making their dirty jokes, along with all the other seething and peacocking and grinning bigots in that overflowing garden, assumed things were as they were, that Dixie was going down, unless they took their stand to live and die.

It's 2:50 P.M. in Washington, 12:50 in the Grove. A thirty-one-year-old slight-framed Alabamian, who also has no idea of what is going on behind the stage, may right this moment be picking his way through the Grove. Here he is, picture him, Charlie Moore, coming on Billy and the boys, sizing up a sudden great shot.

Barnett: Hello, General, how are you?

RFK: Fine, Governor, how are you?

Barnett: I need a little sleep.

RFK [further on]: I will send the marshals that I have available up there in Memphis . . . and they will come with Mr. Meredith and . . . I will have the head marshal pull a gun and I will have the rest of them have their hands on their guns and their holsters. And then as I understand it he will go through and get in and you will make sure that law and order is preserved and that no harm will be done. . . .

Barnett [further on]: General, I was under the impression that they were all going to pull their guns. This could be very embarrassing. We got a big crowd here and if one pulls his gun and we all turn it would be very embarrassing. Isn't it possible to have them all pull their guns?

RFK: I hate to have them all draw their guns. . . . Isn't it sufficient if I have one man draw his gun and the others keep their hands on their holsters?

Barnett: They must all draw their guns. Then they should point their guns at us and then we could step aside. This could be very embarrassing down here for us. It is necessary.

RFK: If they all pull their guns, is that all?

A few exchanges later, the lieutenant governor comes on the line.

Johnson: It is absolutely necessary that they all draw their guns.

RFK: Can you speak a little louder?

Johnson: We are telling them to lay their clubs aside and to leave their guns in their automobiles. But it is necessary to have all your people draw their guns, not just one.

An hour later. It's 1:50 P.M. in the Grove, 3:50 in Washington. Barnett and Johnson are in their campus headquarters; the lieutenant governor has circled the campus in a state police car, barking into a loudspeaker, "The nigger isn't here yet. . . . I plead with you. . . . Someone could easily be killed. . . ." Has the photograph that will end up in *Life* now been made—or is Moore *right now* positioning himself behind the shadowy trooper and elevating the small box to his eye?

Barnett: General, I felt like I ought to call you back. . . . Why can't you wait until Saturday morning. . . . The people probably will find it out.

RFK: There's not going to be any mention of it from here.

Barnett: Certainly not here. Our conversations weren't taken down here.

RFK: You never had anything that's come out of this office and I never said I talked to you. . . .

Barnett: One man said, "You will all compromise in this thing?"

RFK: You are not compromising—you are standing right up there.

A few exchanges later, the lieutenant governor is back on.

Johnson: General Kennedy, we are trying to be completely honest about this thing. We got a few intense citizens here, got a lot of men who are not directly under us who are involved to hold the fort such as sheriffs and deputies. We cannot assure anybody that those people or someone maybe hotheaded won't start shooting. . . . We've got to have time in order to discreetly move these sheriffs out of here. . . .

RFK: You've got a couple of hours to tell the sheriffs and others to go home and suddenly I will call at four o'clock your time and tell them he is coming in.

Johnson: I can't move these people out of there, General. Some won't leave.

Barnett [skipping down a few exchanges]: If half a dozen people got killed it would hurt me, you, the lieutenant governor, all of us.

There is more talk between the two, with increasing panic on Barnett's end. It's 6:35 P.M. in Washington, 4:35 in Mississippi. Barnett has been touring the campus and the town. This thing could get out of hand. The caravan bringing Meredith from the naval air station in Tennessee is on the way to Oxford. Meredith, McShane, and Doar are speeding southward on the newly completed interstate at somewhere between 90 and 110 miles per hour. FBI Teletypes are clacking into Washington regarding KKK Klaverns mobilizing their members from all over the South. Shadows in the Grove have lengthened. Surely, seven lawmen beneath a tree have dispersed, and the man who has frozen them inside his camera has also gone somewhere else.

Barnett: General, I'm worried—I'm nervous, I tell you. You don't realize what's going on. There are several thousand people in here in cars, trucks. . . .

RFK: I had better send them back.

Barnett: There is liable to be a hundred people killed here. It would ruin all of us. . . . A lot of people are going to get killed. It would be embarrassing to me.

RFK: I don't know if it would be embarrassing—that would not be the feeling. [When you listen to this exchange on the tapes, it's as if Bobby is suddenly coming awake from a very bad dream.]

Barnett: It would be bad all over the nation.

RFK: I'll send them back.

Barnett: General, do that, please. I just have to take the consequences tomorrow.

RFK: I'll send them back.

An order was flashed from the Justice Department through military channels to a communications plane accompanying the thirteen-car caravan, and from there it was beamed down to John Doar, who was in the lead car with Meredith and McShane. In the *Clarion-Ledger* the next day, beneath a headline that said "600 U.S. Marshals Group at Memphis," the story began: "James Meredith was batting '0 for 4' late Thursday in his attempt to be the first Negro to register at the University of Mississippi. In fact, the 29-year-old student did not make it to the campus because of a last-minute change of plans by the Justice Department. . . . More than a hundred steel helmeted highway patrolmen with gas masks and long night sticks were stationed at every campus approach. They were reinforced by more than seventy sheriffs representing all sections of the state. . . . At 6 P.M., sources close to the governor said that he had been informed of the change in plans." The story described Barnett as appearing pale and tired. There was a photograph of him waving to the crowds from the back seat of his sedan.

And at the same time, real life had gone eerily on in Oxford. There was a want ad in the local paper that offered "Quail, dressed, $18 a dozen. Phone 234-3434 or office of Lyric Theatre. Ask for Bob Williams." A newsman for the *Chicago Daily News,* Raymond Coffey, filed a dispatch late Thursday evening, describing events away from the campus: "[That morning], in the heart of town, a couple of elderly Negroes set up a watermelon stand on the courthouse lawn, just as they had every day for many weeks. At Jackson and Lamar, a block off the courthouse square, dozens of Negro women gathered, laughing and exchanging small talk to wait for the white women to arrive to drive them to their homes for domestic work. Near the center of town, several Negro laborers worked on the construction of the new Lafayette County Jail. More than 140 newsmen from outside the South milled around the campus restlessly. . . . In the residential areas, garbage cans were set along the curbs awaiting the usual pickup." The piece appeared on the front page of the *Daily News* on Friday. A world away, in Moscow, the communist youth paper *Komsomolskaya Pravda* described in its Friday edition the events thus far in Mississippi, and then concluded: "All this is being done merely to prevent 29-year-old James Meredith from becoming the first Negro student at the University of Mississippi, so as not to stain the purity of the educational establishments of the state."

Taylor Branch, in his closely argued, intricately reported *Parting the Waters,* wrote that Kennedy was drawn steadily against his will and judgment into that weekend's conflagrating events. It's clear from the tapes as well as from the vantage point of years that the Kennedy brothers weren't much interested in civil rights in general (at this point anyway) nor in Meredith's admission in particular—and yet this was a constitutional crisis they had to meet. The overriding fear in the attorney general's mind was that the use of armed federal force would make America look bad in the eyes of the world. "His only alternative," Branch wrote, "was to collaborate privately with Barnett to produce an inspired theatrical effect, worthy of Shakespeare. None but a genius could hope to orchestrate the desired illusion of normalcy and control, especially since Kennedy and Barnett simultaneously sounded public war trumpets that attracted hordes to overrun their stage." But perhaps September 27 is worthier of Kafka's imagination. A whole state was being set up. Not that this could ever excuse anybody for his conduct, and not that seven particular bigots had any kind of starring role in the violent end three nights later. Indeed, most of these seven weren't around. They'd scattered, as they'd been ordered to do by their governor and lieutenant governor. They ended up missing the show. It's another thing the South is pretty good at: anticlimax.

What was Billy Ferrell—and the six fellow Mississippi peace officers at his side—swinging at, on September 27, 1962, before the tear burst? At Meredith's unseen head? Yes. At Bobby Kennedy's functionaries, who thought they could come in and gracelessly intrude their will on Mississippi? Without doubt. But there must have been so many other dreams and dreads possessing each. A hundred-year-old way of life was cracking beneath them, and they knew it, and all they could do was swing.

The full story of the rest of that weekend can be found in almost any comprehensive history of civil rights in the South. Even now, the precise number of troops mobilized and the number of injuries sustained and prisoners taken are still the subject of argument. William Doyle's detailed study of the riot, *An American Insurrection,* published in 2001, reports: "A grand total of nearly 31,000 federal troops were mobilized in the invasion of northern Mississippi in the first week of October 1962, including 11,000 Mississippi National Guardsmen called into federal service and 20,000 regular army troops. Of the Guardsmen, 2,700 were deployed directly into the Oxford area, including the entire 108th Cavalry Regiment and two battle groups of the 155th Infantry Dixie Division. The remainder of the Mississippi National Guardsmen were held at their hometown armories, including Lieutenant Ross Barnett, Jr., in Jackson."

Just to sketch the riot itself, the inevitable end point of what had been building for weeks: Two died that Sunday night—a French reporter for Agence France-Presse named Paul Guihard (he got a bullet in his back near the Peabody Building) and an Oxford bystander and jukebox repairman named Walter Ray Gunter (he was shot in the head on the opposite side of campus). At least 160 marshals and about 50 Army soldiers were injured on the night of September 30. About thirty of the wounded marshals were hit by sniper gunfire. Before it was over, the mob had swelled to about 3,000. The battle, according to estimates in the *New York Times,* resulted in about 370 military and civilian casualties. There were said to be over 300 arrests at the riot and in the several days after. A relatively small number of these were Ole Miss students. Most of the rioters, at least as the night of destruction wore on, had no real relationship to the university.

One of the aiders and abettors was former Major General Edwin A.

Walker of Texas, a West Point graduate, who had commanded the 101st Airborne when President Eisenhower dispatched federal troops to Central High in Little Rock. But after that civil rights crisis, something in Walker took a dark turn. In 1961, he'd resigned from the Army in protest, after being disciplined for insubordination. He devoted his time to the John Birch Society to help combat the communist vermin overrunning the country. In the days before Oxford, he was on the radio from his home in Texas, orating that he had been on the wrong side in the Little Rock crisis. On Wednesday the twenty-sixth, during a call-in radio show on a station in Shreveport, Louisiana, the ex-general called out the citizen-rednecks to the barricades of Ole Miss: "It's time to rise. . . . Now is the time to be heard. Ten thousand strong from every state in the nation. . . . Bring your flag, your tent, and your skillet."

The night before it all erupted, on Saturday the twenty-ninth, the great double-dealer and chief executive of Mississippi had sent 46,000 people into a state of frenzy at the Ole Miss–Kentucky football game at Memorial Stadium in Jackson. At halftime Ross Barnett went down onto the field and stood at the fifty-yard line as the world's largest Confederate flag was unfurled. Billy Ferrell and his wife, Hazel, were in that stadium, and perhaps two other sheriffs from Moore's photograph. Someone who wasn't a sheriff later wrote that it was probably a little like being at a Nazi rally in Nuremburg—those rebel flags in every hand might well have been swastikas. The governor pumped his right arm, with his fist clenched. He cried into the microphone and floodlights: "I love Mississippi! I love her people! I love her customs!" After the game, he called the Justice Department and was patched through to Bobby Kennedy at home. Barnett said that any deals were off. Earlier that afternoon, the governor had been on the phone with the president himself, promising that the registration would take place. Until Saturday, John F. Kennedy had not been asked by his brother to speak personally to Barnett to try to cool events. If a person interested in history and these specific events went now to the right government or university archive, and pulled up Dictabelt 4-A of Presidential Recordings, September 29, 1962, and listened to the stabbing, nasally Massachusetts voice attempting to converse with the mesmeric and oozy Mississippi voice, he or she would surely think: This is all too hilarious, except that it's also all too shameful.

> *JFK:* Well, I'm glad to talk to you, Governor. I am concerned about, uh, this situation, uh, down there, as I know, uh . . .
> *Barnett:* Oh, I should say I am concerned about it, Mr. President. It's, it's, it's a horrible situation . . .
> *JFK:* Right. Well, of course . . .
> *Barnett:* And . . .

JFK: . . . the problem is, Governor, that, uh, I got my responsibility, just like you have yours . . .
Barnett: Well, that's true. I . . .

At the end, Barnett said, "I appreciate your interest in our poultry program and all those things." You can hear Kennedy trying to choke down a cackle. You can picture him putting the phone down and saying to the room, more or less: *You're not going to believe what that cracker just said.*

On Sunday, Bobby Kennedy and Barnett kept trying to find a way out. The attorney general lost his temper. He said the president was going to expose the secret talks.

RFK: The president is going on TV tonight. He is going through the statement he had with you last night. He will have to say he called up the National Guard; that you had an agreement to permit Meredith to go to Jackson to register . . .
Barnett: That won't do at all!
RFK: You broke your word to him.
Barnett: You don't mean the president is going to say that tonight?
Kennedy: Of course he is; you broke your word; now you suggest we send in troops, fighting their way through a barricade.
Barnett: Don't say that. Please don't mention it.

Late Sunday afternoon, Meredith was installed in a dormitory room at Baxter Hall on the back end of campus. The plane carrying him had landed at the Oxford-University Airport close to 6 P.M., and Meredith and his bodyguard of marshals were able to slip into the campus through a rear gate. A force of more than 500 federal marshals had now been assembled, for whatever lay ahead. (Actually, there were very few marshals per se. The force consisted of deputy marshals, border patrolmen, guards from the federal prison system.) Even into middle afternoon, much of the campus was deserted—many students were still returning from the football game in Jackson. Some had driven to the capital on their own, others had ridden a "Barnett Special" train. The relatively empty campus is one reason why the federal forces were able to slip Meredith in undetected. The applicant came to his destiny in a suit and with a slender tan briefcase.

Earlier, about 3:30 P.M., the first transport planes carrying marshals had begun arriving at the university airport. An Air Force Jetstar brought Deputy Attorney General Nicholas Katzenbach. He and other officials and marshals climbed into seven Army trucks for the two-mile ride to campus. A crowd gathered on the central lawn, known as the Circle, which is just west of the

Grove, adjacent to it. They positioned themselves in front of the Lyceum, a stately old white-columned building predating the Civil War, the only survivor of the five original buildings constructed for the opening of the university in 1848. The afternoon lengthened. Some bricks and bottles were hurled at a line of about thirty marshals who were acting as a decoy in front of the Lyceum. They had on white helmets and yellow-orange riot vests, and in the vests were stubby tear-gas canisters. The Lyceum, which is the main administration building, had served as a hospital during the Civil War. When still more marshals arrived in Ford Falcons, students raced out from bushes and smashed the car windshields with bricks and crowbars. After dark, the campus became illumined with military floodlights—and eventually tear gas enshrouded and choked everything. By then, the student rioters were in the minority. Outriders and inriders had taken over what writer Willie Morris later termed "the echo of the Civil War's last battle." If the bigots had had their way that evening, they would have torched the campus, starting with the Lyceum. As historian C. Vann Woodward wrote in *The Strange Career of Jim Crow:* "This was not an attack on Negroes or demonstrators. It was an insurrectionary assault on officers and soldiers of the United States Government and the most serious challenge to the Union since the Civil War. The mob fought with stones, bricks, clubs, bottles, iron bars, gasoline bombs, and firebombs."

At 7:30 P.M., Barnett went on the air in Jackson to announce that Meredith was inside the university, and that he, Barnett, was yielding peacefully to the "armed forces and oppressive power" of the United States. It was the same old rhetorical attempt to offer surrender while simultaneously fanning flames and feigning resistance. (At midnight, he'd issue a "We will never surrender" statement.) Just before Kennedy spoke to the nation on television—the talk was set for 8 P.M. in Mississippi, 10 P.M. in Washington—the mob surged toward the marshals. The orders of the court "are beginning to be carried out," the president said into the cameras even as the first orders to fire tear gas were being given, or perhaps had just been given, two or three minutes before. (There are many arguments about time, and, like so much else, they remain unresolved.) Kennedy appealed to reason and patriotism, saying to Mississippians, "the honor of your university and the state are in the balance." He spoke directly to the university community, referring to Ole Miss traditions "on the gridiron, as well as the university campus." He said that neither Mississippi "nor any other Southern state deserves to be charged with the accumulated wrongs of the last 100 years of race relations. To the extent that there has been failure, the responsibility for that failure must be shared by all of us, by every state, by every citizen."

An Ole Miss author and literature professor named Evans Harrington was listening to the speech at his home near the campus when a Memphis newscaster broke in with a report that matches had been dumped onto a fuel truck, and that the truck had ignited. Harrington, who lived a mile and a half away, got into his car and drove toward the campus. He was terrified but felt he had to try to do something to stop the madness, and another reason why he was bolting from his home was because he couldn't get out of his brain the idea that "Moby Dick had just come to me." He approached the campus from a side drive and was waylaid by a newsman desperate to get back to the Ole Miss Motel in downtown Oxford to use the telephone. Harrington drove the reporter to his room and then came back in toward University Bridge. He abandoned his car somewhere on University Avenue and heard highway patrolmen telling kids to go ahead and smash windows with chunks of construction brick. He saw students whom he knew with rocks, bricks, bottles. He saw a long line of state trooper cars. Troopers were leaning out the windows to yell, "Kill the bastard." He moved on toward the central campus. Along with several other professors—James Silver was one—he tried to speak sense to anyone he recognized as a student. The Right Reverend Duncan Gray, Jr., pastor of the local Episcopal church, was attempting the same. That July, Gray had presided at Faulkner's funeral, intoning the final prayers at graveside in the town cemetery. He read from Walt Whitman: "I too am not a bit tamed, I too am untranslatable / I sound my barbaric yawp over the roofs of the world." Gray had been on the campus since about 6 P.M. Now he stood up on the Confederate monument, on the eastern edge of the Circle, about a hundred yards east of the Lyceum. He tried to calm the barbaric yawp. An arm yanked him down. Evans Harrington, twenty feet back in the crowd, thought: I've got to do something. He thought again, They'll break my jaw. He thought again, If I don't do it, I'll never forgive myself. He thought again, You're already doing something. Just by thinking this way. I've got to keep doing it. I've got to figure a way to do something and not get killed and at the same time not renege on my honor. Someone began to punch the clergyman. Professor Harrington was one of those who stepped in. Remembering, four decades later: "A big old wide football type is trying to shield him. He's cradling Duncan Gray. He's yelling, 'He's a preacher. Don't hurt this man! He's a preacher.' And the aggressor says, 'Didn't you hear what he said last night on TV? He said that that nigger sonofabitch should get registered.' And the big old wide football type cries, 'I know, I know, I hate that nigger too, we oughta string him up, but this is a preacher, don't let's hurt this preacher.' " Gray escaped serious injury, as did Harrington. Within days of the riot, the assistant professor of English, a native Mississippian, along with other faculty members, would sign a document pointing to his university's lies and cover-ups and after-deceptions. (". . . we have evidence that the attempt of men in prominent positions to place all the blame for the riot on the United States marshals is not only unfair and reprehensible, but is almost completely false.") That night deeply and instantly politicized Harrington. He continued teaching at Ole Miss for decades, loving it whole, seeing it whole. That could be said of Duncan Gray as well. The son of an Episcopal bishop, he was later himself named bishop of the Mississippi Episcopal Diocese, and after that he served as president of Sewanee University in Tennessee. But he kept on loving and defending what was good about Mississippi, even as he kept on being appalled by its history.

A little while before Kennedy spoke to the country on national TV, State Senator George M. Yarbrough—Barnett's representative at the scene—had ordered the highway patrol and other uniformed officers to withdraw. The marshals were under furious attack, trying to rely mainly on tear gas. An enraged Bobby Kennedy demanded the troopers' return. Some did return, too late, with no wish to maintain order. Some got caught in the waves of tear gas. They withdrew again, and those who didn't stood by and egged on the rioters. Many sat in their patrol cars and watched the destruction. The governor was in his mansion 175 miles away.

Within an hour of the president's address, the sniper fire had begun. A bullet caught a marshal in the neck. The Lyceum corridors became lined with wounded or exhausted marshals. Charles Moore, who was inside the Lyceum, got pictures of the marshals slumped against the walls in their gas masks, and these images would be published in the next issue of *Life*. Moore was all over the campus that afternoon and night, risking his life. At some point, a false report got out that the mob had located Meredith's whereabouts and was storming the dormitory to string him up. At another point, a bulldozer with the vertical scoop sticking up as a shield began plowing toward the line of marshals. A tear-gas canister knocked the driver from the machine, but the machine, with a life of its own, kept moving, hit a tree, spun around. A marshal jumped atop it and steered it away.

Some units of the federalized Mississippi National Guard arrived—it was close to 11 P.M. They were led by Captain Murry Faulkner, a relative of William Faulkner. After a series of logistical blunders and confused commands, the first Army units arrived from Memphis. "It was like a western movie, where the cavalry arrives in the nick of time," Walter Lord wrote in *The Past That Would Not Die*. It was past 2 A.M. By dawn, Monday, things were calm—and then more destruction broke out in the streets of Oxford, including brick throwing by the sheriff of Pascagoula.

Throughout, James Meredith slept well—so he wrote in *Three Years in Mississippi*. He dismissed the riot in a couple of sentences, as if it was removed from him entirely, as if he was talking from behind a screen, on the other side of a wall, which in a way he was. "The first thing I did [on getting into Baxter Hall late that afternoon] was make my bed. When the trouble started, I could not see or hear very much of it. Most of the events occurred at the other end of the campus, and I did not look out the window. I think I read a newspaper and went to bed around ten o'clock. I was awakened several times in the night by the noise and shooting outside, but it was not near the hall, and I had no way of knowing what was going on. Some of the students in my dormitory banged their doors for a while and threw some bottles in the halls, but I slept pretty well all night." Shortly before eight o'clock on Monday morning, October 1, 1962, Meredith and his protectors walked through the rubble and past the burnt-out vehicles to the Lyceum, where the enrollee held a handkerchief to his nose and became officially an Ole Miss student. As he wrote later, "I wore a dark suit with a blood red tie. . . . I was like a soldier on that day and my clothes were my flag." His bodyguards escorted him to his first class, in Colonial American history. He was a few minutes late and was asked to take a seat at the back. In the days following, Washington and Mississippi worked overtime, each to blame the other. Congressman John Bell Williams, a silver-tongued Mississippi racist, said: "The bestiality, cruelty, and savagery of Justice Department employees under the direction of Robert Kennedy . . . were acts beyond the comprehension of normal minds."

A nd the seven of Moore's photograph? The caption writers in *Life* had it right, or mostly right: "[W]hen the riot broke out, all local and state cops made themselves scarce." Their absence at the center of destruction was not by their design. It was by irony's design.

John Ed Cothran and his deputy Big Smitty had left for home on Thursday evening, a couple of hours after Moore took the shot. John Ed had departed the campus on the orders of the lieutenant governor, who, John Ed says, told him personally to get out of town. (When I asked if Big Smitty had wanted to stay, there was that curving ooze of smile from Cothran.) John Henry Spencer and Jimmy Middleton and Bob Waller had also left on Thursday. They waited at their homes for word from Billy Ferrell. By the time word came, it was too late for them to have any kind of central role. Jim Garrison, who lived in Oxford, was on the campus during the riot—but to what extent he participated in violence, or tried to help stop it, I cannot say. I've never found his name in FBI documents relating to that night. As I've already recounted, his kid sister, Patricia, remembered that his face looked terribly blistered the day after the riot. "He was *in* it," she said. When I pushed for more, she said, "I don't know any more. Jimmy'd never talk about that." By definition, riots are chaotic things, the more so when they occur at night. Unless someone has been caught red-handed in a crime, it is very hard to know the nature of his or her involvement.

James Ira Grimsley's name can be found in many documents—but again I cannot say with any reliability whether he committed serious crimes. I doubt he did, only because he and his wrecking crew got there so late. The FBI and Justice Department documents that pertain to Grimsley's actions are sketchy in detail, and are not to be trusted anyway, since most of them consist of statements by Grimsley henchmen. Ira Harkey's newspaper, the *Chronicle,* ran a front-page story on the day following Meredith's registration: "Sheriff Tells of Riots" was the main headline. "Tried Calming Mob, Grimsley Relates" was the secondary headline. The story opened with a perfectly straight face: "Sheriff James Ira Grimsley said he withdrew Jackson County deputies from Oxford Monday when it became apparent their efforts were futile. . . . Grimsley said he left here with thirty-five deputized men on a chartered bus. . . . He said they picked up twenty men in George and Perry Counties and deputized them. 'We turned down about thirty others because we felt they were hotheads who would endanger our mission,' Grimsley said. Grimsley said they spent four hours in Oxford in a vain attempt to quell a mob which attacked Army vehicles bringing in troops." The day before, October 1, the headline in the *Chronicle* was "Meredith Enrolls—2 Die." Six paragraphs in, there was this: "Grimsley said the men who went to Oxford were hand-picked from about 650 persons who volunteered their services Sunday. Grimsley said earlier he was waiting to be called either by Lt. Gov. Paul Johnson or Billy Farrell [*sic*], president of Mississippi Sheriffs' Association."

It's clear from documents and other sources that Grimsley did get word from Ferrell, and that he did charter a bus, and that he apparently paid for the bus out of his own pocket, and that he and his deputized band left the courthouse square sometime around 8:30 P.M. Several of Grimsley's regular deputies in the Jackson County Sheriff's Department were aboard bus number 1241, which belonged to the Gulf Transport Company in Mobile, Alabama. The driver (his name is blacked out in the documents) claimed not to have seen anyone come aboard bearing weapons. That is contradicted by many other accounts. Everybody on board had some kind of weapon. One deputized man (the name is blacked out) told the FBI he had a .20-gauge Browning automatic shotgun "without plug," but that he intended to use it only in self-defense. The sheriff was said to have left Pascagoula wearing two revolvers—a holster on each hip. A retired reporter for the *Chronicle,* Don Broadus, remembered that he went down to the courthouse square that Sunday evening to watch the bus depart Pascagoula. He was asked if Grimsley was drunk and armed, and he said he couldn't be sure about the former but no question about the latter. On the way north, the caravan picked up more cars and defenders of Mississippi. The bus stopped near Escatawpa, Mississippi, and loaded up on extra rounds of ammunition. According to Grimsley's account in the *Chronicle* on October 2: "We arrived at 2:30 A.M. and set up headquarters at a service station. No one was allowed to wander away from our group. When we got off the bus we saw about 150 young men gathered on a street corner. We went over to the group in an attempt to disperse them. We told them to go home because there was nothing to be gained by violence." Some of the FBI documents indicate that the bus arrived at the outskirts of the university as late as 4 A.M. A retired highway patrolman named Frank Ely remembered in an interview four decades later that he and several other troopers stopped Grimsley's bus at a roadblock. Grimsley was drunk and roaring in the aisles, this ex-trooper said. Ely remembered that he and other troopers ordered the driver to turn the bus around. Ely said he was certain the sheriff and his vigilantes never got inside the campus gates. However, all the available evidence indicates that the bus didn't head back south. It went into downtown Oxford. There, sometime after dawn, the head lawman of Pascagoula was photographed heaving a brick or a piece of concrete through a store window, or so a loyal former Jackson County sheriff's deputy remembers, along with other Pascagoulians. (I have never been able to locate that photograph.)

To quote again from Ira Harkey's book *The Smell of Burning Crosses*: "Our sheriff, James Ira Grimsley, was a hard-drinking red-faced fat man with the colorful glibness found so often in near-illiterate Southern politicians. He had been to Oxford, he had told the press, sorteing from Pascagoula with thirty-five deputized local citizens, picking up twenty or so more on the bus ride north. . . . 'I am proud of the men who went with me,' he had told the *Chronicle*. 'They were hand-picked for their sound judgment. They did exactly what I told them without question. They all said they are willing to go back if I ask them.' " From another part of *Crosses*: "They bragged that at Oxford they'd done more damage than any other outfit that went, burning cars, breaking windows, slugging people." From another passage: "They boasted in Pascagoula saloons that none had outdone them in brick throwing and vehicle burning."

So what is the "truth"? Probably, it's something like this: An alcoholic with a pair of six-shooters on his belt rode through the night to the north of his state, only to be denied his chances. Humiliated, lathered, the high sheriff returned to the Gulf Coast with his posse of ship welders and others to sponsor "a citizen's emergency unit," which by any other name was a Klan Klavern without robes. (In Michael Newton and Judy Ann Newton's 1991 book, *The Ku Klux Klan: An Encyclopedia*, the JCCEU is identified as having been a "Klan affiliate" of the early sixties in Mississippi.) The members of this "unit" talked of returning to Oxford to kidnap and kill James Meredith, and perhaps they'd also burn down the offices of the local newspaper and string up the editor. None of it came to pass and maybe most of it was just the talk of cowards. The FBI came around to investigate, and then word got out that federal contracts at the shipyard might be canceled. The bloated ruffian with the star on his breast became the first casualty of a corrupt town's miraculous conversion to righteous-thinking ways.

I remember the day Billy Ferrell and I talked of the riot, the two of us sitting side by side on a bench on his fishing dock, Billy sneaking his smokes and keeping an eye out for his wife, Hazel, who was up at the house fixing delicious vittles. The peace officer was in restive retirement at his lake house on the Louisiana side of the river. He had that little red psoriasis sore on the inside of his ankle—he kept reaching down to scratch at it. He plowed his puffy hand through his swept dirty-white hair. He was trying to aggrandize his role; he also kept trying to minimize it. It was clear that he was being selective in what he chose to say. I was aware of gaps in logic and time. I didn't know it then, but two months earlier he had participated in an oral history interview with a historian from the University of Southern Mississippi. The historian, who came to Natchez for the interviews, asked about "memorable" events during his tenure. Billy responded that "one of the things that sticks out the uppermost in my mind was when I was sheriff was in 1962 . . . what we commonly referred to as the 'Battle of the University of Mississippi,' during the integration up there of—what was that guy's name?"

"James Meredith," the oral historian prompted. Billy then told the story, his version of it, as he did with me two months later.

Some of what Billy related that day on the dock, thirty-five years (almost to the day and hour) from Meredith's enrollment, did factually check out, as I later discovered. Other parts of it were flatly inaccurate, or inadvertently mixed up in time sequence. Almost all of it—or so I would judge now—was a manifestation of a dying old man's need to sanitize and justify long-ago events that had always deeply embarrassed him and that had circled around to annoy and embarrass him anew before death. On the other hand, Billy didn't have to talk to me about it at all, didn't have to invite me into his house, or down onto his dock. Even in the sanitizing and distorting, I saw a certain kind of redemption, muddy with mixed motives, but redemption all the same.

He explained that the "whole reason" he and the other sheriffs "had gone up there in the first place" was because Sheriff Joe Ford, the sheriff of Lafayette County, had "called me and asked for help from the Sheriffs' Association. Hell, Joe Ford didn't have but one or two deputies anyway [one of whom would have been Jim Garrison]. When you think about it, Oxford is just a little old country town, nothing there. What do they do there? They bale hay and grow beans, maybe, and they got that big university. So that's why we went up there, that's how the whole thing happened, that's how our picture got took. We went up there not to help Ross Barnett prevent the integration of the University of Mississippi but sorta to help Joe Ford stop any lawlessness that might take place. We went up there to maintain law and order, is what I'm telling you."

Billy remembered that he left the campus and returned to Natchez on Saturday the twenty-ninth, the day before the riot—but all the evidence suggests that he departed on Thursday or Friday, as the others had, closer to the time that Moore took the photograph. He came home (it isn't clear if he left Oxford alone or in the company of other sheriffs), and on Saturday afternoon he drove with his wife to Jackson for the big football game. "Hazel and I was at the Ole Miss–Kentucky football game on Saturday night, as was several of the sheriffs around the state," is the way he described it. After Barnett's halftime speech, an announcer on the public address system called out "the code letters of the Lafayette County sheriff's office radio. This was our signal to get in our cars and come back to Oxford. I forget the code now. Each sheriff in the state had his own radio code. Mine was KKE 323. We heard Joe Ford's code on the public address. That meant head back to Oxford. I heard it and I turned to Hazel and I said, 'C'mon, we're going.' She said, 'But the ball game's not over.' I said, 'Well, it's over for us.' "

He took his wife home—it would have been about a two-and-a-half-hour drive from the football stadium—but apparently he didn't start out for Oxford again until late the next day, Sunday. His plan was to drive up U.S. 61 to Port Gibson and pick up Jimmy Middleton and then go on to Vicksburg and collect the sheriff of Warren County. His intention was to lead a "column" of Mississippi sheriffs northward to the fight. But as he was leaving Natchez, or perhaps when he got to Port Gibson, word came from the highway patrol to detour over to Jackson to pick up several prominent state officials, who were gathered in a room at the King Edward Hotel. One of these seems to have been Lieutenant Governor Johnson. Billy remembered that he offered the loan of his Adams County sheriff's car to Johnson, who needed a vehicle to get him to Ole Miss. Billy remembered that another official in the hotel was State Senator George Yarbrough, but this doesn't seem correct, because by late Sunday afternoon, Yarbrough was en route to Oxford as Barnett's official stand-in. (Most accounts have Yarbrough, president pro tem of the state senate, arriving on the campus about 6:30 P.M.) Billy recalled that the other legislator in the hotel room was State Senator Russell Fox of Port Gibson and Claiborne County, and this seems accurate. However, as Billy was relating the story, he kept getting the day mixed up, believing that the riot occurred in the middle of the night Saturday, instead of the middle of the night Sunday.

Billy: "So I stopped at the hotel with Jim Middleton while the others went on to Oxford, and we went in this room at the King Edward Hotel. . . . 'What in hell is going on?' these two important guys, Yarbrough and Fox, said to me. 'I thought you'd tell me,' I told 'em. 'Billy, you're the president of the Mississippi Sheriffs' Association—don't you know?' they said. Well, we called Washington, D.C. We got on the line up there with Senator James Eastland of Mississippi. Big Jim Eastland. One of the most important and respected people in the United States Senate. I didn't know him from Adam, other than that Jim Eastland was our senior senator. His wife answered. They were in bed. It's in the middle of the night in Washington. The riot was going on—we were getting radio reports from Oxford. I get on the phone line with Senator Eastland in Washington—Senator Russell Fox, the state legislator, just stuck the phone at me—and I say, 'Sir, this is Sheriff Billy Ferrell, the head of the Mississippi Sheriffs' Association, and, sir, all I gotta say is we have a tremendous problem up there at Oxford. And if you have any influence with that tousle-headed sonofabitch sitting over there in the White House chair, I wish you'd try to use it, because our whole state is about to go up in flames.' I remember those were my exact words. Eastland said, 'Who's got control of the campus?' I said, 'The rioters have got control of the campus.' Eastland said, 'Well, are the federal marshals there?' I said, 'You bet, they're the sons of bitches that started it all, Mr. Eastland.' "

Billy interrupted this recollection to say, "What Kennedy did was in direct violation of what he said at the Democratic National Convention in San Francisco. [He meant Los Angeles.] He promised he'd never send in troops the way Eisenhower did in Little Rock in 1957. Direct violation, and I want you to know that and put it down in your book, you hear? See, the whole thing wasn't a thing in the world but the manufacturing of political ambitions by Barnett and those Kennedy brothers."

What happened after that? He seemed embarrassed to tell. "Well, kinda funny to say, but I missed out on going to Oxford. It was too late by then. I stayed put. Didn't have my car. In the middle of the night, Kennedy moved a whole Afro-American military police battalion right up sorority row. Now, was that going to incite folks?"

A few days afterward, he went home to Natchez and walked into a bazaar at St. Mary's Cathedral parish, where his wife was seated at a long table with friends. Every head turned as he strode through the hall, the place growing deathly quiet. "One of the strangest feelings I ever had. Have you ever been in the wrong place at the wrong time, and just couldn't figure it out? I go up to my wife and I say, 'Hello, honey,' and, guess what, she's got three of the books sitting there with her, the *Life* books, they're just out on the newsstands, and she plops one in my lap and opens it up to the middle and says, 'Look here.'

And I look. And I say, 'What? Why, that's me with that stick.' And Hazel, she says, 'Yeah, and I'm married to him.' "

That day down at the dock, a year and a half before he died, with the water lapping at the pilings, with his blue heeler splashing around trying in vain to snare a fish, Billy neglected to say that his and Hazel's only daughter was an undergraduate in her first year at Oxford when it all took place. Perhaps this fact slipped his mind. Perhaps he didn't think it an important detail to bring up. I learned of it subsequently, by reading through his oral history with the grad student at the University of Southern Mississippi, but more important, I learned of it from Billy's son and successor in the office of Adams County sheriff. Tommy Ferrell said one day, his feet up on his desk, surprise in his voice that could not have matched the surprise in my face: "You mean you didn't know my sister, Sherry, was up there when Meredith was getting in? Oh, yeah, that was an awfully big part of it for my father, you know, that his daughter was at the school, his concern for her welfare, when James Meredith was forcing his way in."

It was the "forcing his way in" part that put a stronger angle of light into my imagination about Moore's photograph. It was after this I began to think of it much more directly as a lynching narrative, its power tapping straight into the myth of Emmett Till, straight into all the old nineteenth-century Southern myths of the "black beast rapist." In the late nineteenth century, especially in the 1890s, racist hysteria gripped white male Southerners—the spiritual and literal grandfathers and great-grandfathers of the men in Moore's photograph. Almost overnight, whites across the South seemed to develop a fear and hatred of blacks that approached the genocidal, at least in figurative terms. No one knows the exact numbers. According to scholar E. M. Beck at the University of Georgia, in his study *A Festival of Violence*, beginning in the year 1882, and running for about the next five decades, some 2,500 black men, women, and children were lynched in America. The greatest number of the killings occurred in Mississippi. And without doubt the grisliest decade of the lynch festival was 1890 through 1899: at least 100 black men were put to death every year.

It wasn't until 1941, at the back end of this national shame, that the Southern historian W. J. Cash connected the history of lynching across the Deep South to a crisis of white masculinity. In his landmark study *The Mind of the South*, Cash theorized on the white man's "rape complex." He wrote of an endangered male authority and the deep neuroses of gender and sexuality it brought. The condition, Cash argued, was the result of the overthrow of slavery's order. The ultimate and as-yet-unrealized expression of the overthrow of slavery in the white male mind would be the destruction of the white sexual order, which is to say, the taking, somewhere far down the road, but maybe not too far, of his own wife, of his own daughter, of his own yet unborn grand-daughter. Cash explained:

> For the abolition of slavery, in destroying the rigid fixity of the black at the bottom of the scale, in throwing open to him at least the legal opportunity to advance, had inevitably opened up to the mind of every Southerner a vista at the end of which stood the overthrow of this taboo. If it was given to the black to advance at all, who could say (once more the logic of the doctrine of his inherent inferiority would not hold) that he would not one day advance the whole way and lay claim to complete equality, including, specifically, the ever crucial right of marriage? What Southerners felt, therefore, was that any assertion of any kind on the part of the Negro constituted in a perfectly real manner an attack on the Southern woman.

The so-called rape complex seemed to bring out the worst in almost any Southern mob, but in Mississippi, in the late nineteenth and early twentieth centuries, some of the executions and tortures of blacks beggared imagination: death by blowtorch; a scalding with hot irons; a severing of and handing around of the genitals; a gouging of the eyes until they "hung by a shred from the socket" accompanied by a simultaneous corkscrewing of "big pieces of raw, quivering flesh"—so the *Vicksburg Evening Post* informed its readers in a 1904 report of a double Delta lynching. More than 1,000 attended that one, munching on hard-boiled eggs, swilling lemonade and whiskey. The victims were forced to extend their hands while their fingers, one at a time, were chopped off and passed around as souvenirs. Perhaps what is most shocking about some of these lynching narratives in the Deep South at the turn of the century is estimates of crowd size—sometimes in the thousands. Sometimes whole families attended. Men are posing casually, without hiding their faces, smiling, no apparent shame, pointing at the charred or bludgeoned thing up above. Women and children can be seen in the frame. For some Southern lynchings, there were excursion trains to the site, with photographers on hand making commemorative postcards. At a lynching in Corinth, Mississippi, in 1902 (seven decades before Jim Garrison managed Long John Silver's there), "reserved seats were placed for the women who might desire them," according to a newspaper account. "Special trains were run to the scene and hundreds took advantage of the opportunity. The brother of the murdered woman lighted the fire."

In a more recent scholarly work, *Making Whiteness*, Southern historian Grace Elizabeth Hale picked up on Cash's 1941 thesis: "Cash implied that white male power challenged by black men's political and economic advances translated into white male sexuality threatened by black male sexuality. Rape of white women signaled metaphorically white men's fear of the loss of ability to provide for white women and physically their fear, given their treatment of black women, of the loss of white racial purity."

The leering man in his Stetson; the cigar-chomping man in his see-through white shirt; the grim and almost funereal man in the black hat at the back; the stick-swinging man in the middle biting down delicately with his two front incisors—you study all seven of them in the light of the foregoing suppositions and scholarly analyses and isn't each of them requiring the same thing, namely, instant and bloody redress for a perceived wrong? Is it too much to suggest that there may be a faint undertone of sexualized tension in their faces? According to Hale: "Lynching was the brutal underside of the modern South, the terrifying and yet for whites also perversely titillating practice and increasingly meditated narrative that made the culture of segregation work, and even seem sane." According to Cash, "What the direct willfulness of his individualism demanded, when confronted by a crime that aroused his anger, was immediate satisfaction for itself—catharsis for personal passion in the spectacle of a body dancing at the end of a rope or writhing in the fire—now, within the hour—and not some ponderous abstract justice in a problematic tomorrow."

And hadn't *he* understood it as a lynching moment, a lynching narrative, with all that it implied? James Meredith knew what the metaphor of penetrating—or threatening to penetrate—a previously white and "virginal" sanctum of learning meant to the white Southern male mind. Meredith understood about the South and its taboos in ways that an outsider—say, Emmett Till—could never know. Meredith was making an unwarranted advance on Mississippi and womanhood and manhood—and who could say where the advance would lead? To quote again from *Three Years in Mississippi:* "What are the essentials of a lynching ceremony? There must be a common victim for the lynching community and he must be guilty in the minds of the lynchers of threatening the virtue or purity of the white woman. It is important to understand that the whole community is always involved in a lynching, even though the actual violence itself may be done or even observed by only a small group from the community. If the community is not totally involved, it would not constitute a lynching." The day the photograph was taken is the day Meredith described as "lynching time." The fact that an unfathomable man, unfathomably heroic, unfathomably messianic, didn't get lynched, not on the afternoon of Moore's photograph, not three nights later, during the fifteen-hour campus rampage, seems almost an accident of history, the same kind of accident that saw to it that Billy and Ira and John Henry and John Ed and Bob Waller and Jim Garrison and Jimmy Middleton came up missing that night, or mostly so.

In his oral history with the USM scholar two months before we met, Billy never made mention of Moore's photograph. He may have had it in mind, however, when he said that Oxford and Meredith were "something we never have talked about because of the—the people of the state of Mississippi was indirectly involved in that in its entirety and stood the chance of embarrassment to no end." He explained to the interviewer, as he did to me, that it all got out of hand up there because of the violence and bullying of federal troops: ". . . it had progressed from just a simple rejection of a black student into the University of Mississippi. It had really got raunchy by that time. When you can go around without declaring martial law in a state or without declaring martial law in a community and having federalized troops arrest local officials, that sounds more like Moscow instead of Mississippi." He said that his daughter, Sherry, had been spirited out of her dorm and off the campus and from under harm's way by a family friend and former sheriff who was at the scene and had access to a car. (Several years later, when I briefly discussed that night with her, Sherry Ferrell Bernhard confirmed the story.)

Earlier in this book, I asked: Where did the hatred and sorrow go that flowed out of a caught instant under some trees—and out of a lot of other moments like it in seven particular lives that didn't get stopped by a camera and reproduced across two pages in a national magazine? Where did it go, the hatred and sorrow encapsulated and symbolized by that image, and where does it reside today? One answer might be that it went too many places to know. It took on too many forms and faces. It spread outward into too many hearts and spleens, like the capillary seepage of water through stone, which is the way of hatred and sorrow.

Scribes and TV reporters are pursuing James Meredith across campus with handheld mikes and tape recorders and bulky film cameras. He's flanked by his federal bodyguards. You can make out the university buildings in the middle distance. It's not long since the night to remember.

"Sir, there's been a great deal of turmoil and conflict. Two people have died. Do you have any feelings of guilt, have you given it any second thoughts?"

Smiling, moving, not answering immediately: "I'm very sorry that anyone had to get hurt or killed. But of course I think that's an unfair question of me. I don't believe any of you believe of me that I had anything to do with that."

"How are you getting along in school, sir?"

"Just fine, just fine."

"How are the students—uh, talking to you? Is there any reaction?"

"No, just acting like students, I suppose."

"Is this kind of a lonely life for you, despite all these people around you?"

Getting into a sedan, the sedan starting to move away, Meredith answers, "I've been living the lonely life a long time."

Newsweek is on campus to file a first-person report. It's a month afterward. The piece is sensitively done by esteemed civil rights correspondent Karl Fleming: "One can't help but be impressed by the vast personal dignity of this man. He is neither cocky nor egotistical, yet he seems to possess some fantastic inner strength and discipline—never flinching, for instance, when firecrackers go off near him. . . . His quarters in Baxter Hall are depressingly plain. He has a steel bed and works at a metal table. A red lampshade provides the only color in the room. There are two other beds in the room, used by Justice Department attorneys. . . . Some students call him 'Jungle Jim' or 'Blackberry.' . . . 'I don't even hear them,' he says. 'I can't remember one of them.' Does he worry about the possibility of being killed? 'I don't even let myself think about that.'" An Ole Miss professor is quoted in the piece: "They'll never break him. That's for sure."

The following are from declassified documents of the U.S. Marshals Service. This first document, with its rushed typing and imperfect grammar and spelling, is part of a many-paged "Shift Report" dated "10-31-62":

Mr. Meredith left for the noon meal at 11:20 AM. . . . He left mess hall at 12 noon and proceeded back to Baxter hall on foot. While Mr. Meredith was having his lunch a suspicious man 5FT. 11 In. tall approx. 205 lbs. Light brown coat, dark brown pants, white shirt, no tie, brown shoes, and dark brown hat. This man took a seat next to Mr. Meredith with another student, which he did not seem to know. He kept looking at Mr. Meredith and eating his lunch very slow. . . . Mr. Meredith left class at 2:50 Pm and proceeded to the Student Union building to Pick up his mail. As he entered the building a few cat calls came from a group of students. . . . At 3:55 Pm received information of two students one of which lives in Baxter Hall That a student in Baxter who lives on the third floor has 17 sticks of dynamite in his room. . . . Chief Tatum took it [a suitcase] to Robertsons room where Chief Tatum ask Robertson opened it, found inside was an ID card, firecrackers . . . also found gas can (2 gal). . . . About 6:40 P.M. the F.B.I. came . . . in trash can in hall way, in hallway was a gas grenade. . . . in Baxter hall in room 41 . . . there was found 20 shotgun shells . . . then searched Lester Hall, in room 33 a night stick was found . . . a 22 rifle in 3 parts, a BB six gun (Daisy Bullseye). . . . Capt Shiver and Chief Tatum found a machete knife, in room 21 a gas can was found . . . on the west end last room was found a old grenade. . . . 12:25 A.m. 11-1-62 received information from Andy Crosby that there was a bomb in the building and you better get out. . . . Deputys made a check of building at 12:55 A.M. nothing unusual a few fire-crackers still being set off.

Another document (Meredith has been on campus for five and a half months):

As Meredith passed Howry Hall #2, two plastic bags of water were dropped from the second floor hall window. They landed near Mere-dith splashing water on his shoes and lower portion of his pants. Meredith turned and ran into Howry hall with the Marshal. He banged on several doors and asked one boy if he knew anything about the water. . . . Deputy Vandegrift telephoned and said that at 1:00 p.m. today two plastic bags full of water were dropped from the second floor. . . . One struck behind and one beside Meredith and the water splashed on his pants and shoes. He became provoked and ran into Howry Hall and up to the second floor. . . . Meredith banged on a few doors and when a student came into the hall, Meredith said, "Who threw that on me?" . . . Meredith came out and went on to class.

Another document: "Weekly Report—May 15 thru 18, 1963":

Subject observed following Meredith—questioned and identified by Chief Tatum. . . . Stated if he had the money he would have Meredith killed. Someone had to do it so it might as well be him regardless of what the penalty was. Checked and released by Chief Tatum. No other unusual activities.

Another document (May 19, 1963):

Meredith drove to Oxford from Jackson, Miss., in his new 1963 Thun-derbird. A crowd of about 50 students gathered around the car in front of the Student Union directing derogatory remarks to Meredith about he and his car. About 20 students gathered at Baxter Hall and the same things transpired. During the night eggs and soap were thrown on the car. No further incidents.

Native son Willie Morris wasn't in Mississippi when James Meredith forcibly penetrated Ole Miss. Three months afterward, Morris wrote a piece in *Dissent* magazine called "Despair in Mississippi: Hope in Texas." "I bought a newspaper one afternoon in San Francisco and read the wire service account of how a hundred or more students had surrounded Meredith's table in the school cafeteria. Shaking their fists, quivering like young mammals in heat, they had chanted: 'Go home nigger. We don't want you here.' . . . There sat Meredith, and there he no doubt still sits; one can only imagine how he, as a human being, must have been torn inside. . . . With a handful of exceptions, Mississippi is a monolith; its soul-force is its burning and ravaging and gnawing hatred. . . . There is only this overriding consideration: to keep the black man down; so determined are they, so great is their fear and hatred, that even with the more sophisticated among them life is a thing of empty social ritual, intellection is shabby and false, and even in their hate there is an almost lifeless formalism. Growing up in Mississippi, you have the hatred nurtured in your bones. If it is not your parents who do the nurturing, then it is someone else; it is almost *everything* else."

In December, roughly three months after he'd been on campus, a journalist for *The Reporter* magazine asked if he was lonely. Meredith answered, "It wouldn't be right for me to be lonely. . . . I get low sometimes but then I tell myself, 'You got to stay operational.' "

At a Baxter Hall press conference on January 7, 1963, the student-soldier handed out a statement to the press: "I have decided not to register for classes during the second semester. . . . We are engaged in a war, a bitter war. . . . The enemy is determined, resourceful, and unprincipled. There are no rules of war for which he has respect." Afterward, a marshal wrote a memo to his superior: ". . . one minute he talks like he will leave and the next minute like he will stay." At a press conference in Jackson, on January 30, Meredith announced that "the Negro" was not returning to Ole Miss. He paused, smiled. However, "I, J. H. Meredith, will register for the second semester." In June, right before the summer session started, *Saturday Review* magazine wrote: "How does a man manage to keep himself so rigidly on guard. . . . Only a terrifying dedication can sustain that man." On August 18, 1963, the most famous student in the history of the University of Mississippi walked in a cap and gown with his classmates through the Grove. Seventy-two-year-old Cap Meredith was in the audience, holding on his lap his three-year-old grandson. When Meredith's name was called, he went across the stage and accepted his degree with a handshake from the university chancellor. "One of Ross Barnett's NEVER! buttons was on my lapel," he said many years later. "I wore it upside down." The graduating moment in the Grove was but Meredith prologue to all the bewildering after-years.

For a time, he lived in Washington, D.C. He gave speeches. Tired of this, he accepted an offer in 1964 to go to Nigeria to study at Ibadan University.

He came back to America to take up the law at Columbia University. He led a March Against Fear through Mississippi. This was in the early summer of 1966, and the stated plan was to walk 225 miles in the June heat. He wore a pith helmet and black sunglasses and carried an ivory-headed cane. A man hiding in bushes by the side of the road rose up and hit him with at least twenty pellets of bird shot from a shotgun. "Is anyone getting help for me?" the victim cried, falling against a car. The AP reported him as dead, but the wounds turned out not to be mortal.

At Columbia, still in law school, he announced he'd run as a Republican against Adam Clayton Powell, congressman from Harlem. He got himself nominated, but baseball immortal Jackie Robinson, first man to smash the color line in the majors, convinced him to withdraw about six days later. In July 1967 (still in New York), he took out a newspaper ad in Mississippi urging voters to support Ross Barnett, who was trying to make a political comeback in the governor's race. After Oxford, Barnett had been all but politically finished. He'd embarrassed Mississippi, but worse than that, he'd lost. He finished a weak fourth in that summer primary in 1967, despite or maybe even partly because of the stunning endorsement.

The Columbia law student owned a six-story apartment building in the Bronx, among other New York holdings, and eventually he was denounced as a slumlord. (In 1969, he would spend two days in jail for harassing his tenants, accused of trying to force white residents out of the building and of failing to provide hot water and elevator service.) In 1968, he won his law degree (he would claim later that he got it without ever cracking a book), but this accomplishment seemed only to presage a series of further run-ins with the law. Back in Mississippi, Meredith began trying for public office—he put his name in for at least five races between 1972 and 1979. In 1974, he declared bankruptcy. In 1979, his wife suddenly died, and that same year he got arrested at a Pizza Hut for causing a scene when the manager wouldn't honor his two-for-one coupon. By 1982, on the twentieth anniversary of the entry into Oxford, he was running a Jackson bar, the Broad Street Club. He was also putting out a publication called *Outlook* and he'd started a talent agency. "I'm going to try to be like Colonel Parker," he told a reporter for the Gannett chain of papers, who'd come to do a feature. "Soldiers don't have regrets," he said. "They only win or lose." He was asked about the significance of Oxford. "I'm twenty years older, that's the significance," he said. Of his ex-antagonist Ross Barnett, he said, "A very brilliant man who safeguarded the whole state of Mississippi." Barnett was eighty-four by then, still a handsome six-footer, practicing law out of the Barnett Building in Jackson. He, too, had acquiesced to some interviews on the twentieth anniversary. He said he had no regrets. He told one interviewer he'd just read a book about the skull of blacks being not quite able to hold what the skull of a white man's can hold on account of a black skull has a known genetic cave in it.

Meredith in these years tried investment banking, restaurant life, radio and TV repair, the cosmetics business, farming, catfish sales. He became a product distributor for Amway. He went into religion, starting his own church, the Reunification Church Under God. It had no buildings and held no religious services. "My thing is, I'm on a crusade," he told a reporter. "I don't any longer have to decide if I want to be an ordained minister to carry out my calling, and that's what it is to me, a calling." He tended toward jumpsuits and berets. He sought to secure a job on the faculty of Ole Miss, but it didn't pan out.

In 1984, the University of Cincinnati offered him a year-long contract as a lecturer in Afro-American studies. (He'd sent out letters to something like eleven schools, offering his services.) He moved to the Midwest with his family and named the wood-frame house in which he established his office the James H. Meredith Office Building. Problems arose. His car was vandalized. He called a press conference to denounce racism in the city. He charged the university with failing to graduate a single black athlete since 1964, although at least twenty had graduated in the previous decade. (It was still a pathetically small number, a fact that seemed to be overlooked in the bad press against him that arose.) At the university, his course was called "The Law and Black People." He couldn't seem to master the material past the first ten or fifteen minutes of each class. His students began reading newspapers while he rambled. By late fall, another instructor had been brought in to take over the course. Police officers had to remove him from a health club when he wouldn't produce a membership card. Actually, he was a paying member of the club, but he said he was trying to make a point. In June 1985, the university chose not to renew his contract, and Meredith charged a conspiracy. "What it boils down to is that certain blacks decided they didn't want me here," he said to the press. "So they got together with certain whites and decided to eliminate me." This was denied by the university administration. The local paper ran a front-page feature entitled "Life of James Meredith Defies Easy Categories." He told the reporter, "I have always felt like a prophet or a messenger." He claimed in that piece that his personal worth was $900,000. He ran for the Cincinnati school board, but it didn't work out. He went on a call-in radio show and traded astonishing insults with local bigots. He told his listeners that he wouldn't have signed the Civil Rights Act of 1964 if he'd been in Congress, and he also said that he'd prefer to see George Wallace or Lester Maddox on the Cincinnati City Council than the nine men who were serving there. He continued giving speeches around the country, with Cincinnati still the base of operations, although the lecture fees had dropped radically and the audiences were turning paltry. In 1988, he was at Webster University in St. Louis.

A female African-American interviewer asked him about "the movement." He was in a lawyerly three-piece blue pinstripe, with a wreath of handsome gray beard. "I have never participated in any of that," he said. "In fact, I always considered that below my dignity—you understand that? I have *never* protested anyone. You understand? No one is big enough for me to protest." He lolled his tongue at this comely interviewer, winked at her. Later on the tape, he seems suddenly scared, confused. "It was too overwhelming," he says to her, looking down. He means Oxford.

The year before that interview, on November 6, 1987, Ross Barnett had died at Doctors' Hospital in Jackson. "He just quit breathing," Ross Barnett, Jr., said of his eighty-nine-year-old dad. "He'd gone as far as he could go, I guess." If he could have gone another few years, the old seg would have seen his maverick, middle-aged daughter, Ouida Barnett Atkins, become a teacher of world history at almost entirely black Lanier High School in inner-city Jackson. ("People ask me if what I'm doing is an apology for my father," Atkins said, when I asked her about it. "The answer's no. What those people did back then, uh, that was their deal." She didn't sound defensive.) After Ross Barnett died, a black couple bought his home in north Jackson.

By 1989, many things had gone wrong and scary in the Meredith family. James's oldest son, John, twenty-eight, was struggling to find himself. His twin sons, Joe and James Jr., almost twenty-one, faced huge legal and medical problems. Joe, an upperclassman at Harvard, had come down with lupus and had been forced, at least temporarily, to suspend his studies. James Jr., in his third year at the University of Pennsylvania, was facing sentencing for a crime in Alfred, Maine. Two summers before, in late August 1987, James Jr. had been driving a Datsun 280-Z in which two passengers were killed. They were his roommates. The son, driving under the influence of alcohol, missed a turn. The car left the road and smashed into a large boulder. The accident happened at night, as the three were coming home from a restaurant called Mrs. B's, where they had been employed. They were celebrating the end of the summer season, before James's return to school for his sophomore year. He survived the crash with minor injuries. A year and a half later, on the second day of his manslaughter and drunk-driving trial (it opened in January 1989), the defendant pleaded no contest to two counts of manslaughter and one count of driving under the influence. His father, in attendance, suggested to the local press that there had been racial bias in the handling of the case. Seven months later, after much negotiation between lawyers, the son received a greatly reduced sentence, with no jail time.

This was the same month, August 1989, that James Meredith, in Ohio, announced that he was pulling up stakes from Cincinnati and going to work in Washington for a senator. Deeply worried about the medical and legal bills,

Meredith had sent a letter to each member of Congress and to every governor in the country. "If God sees fit to allow me longevity and good health," he said, "I will be in the future the most important Black Leader in America and the World. We need to know each other."

Soon there were headlines: "Man Who Integrated Ole Miss Now at Work for Jesse Helms." The race relations adviser to the Senate's most prominent racial obstructionist was on the payroll for a reported salary of $30,000. It wasn't a lot of money, and to complicate matters, Meredith's wife, a TV reporter, had a new job in San Diego, and so the family had to maintain separate residences. To defray some of this, the new Hill aide to a North Carolina racist went around lecturing about race. At Florida State University, he told the law school student body, "For the last ten years my enemy has been the white liberal. And I plan to crush them, and wash them out, because they are destroying my people." At Mount Holyoke College in Massachusetts, he said, "My enemy then was the white supremacist, my enemy now is the white liberal. The white liberals are about 1,000 times worse than the white supremacist." In Boston, he said, "The making of slavery as an institution does not have near the significance as is placed on it." At a State Department briefing on U.S. policy toward Africa, he told the audience he was a genius with a 141 IQ. He wished to be referred to as "Dr. Meredith." On U.S. Senate letterhead, he wrote to an energy specialist in Senegal: "Without a doubt I am now in the most powerful position that any black person has possessed in the history of Western Christian civilization. Time will tell whether I am a match for my responsibility and opportunity." Time did seem to tell—the relationship with Helms was dead by the fall of 1991. Meredith said he was quitting the staff because the senator was "too liberal." A month later, he drove to Louisiana to throw his support behind candidate David Duke, onetime neo-Nazi and imperial wizard of the KKK, who now wished to be governor of his state, and beyond that, president.

Not long afterward, a white Southerner named John Ed Bradley interviewed Meredith for a story that was published in *Esquire* in late 1992. His magazine piece on Meredith is one of the few that has ever sought to touch the hatred and sorrow and fear beneath the surface. The journalist took Meredith to dinner, and Meredith began telling of the bird shot he sustained from the shotgun blast in the 1966 March Against Fear. He touched his scalp, ran his fingers over the back of his head. "Feel this right there," he told the author. Bradley did. "They're all under the skin, it's a BB. Here's one here—see that, right there." He said, "It keeps a continuous sore, and I can't sleep more than an hour or so at a time. Occasionally, one will come out, just pop out of the skin, like when you get a splinter and you pick it out." Bradley watched a tic come to Meredith's lips, the slightest tremble. The journalist looked away. He was sure Meredith was about to cry. "Used to find them on my pillow," Meredith said. "What?" Bradley said, staring at his plate. "The BBs." When he looked back at Meredith's face, Meredith wasn't crying. He was smiling.

I once showed Charles Moore's photograph to a man named Will D. Campbell. He is an ordained minister and a prolific author and a lifelong student of the South. For many years, he has lived outside of Nashville, but he is Mississippi in his origins and predilections. In the fifties, he had been a chaplain at Oxford. Now, in his little writing cabin, which is a hundred or so yards from his house in Mt. Juliet, Tennessee, the historian and man of God and lover of Mississippi and the South spread the magazine out on his knees and said, moving his head side to side, "Well, these are our people, aren't they?" There was something so accepting in it.

I once showed the photograph to a Southern historian and Mississippi native named David Sansing. He is another gentle and gracious man. For years, he taught at Ole Miss; he is mad for the school, its traditions, its football glories, and finds that he can't stay away from it even in his retirement. A couple of years ago, Sansing authored the sesquicentennial history of Ole Miss. He said that he has his young grandkids already preregistered for enrollment. He got very excited looking at the picture, which, curiously, he'd never seen before. He hunched forward and touched it, as so many have done. "You know what this is?" he said. "It's life imitating life. These guys are posing for this picture. They know the rest of the country knows what they look like, and, hell, they're just gonna show them that that's exactly what they look like."

I stood up from the table we were sitting at in the Alumni Center. "These are American white Southern bigots," I said.

The retired professor stood up. He looked down at the photograph. "Yep, authentic bigots," he said.

"But they insist on being taken as individuals?"

He hesitated. "Yes and no. What is that old thing? There's security in numbers. Safety in it. They want to stay part of the group. Because they break down into their humanity when you get them one-on-one. They're a little afraid of that. I think they'd rather stay part of the mob. This guy swinging that stick knows in his heart it's wrong. He can't help it. See, these guys are both individuals, and they are part of a much bigger face. They're just freckles on a larger face. They couldn't do what they're doing if their wives and communities weren't endorsing it." None of this was said with rancor, and indeed I got the feeling that if the faces in Moore's photograph could come to life off the flat page, Sansing would immediately be inclined to invite them into his home, to get a better fix on them, maybe.

"You sound like a man in conflict," I said.

"Damn right," he said. "Faulkner wrote about me. Remember his Nobel Prize speech? He talked of the human heart in conflict with itself. That's Mississippi."

I once showed the picture to John Herbers, another wise, gentle Mississippi son and retired reporter for the *New York Times*. Herbers spent most of his journalism career covering the South. He was at the Emmett Till trial as a young reporter for the wire services. "The hate always runs so deep in Southern cops," he said.

"Why?"

"Well, because they come by and large from a blue-collar background. They've put on the badge and risen above it a little in their white shirts and ties, but they still know where they came from and so in a sense you could say they hate themselves. It's a form of self-hate and outer-directed hate at the same time. The line between a criminal and a cop is always very thin. They're very much alike. They're prey to the same impulses and secret desires. With the badge on, they can slip over that line. They're halfway over before they realize." Herbers looked again and laughed. "None of them could expect to live very long—they all ate too much pig fat."

I once showed Moore's picture to another photographer—D. Gorton. He is a native Mississippian, white, from Greenville, who grew up in the fifties and who was at Oxford as a student at the time of the riot, and who afterward went to work in voter registration for SNCC, and who, much later, became an esteemed photographer at the *New York Times* and other newspapers. After we talked, he sent a letter. "We find ourselves drawn more and more into discussions of redemption," he said. "The pressure on whites in Mississippi was so extreme that to act in a moral way approached self-immolation. . . . A double-bind was presented: to act was to cross lines that might never be recrossed. Not to act was to be complicit. Moreover, judgment of your actions was largely made by outsiders in a secular environment. Meanwhile, one's black neighbors had been burdened by these very issues for their whole existence on this unwelcoming soil."

After Oxford, massive resistance was mostly finished in Mississippi. So was the Citizens' Council mainly finished—certainly you can begin to mark the waning of its power from that moment. That seems a large part of the meaning of Meredith's entry—the resistance wave had crested, and nobody really understood so at the time. In many ways, Meredith at Ole Miss—a somewhat forgotten moment in America—was the culminating event of civil rights in Mississippi, even though still ahead were so many bad and notorious moments for Mississippi and for the rest of the South and for the country itself. Ahead in Mississippi was the reemergence of the Klan—the revival began in

Billy Ferrell's Natchez and spread through the state. Ahead was the astonishing hate of already astonishingly hateful places like Greenwood. Ahead were Bull Connor and the dogs of Birmingham. Ahead was the slaying of Medgar Evers. Ahead was the murder of four little girls in the bombing of the Sixteenth Street Baptist Church in Birmingham. Ahead was Freedom Summer of 1964 and the murder of Schwerner, Chaney, and Goodman in Philadelphia, Mississippi. Ahead was Bloody Sunday in Selma on March 7, 1965.

And yet also ahead were the triumphs and the moral turning of a country: the August 28, 1963, March on Washington ("I have a dream," Dr. King cried to the more than 200,000 faces gathered below him); the signing of the Civil Rights Act of 1964 on July 2 of that year; the passage of the Voting Rights Act of 1965. That civil rights legislation became law on August 6, 1965. In March of that year, only 6.7 percent of all eligible blacks in Mississippi had been registered to vote; but within two and a half years—by September 1967—the percentage would be 59.8 percent.

Ahead, too, were the burnings in cities—Newark, Watts in Los Angeles, Detroit, Hough in Cleveland—and in the wake of these northern fires, a slow fragmenting of the movement. The Black Panther party rose, and with it Stokely Carmichael, once of SNCC, calling by then for apocalypse in the ghetto. On April 4, 1968, Martin Luther King, Jr., died on his motel balcony in Memphis, and two months and one day later, on June 5, Bobby Kennedy was assassinated in the pantry of the Ambassador Hotel in Los Angeles, falling backward with a quizzical expression on his face. He lived for about another twenty-six hours—until 1:44 A.M. on June 6. And then there was the funeral two days later at St. Patrick's Cathedral in New York. And that same afternoon, there was the train ride southward, attended at towns and crossings by the silent and curious—perhaps a million trackside mourners in all, black and white alike.

It was a blur of time in America, from the front end of the sixties to the back end, during which so much about our national life went helter-skelter. By the back end of the decade, Vietnam was the hemorrhage no one could stanch, and it had superseded almost everything, including the struggle for civil rights, which had been won and not won.

Several years ago, I was visiting a civil rights museum in Memphis. I was standing at the exhibit panel that told about Meredith after he'd made it into Ole Miss. On a green card in white lettering, I read: "For almost a year, Meredith has lived in a kind of 'No Man's Land.' He found few friendly faces on the white side. . . . He never admits to the pressure or tension he feels. He either denies it or makes fun of it." In the next room, I could hear the recorded sound of fire hoses knocking people over. It was an exhibit about Bull

Connor and his cops and dogs in Kelly Ingram Park, seven months after the events at Oxford. Charles Moore had taken the photographs of the Birmingham police dogs with their teeth bared, lunging against their choke chains, ripping the clothes of demonstrators. Historian Arthur Schlesinger, Jr., later said, "The photographs of Bull Connor's police dogs lunging at the marchers in Birmingham did as much as anything to transform the national mood and make legislation not just necessary, which it had long been, but possible." After Ole Miss, after Birmingham, Moore had moved to other racial battlegrounds. He was at the Selma-to-Montgomery march in 1965, and yet by then he could feel something dying in him.

A month after that assignment, he was sent by *Newsweek* to shoot the civil war in the Dominican Republic. He was on a balcony in his hotel in the dark, watching machine-gun fire in the distance. "But I was tired of being involved in violent things," he would say years later, trying to explain. He left the Dominican Republic and went back to Miami. He bought an around-the-world ticket on Pan Am and didn't return to America for eight months. For the next several decades, he made Southeast Asia his base of photographic operations. He shot many national and international magazine covers. He made portraits of celebrities and movie stars—Kim Novak, Raquel Welch, Lauren Hutton. He did corporate photography for *Fortune* 500 companies. He became interested in landscape and nature photography. He lived, among other places (these are not in any strict order), in Singapore, San Francisco, New York, Los Angeles, the gold mining country of the Sierra Nevada of California, western Massachusetts, the mountains of North Carolina. He collected overdue awards, not enough, not the truly big ones he deserved. He gave speeches and starred at various symposia—always with his winning modesty. He got married and unmarried—more than once. Many years removed from that summer-of-'62 freelance try in Manhattan, he wrote a letter to his brother Jim, five years younger and his closest friend in life: "I ran away from the pain of a very bad marriage, and into the more painful life of being away from my children whom I loved so much." In the spring of 2000, a wanderer and wounded man and yet still an intensely curious and kindly soul moved back home to northwestern Alabama, thinking at last he'd settle, and this is where we first met, a few months after the move, in the town of Florence, as he was getting a deck built on the back of his new house, as he was shelving books in his living room. I opened a coffee-table book. It was a retrospective of the work of the great portrait photographer Arnold Newman. Newman had written in the flyleaf: "For Charles. I'm floored and flattered to be asked to sign this book by such a great Master, with humble respect and admiration and from an old friend. Arnold."

Standing before the Meredith panel in the Memphis civil rights museum that day several years ago, reading the words "never admits to the pressure or tension he feels," listening to the recorded sound of pressurized fire hoses and the barking of dogs in the adjoining room, I began to come slowly to a new feeling about the unknowable figure who lives behind drawn blinds on Meadowbrook Road in Jackson. Although Meredith can't be seen in Moore's frame, he is in the picture. He is, you might say, filling it up, controlling and directing all of its spaces.

I once believed that the pressures of Oxford had cracked Meredith. I think the closer truth is that his dilemmas and demons were already present. Oxford, and the aftermath of Oxford, exacerbated and catalyzed all he became. The cruelty of the ordeal at Ole Miss got welded onto the already mystical-messianic temperament, and what resulted, in the long after-years, was a life no one has been able to decode, not least the man himself. Increasingly, he became a marginalized figure in America, and the sheer frustration of that must be overwhelming to him behind those drawn blinds. This fact needs be put into the mix: The world has never had enough compassion for Meredith. He himself has seen to that. In John Ed Bradley's 1992 *Esquire* piece, there are phrases like this: ". . . no more than a dressed-up errand boy for a race-baiting southern senator." And: "Sadly, the diatribe seemed the ravings of a megalomaniac devouring whatever shred of a reputation he had left. And the vicious irony was that the more Meredith confessed his ambition to be the savior, the more people turned away—not in political disagreement but in pity and confusion." Those judgments are as tough as they are fair. The easier path for most white journalists, as the decades went on, was to write the confoundment–contradiction–crack-up story, with mockery at the margins, and with little or no attempt to recognize their own complicity in the terrors of a whooshing bat that in a sense has never stopped whooshing. Let that thought be stated another way: Aren't all of us who are white in America in Moore's frame too, unseen yet present, standing in the ring of batterers, maybe even trying on our own leer or sneer, just to see how it fits?

A nd so a personal story. On October 16, 1992, in a mid-South farm town called Morganfield, Kentucky, a thirty-one-year-old man named Terry Frazier gained entry to a house at the corner of Poplar Street and West O'Bannon Street. At home that early afternoon were two people—a two-year-old named Steven, asleep in a bedroom, and Steven's thirty-one-year-old mom, who was doing housework. Her name was Tina M. Waggener, and she knew the intruder well. She'd gone to Union County High School with Frazier, as had her husband, Doby Waggener, who, at the time of the robbery and murder, was cutting hair in his barbershop. Frazier, who is now in a Kentucky penitentiary, is black; his old classmate Tina, whom he murdered about two o'clock for reasons that are still murky, was white. It is not known if he intended to attack her sexually, although that has been much speculated. What is known is that he stabbed her repeatedly in the face and throat. He pursued her out into the yard where he caught her and perhaps stabbed her again as she screamed and clawed for a fence. That's where they found my first cousin, next to a fence, eighty-nine feet from the house. I remember the chillingly soft way my father said, when I asked him for facts, "I think he got her climbing the fence, son."

Tina was my Uncle Leon's child. My Uncle Leon Hendrickson, who is my dad's brother, along with my Uncle Jimmy Hendrickson and my Uncle H. C. Hendrickson, have lived in Morganfield all their lives. The Morganfield phone directory has many listings for the name Hendrickson. That Indian summer afternoon, my three uncles were hauling corn to market. My father's family is descended from farm people who go far back in that rural region of Kentucky. My father is third-oldest and eldest surviving son in a family of eight boys and one girl, some of whom, including my octogenarian father, have been out of Morganfield and off the farm for decades. But each of them was formed and deeply marked as a Depression-era child in that segregated place. A generation later, in my own fifties childhood, when I was riding on the fenders of my uncles' tractors for several weeks out of every summer, Morganfield remained a deeply divided community. My older brother Marty and I were Illinois boys, and we couldn't wait to get down to the pleasures of the Kentucky farm.

Tina Waggener's 1992 murder shocked Morganfield. It was so out of the order of things, so against the town's social and moral history. Three years after her death, I was standing one night in a West Coast bookstore when a black-and-white photograph of some men in a half circle took strange hold of me. And do you know what? For the first several years of my Mississippi travels, I missed the most obvious and central thing about this photograph, obvious and central insofar as my own history is concerned. I suppose this is exactly why I missed it, because it was and is so obvious to my own history, namely, that the man in the middle, swinging the bat, biting the Lucky, bent on his murderous vengeances, could be my own dad as a younger man. The physical resemblance is remarkable.

But the "real"—what assaults the eye before the eye begins its work of selection—is never on the verge of dissolution, still less of appropriation. The real is raw, jarring, unexpected, sometimes trashy, sometimes luminous. Above all, the real is arbitrary. For to be a realist (in art or in life) is to acknowledge that all things might be other than they are. That there is no design, no intention, no aesthetic or moral or teleological imprimatur but, rather, the equivalent of Darwin's great vision of a blind, purposeless, ceaseless evolutionary process that yields no "products"—only temporary strategies against extinction. Yet, being human, we think, To what purpose these broken-off things, if not to be gathered up, at last, in a single ecstatic vision?

—Joyce Carol Oates, "They All Just Went Away"

I intentionally avoided children of famous perpetrators, like the sons of Rudolf Hess or Josef Mengele, who had already been the subject of media attention, because I suspected that they had developed an "external self" in talking about their fathers and the Third Reich. I looked for people who had been left alone, for whom the past might have become part of an internal dialogue.

—Dan Bar-On, *Legacy of Silence: Encounters with Children of the Third Reich*

Wars have their endings inside of families.

—Cynthia Enloe, "Women After Wars: Puzzles and Warnings"

History says, *Don't hope*
On this side of the grave.
But then, once in a lifetime
The longed-for tidal wave
Of justice can rise up,
And hope and history rhyme.

—Seamus Heaney, *The Cure at Troy*

Part Three

Hopes of the Sons

Five years before James Meredith at Oxford, and two years after Emmett Till at Money, Dwight Eisenhower ordered 1,200 paratroopers of the 101st Airborne into Arkansas during the desegregation battle at Little Rock's Central High School. Despite a court order, Governor Orval E. Faubus had dispatched the state national guard to the steps of the school to bar nine black students, thus forcing the president to deploy federal troops. There's an image from that civil rights standoff in the early fall of 1957 that turned into an icon photograph; the Associated Press later named it one of the top hundred pictures of the century. A white student named Hazel Bryan, her face contorted, spews venom at the back of a fifteen-year-old black student named Elizabeth Eckford. Eyes hidden by dark glasses, clutching her books, looking slightly downward, Eckford proceeds toward the entryway. Behind her is a column of bigots, and in the center of it the white girl, who looks about seventeen and has on a pretty dress and who holds out in front of her a rolled newspaper, as if she might swing it at Eckford's neck. But what the world didn't find out is that six years after the photograph, in 1963—which was the year of Bull Connor's attack dogs and fire hoses in Birmingham, the year of America's complicit role in the overthrow of a puppet president of South Vietnam named Ngo Dinh Diem—the female hater, by then married and a mother, contacted her victim by phone to offer an apology. The apology was cautiously accepted. The years passed. The white woman told friends and family that she continued to feel like a national "poster child for the hate generation, trapped in the image captured in the photograph, and I knew that my life was more than that moment." She longed for a face-to-face reconciliation. In 1997, the opportunity came. The private meeting—arranged by the man who'd made the photograph, Will Counts—was in anticipation of the fortieth anniversary of what had happened in Arkansas. (Native son Bill Clinton attended the ceremony.) Ahead of the official events, Elizabeth Eckford and Hazel Bryan Massery met at Eckford's home. "Elizabeth, thank you so much for agreeing to meet with me," Hazel said. Elizabeth replied, "You are a very brave person to face the cameras again." They drove to Central High and stood together out front of the entryway. Their thickened bodies touched. They laughed—two middle-aged women of opposite color from the same city who'd suffered separate shares of life's setbacks—while Counts took pictures. The following year, they appeared on programs at several universities and participated in a workshop on racial healing.

This is a redemptive story in the arc of sorrow that defines us as Americans more than any other sorrow, and some of it has now been told in a small, beautiful book entitled A Life Is More than a Moment. But there is no similar redemptive story to tell about any of the faces in Charles Moore's photograph. These seven lived on, each for his allotted span. They didn't approach or outwardly regret. Anything in the direction of atonement or expiation—even if never named that or understood as such—was left to sons, or to sons of sons, or to sons of sons of sons.

Sometimes Trashy,
Sometimes Luminous

And when the morning light comes streaming in
I'll get up and do it again

                              —Jackson Browne, "The Pretender"

A picture of a working man: He was in his third bad marriage, still in his mid-twenties, that winter night in 1989 when John Ed Cothran's grandson and namesake got off work at the produce company and went out to the parking lot to find his car dead again. It was a cold January midnight, snow on the ground, something like seventeen degrees out. In Mississippi, that's the Arctic. The car was a '78 Mustang that looked good but didn't run worth a damn. John Cothran got out and kicked at the door and trudged home, where probably there was a fight with his wife. In daylight, he went back to the parking lot and tried to get it to fire, and when the car wouldn't, he opened the trunk, retrieved a tire iron. "I just worked my way around," he says. "I busted the windshield, the back glass, the hood, the front door on the driver's side, the door on the passenger side, just every place where there was metal or glass and I could hit it with a tire tool." Two of his coworkers came out and stood a safe distance away to watch the demolition derby. They were laughing. The teller of this story is cracking up as well. "The thing had four hundred dollars worth of tires on it. If I had a blade, I'd have cut them, too. So what have we got here? A tore-up car that still won't crank. Stupid. I put the tool back in the trunk and went on in there to my job. See, what I'm telling you is I had a temper like that back then that was just out of control."

Ever bubble up now?

Quickly: "I won't let it."

Here's a second picture of a nearly forty-year-old inheritor, descended from the figure in the photograph who's got his back turned:

Several summers ago, John and the woman he was living with—her name was Kay—decided to try to take a real vacation, "like regular people." It was a long weekend motor trip, "a sorta unplanned thing." They almost didn't go— he was going to cancel so that he could help his fourth ex, from whom he'd been divorced less than a year, move out of her house and into a new place. He'd earned eleven days off from his supervisor's job at the Home Depot, and he'd used up almost all of it by helping out his parents or his most recent ex with one thing or another. He did get in one good day of jig fishing for crappie with his daddy on Grenada Lake. That relaxed him some. John was living then in Arkansas, across the Mississippi River from Memphis. Kay had small children, and he was trying halfheartedly to connect with them. John's own two older children, Ashley and John Jr., whom he'd been with once in the previous three years, and who are by his third wife, were visiting from Tupelo, Mississippi, on the weekend that he and Kay decided to take off. Their destination was Six Flags amusement park in St. Louis.

They headed out in Kay's van, much later in the day than they'd intended. They drove hard, but it got dark too quickly, and then the kids were turning cranky, and everybody was hungry, and so he and Kay started looking for a place to stay, hopefully one that would be close to a McDonald's or a Wendy's. They were somewhere in Illinois. All the motels were either full or way beyond their means. John kept driving. Everyone else in the car fell asleep. On the outskirts of St. Louis, he saw the Arch, that huge silver curve gleaming on the other bank of the Mississippi River. Right there, crossing over from Illinois into Missouri, the whole trip almost felt worth it. John's fourteen-year-old woke up to see the Arch in the headlights and said, "We're here, Daddy, we're here," and then Ashley went back to sleep.

He drove across the river and into downtown St. Louis. He got out and asked about lodging. The rooms were unbelievably expensive. He drove on, got out, kept asking, kept coming back to the car without a motel key. At this point, he was actually driving back south, toward where they'd come from. He told Kay, "I'm only going to stop at one more place, and then I'm going to drive straight back to Arkansas without stopping." He went into the next motel he saw and the guy said $200. "Are you crazy?" Kay said when he reported the price at the car window. He went back in and took the room anyway, paid cash, and the six of them got a beautiful room with two king-sized beds. It was now about 6 A.M. A couple of hours later, the kids were all over the grown-ups. They wanted to go to the park. At the park, John bought the admissions. The tickets were over twenty bucks apiece, even for the kids. John said to Kay, "Nah, I don't want to go on any rides in here, I'll just sit on one of these picnic tables with your baby." Kay said, "But we've come all this way." John said, "Nah, I like this fine, I ain't sweating it, you go on and have a good time." And that's what he did—sat for most of the day in the July sun at a picnic table just inside the gate of Six Flags, tending Kay's nineteenth-month-old. A month or so later, when they broke up after a nasty fight (they'd been together about four months), John took out of Kay's apartment in Marion, Arkansas, everything he could stuff into an overnight bag: rolls of toilet paper, soap, salt and pepper shakers, paper towels, shampoo, toothpaste, pillowcases. He probably would have taken the front door off the hinges if he'd needed a front door, and if there'd been a screwdriver handy, he says. Kay had already left for work, and soon, so had he: gone, in a rage again, in flight again, back home to Mississippi.

John Cothran, with his lifelong rage and impulses for goodness as well as flight, is a stubby, bouncy, balding, extroverted man with pale features and a scraggly reddish beard and a mustache that looks made of straw—auburn straw. You could imagine him as a muscular fireplug, and that would be a start. To see him in Bermuda shorts is nearly to stifle a laugh: squat, pasty legs covered with curls of blondish-red hair. He has sensitive skin, which is why he doesn't like to shave and often looks shaggy. He's got a recessed tooth on his front left side. Early in the day, the gregarious fireplug with the recessed tooth can look especially shaggy, not to say green-glassy-eyed, not to say ready to knock your own teeth out, and this will probably be due to a lack of sleep and maybe a little too much beer the night before. He doesn't sleep well to begin with—he's usually too popped up from his long hours at work. Some nights he doesn't get home until midnight or one in the morning. He'll toss and turn on his black rubber water bed and then he might get up as early as 4 or 4:30 because he's got a 6 A.M. department heads' meeting at the Home Depot. The store he's assigned to is about forty-five minutes away, in Southaven, Mississippi, up in the Memphis metropolitan area, just below the Tennessee state line. He'll rattle up the interstate in his old beater through the north Mississippi darkness: *Good morning, America, how are you, don't you know me, I'm Johnny Cothran, your native son and working stiff.* He'll make it to the store in time for the meeting, and then he'll start his regular shift—say, from seven to three—and then he'll maybe take an hour break before he goes across the parking lot of the same suburban shopping mall, to the Kroger supermarket, where he'll tie on an apron and begin stocking shelves for another five or six hours. Then he's off—until the next day. He doesn't work like this week in and week out, but he's been doing versions of it, on and off, for many years now. He has no choice. He's a man ever strapped for money. He pays child support for four kids to two women.

"I only count the last two," he says, wishing to get off the subject of how many times he's been married, of how confusing it all seems now, not least to himself. He's been married to four women thus far. Why doesn't he wish to count his first two marriages? "Too far back," he says, shooting a brownish-yellow stream through the split in his front teeth. He's grinning his easy, infectious grin. The stream of juice is from a glop of Skoal Long Cut tobacco bulged in his lower lip. He sends it out in an arc, and the juice hits the ground about four feet from his tennis shoes. His beat-up sneaks look to be about a size six or seven—this compact man with the Popeye forearms has small hands as well as feet. He wouldn't spit the juice from his chew if he were indoors. One of the things you discover about him, no matter what's on the outside, is his inclination for neatness. He desires order in his disordered life. If you go into his bare bathroom and open a closet, you'll find towels and facecloths folded carefully on a shelf. They are thin, practically worn through, and there aren't many. Same thing with his toothbrush and comb and toothpaste: lined up on the back of the toilet, on a paper towel, as if a cleaning lady had come through and straightened things.

At the Depot, which is how he refers to his primary place of employment, they slice up his check three ways. "Two of my ex-wives get cut a paycheck just like I do," he says, with something like mystification in his voice. John never sees the taken money—the Depot just records it on his pay stub. In its own way, this is relieving. "Courts say you gotta pay child support as long as they stay in school—you mess up and they'll lock you up," he says. "I'm gonna be on their butts to stay in school as long as they can."

Not like their dad, who left school behind at fifteen, hell with it, I'm through, middle of the day, fuck you, you can have it. "Yeah, I went eight weeks in tenth and called it quits," he says. "I had failed ninth, and repeated it, and passed, and went into tenth, and just hated it. Bad teachers, no one who'd believe in me. An English teacher who didn't take any interest at all. I fell further and further behind. Maybe a lot of it was me, my fault. But I felt stupid, I hated it, it was humiliating, I got up one day and said, 'You can have it, I quit.' She said, 'What do you mean?' I said, 'I quit, I've had it.' They were all sitting there and I just walked right out. Didn't even bother to check books in. I called Daddy. He said, 'I'll come get you.' He did, right away. He also said, 'If you don't have a full-time job by this time tomorrow, don't come home.'"

By the next day, Johnny Cothran was sacking groceries and helping the old ladies load them into their cars at the Big Star supermarket in Greenwood. The teen started at a buck-ninety an hour and three and a half years later he was up to three seventy-five an hour, and he'd progressed by then to one of the best and fastest shelf stockers in the place, and by then, too, he was in and out of a first marriage—which had lasted roughly six weeks. The old Greenwood ladies, whose bags he used to load, liked him a good deal—there's always been a natural kindness, even softness, in this rough man's rough character. That could be said to be the leitmotif of his life, of his story: a remarkable and complex humanity that's obscured, masked, by the chaos of his history, so much of which he's brought on himself. The chaos, that is.

A lot of Cothrans have gotten only as far as tenth—the grade seems to be a family demarcation line for formal learning. John's mom, Alice Cothran, a housewife, quit in tenth. His father, Billy Cothran, who has spent much of the last decade selling cars and pickups in the town of Grenada, quit in tenth. His sister, Carolyn, a medical receptionist in Jackson, quit in tenth. His paternal granddad quit in tenth. That was back in the twenties, at a different Delta high school. The future sheriff of Leflore County left school and went straight to work on the land (and in a sense never got off of it, not even in all those years he was a lawman), while his namesake and spiritual heir, five decades later, left Greenwood High and went straight to work as a time-puncher. That was two and a half decades ago, and whatever else you could say about him in the time since, you couldn't say the grandson is afraid of work.

The year he left school, 1978, was also the year the progeny grew an Afro all the way up. It was bright and bushy. They called him Fro. His girlfriend's mom called him Fro With Legs. "That head of hair I had then was so thick, when I'd wash it, it'd take thirty minutes to dry," he says. In snapshots, the Afro looks almost like a fright wig or Ronald McDonald's headgear. His face was narrower then, and the auburn hair literally surrounded the soft, boyish features. What made him decide to grow it? "I don't have a clue," he says. "I couldn't tell you, other than the girls I ran around with liked it." He knew he looked fairly ridiculous, this short white kid walking around nearly all-black Greenwood High with his 'fro. Did he get heckled? "I got it from every angle possible." Did he get in fights? "No, I try to avoid fights. Because I have such a temper. Put it this way. I'm afraid of fighting."

This is another paradox, or at least a surprise, the curious mixture in him of fear and fearlessness, of terrible temper and what could almost be called delicate sensibility. John played Little League baseball in Greenwood—but he wouldn't go out for pony league, the next level up. He was afraid of getting hit by a pitch. On Grandpa's farm, where he worked as a kid for extra money, he'd do almost any chore asked of him except to drive the cotton picker. He was scared it would flip. "It was a three-wheeled thing, and I was sure it was going to turn over and crush me." Once, in sixth grade, the bantam with the bad temper walked away from a fight on the school playground with everybody watching. "I got popped three times before I knew. Black eyes. Pop, pop, pop. I put down my fists and walked away." And yet, as an adult, he's been willing more than once to defend an ex-wife against a bully boyfriend. Usually, it never came to an actual fight, he says—just tough-talking on the phone or in person. And he tells this story too: At one of the grocery companies where he worked for a few years in his twenties, there were many blacks earning minimum wage, or less. The teenage son of the white boss of that company loved going off on the black workers. The son was even fouler in his use of the n-word than the father, who owned the business. One day John, who'd risen to become a mid-level supervisor—with about fifty employees under him, all but five of whom were black—stepped in front of the son. The son was almost twice as big as John. "I told him to lay off. He was just abusing the shit out of one of my black workers. He was going off on one of the oldest men there. He was saying things like 'You goddamn worthless nigger.' The man couldn't quit because he had to have the job. The owner's son told me to mind my own business. He was seventeen. I said, 'Now, there's no question if we go at it here toe-to-toe you'd whip my butt. I'm not questioning that. But I don't think you'd better fight with me, because there's enough stuff laying around here on the floor, and if we get started, I'll pick up a pipe or a board or the first thing I can get my hands on and I'll crack your damn skull in two.' " The owner's son cursed at him and walked off. John didn't get fired. Good thing, because he was in his third shipwreck marriage and a father by then.

Another admirable quality: He tends not to duck a question that he knows is going to cast him in a bad or embarrassing light—and the answer, when you check later, turns out to be mostly accurate. You ask if he's ever been in jail and he pauses. The Cothran curve of smile. "Only once. Four days once in a jail in Webster County for driving on a suspended license. I was coming back to Greenwood in a truck for the produce company. I'd been over to Alabama. I was driving almost dead on empty, so I fell in behind an eighteen-wheeler to pick up his wind draft. State trooper pulls me over and took me to jail when he found out I was on a suspended license for unpaid tickets. Thing that hurt me is I had to stay in that jail four days. Nobody from my family would come to bail me out."

You ask about the first two marriages—the one that lasted a month and a half and the second, when he was nineteen, that went about nine months. What he chiefly remembers about these marriages is the fighting and his substance abuse. He recalls that his first wife—she was also eighteen—had a child from another union. "What happened with wife number one?" he says, cocking his head sideways. "It was grass and speed and booze. Basically, I was a speed freak. I'd party to four or five in the morning and then get up and try to go to work." They fought, he left, he came back for a week, they broke up again, she left with the child for Louisiana. John went from 145 pounds to 118 pounds. (His weight always tends to balloon or plunge during periods of emotional stress.) Once, in the middle of it, his father came to the door. "I want to see my son," Billy Cothran said. "Well, he's standing right here," the son said. "No, this is not my son," his father said, turning and going to his car. Afterward, John says, he began kicking most of the dope habit, if not the excessive drinking. The last time he saw his first ex was a few years back, at a balloon festival in Greenwood, when his fourth ex was pregnant with the twins, Sara Elizabeth and Joseph Tyler. Sara and Joseph are the children John calls "my babies," even though they're in the early years of primary school. He is extremely devoted to his babies, and some of that must have to do with the recognition of how badly he's screwed things up with his two older children. Ashley Nicole and J. J. live several hours away, with their mom, in the eastern part of the state. J. J. has had serious health problems from infancy.

"I hate myself for it now, because I realize I can never get that time back with them," he says one day, standing in the middle of the room and nearly spitting out the word "hate." He's referring to the long period when he didn't see them. But on another day, in a calmer voice, he says, with no judgment of the various parties involved: "Well, it wasn't all my fault that I didn't see my older ones for three years. Put it this way. My last two ex-wives just didn't click." John's last two ex-wives are very different personalities, according to John. The third is a "real country girl type," he says, while the fourth is much more uptown. He started courting his third when she was sixteen. She got only as far as sixth or seventh grade in school, he says. "Me and a buddy was dating her and her cousin. I was with the cousin, he was with her. One night I said to my buddy, 'Hey, something's wrong here. We're dating the wrong women. We ought to reverse this thing.' So the next night we went back out there to pick them up and we traded dates, and that's the way it was." This is the way he tells stories, without artifice or irony, straight ahead.

One of John's expressions is "put it this way." "Put it this way," he'll say. "I was a great-uncle at thirty-six." Meaning that his sister's child had a baby as a teenager. John's only sibling, two years older than he is, got married at fifteen to a boy who was seventeen, and in the next generation her daughter repeated the pattern. Teenage marriage runs deep with the Cothrans. John's mom, Alice, was a bride at sixteen.

"Put it this way," he'll say. "Most of my career has been spent in the grocery business." He has sacked and shelved at Big Star, Wal-Mart Super Center, Jitney-Jungle, Piggly Wiggly, Kroger. This is one reason why he has such powerful legs and forearms: all that "throwing" of twenty-four-can cases of, say, Del Monte peaches or Franco-American SpaghettiOs. You rip open the box. You price the lids with a stamper. You rack the cans on a shelf. "What you're doing is dropping to a concrete floor with a case of stock," he says. "More or less, as I pick it up and see where it goes on the shelf, I drop right with it." This has killed his knees and half wrecked his back, but he can still get the case off the dolly and throw with the best of them. "It's about speed and know-how," he says. "You take the flat-knife box cutter and make a rectangle and you cut the top off in one cut. You're turning the box as you cut. You use your thumb as a guideline, a straight-edge. As you're pulling the lid off the box, you're reaching for your stamper. It's in a leather holster on your apron, and you go right down the lids of the cans and put the price on. Bam-bam-bam-bam."

John has driven a twenty-four-foot "bob" truck for an interstate produce company, getting to glimpse parts of America that he never expected to see: Texas, Alabama, Florida, Georgia, Oklahoma. On that job, he and a partner would do turnarounds, catching fifteen-minute naps at rest stops before heading back to Mississippi. This is because the owner refused to put them up on the other end, he says. But he loved the feeling of freedom the road provided.

When he first broke into grocery work, all they'd let him do was sack on the front end. Three years later, Jitney-Jungle offered him five dollars an hour to stock shelves. That was a dollar and a quarter more than he was making at Big Star. He quit in the morning and began throwing for the competitor that same afternoon. He thought he was rich. This was 1982, and he'd been out of school for almost four years, not yet twenty, divorced twice. After several years at the Jungle, they made him head stocker. He was outworking everybody in the place.

At Big Star, the managers used to hold weekly time tests. The idea was to see how many cases of stock you could throw in half an hour. The fastest stocker in the store would get a free lunch or sometimes even an afternoon off. John got to where he could throw thirty-five to forty cases in thirty minutes, which was usually good enough for second place. There was another guy there whose name was James. "He was from Illinois. He could throw fifty cases in a half hour. Now, that's pricing. And the thing was, James never looked like he was working. We got to be pretty good friends. He was black. He was in his twenties. I forget his last name. I'd be sacking on the front end, next to the cashiers, and when it got slack, I'd ease down the aisles where they were stocking. I asked him if he'd show me how. He said okay. That's how I learned. I'll never forget that guy."

John Ed Cothran's grandson has never been to an art museum or the ballet or a symphony hall. "No, never been to anything like that," he says. Pause. Grin. "I have been to an aquarium. At the Memphis Zoo. Now, that just might be a fish thing." What about classical music—ever tuned it in on your car radio? "Yes, I've tried to listen to that," he says. "That don't click." But a memory has bulbed inside him—he's making a connection to the question. He puts down his knife and fork, props them on opposite sides of his dinner plate. He's been sawing on a piece of chicken-fried steak at a truck-stop restaurant, which is around the corner from where he sleeps. "Have you ever seen the moon through a telescope?" he asks. He tells this story: A few years ago he was bunking with a guy named Perry, who drove a truck. Perry had all these interesting friends. One was a guy who worked at some kind of drafting job. "He's an artist," John says. "Well, he more or less draws. Some kind of drafting job, I think. His name is Gary and he owns a telescope. I refer to him as an old burnt-out hippie, you know, long hair pulled back, sideburns. We used to spend a lot of time over at Gary and his wife's." One night, he and Perry and Gary were drinking beer and shooting the shit. Gary didn't like the music on the radio. He told his wife to cut off the radio and to go get the telescope out of the closet. The three males went out into the yard. It was a beautiful and clear night. Gary said, "You ever looked at the moon, Cothran?" John: "Course. I'm looking at the moon right now." Gary: "No, I mean have you ever seen it?" John: "Okay, show me what the moon looks like." Gary focused the telescope and said, "Take a look."

John stayed out there for three hours. They couldn't get him to go back inside. Everybody had to go to work the next day. "Put it this way," he says. "I never knew anything like that could be so beautiful, never had any idea. That moon was luminous. I guess I never really got onto the word 'luminous' until I saw the moon in a telescope."

A luminous and soft Sunday evening in September several years ago, at John's place. One saggy yellow sofa. One bad painting above the sofa. One blurry TV. One water bed. A couple of dinner plates and knives and forks and spoons. Some napkins and a roll of paper towels. Some bath towels and facecloths and toiletries. An automatic coffeemaker and a box of paper filters. A couple of food items in the fridge. And Fred the philodendron.

These are roughly the furnishings of Unit C, 311 Evelyn Street, Senatobia, Mississippi. It's a duplex, what's known in the South as a "shotgun" house: three small rooms lined up one behind the other. Out on the concrete stoop, illumined by a yellow bulb, there's a shiny green barbecue grill, unused. The rent here is $300 a month. The renter's blue Nissan King Cab pickup is out in the driveway. In the bed of the truck, which is rusting out and has a bad transmission, are four or five bags of garden mulch from the Depot. His fourth ex is supposed to come over and pick them up tonight.

She gave him the execrable painting over the sofa. "She said it would go real nice in my living room," he says.

"Well, it's a roof," he'd said the day before, opening the screen door, and then standing aside and letting his guest go first. But that was a quick look. Tonight he has a lot more time to talk. This is the third conversation in four days. John was off today. He slept in and spent most of the afternoon across town, at his ex's, playing with the babies. Last night, after he got off work, he and a buddy went to a beer joint up near Memphis. "If you're paying," John had told his buddy, since he didn't have any money. His buddy was. They were hoping to run into loose women, but no luck. He got home to Senatobia at about three in the morning. Senatobia's a little burg right off I-55, straight south of Memphis. If you were hurtling to New Orleans and had last gassed up, say, in rural Tennessee, you might have a reason to pull off and refuel your belly and car at the BP truck-stop station adjacent to the exit ramp. When he's in Senatobia and goes out to eat, John heads for the BP station.

You keep thinking that the shiny, green, unused barbecue grill out on his stoop looks all wrong amid these lean cultural holdings.

"That's Fred," he says, nodding at the plant in the blue plastic pot on the kitchen counter. Fred's been around since 1993 and, like his owner, has gone through extremely bad days. "Bought him at a little old flea market place out there on Park Avenue in Greenwood." He gave Fred to the woman destined to be his fourth wife while they were still courting. Every time they'd fight, Fred would go down, get weak. They'd make up, Fred would perk right up. Once, after a fight, he seized Fred and took him to his place. "She comes for it, and we're pulling at it, and she says, 'It's mine, you gave it to me,' and I say, 'No, by damn, woman, you won't have it,' and she's still trying to get it away from me, and I pull away from her and throw it clear across the room and it smashes against the wall." But Fred survived. John married his fourth wife, and every time they fought, Fred seemed to wilt, and then they'd make up, and he'd get good again. "Sounds crazy, I know," he says. About three or four months before he moved out—that was the summer of 1998—Fred was apparently pretty yellow, but John was so enraged then that he didn't notice. After the divorce, in November of that year, he asked for custody of Fred. He's been nursing him back ever since. Fred's up to about a half-dozen fresh green leaves on his spindly stalk.

The working man is in shorts and sneakers and a sleeveless blue jersey. He looks puffy. He's up 20 pounds, he says. He's carrying 175 pounds on his five-foot-eight frame. He's been as high as 190. It's the stress of his supervisor's job at the Depot that's causing him to go up again, he says. Six months ago, they made him head of the kitchen and bath department. He was proud, but there's so much damn paperwork to fill out. Writing evaluations for his workers—"associates" is how they're referred to at the Depot—drives him crazy. "I write real short sentences," he says.

He's at the kitchen counter, brewing a couple quarts of tea. "I have me a glass of brewed tea and a BC tablet every morning of my life," he says. "That's breakfast. BC headache tablets are about as far as I go now with drugs." He pours sugar from a one-pound sack into a green plastic pitcher—doesn't measure it out, just holds the sack in two hands and dumps a large amount in. He adds the water, then stirs the water and sugar into a solution, then pours it into the back of the coffeemaker. He dumps loose tea into the filter part of the apparatus. "Done," he says. While he's cleaning up, you ask whether nursing Fred back to health isn't connected in some way to the telescope story, or to the sixth-grader who put down his fists and refused to fight in the schoolyard, or to the kid who wouldn't go out for pony league because he was scared of getting hit by a pitch. He considers this. "I have been told I'm very kindhearted," he says. He wipes off the drain board with a rancid-looking sponge. "I ain't got two chairs," he says. "I'm a poor man. We can go outside and talk if you want. I can drop the tailgate of my truck and we can do redneck style."

Outside, in the saffron evening, with the electric drone of the crickets and cicadas just coming up, the talk winds this way and that. He tells of an old teacher—dead now—"who believed in me, only one. He taught history and science. It was eighth grade. He called me aside and said, 'You can do this stuff, Cothran.' After that, I never got below a ninety on a science paper for him. Every other teacher I ever had, I felt stupid."

He recounts the hotheaded thing he said to his last ex's lawyer during divorce proceedings the previous year. "I told him I'd do whatever I had to do in order to 'take' my kids. I didn't say, 'I'll do whatever I have to do to see my kids.' I got mad. I said, 'Listen, they're my kids just like hers, I'll do whatever I have to do to take my kids, you got it?' Her lawyer said I'd be sorry for saying that, and of course he was right." According to the divorce decree, John has to have his ex's stated consent every time he wishes to see his children—and it has to be done with her supervision.

He tells of a fellow worker at the Depot with whom he's gotten friendly. He's full of tattoos. He's from San Diego and has five kids. The Depot moved him from California to Memphis when the company was opening more stores in Tennessee. "You look at him and you'd think he was a grunge rock freak. But, see, it's all Christian-based. You gotta take a closer look. It's stuff like 'Sin Kills' and 'Jesus Protects.' Me and him was taking freight out to the dock one day, and I said, 'I'm tired of this fucking shit,' something like that, I can't even remember now what it was I was mad at. And he looks at me and he says, 'You just enjoy cussing like that, don't you?' I look back at him and said, 'I've never thought about it.' But that was it. Now, I just won't swear in front of him or do any kind of dirty talking, because I know he doesn't want to hear it."

He describes a black man he used to work with at the produce wholesaler in Greenwood. "His name was Jerry. We called him J-Boy. Huge guy. I got mad at him once and yelled bad things at him. Next day I said, 'J-Boy, I apologize for yelling at you. I'm a supervisor here and you're an employee of the company, but I didn't show respect to you.' So he comes over and hugs me. He ended up saying, 'I love you, Cothran.' After that we really got to be friends. I'd say to him, 'You sorry-ass white boy,' and he'd say right back, 'Yeah, you ain't nothing but a sorry-ass nigger.' "

There's a loud *pop* from the darkness. It seems to have come from another street. "Transformer box went out again," he says. "Let's go look." On the next block, a small crowd of kids and adults are gathering below a utility pole. There are still sparks jumping from the box at the top of the pole. The kids lean on their bikes and watch; the adults greet one another. It's like Sunday evening free neighborhood fireworks. "We come out to watch the transformers blow," John says.

Back at his place, the talk again trombones toward one thing and the next, but the subtext of the conversation, race, is a word that hasn't been uttered, not in any direct way. Headlights illumine the corner at Evelyn Street. Is his fourth ex coming for the mulch? The car is about a hundred yards away. The subject of race and racial attitudes has just slid into the conversation: The visitor has said there's something he'd like to discuss.

"What's that?" says John, knowing exactly what it is. He spits the juice. "I think we timed that just about right," he says. "My ex is here." The car comes closer, and he realizes it isn't hers. "Damn." He grins. And yet, with the word having been said out loud, he seems almost eager to discuss race—as if there's something freeing in it. "Now, okay, as far as the race thing goes, you want to talk about it, and maybe you don't agree with me on this, but I don't believe in the business of, what's the word I'm looking for, you know, when the blacks and whites are getting married?"

Interracial marriage?

"I don't hold with that. I see it all the time in the store. They come in, white woman with a black husband."

On the n-word: "I used to use it all the time, but I've gotten away from it." Why?

"I guess, well, sort of realizing how offensive it is to that race."

Has he felt this way for a long time?

"No. I'm talking probably in the last ten years—maybe even five, maybe even less than that. I catch myself at work all the time. I'll say to one of my black workers at the Depot in my department, 'Listen, there's a black guy over there in the next aisle in a blue shirt. Go help him.' And I catch myself—but it's always after the fact. I say to myself, 'Now, why'd you have to bring color into it? Why didn't you just say, 'Go help that customer in the blue shirt?'

Probably ten years ago, shit, maybe five, I'd have said, or wanted to say, or probably would've thought about saying, 'Go over and help that nigger standing over there, nigger, hear?' Course, you couldn't say that and work at the Depot. They wouldn't stand for it. We have these training sessions twice a month—eight hours on respect for customers and coworkers. And don't get me wrong, what I'm trying to tell you here. I'd say we have blacks in Mississippi, and we have some niggers in Mississippi, in the same way that we have white people, and we have white trash here. But I don't use the word nigger anymore. Or I try not to."

Does he slip?

"Course I slip, what do you think?" Then: "But I guess where I'm at now, I wouldn't want that said to me, either. I guess that's the reason I don't say 'nigger' any more."

Could the change in the way he looks at all this have something to do with the pain of his own failures? "Maybe."

Then: "Maybe it's been happening for a long time, and I never noticed. I remember being around blacks all the time on the farm who worked for grandpa. It was easy to say 'nigger.' I ran around in school with guys who did it for sport. But even then I guess it was starting to bother me. Not that I stopped using it. It was just bothering me a little. I remember out there in Greenwood where Highway 82 and the Humphreys Highway come together. You go down Bowie Lane and it takes you right into the heart of what they call Niggertown. We were out there one night, bunch of us. There was this black guy on a bike, older guy. One of my buddies worked for the city and he had a can of mace to repel dogs with. We got the car up alongside the old man on the bike and my buddy sprayed mace at him and the guy crashed his bike and started yelling and everybody in the car's just roaring. I said, 'Y'all take me home. I don't want any part of this.' They said, 'Hey, John, it ain't nothing but a nigger.' I said, 'I don't care, take me home.' See, if I have to act like that to get in trouble, I don't need it. Because they're going to bring me down with them. I mean, even when Daddy wants to tell me a dirty joke now, even if it's got nothing to do with blacks, it makes me feel uncomfortable."

He gets up from the bed of the truck. "Guess she's not coming," he says. "Let's go inside. I want to get something."

He's in the back room, where he sleeps. You can hear him rooting for something. In a minute he's back and standing in the middle of the living room. In his hand are some sheets of paper. They look like they've been torn from a notebook. He hands over several of the sheets. They're poems. "Like you said, you thought I had this sensitive side," he says. "I think the first one of these I wrote her, I called it 'You,' " he says. "For my fourth. I wrote these for her."

"You" is in three stanzas. It begins: "When I'm with you I can not see / I get all nervous when I'm with thee / I get all jittery I don't know what to do / I can't explain how I feel when I'm with you."

"She read it and she said, 'Where'd you copy this from?' I said, 'Right outta here. My heart.' She said, 'You're lying.'"

Almost choking, standing in the middle of the room, he says: "You're the only person I've showed this to." Then: "I snuck them out of the house on Bowden Street that we were living in when I left. I'm not sure she knows they're gone."

There's another poem called "Friends Forever." It opens: "To have a friend like you / Is as special as they come / I would not know what to do / If this was undone." The verse is four stanzas long and is initialed at the bottom, "J.T.C."

"Not bad for a dumb-ass dropout," says the head of the kitchen and bath department at Home Depot, who makes about $11 an hour and hopes to gross about $30,000 for the year and who goes now to the screened door of his $300-a-month rental and arcs a stream of gloppy liquid out into the yellow-bulbed semidarkness. Arcs it nifty as you please. Slickers couldn't do that on a bet.

In *Notes of a Native Son,* James Baldwin wrote, "I imagine that one of the reasons people cling to their hates so stubbornly is because they sense, once hate is gone, that they will be forced to deal with pain."

Back up a generation, to John's mother and father. Billy and Alice Cothran, deep believers, Christian fundamentalists, live in a small community called Gore Springs out toward Carver Point, on Grace Road, far back in the country, about an hour and a quarter away from their only son. (Billy and Alice, in turn, live about seventy miles and about an hour and a quarter away from Billy's dad and stepmom, John Ed and Maudine, who are in the middle of the Delta. These upper Mississippi distances tend to get bridged in Cothran pickups.) John's folks are great-grandparents, but not at all what you'd think of as elderly. Billy's in his mid-sixties; Alice is in her late fifties. Billy looks like a younger, fitter version of the old lawman: bald and reddish cueball head, gold-rimmed glasses, stocky frame, thick ankles, shiny shins, meaty fingers, muscular forearms with curls of the trademark Cothran blondish hair. Alice has a sweet, round, grandmomish face on her small, round figure. They seem to have a comfortable life and appear content with each other, but when you spend time with them, it becomes increasingly clear that their hearts ache over the fact that their two children don't attend church or profess much belief in a savior and have somehow been married seven times in the aggregate.

John's parents worship at the Church of Christ. The Church of Christ goes strictly by what the Bible says. Literal interpretation, as Billy says: "You don't add to it, you don't take from it. If it ain't in the Bible, you don't do it." Divorce is not in the Bible. Having children out of wedlock is not something sanctioned by the Bible. There's no instrumental music in Billy and Alice's church, and that's because nowhere in the Bible is there a reference to instrumental music.

One way to find their place, which is east of the town of Grenada, is to look for a sign nailed to a tree: JESUS IS LORD OF THIS COMMUNITY. You take a left there and a quick right and another quick right and then stop at the handsome brown house that has bulged itself outward over the years from a double-wide trailer. Thanks to Billy's carpentry skills and to Alice's homemaking skills, the place looks like anything but a mobile home now. It's a little Shangri-la in the woods, with a trickling stream running through. Billy has done the additions himself, wiring walls, making corners mortared and tight. Inside, there are many knickknacks and homey touches: Alice's extensive collection of Aunt Jemima dolls, Billy's wood carvings of toy boats, other objects.

He's always been handy as a box of tacks. Back in the fifties, after he'd dropped out of school and gone into the Air Force, he trained to be a radio operator and picked it up in no time. This gave him a trade when he got home to Mississippi at the dawn of the civil rights era: TV and radio repair. He had his own Greenwood shop, Cothran Electronic Service, until he went to work for his dad in the sheriff's department as a deputy and a jailer. He sold the business "to the boy who was working for me," although he still did repair work on the side. He liked being a lawman and making extra cash by fixing up people's TVs. He didn't like working on the TVs of people on the south side of the river, because they had a way of not paying, he says. Anyway, he got called up to service again, and that put sheriffing and TV repair on hold. This was during the Berlin Crisis, and when he got back to Mississippi, everything about his country seemed different.

He'd gone to Uncle Sam the first time in the fall of 1955, a seventeen-year-old who'd always struggled with the books and had been left back a time or two. A month and a half before, in late August, Emmett Till had been murdered in the Delta and dumped in the Tallahatchie: another kind of pattern. That same summer, John Ed Cothran, who'd helped recover the body and who was chief deputy of the county to Sheriff George Smith, had run for sheriff—unsuccessfully. He'd come in third in the August primary. Then Till was kidnapped and killed. To reprise: The corpse was found on August 31, and that afternoon's front page of the *Greenwood Commonwealth* described how "Deputy Sheriff John Edd Cothran and Deputy Sheriff Ed Weber went to the scene and carried Mose Wright, uncle of the youth, along in order to make identification of the body. It was brought back to Greenwood and turned over to the Century Burial Association." Two days later, on Friday, September 2, John Ed's picture was published on page 35 of the *Memphis Commercial Appeal,* squatting next to a gin fan in his snap-brim fedora and white summer shirt with the sleeves rolled up his muscular upper arms, with his Leflore County deputy's badge visible on his left breast. "USED IN SLAYING," the caption said. Who could have known the import of the moment?

Not Billy Cothran, who had a wild hair in him and wanted only to escape from school and the Delta in 1955. Twenty-three years later, the same high school, another autumn, his fifteen-year-old son would have similar longings. Billy worked briefly for an uncle in construction (he'd gotten a job by the next day, because that was how John Ed had laid down the law), then told his father he didn't want to be crawling around on roofs when the cold weather came. Since Billy was under age, John Ed had to give his written consent for the enlistment. Billy did basic training at Lackland Air Force Base in San Antonio, then went to electronics school at Scott Air Force Base outside St. Louis. The following July, the recruit pulled out of the Brooklyn Naval Yard bound for Europe on a ship filled with servicemen. He spent much of his tour in Germany, which he loved. Sometimes fellow G.I.'s asked him about the South and race relations, and he'd say, "In Mississippi, we've got black people, and we've got niggers." He was thirty-seven months overseas, and when he got back to the States, in August 1959, he was twenty-one and a man and figured he'd sown his wild oats and was ready to settle down. His dad had just won the county primary for sheriff, even as the noted and folksy damage-suit lawyer Ross Barnett in the capital city had triumphed in the gubernatorial primary.

Billy lost no time courting his future wife. He and Alice were married six months later on February 12, 1960, which was also five weeks after his dad had taken the oath of office as sheriff of Greenwood and Leflore County. Eisenhower was president, and his handpicked successor was Richard Nixon, but Senator John Kennedy was running hard for the nomination of the other party. (In six months' time, James Meredith would come out of the Air Force and back to Mississippi with one mission.) Billy and Alice were married by a JP in the kitchen of the county jail. They'd both been talking to their preachers about a ceremony—Alice was Baptist, Billy was Church of Christ—but Billy was impatient and said to Alice, "Honey, let's just get it done." In attendance were the groom's parents, John Ed and Maggie, whom people called "Mack," just as those who've known John Ed well have always referred to him as Jack. Besides Jack and Mack, the marriage of the twenty-one-year-old to the sixteen-year-old was witnessed by the jail cook and the new sheriff's deputies: Noel McCool, Boll Weevil Stowers, Jack Poss, Ed Weber, and Wardine Smith. Big Smitty hulked in the small space with his massive stomach and hooded eyes, and even now, more than forty years onward, Alice can see him looming there. Her parents did not attend the Friday-morning nuptials. It snowed like hell in Greenwood that afternoon, but the newlyweds had already gone to bed and pulled the curtains. That evening, the new husband stepped outside in his bare feet—and crunched into snow: "What the hell is this?" he called in to his bride, roaring with laughter. It felt like a sign from above.

On Monday, Billy went back to work at his TV repair shop. Soon, though, he became a full-time deputy to his dad and moved into the jail with his wife. A year later, in February 1961, Billy and Alice's daughter, Carolyn, was born and the infant was brought home to the living quarters in the jail. Billy had lived there as a boy, when John Ed was a deputy to Sheriff George Smith, but his wife could never get used to the idea of being so close to prisoners, especially with a baby daughter. The jailer's apartment had a living room, two and a half bedrooms, two baths. The white men's cell was on the same floor. The black men's cell was upstairs on the fourth floor, as were the white women's cell and the black women's cell. Alice knew the prisoners couldn't get to her—there was a double-steel door going into her living room—but there they were, above her head, just across the hall. They'd bang on the bars with their tin plates and scream profanities and carry on to all hours. A decade before, when Jack and Mack had lived in the jail with their children, the screaming and the banging had seriously upset Maggie, and Billy wonders now if this didn't have something to do with his mom's early demise, from colon cancer, at age fifty-three, in 1972.

There's an odd pattern of death among the Cothrans—the dying always seems to occur on birthdays of other family members. For instance, Maggie Cothran died on the birthday of her grandson, John Cothran. Maggie's own mother, Willie Mae Granthan, had died on her daughter's birthday. John Ed's father had died on John Ed's birthday. Billy and Alice's explanation of this phenomenon is that the ways of God are unfathomable.

In the fall of 1961, Billy got called back to the Air Force. He was gone a year, until October 1962, right after James Meredith had caused all that trouble at Ole Miss and right as the Cuban Missile Crisis was happening. By then, the local papers were full of headlines such as "Negro Marchers Found Guilty," and by then, too (as Billy was wont to say after he got home), seems there were a helluva lot more niggers in Mississippi than black people. He put on the star again (Boll Weevil Stowers had become the jailer in his absence) and worked for his father until August 1963. By then, John Ed's term of office was nearly over, and it was state law that he couldn't succeed himself, and so the son decided to interview for a civil service job at the Greenwood post office. On August 7, 1963, three and a half months before John Kennedy died in Dallas, Billy and Alice's redheaded son was born, and they named him after Billy's father.

This is the past, as it wraps in and around other pasts. These days, lawman no more, not for a long time now, not a postal worker either (that experience ended badly), Billy Cothran is in the car business. On his business card for Grenada Nissan, it says: "W. T. (Billy) Cothran, Sales Representative." He's nearly always number one when the monthly totals are added up. He figures he's moved something like 1,500 units off the lot. Once, in a lapse of faith, he left Grenada Nissan and went over to Sunset Chrysler to try his hand. In the good weather, he's at the dealership from early in the morning until seven in the evening. He sits there and waits on them to come in. He doesn't go in for the hard sell. He likes to sidle up and be friendly, get them into the vehicle (VEE-hicle is how he pronounces it). If he can get them behind the steering wheel in the first ten or fifteen minutes, he figures he may have a deal. He's been accused of losing a few deals because he wasn't aggressive enough. But he can't stand to pressure them, especially these young couples who come in with babies. They remind him of when he was a broke young buck starting out with Alice so many years ago.

He'll pass the time between nibbles sitting in a Naugahyde chair out in the rugless, open showroom, or he'll stare at daytime TV, or he'll do paperwork in his corner office, which has a good view of the lot, where he can watch them coming in. One wall of his office is covered with plaques. According to Billy, the bosses pretty much stopped handing out sales awards because he'd won almost all of them. It was demoralizing to his colleagues. "I do believe my daddy could sell a man the hat on the top of his head," John Cothran says of his father. The Grenada dealership doesn't have a quota system, not per se, says Billy. It does have a "demo" program, meaning that if you sell seven units in a month, you get to drive back and forth from home in a model of your choice. Billy always chooses a pickup.

His office at work is full of what you might call Billyness: little shellacked wood carvings and some mounted corny jokes. He's got a jar of "dehydrated water" on his desk. (It's just a jar.) At Christmas, he likes to decorate the office with his wife's arts and crafts: a string of colored bulbs, for instance, arranged in a wreathlike cluster of plastic cups. Billy also passes the time between customers by working on his newsletter, which he subsidizes from his own pocket. "Published Monthly By: W. T. 'Billy' Cothran, Sales Consultant, Grenada Nissan" it says on the front of the newsletter. On the inside, it might say, "GREAT THINGS ARE HAPPENING AT GRENADA NISSAN!!!!" Before telling what they are, he'll spin out the latest news from the Mississippi Redneck Mother. He invented her for his newsletter. A sample of her wit and wisdom from an installment several years ago, following the presidential elections: "A Mississippi Redneck Mother writes another letter to her Son that went like this: Dear Son, MERRY CHRISTMAS. Do you know the difference between Al

Gore and a new-born puppy? Well, let me tell you. After three weeks a new-born puppy opens it's eyes and quits whining. I read in the paper where they ain't having a Nativity scene at the White House this year. After searching far and wide, they couldn't find no Wise Men in Washington. Have you noticed that late-night television has become very educational? It teaches the very important fact that we should go to bed earlier. Will write more next time, Love, Ma."

On Sunday, day of rest, the Lord's day, following morning worship, Billy might fiddle with something around the house, or drive to Moorhead to visit his father, or sit back and listen to country music (he loves ol' George Jones, considers Willie Nelson too uptown), or go jig fishing on Grenada Lake. He's a crappie man, doesn't fool with bass. "Them things stink," he says in his best Mississippi redneck accent. Occasionally, he'll stick a minnow on the jig, though mostly he just uses the jig rig itself and sinks it deep. He'll sit there, waiting on them. Occasionally, his son will get time off to go with him, and then Billy might tell a couple of dirty jokes, which may or may not have the n-word in them, and, even if they don't will still make his son uncomfortable, just because of the dirtiness. Not that John would say so to his father.

Today is a Sunday, an afternoon in April several years ago, the first meeting with Billy. This initial visit to the Shangri-la in the woods, on Grace Road, is taking place *before* the first meeting with Billy and Alice's son. Indeed, one of the things urgently and secretly hoped for from this visit with John's parents is John's home phone number. (One of the things to be discovered today is that John doesn't have a home phone.) So far, in terms of the chronology of events, the infiltrator has spent many hours in Moorhead with John Ed and Maudine, although increasingly over these past months he has felt the need to move down the family ladder, most especially to the third generation.

The talk has been going pleasantly enough for about two hours. Billy's on a green metal two-seat glider on his porch. He's in an open-collared shirt with a green ballpoint hooked in his shirt pocket. His wife, wearing tinted yellow glasses, is in a chair beside him. She's brought iced lemonade to the porch. It has mostly been family stories. Everyone on the porch, however, is aware of the subtext, which has just come forward in an unshellacked way.

Billy: "I don't care whether you write it or don't write it or whether you forget it or what, I'm just gonna say it. I think the morals of this country disintegrated with forced integration. And the reason I think this is because black people as a whole don't have the same morals as white people—or maybe I'll say it this way: the morals that white people used to have." Here's an example, he says: Just last Friday Alice was in the deli line at Piggly Wiggly and here comes these two blacks, maybe in their twenties, maybe some kind of construction workers, they're coming up behind her and they're using all this f-word profanity—the *effing* way the line is so long, and the *mother-effing* way they're going to have to use up their whole lunch hour getting a sandwich. Everybody else was just waiting their turn. The whole store could hear it. Shameful conduct. "Poor Alice had to listen to that disrespect," Billy says, and there is something hard in his voice. Alice is nodding at the truth of it, and even behind the tinted glasses it's easy to see the narrowing glint in her eyes. Her voice has grown that way, too.

Billy: "It's what I mean when I say black people don't have the morals white people have—or anyway, used to have. You see, if Greenwood, Mississippi, in the nineteen-sixties would have been let alone to solve its own problems, we wouldn't have had all those problems with the federal government."

"Let alone to solve its own problems," Alice repeats.

The visitor says he'd like to read these words back to Billy. "Exactly. Exactly right," he says, after he's heard them.

The visitor asks if it isn't somehow wrong to make such generalizations about a whole group? Individuals, okay. But a race? A small, strained silence. Alice's hands are folded in her lap. The swing is making creaking noises. Billy: "I don't want you to leave here with the idea that I'm a racist or against all black people. That's not the kind of people we are at all. That wouldn't represent what we think. I wouldn't want to see that representation go in your book. Here's something you wouldn't know. Alice and I defended the right of black folks from Winona, Mississippi, to come to our church at Red Heel. They were Church of Christ over there, and they wanted to come to worship at ours. We have just a very small church, and this caused a split. But I thought it was right, and Alice did, too. We stood up for it. If we were racists or against black people in general, we wouldn't have done that."

Alice is nodding.

"At post office banquets, I'd sit right across from black folks, no problem," Billy says.

Alice, her voice softening: "You can approach it like this: Who's going to go to heaven? Aren't black people going to go to heaven? Doesn't God want black folks in the kingdom? Sure, he does."

A little later, inside the house, Billy retrieves his son's current phone number. He has it on his speed-dial on his cordless phone. It's the place where John is shacking, over in Arkansas, with that woman with the kids. John's parents and the visitor spend a little time leafing through old family photo albums. From one of these albums, a postcard drops out and paper-airplanes itself to the floor. It lands on its face. Alice reaches down to pick it up. On the front of the postcard is a picture of onetime presidential candidate and famed Alabama segregationist Governor George Wallace. On the back is a machine-generated thank-you note from the governor, with a machine-stamped signature. Billy squints at the card. "Oh, I remember what this is. I donated a little money to his campaign back then. I didn't have much to give, but I gave some."

Alice says, "Well, I guess this is kind of interesting right here, isn't it, this card and what we were talking about a little while ago." She is smiling.

When Billy and Alice's son bolted from his fourth marriage, just about to turn thirty-five and a father of small twins, he was living in a modest but attractive one-story redbrick house on Bowden Street in Senatobia. There was a tire swing under a big tree in the front yard; there were three-wheelers and other toys in the carport; there was a blue Nissan pickup parked in the driveway at odd hours. A person could have driven by that house in the summer of 1998, looked at the swing and the piled toys, and formed a very wrong impression about the lives therein, some sort of fantasy that they were happy lives.

Some months have passed, although it's the same calendar year. The Cothrans have continued to allow the visitor in. The visitor has been with Billy and Alice's son on half a dozen occasions. It's the Christmas season, an important time of year at the Home Depot. On several occasions, the infiltrator has arranged to meet John Cothran at work, and thus has been able to observe an old sheriff's namesake interacting with customers and employees, some of whom are black.

A few months back, on another visit to the home of John's parents, there had been some lengthy and unvarnished talk about Big Smitty. This was asked: Why would John Ed have kept such a hateful bigot on his payroll? Billy answered: "You'd have to understand something about my dad. He's a trusting individual. He wasn't necessarily going to ask what was going on behind his back."

But what about what other people would have told him?

"Well, that's the thing," Billy said. "Some others weren't going to talk about Big Smitty, what he was doing or not doing to the blacks."

Why not?

"Well, afraid of it getting back."

Retaliation against them if Big Smitty found out?

"Yes," Billy said.

Billy and Alice were asked about their son's anger, and about the blur of marriages. "I don't know," Billy said quietly. "I've thought about it a lot."

Alice said: "It may have something to do with squabbling. Billy and I fussed at each other when we were early in our marriage, and maybe they were affected by it—our daughter, Carolyn, and Johnny. Now, as far as John's anger, I don't know. There just seems to be a kind of torment there in our son."

Billy said, "Anyway, we're sorta beyond that now. The squabbling."

But could the squabbling really account for all the anger and divorces? Doesn't every family have its share of parental squabbling? "It's about the only thing I can think," Alice answered. Her husband began talking about how it says in the Bible that the only reason for a marriage to be set aside is infidelity, is adultery. "I can see sometimes where it might be better for two people to be apart," Billy had said.

Now it's a Friday afternoon, two weeks before Christmas, and the supervisor of kitchens and baths at the Southaven Depot store should have been through the front door an hour ago, when he clocked out, but he keeps hanging around his department, shooting the shit, as he likes to say. John doesn't have to work at Kroger today. He's talking to Buddy Harris (this is not his real name), who has worked for the Depot for three years. Buddy recently graduated from a community college with an associate's degree in design and drafting; he's progressed from unloading carts in the parking lot to the paint department to John's department. He seems eager and bright and a little bashful. He is a young black man who seems barely out of his teens.

He tells John he made a $4,000 sale at the end of the night last night. John had clocked out in midafternoon.

"Way to go," John says. They high-five.

"Incidentally, we were first in the division last week," John says.

"Yeah? Wow," Buddy says.

"Yep. Cordova did eighty-six, we did ninety-five thousand. They usually blow everybody out of the water," John says.

The supervisor goes to another part of the department. Of his boss, out of earshot, the employee says, "John's a real nice guy. Down to earth. We don't have any issues at all."

Ariel Jeffords (not her real name) echoes that. She's much older than Buddy. She's white and is married and has worked in various retail jobs. "You might think a guy like John would be sexist," she says. "He's about the kindest guy you could ever find in a boss. I know about his marriages. I hear him talking on the phone to his kids. He loves those twins. In the store, he gets in there and just works with everybody. He's great with pitching in and helping with freight. Only thing, I guess I worry some about whether he can handle the stress of all he's gotta do as a supervisor."

Close to two hours after he has punched out, the supervisor exits the store. At a nearby restaurant, while waiting for a burger and fries to arrive, he makes a puddle of ketchup on his plate and pours salt into the middle of the puddle. "I went and bought Christmas for my kids," he says. "Got them those electric four-wheelers—got Tyler the jeep, got Sara the Barbie car. Well, they're both the same thing, just different color and design on them. One of them I've got covered up with a horse blanket in my bedroom next to the water bed. The other one's still in layaway at Wal-Mart. My ex and I went shopping together. We'll get that one out of layaway next week, on payday." He shrugs. "My kids ain't going to be this age but once."

Money's real tight right now, he says. "I bought me a twenty-five-dollar electric heater for my bedroom. Bought two of them—one's a twelve-hundred-watt, other's a fifteen-hundred-watt. It's all I need. The water bed heats the room up pretty good anyway. With those space heaters, I don't have to turn my gas on at all."

Few days ago, he bought himself a four-foot tree and all the trimmings. "Thirty bucks for everything, including the blinkers. The tree folds down. It comes in a box. [My ex's] got a six-foot artificial at her house. I took mine out of the box and fluffed it up and called my ex. 'I need some help,' I said. 'I got an artificial tree that looks like dog shit.' She told me to get some candy canes. I went to the dollar store and bought a box of candy canes and put them on." Then his ex and the kids came over to take a look. His ex stood in the doorway of his apartment while the kids ran into the living room to look at the tree. "My ex said, 'You gonna behave now?' I said, 'Of course. I'm not gonna run off with them, you know that.' It was real nice between us. She said, 'Okay now, I'm going home to take a nap.' First time since the divorce she let me play with the twins without her being there." This last part is said with a glow of pride.

He's asked if he has ever sent out Christmas cards. Shrug. Grin. "Never thought about doing anything like that." How about getting them? "Oh, sure, I've had them. I'll get a Christmas card in the mail this year. I'll get one from my mama."

The talk returns to his anger. "It just follows me. I've tried to stop it. I'm getting better." He tells of a 1978 Chevette he once owned, and how he broke the windshield. He'd been out drinking with his buddies. This was in his third marriage. He and his wife were on food stamps—and he was pissing away with friends whatever little money they had. He went to pick up his wife in the Chevette and she started yelling at him. "I've got my two hands like this, on top of the steering wheel." He swung and broke the windshield, "shattered it, sitting there in the driver's seat, cause she's yelling at me and we're broke and I've been drinking. I say, 'Great. I smashed the windshield. Here's another hundred fifty dollars we gotta find.'"

He hesitates. "In the past, I've gotten mad enough to hit her—hit any of them—and turned away and went outside and hit something." He says he has never hit any of his wives—and wonders how he managed not to.

Where does such rage come from? He shrugs. "Basically, I think it was the drinking. Because back then I was drinking every day."

Were you an alcoholic? "Oh, yeah."

An hour later, at his place in Senatobia, he opens the door and puts on the light. He bends down and puts a plug in a socket, and then his four-foot artificial tree is glittering in a corner, with two red stockings taped up beside it. He puts another plug in a socket and a little electric heater begins to glow orange. "That star cost me three dollars and those string lights a buck and a half apiece," he says, sitting across from the tree on the yellow sofa. "Two sets of them." He gets up and goes across the room and lights a red candle on top of his TV.

For a while, there isn't much talk. Then he says he'd love to get out of this dump and buy a trailer—"one of those Jim Walter mobile homes on a pond around here. Really, I don't even know if there are any ponds around here." Pause. "I haven't asked. I don't want to get my hopes up." Pause again. "I've had a lot more downs than ups, but I think I'm a helluva lot better than the guy I've come from—this dumb-ass dropout who was getting married all over the place and didn't have any money or any kind of job prospects."

With no prompting: "I don't know if it's a matter of growing up and realizing it's not a right thing to do, calling somebody a nigger." The other day, he was talking by phone to another supervisor. The supervisor was a couple of aisles over. John wanted to send a customer to see him. "I said, 'You'll recognize him. He's about my build and he's got a blue cap on.' That's all I said. I didn't say the guy was black. Proud of myself."

He says he'd like to get in his truck and drive over toward his ex's house—not to go in or anything; that wouldn't be appropriate and she probably wouldn't allow it anyway. "She's on the other side of town, in a new housing development. She just bought a beautiful new home—well, her and the bank did. C'mon, I'll show it to you." On the way across town, his Nissan belches and rattles. He's wearing an old coat and an orange Home Depot hat. He's got country music on. He seems almost ready to start singing with the music. He doesn't stop in front of his ex's house, just slowly drives by, making a turn at the cul-de-sac. As he turns, he tries to get a glimpse of his children through the front window. He drives to the next block, parks the truck diagonally, cuts his headlights and engine, rolls down his window. Peering now in darkness through the side yard of a neighbor, he points out his ex's six-foot artificial tree. It's glowing in a window in the rear. "My babies are in there," he says happily. "They gonna have Santy Claus two places this year."

Early the next morning, Sarah and Tyler's dad is at the Depot. Most of his shift is spent working in the store parking lot with a man named Maurice, a supervisor in walls and floors. The two are managing a "fire sale," trying to snare customers before they get inside the front door. Maurice is a muscled black man who looks about forty. In forty-degree cold, he's walking around in a T-shirt. In terms of size, he makes almost two of John. They trade insults. They bring each other coffee, tell raunchy jokes, talk Depot politics. "You poor-ass honky, you don't know shit about being a salesman," Maurice says. "I can whup your black ass in sales," John says.

Later in the morning, he runs into one of his best and oldest Depot friends, Charles Hawkins. They pass each other in the lunchroom. Hawkins has a dollar bill in his fist that he's going to insert in a vending machine. John, with surprising speed, a little cornerback running for daylight, snatches the bill, heads for the door. "I'll just be relieving you of this," he says over his shoulder to the black man. And the black man says, "Oh, I know you think you will, you miserable honky." John hands it back. A moment later, out on the floor, John says: "Since I came here, me and Charles Hawkins have been just like that." He crosses two fingers. "We were in lumber together."

In a better world, it could end there. Six months later, on a June evening, I pulled up to his place in Senatobia. The apartment looked vacant. No one answered the door. I went across the yard and spoke to a neighbor, who told me John had moved out some months before. He was in a mobile home in the country, the neighbor said. It was in a community called Strayhorn, about seven miles from Senatobia. Since there seemed no way to get hold of him (the neighbor was pretty sure he still didn't have a phone), I drove out toward Strayhorn, hoping John wasn't doing a shift at Kroger that evening. I wondered if he had received the several letters I had sent him since our last talk.

As I drove into the countryside, I reflected on what I'd witnessed in Jackson that morning: the arraignment of a former Klansman named Ernest Avants on a thirty-four-year-old murder charge. The victim, Ben Chester White, a sixty-seven-year-old black farmhand with no involvement in the civil rights movement, had been killed by a group of Klansmen on June 10, 1966, in a national forest in the Natchez area. Avants was the only suspect still alive. White had been murdered, the theory went, because the Klan was trying to lure Martin Luther King, Jr., to Natchez. The Klan wished to assassinate King, and they thought that killing White, an innocent old man, might be an effective bait. There are other theories about the slaying, too—but the point is, it was just one more unsolved Mississippi murder, with characteristically grisly details. (The victim was all but decapitated from the final gun blasts.) So I had watched that morning in the James O. Eastland U.S. Courthouse in downtown Jackson as a shackled Ernest Avants was led in for a presumed date with justice at last. He was sixty-nine, hunched, confused, in work boots and bib overalls and a sleeveless denim jacket. He wasn't wearing a shirt. It was as if he'd been outfitted for this time warp by central casting. Beyond the railing, stylishly dressed black reporters, both male and female, from Jackson TV and radio outlets wrote notes on legal pads as the federal murder indictment was read aloud to the prisoner. Once before, in 1967, Avants had been tried and acquitted for White's murder, even though he had submitted a statement to FBI agents acknowledging that he had shot White with a shotgun (claiming, however, that he had fired after White was already dead from other blasts). The State of Mississippi had conducted that trial. He was being charged anew with the crime because latter-day researchers and federal investigators had made the discovery that White was killed on federal property, in the Homochitto National Forest. Thus federal prosecutors also had jurisdiction in the case and thus Avants could now be indicted on a federal murder charge for a civil-rights-era crime. The killing of Ben White was the eighteenth slaying from the South's civil rights years to be reinvestigated since 1989. Three of those cases, in Mississippi, had made their way into the courtroom and had found convictions. (The most significant conviction was that of Byron De La Beckwith in 1994 for the 1963 murder of Medgar Evers.) "Mr. Avants, you're able to read and write?" the U.S. magistrate asked. "Yes," he said. He pled not guilty. The judge set his bail at $100,000. "No time is too late to vindicate our country's repudiation of acts of racial violence," U.S. Attorney Brad Pigott of Jackson said afterward to the press.

I mused on that as I drove into gathering dark.

It was pitch dark when I found John's place. I knocked on the screen door of a double-wide. There didn't seem to be any lights on. He came to the door and I sensed something ominous. He'd gained weight and his eyes were red and his skin looked blotchy. We shook hands and he invited me in. A patch of color glowed behind him. "Sitting here watching the TV," he said. "I couldn't tell you what's on." He shut off the box. "I told you I wouldn't be living long in that hole on Evelyn Street. How do you like my new digs?"

I said I liked them.

"It's an all-white community. That was part of the incentive."

Briefly, he grew animated. "I got three acres here. Got this double-wide and the land it's sitting on for $68,000. They moved the house onto the property for me. Didn't have to put hardly anything down. Got the furniture free. I've already thought about selling it for the profit. It's almost brand-new. I think I could get eighty-five or ninety right now. If I don't sell it, I got lots of plans for it." He said he wanted to improve the site, put in a driveway, shrubbery.

He showed me around inside. The place was extremely neat. His water bed was in one bedroom. In the other bedroom was a queen-sized bed, with a matching chest of drawers. "This is my bedroom suite," he said. "I ain't sleeping in here, though. That damn bed gives me headaches."

He said he had two beers in his refrigerator, and we sat in the living room drinking them. I had to keep the conversation going. There was a heaviness in the room, an awkwardness between us. I asked about his kids. They were good, but he was having arguments with his ex. I asked about work and some of the Depot employees I'd met on earlier trips. Work was lousy, he said. He was getting more and more fed up with being a supervisor. He'd gone in and tried to resign being a supervisor, but the bosses wouldn't let him. There was a new store manager, somebody they'd sent from the company headquarters, and this guy was bearing down on all the department heads. Taking away some of their responsibilities, making them do more Mickey Mouse shit, even more paperwork than before.

"How's Buddy Harris?" I asked.

"Transferred to the Cordova store. That's fine with me. He said I was riding him too hard. We discussed it face-to-face one day. I said, 'Yeah, but why am I riding you so hard, Buddy? Because we've sent you for six weeks of training at company expense, and you aren't wanting to work hard enough. And anyway, I'm not riding you.' Buddy's got an attitude. He thinks I don't like him because he's black."

"How's Ariel Jeffords?" I asked.

"She's a know-it-all now," he said. "You can't tell her a thing. There's this new black associate in my department, a woman. She's like Ariel, only Ariel's white. She said I was sexist in my relationship with her. I told her she could file a complaint. That kind of shut her up."

We talked a while longer and I finished my beer and then said I had to go back to town and find a room because I had a lot to do the next day. I said I wouldn't wait so long next time to see him. We shook hands. I drove back to Senatobia and slept in a Motel 6 beside the interstate, only I didn't sleep. I tossed for most of the night, listening to the whine of big-rig trucks beyond my door. After a while, I turned on the lamp and retrieved from my bag a copy of *Let Us Now Praise Famous Men*. I reread that section near the beginning when Agee speaks of going down to Alabama in the summer of 1936 armed with his arrogance and presumptions, hoping nonetheless to achieve a truthful and "independent inquiry into certain normal predicaments of human divinity." But the lyrical words in that lyrical book, where the "truth" of the South and those sharecropper lives keeps double-backing on itself, exploding on Agee, exploding on the reader, provided no comfort.

They call him Ty. He's the Ferrell who lives so far from home, the one in the family who so often seems close to tears, whose particular field of law enforcement is apprehending desperate people, aliens trying to get to the other side of a tantalizing dream. A bat bristling in the afternoon sun of September 27, 1962, had brought me here, two generations and forty years onward, in this desert scape called Santa Teresa, to the ironic predicaments of this soft, sensitive, doubt-filled grandson, a U.S. Border Patrol agent. William T. Ferrell III doesn't really look like Billy, though, not the Billy limbering up, that Lucky on his lips.

The Distance from
Natchez, Mississippi,
to Santa Teresa, New Mexico

There have been times, out there looking for them on horseback, or spraying around the desert in pursuit of them on an all-terrain vehicle, or tracking them on foot, alone, sometimes with a partner, sometimes in the middle of the night, armed with his cuffs and flashlights and billy stick and water bottles and radio and standard-issue .40-caliber Beretta, armed—you could say—with nothing past his wits and family genes, but loving it all, the hunt and chase, the implicit danger, the primitive and atavistic and somehow authentic cop-cowboy feel of running lawbreakers to ground, when Ty Ferrell will ask himself: But what's wrong with it, really? What's wrong with trying to better your life, make a better world for your family? We've made it a crime, coming across the border illegally. It's my job to stop it. I do. But wouldn't I be doing exactly what they're doing if the situation were reversed? Why shouldn't these people have a moral right to try to make their lives better?

Billy Ferrell's grandson and namesake and Sheriff Tommy Ferrell's namesake and only son—who did the unthinkable male Ferrell thing a while back of learning how to change his infant daughter's diapers; the Ferrell who's always inclined to stop in the road and rescue a stray kitten—has just turned his palms upward. He's grinning, although a moment ago he was choking back tears.

This U.S. Border Patrol agent is sitting in a restaurant in a shopping mall on the edge of El Paso, Texas. It's our first face-to-face meeting; the interview is less than thirty minutes old. Out in the parking lot, on the back seat of a rental car, is a magazine, and in the magazine, spread across pages 40 and 41, is a picture of his grandfather bristling his bat in all of his ego and arrogance, in his intolerance and racial fears.

"You see my dilemmas," the inheritor says, not specifying.

The word "compassion" enters the conversation, in this context: "So when you catch them, you have compassion for them, even though you still love being able to catch them?"

He answers: "I don't know if I have a compassion for them. I think I have an understanding. You're not angry at them. The only ones you half can get angry at are the ones you catch who are just going into El Paso to beg or steal. But even then, the majority of them are doing that to feed their families. Like I say, it's just what I'd be doing." He hesitates. "I'm not sure I should say this. Just because a guy's got fifty pounds of marijuana in his backpack, does that make him a bad person? I almost hate to say that because it sounds soft. But how much different is it from the five guys you caught the night before at Cristo Rey, who were just trying to get to Denver to make a living? Yes, smuggling drugs into America is a crime. It's our job to stop it. But I'm raising a different question."

A moment ago, Ty Ferrell choked back his tears at a mention of his grandfather's funeral. He flew home for that funeral with his wife and baby daughter. He choked tears back again at mention of his father, who meticulously took care of the details of Billy Ferrell's huge and front-page Natchez burial at 3 P.M. on March 2, 1999. "Oh, I hate him for his pride," the son and grandson suddenly said of William Thomas Ferrell, Jr., head lawman of Natchez and the county since 1988, who took over from Billy when Billy had had enough, and whose fame and ego—Tommy's, that is—now spread far beyond Adams County and Mississippi and the South as he ascends to the presidency of all the sheriffs in America.

The son and grandson had gone on: "In so many ways, I've never been able to please him. I can't live up to him. The way I see it, I'll never be able to measure up. My dad scares the shit out of me. He can break me down on the phone. He scares the shit out of my little daughter, and he doesn't even mean to." His voice broke when he said "my little daughter." Despite the harshness of the words, there seemed a lack of judgment or condemnation in his voice. And just as quickly as his eyes had glistened, they dried, and he recovered.

This is a Ferrell who raises many un-Ferrell-seeming questions—and in whom a certain unspecified, existential torment seems continually to exhibit itself. But don't get the wrong notion. He is a Ferrell all the same, which is to say he's a law enforcer, by any other name or mask or current domicile or specific job description. That, too, seems a larger truth the more you get to know him. It's in his pores and bloodstream, being a law enforcer. It's something he feels he almost has no control over, in the same way he often feels he has no control over the propensity to cry. He has tried to be some other things in his life, do some other things. But he has always come back to the family business. What we resist in this world, we are often stuck with.

He is talking of that work, in its current guise: "Ninety-nine percent of them are very passive people. They're not criminals. They're just trying to get over." That's how they'll say it, sometimes, in their scrap English, when he's got the light trained on their faces, when they're looking back at him, petrified, in the washing cone of his beam: *get over.*

"You try to get north of them," he explains, something almost dreamy coming into his voice. "You hopscotch it with the other agents. You're on radio contact. It's a big rush, it's very exciting, you get out there with a gun, and if it's at night, with a flashlight. It has a tremendous potential to be very dangerous. If you stopped to think about it, you'd never put on the uniform and go to work. It would spook you to death."

Later, on another visit, when you are discussing again the implicit tensions of having sympathy for those who are so atavistically and pleasurably being run to ground, this is asked: "What do you usually call them, the ones you're hunting?"

"Aliens," he says. "I'll call them aliens most of the time. Sometimes, I say illegal aliens. On the radio, though, I call them wets. On the radio we all call them wets. We're not trying to be politically correct then. We're trying to catch them."

What would he do if he were chasing a wet on horseback in the middle of the night and the wet wouldn't stop? "I'd run my horse into him," he says, with a little *of course* in his voice.

"At night, we use infrared motion sensors to get them," he says. "We call them 'hits.' You get hits on the sensors."

They'll "bush up," he says. "Bushing up" is when your quarry is trying to elude your beam by hiding, maybe facedown, behind some stunted growth of mesquite or cactus or other desert flora.

"They're mainly men," he says, "although women and children, too. We'll get pregnant women coming over just before birth so that they can claim their child as a U.S. citizen."

And he understands that? "I guess I'd do it too."

He has come on "whole families, hiding out there in the bushes." Maybe they're Indians from the Mexican state of Oaxaca, which is deep in the interior of the country. Maybe they've ridden a bus up to Ciudad Juárez, which is the Mexican border city opposite El Paso. Hoping to cross undetected, they've made their way out of the lights of the city into the nearby New Mexico desert, where Ty patrols. "There they are, they're in your flashlight, the grandmother, the father, the teenage son, the mother nursing babies with snot running out their noses. I've found that. I've had that. They can be very offensive in their body smells. All they want is to get over and beg for a month on the other side, sleep in a gas station lot, or a drainage ditch, make enough to go back home and live for the rest of the year."

What happens next?

"We'll either process them and send them back or, if we've caught them many times before, we'll put them in jail. It just depends."

Appended softly: "None of it seems exactly fair, does it?"

Hemingway once said, "Certainly there is no hunting like the hunting of man and those who have hunted armed men long enough and liked it never really care for anything else thereafter." Billy Ferrell's progeny owns a T-shirt with the quote lettered in green on the back of it. He got it when he was finishing up his seventeen-week training course at the U.S. Border Patrol Academy in Charleston, South Carolina. The shirts were being sold semilegally in a store on the academy grounds—until they were deemed too impolitic, and maybe a little too truthful. Ty doesn't wear the shirt much, but he isn't inclined to get rid of it.

There are probably a lot of ways to think about the riddle of his story, but one of them is that an immensely likable and palpably conflicted man has picked up his family's whole history with race and carried it about 1,000 miles westward, into a twenty-first-century setting, a new-millennium setting. In the old century, it might be said, America's core tragedy was painted in black and white. But in the new, as Hispanics have overtaken African-Americans as the country's largest minority, that tragedy has shaded itself with additional colors, not least the color brown. Not that Ty is seeing it or thinking of it this way. He's living his life, doing his job as a fourth-generation Ferrell law enforcer. (Fourth generation at minimum; his paternal great-grandfather, whom he never knew, was a part-time deputy sheriff.) He's doing it in a place where not just the colors, but the landscape and light are so different from all that he's ever known. What he misses is the South's density, its greenery. On the border, the light isn't filtered through moisture and overhanging trees. It isn't "latticed with yellow slashes of dust motes," as Faulkner wrote of the lovely, late, still, dead Mississippi afternoons. "If it's east of Texas, it's home," Ty says. "Home to us can be anywhere in the South. If it's not east of Texas, it's not doing us any good." Until he moved to the Southwest, he never knew what the longing for a place could be like.

One of the reasons why this skilled and homesick law enforcer, who's in his mid-thirties, with a wife and child he is devoted to, is so quickly likable is because his ego seems nothing like that of his two same-named forebears. All of that celebrated Ferrell peacocked strut and hungering need to be at the center—that wouldn't describe Ty. "Oh, I've got the ego, the Ferrell ego," he assures you. "It's just that I've got the fear, too. I'm always worried and worrying. I'm a tremendous worrier. I worry about things I have no business worrying about. And I guess that works against the ego and is always sort of pulling at me." He adds, "When I'm doing my job, I'm a different person. I guess it's a persona coming out of me."

On the phone, before the first meeting (which was in late 1999, about eight months after his grandfather was buried), he'd said, as if in warning: "I have trouble with my emotions. My emotions come out when they're not supposed to."

D oing his job, a persona coming out. The federal agent—who is in the employ of the Department of Justice—was on foot one night when he came on four illegal immigrants and instantly understood something was different. His partner wasn't close by. He'd gone on duty as he always does, with five full magazines of ammunition. He's very skilled with firearms, having grown up around them, having hunted for small game since he was a boy. (He has served stints of TDY, temporary duty, as a firearms instructor at one of the two training academies in the United States that the Border Patrol maintains.) He'd packed two flashlights—the one with the big beam that recharges on his belt when it's not in use, and the smaller 3-D cell Maglite, which he always keeps in a little holster Velcroed to his waist. He had his billy, which is made of steel and known in the Border Patrol as a "baton." You could crush bone with it. There are firm guidelines and periodic refresher courses concerning the use of the batons, Ty says. "Basically, you hit them in parts of the leg or arm where there's a lot of flesh and muscle. I've almost never used it. I feel I don't have to."

He didn't take along a can of pepper spray. It's standard issue, but he is disinclined to use it on recalcitrant subjects. When he was a cop back in Mississippi, he didn't like to use it, either.

It was three o'clock in the morning when he came on them. Two of the four had on ski masks. One had a backpack. Was there a gun in it?

"*Levántense!*" he cried. The four got up.

One started talking to the others in English. It wasn't pidgin English, it was real English, with a thick Hispanic accent. Were these "mules" carrying dope across? Was there an American among them?

"*Manos arriba!*" he commanded. In his time on the border, he's gotten handy with commands in Spanish, not that he could carry on a real conversation. The four put up their hands. But they weren't responding fast enough, didn't have enough terror in their eyes. He got out his gun, and he yelled at them again, throwing in some profanities. He can't remember what he said. All he remembers is the force that came out of him and the ability to act on instinct and adrenaline.

"Pongan sus manos detrás de las cabezas! Ahorita!" he yelled. Three of the four put their hands behind their heads—pronto. That's when the fourth took off running. Then one of the others started to come around behind Ty. The lawman lunged at him, swung him around, stood the guy in front of him as a shield. He told the other two to lie facedown. He was yelling all over the place now. He got out his radio and called for help. When the backup came, the aliens were cuffed and shoved into the van. Ty took off after the one who'd fled. He was bushed up.

"I found him facedown. He was a little uncooperative. I had to whack him a couple times."

As it turned out, there wasn't dope in the backpack, and none of the four aliens had a gun, and all were Mexican, and all were in the "system." Meaning that the USBP had a prior record on each. The agent had fretful dreams for a few nights afterward.

Having just finished telling this story, he has anticipated your question. "Now, I could be lying, right? How would you know if I mistreated any of them, once we had them in custody? I could have roughed them up a little, if I wanted to. But I did not mistreat them, no matter how scared I was. I refused to let myself go over the line. I have never let myself go over that line as a law enforcer."

Once, on the Mississippi Gulf Coast, when he was working as an inexperienced lawman, Ty (who was maybe twenty-six) watched an older cop slam an Asian teenager into the back of a squad car. The kid, who was in cuffs and who didn't speak English, began squirming in the seat. The veteran policeman jerked him out of the car, got him by the hair at the back of his head, started smashing his face against the trunk. *Whawk, whawk, whawk.* (The teller of the story is making this sound in the back of his throat; you could mistake it for the sound of a wooden bat cracking bone.) The prisoner came up and spit out two teeth. He was bleeding. He urinated on himself. He started bawling. The young officer, who wondered if he might faint, or vomit, walked away. It turned out that the reason the kid had been squirming in the back of the squad car was because he had to go to the bathroom—and couldn't communicate it. For the next two weeks, Ty says, he talked almost nonstop about that incident with another young officer who was present, and also with his wife. It was his sense of helplessness that was so awful, he says. He didn't know how he was supposed to react. He was trying to fight his own instincts. He didn't even know the abusing cop's name. He also knew that if he tried to say something to him, much less report him, the cop would have confronted him with something like, "Hey, haven't you ever seen blood before? This is what we do." So Ty didn't do anything, except let himself be tormented. Until the feeling wore away.

Pause. "I mean, okay, sometimes you'll be out here, on this job, and you get some little Mexican sixteen- or seventeen-year-olds who are doing nothing but coming over to steal cars or whatever. And they'll look back at you as you're putting them in the van, and they'll be sucking their teeth, and there's nothing really wrong, in my view, with rapping or slapping one or two of them with the back of your hand. I'm not saying I'd take the stick to them. I'm saying maybe I might want to take the stick to them. But I wouldn't, not unless there was absolutely no other alternative. I'm a lot older now. I think I know how to handle myself a lot better. I'm stronger at what I need to do."

On a different visit, talking again of the conflicts inherent in being a hard-soft cop, a hard-soft Ferrell, he'll say: "It's a law enforcement deal. The way I've always done it is to treat them with respect right from the start. And yet if they don't respond to that, then I have to adjust my treatment and manner accordingly—to what I need to accomplish to get the job done. You remove all doubt—immediately. You'll be able to know how they're going to react. Then the situation either de-escalates, or you have to ratchet it up. It just depends on their response. What I'm trying to convey to them right off the bat is: 'Look, this is my job. This is what the government of my country has hired me to do. I'm an agent of the U.S. government.' In the best situation, it never has to go beyond that."

A picture of what that agent looks like: brush top, fair features, moonish face, bowling-ball head with jug ears, semiwatery blue eyes, buff torso tapering to a slim waist. You see Ty and you get a quick sense of the family's Scotch-Irish lineage. He's got a high-timbred voice. He's on the short side, about five feet seven and a half. If he gained ten pounds, he might be at risk of seeming fat, but as it is, the cop looks very solid, looks very much like a cop, whether in his Border Patrol uniform or out of it. Out of uniform, he likes to wear T-shirts and tennis shoes and ball caps, the latter to shade his wide forehead, which can singe and blister in the desert sun. For all the discernible gentleness in him, there's something very Ferrell and masculine about him, not least in the way he moves, taking ownership of physical space in subtle, forceful ways. It's the same physical claiming of space I've experienced with both his father and grandfather. He used to be called "Waddle" by his grandpop, when he was waddling around the sheriff's office in Natchez in the early seventies with a toy star and a plastic six-shooter. But Waddle doesn't waddle now.

On a bookshelf in Tommy Ferrell's office in the sheriff's department in downtown Natchez, there is a framed photograph. Three cops with the same name are holding guns and wearing military outfits and gazing heavenward. It's a staged thing, done in dark hues. It's a little like one of those Civil War fake fronts that people stand soberly in front of in costume. The picture seems both scary and a little comic. It's as if the three Ferrells—Billy, Tommy, Ty— each with his piece and head lofted upward at nearly the same tilt, are on a direct beam with the Almighty. But even looking at it casually, you can see something different in the face of the youngest William T. Ferrell: softness. It's almost as if Ty is playacting the part of a lawman—which isn't at all true.

Another kind of picture: If you drive northward out of downtown El Paso, Texas, along old historic U.S. Route 85—where the road is known as Paisano Drive—you'll have the strange sensation of being able to look directly into another country. Two nations, two peoples, side by side, literally and figuratively. The civilization of Mexico is just over there, on your left, on the other side of a fence that you can see through, on the opposite bank of a famous and shallow and listless brown rope of water known as the Rio Grande—Big River. If the weather is sunny and warm, which it nearly always is in El Paso, you'll see clotted humanity on the bank.

Old tires are floating in the river. Mothers are washing clothes. Little kids are swimming and wading and laughing. Knots of men, talking, are passing the day, their faces shaded by straw hats. On this side—God's side, you'd say— there's a superhighway directly above Paisano, with its frightful roar of cars doing seventy-five. It's Interstate 10, which runs through downtown El Paso. (Going the other way, I-10 will take you to California, through New Mexico and Arizona.) The University of Texas at El Paso is also directly above Paisano Drive, pitched into hillsides, with its fine big buildings and promises of future good jobs to those who apply themselves.

If you continue slowly along this route, you'll have the almost disorienting sense of being able to reach out and touch the hands and faces on the other side. Literally, you could pitch coins across if someone didn't want to stop you. There are cameras positioned on high poles along the route. There are SUVs with U.S. Border Patrol insignia on them, and sitting inside the vehicles are USBP agents. The vehicles are usually parked at right angles to the road. Along the route are also signs nailed to utility poles advertising discount bus fares to Denver and Las Vegas and Los Angeles.

Just beyond the figures on the bank, on the counterpart of Paisano Drive, dilapidated cars and trucks and crazily painted school buses will be belching and fuming along at what seems like five miles an hour, past the Pemex gas stations and convenience stores and squalid housing. The school buses, which serve as public transportation, are conveying the people of Ciudad Juárez, a hazy, horizontal sprawl of 1.7 million people. El Paso and Juárez, two sides of a vast border city. El Paso's population is 700,000. It's the seventeenth-largest city in the United States. Its per capita standard of living is far below that of many places in America—but life there must seem rich beyond imagination to the people on the other side of the tantalizing dream. Seventy-six percent of what was once called El Paso del Norte, the Pass of the North, is of Hispanic descent. The two towns form the largest border community anywhere in the world. Increasingly, they form the united states of "Amexica." Over four hundred years of history have interlocked them.

Ty and his wife, Carla—she's from back home, too—came to the American side of Amexica when he finished his training at the Border Patrol Academy in mid-1997. He was twenty-nine. He was a college dropout who had worked as a cop in his native state in two incarnations for the previous five years. He had recently quit officers candidate school in the Mississippi National Guard, which he had gone into at seventeen, while he was in high school, once again trying to do what he felt might please his father. (His father has had a long history in the army and the guard.) The reason Ty dropped out of OCS six months shy of obtaining a commission, an act that was incomprehensible and enraging to his father, was because he'd get so wrought up with stomach cramps every midweek before the weekend's military obligations—not that his father knew it. The son kept it a secret. "I aged," he says. "My psyche aged ten years," he says, coping with the stress of OCS training in the guard. Sometimes he would almost bawl himself to sleep.

The graduate knew almost nothing about life in the border Southwest and found the desert an extreme culture shock, and not just the look of it. It perplexed him why those who were in the overwhelming majority seemed to be making instant judgments about him because of the color of his skin, because of the fact that he talked Anglo—and a funny Anglo at that, one with a Southern drawl. There were fifty-six agents in Ty's graduating class, and more than half were assigned either to the El Paso station of the USBP or to the sector immediately west and northwest of El Paso, which is the Santa Teresa, New Mexico, station. By the luck of the draw, Ty got posted to the latter, which allowed so many atavistic cowboy-cop genes to click in. While the El Paso station is entirely urban and is about thirteen miles in length (with hundreds of federal agents patrolling its border twenty-four hours a day), the Santa Teresa station, next door, is almost entirely rural. It begins at the edge of the city and runs out into the New Mexico desert for about sixty-seven miles. It's full of arroyos and washes and draws and mesas, not to say rattlers. If you're a citizen of Mexico and you get caught coming across the border in the Santa Teresa sector, you'll still be known as a wet, short for wetback, by agents talking to each other on the radio, at least according to agent Ty Ferrell. It's a technical irrelevance that there isn't any water to swim or wade across.

On the western edge of El Paso (which itself is at the very tip of west

Texas), there is a place called Smeltertown and Monument One. Historically, it's a popular crossing spot. This is where Mexico and the states of Texas and New Mexico come together. There are mountains, and the river, and the crossing can be punishing. West of here, the border between nations ceases to be a river. The Rio Grande, which forms the natural boundary between America and Mexico through all of Texas, cuts north at Smeltertown and goes up into New Mexico. In the Santa Teresa station, the border between two countries is a fence line—and often no fence at all. The Santa Teresa station is maintained twenty-four hours a day by several hundred agents. Really, says Ty, it's like trying to catch minnows with a salmon net; it's like trying to bail out the ocean with a Dixie cup. Too many of them, too few of you. There are two other Border Patrol stations in New Mexico—at Deming and Lordsburg—and their areas of jurisdiction are even emptier and wilder than Ty's station. But the Santa Teresa station—beginning on the rim of exurbia and running straight west into the desert—is wild and empty enough.

For much of the Santa Teresa station, the line marking American soil is invisible. Now and then, you'll see a little green sign: BORDER OF THE UNITED STATES OF AMERICA. All along the Santa Teresa line, hidden behind boulders, along trails, behind bushes and trees, are the infrared motion-detecting sensors. "Freds," they're called by Border Patrol agents. The Freds may be protruding an inch or two up from the sand, like spooky little eyes. When a foot falls near a motion sensor, alerts go off at command and control centers. The operator who is monitoring the sensors relays by radio message to an agent that the 489 Port One, for instance, has just had three hits. The agent in the field may be parked nearby in an SUV, or he may be patrolling the same area on foot or on horseback or atop an ATV. Sometimes the wind will trigger a Fred; sometimes a four-legged desert night creature will falsely set it off.

First day on the job, Ty was in on the apprehension of fourteen illegal immigrants. A Fred had been tripped and the illegals were all caught nearby. They were rounded up and loaded into the vans. That night, the border patrolman went home and told Carla he'd do the job for free. Carla, who's known Ty since she was fifteen (they dated on and off for nine years through high school and college before they married), thought to herself: Gee, I've never heard the free word before.

When he started, Ty says, they were catching as many as three hundred aliens a day, about one hundred per shift. Now, he says (late fall of 1999), "we're lucky if we get eighty on all three shifts." It doesn't mean that the flow of human life coming across the border has lessened—it means that it has shifted. Word among the crossers has passed: The Deming and Lordsburg sectors, further west, afford the better chance of getting over. Further west, into rural Arizona, proceeding toward California, the apprehension rates have been enormous. And they keep growing. (In the summer of 2000, the *Washington Post* reported that, on a single June night, in the vicinity of Douglas, Arizona, 1,400 illegal crossers were stopped. In one month—May 2000—in Cochise County, Arizona, the Border Patrol detained and returned to Mexico about 43,000 crossers.)

When Ty arrived in the Southwest, the El Paso station averaged more than a hundred getaways a day, he says, "although those are only the getaways that are seen. You work the El Paso station, you're mostly a security guard. You're watching a fence. It's not really law enforcement, in my view. It's not like being a cop at all. We have to do some of that, too, out here—sitting in the truck, parked, waiting for them. Sitting on the line, in the van or a truck, is a bore. We all take our shifts doing watches. There's a watch up on the top of Monument Three. You just kind of sit there, like a sentry. But then, other times, you get to do all this other stuff. You learn some amazing skills. Like sign cutting."

He's talking about the art of tracking. Agents sometimes speak of it as "cutting the sign." Watch an inheritor cutting the sign right now. He's bent over, studying a little indentation in the sand, which is a human footprint. He hasn't gotten off a horse to do this; he has climbed out of a four-wheel-drive vehicle. This footprint, which an ordinary person might have missed altogether, is about three feet inside the border of the United States. In another sense, the footprint seems a planet away from whatever once got formed in the sign cutter's gene pool—but that's an illusion. The agent of his government is reading a quarter-inch-deep blemish in the New Mexico sand with all his senses, as if it were strange braille. He's off duty today. He's in his ball cap and jeans and T-shirt. It's a Sunday. He has taken his visitor out to the line in his own vehicle, a green Suburban, which he purchased from the Border Patrol. He loves going to the line, whether he's on duty or not. There are times, says Carla Ferrell, when her husband will get off work at, say, midnight and stay in the shop (which is to say the Santa Teresa station headquarters), shooting the shit nearly till dawn with fellow agents who've just come off duty.

He's down on one knee. He's so focused, intent. "This track's not fresh," he says. "Somebody came across, I'd say, maybe as much as half an hour or an hour ago."

How does he know?

"These tiny little beetles and bugs. That's one way you know. It takes a while for beetles and bugs to find their way into a track. Then, too, you can see how the wind has swept the edges of it just a little. That also tells you it's not fresh. He went out that way." He's pointing in the direction of what seems like desert nothingness.

The footprint, which seems to be the only footprint in sight, is at the end of a high fence line. The footprint is perhaps a quarter of a mile distant from a wretched-looking "town" called Rancho Anapra. Rancho Anapra is on the Mexican side. Jurisdictionally, the rancho is part of the city of Juárez. It's a *colonia*. What the colony of Anapra looks like from the American side is a moonscape of hovels glued and stapled together from corrugated tin and plywood and cardboard and dried mud and whatever else might have been handy or cast off. The dwellings in Anapra seem like a weird and oversized preschool art project. The settlement itself looks built into prehistoric anthills.

The fence line is used in a kind of funnel effect, Ty explains. "If they're in Anapra, they know they can't get through the fence, and so they come down here, to where it stops—or else to the far other end. All they have to do is walk across, if there's no agent nearby. We can't cover all this ground at once. They could be hiding anywhere in here. See that tree over there?" He points to a pathetic-looking tree, maybe thirty feet away, on the Mexican side. "There could be one hiding behind there right now."

Walking over there to find out would be a violation of international law. That tree is Mexico. There are no *federales* patrolling on that side, not at this moment, or none that can be seen.

How did just a single footprint get here? He laughs. "They're ingenious. They're always thinking of new ways to get over. They'll take their shoes off and walk across the road and go fifty yards into the U.S. and put their shoes back on. It's much harder to pick up the track when they do that. They'll break off branches and sweep behind them as they walk. It's called 'brushing out.' They'll tie cardboard to their feet, but if you're good at cutting the sign, you can tell that right away. They'll bring a roll of carpet and unroll it and the last guy across will roll it up. Those are usually narcotics people, because one person is not going to carry more than eighty to a hundred pounds of dope across. So they'll come in fours, maybe. Two will carry a hundred pounds each in a backpack, and the other two will carry the water, because they may have to walk twenty miles in the desert before they'll be able to unload it. If they don't have water, they can't live. They'll tie cow hoofs on their feet with sandal straps and try to get across. They'll guide themselves by the lights of the city, or by Mount Cristo Rey, or by a big white tower ball out by the airport."

You get "the bike guys coming through," he says. He tells of an old man named Brujillo. "We call him the woodcutter. He's been crossing twenty years. He may be eighty. Nobody knows how old he is. He picks up scraps, pieces of wood, old tires. He's allowed to cross. We don't apprehend him. He'll go early in the morning, at daylight, and come back in the afternoon or the middle of the day. We just let him go. He pushes a three-wheeled cart. It's kinda like a cart on a bicycle. Every day, he scrounges all this stuff from the American side, and then he goes back to his home in Anapra. Every once in a while, there are agents who will pick him up. I never bother Brujillo. In fact, I gave him some gloves. He came up to my truck complaining how cold it was, and I said, 'Here you go, woodcutter.' They were my search gloves."

Search gloves are what Border Patrol agents use when they're looking through the pants pockets and jacket linings of suspicious aliens. The fingers of the gloves are reinforced with thick leather: protection against razor blades and knife points.

They "run drags" to catch the aliens, he says. They attach truck tires to cables and pull them behind their trucks along the unfenced portions of the line. The sand gets raked clean and you can thus track for new prints. "We have all this technology. And a lot of it still comes down to hopping out of a thirty-five-thousand-dollar vehicle and trying to read a footprint in the sand. It's part of what I love about it."

A moment later: "Even if we catch him, chances are we'll put him back on the other side. We have a threshold. We'll let a guy come across maybe fifteen times before we put him into the system. Different stations have different thresholds. We have a fingerprint system. Nine times out of ten, they're in the system, they're not a first-timer. If he's put into the criminal system, he'll do ninety days. Nine times out of ten, he gets out and tries to get right back over. Then we'll put him in for six months, maybe." It annoys him, "the fact that he gets out and tries to come right back. But I also try to think of it like this: If he goes to jail in the first place, you're denying his family the chance to have something better. I want to catch him." Pause. "I guess there's a part of me that doesn't want to do anything else after I catch him but cut him loose."

Pause again. "Let him do what he has to do."

He has come on Guatemalans and Salvadorans and Hondurans and even Chinese in the bush, Ty says. There they are, the Chinese, staring up at him in their Asian garb and faces. Maybe they've made their way from mainland China to Mexico City. Maybe they've paid somebody in Juárez $2,500 so they can be smuggled into a stash house on the other side, in a community called Sunland Park, New Mexico. What they're really hoping for, he says, is to catch a bus to Las Vegas, where dishwashing riches wait for them in big hotels. "OTMs" is what Border Patrol agents will sometimes say when they're talking of nonwets they've taken in. OTM: Other than Mexican.

He stands up. "Let him go, whoever he is. I'm one guy. I can't stop the Mexican nation from coming into the United States."

He climbs back into the Suburban, drives a quarter mile down the fence line, stops directly across from the hovels of Anapra. He gets out. "I want you to hear something." On the other side of the high white metal fence, which you can see through, is a welter of high-pitched, unintelligible sound. It's coming from the direction of the dwellings, inside of which are human beings, but almost none of whom can be glimpsed from here. The noise sounds like transistor radios on bad frequencies, babies squalling, animals bleating, old women crying hysterically to themselves.

On this side of the fence, desert silence. On this side, the tantalizing dream, America. Over there, twenty-five yards off, the hovels, the caterwauling, of Rancho Anapra, *colonia* of Juárez.

The agent is standing against the fence, looking through. He doesn't seem like a cop, he doesn't seem like a Ferrell—but that is illusion. He is speaking softly, almost to himself. "It just goes on like this all the time. I've come out here to listen to it."

Pause. "They don't have toothbrushes over there—we've asked," he says.

Pause. "They burn tires for their heat and light," he says.

Pause. "No medicine over there," he says.

Pause. "No sewage, no electricity, no running water," he says.

Pause. "I don't understand it. You would think with the two countries so close together, one would pull the other up. Somebody can be born right over there, and somebody else, born right over here, and living their lives so close."

And you say, "But isn't this Mississippi, same injustice?"

The offspring of a man in a photograph turns away from the fence. He's looking directly at you. "Yeah, I guess you could say that, come to think. I don't know that I ever thought of it in those same terms until just now. But, yeah, okay."

A snapshot in time—current time, past time—of his particular Mississippi, the one down in the southwestern corner of the state where almost every Ferrell is from. In a way, it's as if Natchez itself, its curious character, wants to offer clues.

The physical beauty and charm of a place are often a cruel mask for all that lies beneath them, inert, or seemingly inert. You come into the town where the last three generations of William T. Ferrells were born and reared, and it's like stepping into some lush antebellum dream on a high-up Mark Twain summer morning. Arguably, there is no more beautiful spot in Mississippi and perhaps only a few more beautiful towns in the entire South. From a fence line at Anapra to the east bank of the Mississippi, where Natchez is, is about fourteen and a half hours by car—Ty knows the way. Basically, it's a direct shot eastward. Once he hits Dallas, his heart begins to lift, because he can see trees and sense something faintly green. Once he gets to Shreveport, Louisiana, and then on to Alexandria, everything begins to feel intensely familiar.

The oldest civilized settlement on the Mississippi (two years older than

New Orleans) sits on bluffs two hundred feet above the river. For a first-time visitor, the vista can be breathtaking. The Louisiana side of the river is flat and weedy, while Natchez rises in the morning mists. Natchez, with those surreal, *Gone with the Wind* mansions, the largest and most stunning collection of pre–Civil War homes in America. Natchez, where sternwheelers trimmed out in gingerbread are bobbing almost imperceptibly at anchor, making you wonder what century this is. (The boats are visiting floating tourist hotels—such as the *Delta Queen*—that ply the Mississippi in the good months of the year. There's also a permanently moored casino at the foot of Natchez, in the old pirate-and-harlot quarter known as Natchez Under the Hill.)

You almost wish to be lulled into a historical forgetting, such is the instant outward grace. "The beautiful architecture and careful restoration makes the city an ideal site for telling America's story" is how the brochures from the visitors' bureau put it. "At one time, the greatest concentration of millionaires in the United States lived in the townhouses and plantation homes of Natchez." This was just before the outbreak of what is still known as the War Between the States. Almost right up until the day the cannons fired at Fort Sumter, the aristocrats of Natchez lived as if they were an extension of Georgian Britain. They loved the hunt. The ritual wasn't conducted on foot, in the style of the shabby little people of Natchez. It was conducted on great steeds with packs of dogs running out front. The brochures and the tour guides who convey you on trolleys around Natchez aren't interested in having you think about whose collective back all this was built on, don't wish you to focus on the other Natchez, the hurting and haunted and gothic and bloody one. There are many Natchezes, for in truth the home ground of the Ferrell family is an almost schizoid-seeming place—perhaps more so than any other town in Mississippi, which is saying something. Maybe this has something to do with the culture of the river itself—the Mississippi was always floating in the next round of dreamers and schemers, card sharks and prostitutes and cutthroats and carpetbaggers. In *Life on the Mississippi,* Mark Twain wrote of Natchez Under the Hill: "It had a desperate reputation, morally, in the old keelboating and early steamboating times—plenty of drinking, carousing, fisticuffing, and killing there, among the riffraff of the river." If river towns are different, Natchez seems the most different. In this sense, there is something far more open about it than there is about other deeply divided and racist Mississippi towns—Greenwood, for instance, up in the Delta, which isn't on the big river, and where you can feel the eyes upon you almost as soon as you park your car. Natchez welcomes its outsiders, if they have dollars. Outsiders weren't so welcome during the civil rights era.

It's gothic and haunted. Take the great Rhythm Club Fire for example. It was a black dance hall, on Jefferson Street near the Triangle service station.

The flames broke out on April 23, 1940. This was long before civil rights, of course. (Billy Ferrell, not quite seventeen, was soon to quit high school and go to work and then to marriage and Uncle Sam and the war.) As the papers related, "203 negroes bought 50 cent tickets to eternity." They died stampeding toward the only door or clawing at the two-by-fours nailed across the windows like burglar bars. They'd come that night to hear the Walter Barnes Orchestra, a noted black swing band. The organizers had decorated the place with Spanish moss, and the moss had been sprayed with gasoline to kill the mosquitoes, and apparently somebody emerged from a bathroom in the middle of the dance and lit a cigarette and flipped his match. The match got into the moss. "CRIES OF BURNING NEGROES HEARD FOR BLOCKS. IDENTITY OF DEAD UNKNOWN EARLY THIS MORNING," the paper said. Those 203 names are on a tarnished tablet of gray stone on the bluffs overlooking the river, overlooking the landing where the tourist sternwheelers tie up. There is a little carved wreath below the two columns of the listed dead: Johnnie Boy Logan, Casiana White Turnipseed, Thelma Lloyd, Willie May Jackson, McKinley Kingsberry, Annabelle Fisher Knight—and all the rest. Who were they?

That's what you ask a man shining his heap with a rag one day near the stone. "My aunt and uncle," he says thickly. He has no teeth. There is an eye missing from his face. He points at the tablet. "Only one way out. Happened way back. I be eighteen. For years, people be walking round Natchez with scars on their bodies from the flames. Don't see them around anymore." He takes your notebook and draws a map, writes out the names of his aunt and uncle.

Near the Rhythm Club Fire monument is another. It commemorates Richard Wright, author of *Native Son* and *Black Boy,* who was born in 1908, "near Natchez, where he spent his early childhood. His lifelong quest for freedom led him to Paris, France, where he died in 1960." Post-totalitarian Natchez has appropriated him. At the big visitors' center, down closer to the water, they've had this same gall—putting the bit about Wright and his lifelong quest for freedom into a film and exhibit. But to read the native son's novels is to know the purity of his lifelong rage against Mississippi and the South and all of America.

Quite aside from its record of sixties civil rights brutality—one of the worst in the state in terms of how many burnings, bombings, beatings, floggings, outright murders—Natchez has apparently always had about it a whiff and aura of "sin," for lack of a better word. ("Dee-caydent," is the word Billy Ferrell used, sitting down on his dock, his love for his hometown welling up in him with a big grin.) It's the same aura of sinfulness and decadence you get almost immediately in New Orleans. In a way, Natchez is a little New Orleans, in its fleshy appetites. Tony Dunbar, a New Orleanian who has written several fine books about Mississippi, has said that New Orleans "smells of salt air, coffee, garlic, crusty bread, gardenias, sweet olive, and the river." There is a similar sensuosity and sensuality about Natchez, just not quite as pronounced. In the early 1800s, Frances Trollope, mother of novelist Anthony Trollope, came from Britain to visit the Americas and wrote of Natchez: ". . . the abundant growth of the pawpaw, palmetto and orange, the copious variety of sweet-scented flowers that flourish there, all make it appear like an oasis in the desert. Natchez is the furthest point to the north at which oranges ripen in the open air."

This is a town famed for once having had one of the greatest whorehouses in the South. Nellie Jackson's place, at the corner of Monroe and North Rankin Streets, operated right into modern times and all through the long reign of Sheriff Billy Ferrell, right up until the late 1980s, when an aggrieved client burned the brothel down, and Miss Nellie with it. Miss Nellie, as she was respectfully known, used to ride on a float in the big Natchez Christmas parade (just as Billy did, when he had the honor of portraying Santa seven years before his death), another way of saying that Natchez has never been afraid to showcase and parade its sin—certain kinds anyway.

In Natchez, you see Queen Anne houses with delicate filigree standing next to homes with a kind of French Quarter motif standing close to commercial buildings that are supposed to be peerless examples of the Greek Revival architectural style. Historically, in Natchez, blacks and whites have always lived near each other all over town. There are black quarters of Natchez, but the larger pattern of interracial neighborhoods prevails even now (although it's less true in the subdivisions). The pattern is rooted in the days when slave shacks surrounded the planters' houses.

So something is instantly kicky and jazzy and Dixieland about this place, which has less than 20,000 people now and is no longer the main river port between Memphis and New Orleans. Something is also immediately blue-collar and factory-worker-sultry about it. The rise of modern industrialization was a postwar phenomenon, after cotton and oil had faltered. The blue-collarness is mixed right in with, snugged up to, the tourism, the visual splendor of the antebellum homes with their manicured gardens. The houses have names like Rosalie, Monmouth, Montaigne, The Briars, Stanton Hall. (The last one takes up a city block.) People from around the world come to Natchez for the twice-annual tour. The mansions—about thirty-two of them—form the heart of the Natchez Pilgrimage, sponsored by the town's garden clubs. Off the buses the pilgrims roll, to peep inside the slightly faded drawing rooms while latter-day family members, in costume, show off the handed-down china, crystal, the dark portraits of their cotton-owning and indigo-planting ancestors. Blacks are not a part of the Natchez Pilgrimage. Natchez has so successfully marketed its history, one slice of it, that tourism makes up about 50 percent of its economy. In the old economy, the mansions had bells on embroidered pull strings, so that a slave (or, later, a domestic, who was a slave just by another name) could tell by the tone of a particular bell where in the house he or she was wanted.

All of the un-chamber-of-commerce history of Natchez is there, under the surface, like malaria. If you approach the touristy town from the other side, off the Natchez Trace Parkway, you'll end up on St. Catherine Street. On St. Catherine, across from E-Z Credit Motor Company, there's a plaque marking the Forks of the Road. It says: "Site of the South's second largest slave market in the nineteenth century. Enslaved people were also once sold on city streets and at the landing at Natchez Under the Hill. Natchez slaves were freed in July 1863, when Union troops occupied the city. The Forks of the Road market then became a refuge for hundreds of emancipated people."

Elizabeth Proby, direct descendant of one of the emancipated, lives in this neighborhood. She's in the small print of civil rights literature—and deserves far more. In 1965, she was one of hundreds of Natchez blacks who marched in protest against the latest round of car bombings and economic repressions and random beatings. Late summer and the fall of 1965 were a very bad time in Natchez. The marchers were rounded up and arrested. Because the local jails weren't large enough, the protesters were held temporarily in the civic auditorium and then removed to Parchman penitentiary in the north of the state on commercial buses—three busloads on a Saturday, two on Sunday, one on Monday. At Parchman, the males were made to strip naked, and the women were made to take off their outer clothes. Both males and females were force-fed laxatives. The single latrine in each group cell—as many as eight were shoved into one cell—quickly backed up. There was no toilet paper. Feces ran onto the floor. Female prisoners later testified that they were using their rations of bread and biscuits to wipe themselves. They testified in court documents that they had to tear up their panties for sanitary napkins. The guards watched this sport unfold. Elizabeth Proby was a young woman. She was later part of a lawsuit filed against the city of Natchez and the prison, and she remembers that eventually she got a reparation check for something like $20. "They didn't make me take off all my clothes at Parchman, no," she says, as if it's important to make the distinction. "I had a light brown corduroy jacket with half-sleeves, and just a bra underneath, and so they said I could keep that on. I was appreciative. That night, when it got so cold, when they were turning the exhaust fans on us to make us shiver, I was sharing the jacket with other girls." After she got out of Parchman and had come home, Proby tried to go back to her job at Krouse Pecan Shelling. But they fired her for having caused the city so much grief. She did maid work and registered at Alcorn A&M University and eventually got certified as a schoolteacher. She is in retirement. You ask her one day, having just knocked at her door, having been invited in, if she thinks that some of those who were guilty of treating her that way back then might have any regret now. "I expect they do. I expect so. If they have any kind of heart, and most people do," she says, letting it go at that. "I try not to keep grudges," she adds.

In 1959, when Billy Ferrell campaigned for sheriff the first time, the median annual income of blacks in Adams County was $2,000. More than one-third of black housing in the city was deemed "inadequate for human shelter." This is from a report filed in the mid-sixties by the United States Commission on Civil Rights, when commissioners came to Mississippi from Washington to conduct ineffectual but well-meaning hearings.

The city famed even in Europe for its gracious and extant old nineteenth-century pre–Civil War Southern ways is also the white-trash Mississippi town where the revival of the Klan began in the sixties and then spread throughout the state. The rebirth began in the second half of Sheriff Billy Ferrell's first term, largely in response to the shame and embarrassment suffered over a black man who'd forced his way into a white institution of higher learning on October 1, 1962. By then, the factories of Natchez were providing jobs to unlettered workers from backwoods logging communities who were eager to drive a couple of hours each way every day for hourly wages. After Meredith at Ole Miss, Natchez's factories—International Paper, Johns Manville, Armstrong Tire & Rubber—became potent breeding grounds for Klan membership, and so, too, the local police and sheriff's departments. There is little question that the police force and sheriff's department had current or former Klan among its ranks, at least according to investigative reports by the federal government later in the decade. These cops were identified as being either current or former members of Klan Klaverns in and around the time of Meredith at Ole Miss, and afterward, too, and, in a few cases, apparently, there were cops in the county who were in the Klan even before Meredith. But Meredith at Ole Miss was the catalyst for a Klan resurgence across all of Mississippi, and the resurgence began in the beautiful, bluff-hanging city of Natchez. Nobody knows for sure how many Natchez Klansmen were walking around in the heat of the mid-sixties night, with and without sheets. In 1965, *The Reporter* magazine, after an investigation, wrote: "With some four hundred local Klansmen, Natchez has possibly the highest per capita Klan population anywhere in the South." The House Un-American Activities Committee, in hearings in Washington in early 1966, published long lists of Natchez residents reputed to be currently or formerly in the Klan. It released a list of over seventy names of employees at International Paper—just one manufacturing plant—who were either present or recently resigned members of either the White Knights of the KKK or the United Klans of America.

The Grand Dragon of the UKA, realm of Mississippi, lived right in town— local boy, former truck driver, former Johns Manville factory worker. He wasn't hiding a thing. His name was E. L. McDaniel. They called him "Eddie." He had a big office on the second floor of 114 Main. The curvy building, with its Art Deco frosted glass, is still there, only now there's a Santa's Station on the premises. The building is down a little way from the Pig Out Inn. You go a block in the other direction and you're at the Natchez Museum of Afro-American History and Culture. In Mississippi, everything changes, and nothing changes.

Eddie McDaniel and Billy Ferrell grew up together, although they weren't especially close. Two of the Dragon's younger brothers—not identified as Klan members in government documents—worked as deputies for Billy and, later, for Tommy Ferrell, when Tommy took over the top job. One of these brothers, Jerry McDaniel, served as Tommy's chief criminal deputy for many years, until his retirement in the late nineties. The other brother, Bill McDaniel, remained on Sheriff Tommy Ferrell's payroll.

I went one summer night to Jerry McDaniel's house and saw the retired chief deputy grit his jaw and fold his huge hands across the dining room table and bead me with suddenly hard eyes as he said: "Only one thing in my life I ever swore to was a badge. No secret organization nowhere, no time, nohow. You got that? My brother was my brother. I loved him. I didn't necessarily agree with him. It's wrong to tar somebody with a brush if you don't have any proof. McDaniel brothers have been living with that crap for their whole lives." He paused. "My brother Eddie was just like a lot of other frustrated white Mississippi men of his time."

Jerry McDaniel, who retired as a cop in 1997 after a twenty-one-year career at the sheriff's department, lives in an attractive brick rambler on the edge of town. He said that he'd gone to work officially for Billy in 1976, but for a good while before that, when he was a city fireman, he'd worked as a special deputy to Billy. After 1988, when Tommy took over, Jerry rose to chief deputy. He gave me one of his cards. On the top it said, "William T. 'Tommy' Ferrell, Jr., SHERIFF." And right below: "JERRY MCDANIEL. Chief Criminal Deputy." He seemed to be enjoying his life in retirement. He and his wife liked taking motor trips up to Branson, Missouri, where Eddie McDaniel was spending most of his time. Jerry and his wife would hook up a motor home alongside his big brother's in Branson and get in a good family visit. According to Jerry, Eddie thought of himself as a friend of Sheriff Tommy Ferrell. Until the moment I brought up the KKK, the evening at Jerry's had gone fine. I slid into the subject by saying, "I'd like to ask you a question or two about race." He'd said, "I don't like that subject, go ahead." But by the time I said goodbye, maybe forty-five minutes later, everything was fine again. "Come back," he said at the door, standing there with one arm around his wife, as so many Mississippians seem to say at the door.

In the height of the troubles, Eddie McDaniel, who'd also once been a city fireman, had a nameplate on the desk of his inner office at 114 Main that said GRAND DRAGON. There was a sign on the outer door: NO PROFANITY BEYOND THIS DOOR. The Dragon was known to have a black kid of fifteen whom he watched out for and had sweep up the place for him during the day. The Dragon wrote letters to the editor of the *Natchez Democrat* like this: "Be it known, as of this wonderful day of Our Lord, October 2, 1964, that we in the United Klan of America have no knowledge what-so-ever of the violence which has plagued our State." He'd sign them, "For God and Country, E. L. McDaniel, Grand Dragon, Realm of Mississippi." On his Klan letterhead, he wrote to the governor, Paul B. Johnson: "Dear Governor: I am writing requesting an audience with you which I believe will be of great importance not only to you and the United Klans of America, Inc., but to the entire citizenry of Mississippi. If at all possible, I would like to have this audience set on a Saturday morning due to the fact that I work five days per week. An immediate reply is requested." It was signed, "For God and Country, E. L. McDaniel, Grand Dragon, Realm of Mississippi."

Natchez is that elegant civilization of well-bred people at a curve in the river where you could awaken on sweet mornings in the sixties to find hate literature stuffed inside your screen doors or inside your mailbox or stuck onto a stick out on the lawn. The dispatches were from the Mississippi White Caps, just one more terrorist organization spawned during the civil rights period. (HUAC, in its 1966 hearings, identified at least four Klan terrorist groups operating in Natchez—but there must have been many more than that, if you counted in all the splinter and sympathizing groups.) The typical literature from the White Caps would close with statements like this: "All the crooks and mongrelizers who have not been mentioned in this paper need not feel left out—there are only twenty-four hours in a day. We will get you next if you do not correct your ways. Some who read this will wonder why we did not sign our names. The reason is that if we were known, we could not continue to get such information you have just read. We will tell you this much: WE ARE THE HUSBANDS, BROTHERS, FATHERS, COUSINS, NEPHEWS, AND EVEN GRANDFATHERS OF THE CITIZENS OF THIS COMMUNITY." Back then, the town had signs at the outskirts that said THE OLD SOUTH STILL LIVES IN NATCHEZ. Yes, it did. Nine men met one night in a service station garage to form the APWR—Americans for the Preservation of the White Race. This was May 1963, in the last eight months of Billy Ferrell's "first administration," as Billy was fond of describing it years later. The president of the APWR wrote to the *Democrat* explaining what was going on in the civil rights troubles. It was the agitators who "took God Almighty out of everything."

In Natchez, civil rights organizations such as SNCC and CORE would put out their Monday-morning recaps of recent violence: "Five-gallon can of gasoline, a bomb-like apparatus, found under Blue Moon bar here. Bar belongs to Jake Fisher, whose brother's bar was found bombed in Louisiana over the weekend."

The now-declassified files of the Mississippi State Sovereignty Commission are full of letters from its director and other officials to the law enforcers of Adams County—such as this one, addressed to "Honorable Wm. T. Ferrell, Sheriff and Tax Collector, Natchez, Mississippi." It was written on June 13, 1961, in the second summer of Billy's first reign: "Dear Sheriff: Please furnish this commission with information on A. C. Curtis, male, colored, of 66 Brenham Avenue, Natchez, Mississippi, owner of Curtis Funeral System at 106 E. Franklin Street, Natchez, Mississippi, as to any information you may have regarding this subject's activity with the NAACP, if any, or other subversive organizations." Two weeks later (June 30, 1961), this letter from the Sov-Com: "Dear Sheriff: Please furnish this commission with information on *George F. West*, male, colored, of 409 No. Pine Street, Natchez, Mississippi, as to whether or not this subject has paid 1959 and 1960 poll tax; also, if he has any criminal record with your department. Any general information you can supply on this subject's activities with subversive organizations, if any, will be appreciated." The sheriff of Natchez or his functionary always replied. Billy closed one such letter that summer, on June 6, 1961: "Assuring you of the complete disposal of the entire facilities of this department at all times in matters of mutual interest, I remain, Sincerely yours, Wm. T. Ferrell, Sheriff." He signed it with that elegant penmanship of his, learned in Catholic grammar school. Four months later, a Sov-Com operative journeyed to Natchez to check personally on the racial situation and then wrote in his report: "Deputy Robinson stated that he and Sheriff Ferrell were keeping a close watch on any activity that might come from the NAACP, or any subversive organizations, and they would enforce the law to the letter, should the NAACP or the voters registration school cause trouble in Adams County." The field agent came to the county on October 10, 1961—which was almost exactly a year before the head lawman came back to Natchez from the troubles at Ole Miss and walked into a church bazaar where his wife presented him with a picture of himself swinging a bat in the latest issue of *Life* magazine.

It's unarguable, in the cold light of history and masses of declassified documents, that there was deep collusion between local law enforcers and the state spy agency located in Jackson, whose charter and mission were to disrupt the civil rights movement. The men who ran the Sov-Com were government employees, with offices in the state capitol building, a floor above the governor. Some were investigators; others were paper pushers who'd kiss their wives goodbye every morning and put on their fedoras and climb into their sedans and go downtown to turn in a day's work, no less than their colleagues at the oil and gas commission or the swine and poultry commission. In the paranoid pitch of civil rights, the Sov-Com bureaucrats and field agents (who in some cases were ex–FBI men) were one more layer of supremacists with mellifluous speech and wonderful manners, doing what they could to guard the gates of the closed society. Theirs was a homegrown CIA op, with its Orwellian name: the Sovereignty Commission. The agency functioned, sometimes haplessly, sometimes perniciously, from 1956 to 1973 and then went out of business for good in 1977. Together with the Citizens' Council and the Klan, it formed a triumvirate of repression. The difference was that the Sov-Com was funded by tax dollars. The governor sat on the board and served ex officio as chairman. The lieutenant governor was the vice chairman. The state attorney general and the speaker of the State House of Representatives and various legislators and noted lawyers held seats. There are 87,000 indexed names in the commission's declassified files (although not 87,000 individuals; each variation on a name constitutes a separate entry). Altogether, 132,000 pages have been released. It's not possible to know what was lost or destroyed before court orders and lawsuits opened up the files.

It was *all* collusion against blacks and the outside agitators, and the colluding included large numbers of FBI agents assigned to the state—this also is unarguable in the long view of history and documents. Instead of protecting the rights of blacks and others in the movement, the FBI often secretly plotted against them with local law enforcers. Bob Moses, leader of the movement in Mississippi, once said: "It's for reasons like this that we believe the local FBI are sometimes in collusion with the local sheriffs and chiefs of police." That was understatement. Moses was talking of a notorious civil rights murder in Amite County, which sits just to the southeast of Adams County. There's long been a strongly held belief that the FBI leaked the identity of a black witness—which put an immediate death warrant on the black man's life. Such things happened all over the South. There were certainly exceptions. But led by J. Edgar Hoover, whose contempt for movement people and their cause was widely known—chiefly because Hoover made little effort to hide his contempt—the FBI was generally slow to act whenever violations of black rights were reported. Often, the agency was openly hostile to any civil rights complaint, the more so if the investigating agents were Southerners. The September 15, 1963, bombing of the Sixteenth Street Baptist Church in Birmingham—in which four little girls were killed—brought national outrage, but no case cracking from the FBI. A Justice Department investigation later revealed that Hoover had secretly blocked efforts by the local Birmingham office to bring a case against the alleged bombers—no matter the urgings of Presidents John F. Kennedy and Lyndon Johnson for prosecution.

The next year, during Freedom Summer, Hoover himself came to the Mississippi capital to open the largest field office in the country. Schwerner, Chaney, and Goodman had been murdered in Philadelphia, Mississippi, but their bodies had not yet been found. Hoover's message was reassuring to whites in the state. The agency was their friend. He said that the Bureau was opening an office in Jackson because "criminal scum" would be coming in. He promised that "we most certainly do not and will not give protection to civil rights workers. . . . The FBI is not a police organization. It is purely an investigative organization." Privately, he told the governor and business leaders and law enforcement officials that Klan violence must cease. Hoover was under pressure from the White House and Congress and his reputation was on the line. By the end of Freedom Summer, 153 agents were working out of the Jackson office.

In Natchez, there was an FBI agent and Mississippi native named George Gunter. He had grown up in town, knew Billy well, was a college football hero. It was natural that he should be assigned as a resident agent in Adams County. In March 1959, when the FBI presence in the state was still very small, the Sovereignty Commission asked Gunter to deliver names of Natchez teenagers who were scheduled to attend a youth march in Washington, D.C. From a Sov-Com document dated March 18, 1959: "Mr. Gunter has advised that he will confidentially inform [the commission] should he obtain any information of any Mississippi Negroes participating in this March. Mr. Gunter also advised on one H. Climans, who resides on an RFD route out of McComb, Mississippi, and who takes the *Daily Worker*, a Communist newspaper. Undoubtedly, if this individual takes a Communist newspaper, he is in favor of integration."

In the fifties, the Star movie theater had a shoulder-high white fence down the middle, Natchez whites on the left, Natchez blacks on the right, both watching a Saturday afternoon oater, the whites pegging ABC gum (already-been-chewed gum) at the blacks. Billy Ferrell was rising as a local lawman—serving under now-gone bigots and esteemed citizens named Audley B. Conner and W. I. Hebert and Billy Priester. (Priester was sheriff when Gunter promised to supply the Sov-Com with names of black kids.) Also in the fifties, another local boy, this one from Ferriday, Louisiana, just across the river, with a wild hair in him, used to wail and wallop his Saturday night honky-tonk piano at a juke joint called the Blue Cat Club. The Blue Cat was under the hill. It's still going, only it's called the Blue Cat Lounge, and it's come up top now, on the bluffs, to Franklin Street. But Jerry Lee Lewis doesn't wail and wallop there anymore, and Billy Ferrell, who thought Jerry Lee Lewis was okay (if a little dee-caydent), is several years in his grave. Billy's wife, Hazel, was about half kin of Jerry Lee anyway, and so this would have forgiven the decadence right off, because loyalty is such a core virtue in the South. The Blue Cat's current incarnation has a fine juke box and cold beer at good prices, and also townies who sit on the stools only too happy to give a visitor guffawing directions to "Martin Lootin' King Street." (You said you already knew, and let it go at that.)

Maybe the seemingly schizoid character of Natchez has something to do with the fact that, almost from its founding, in 1716, the settlement was trading hands, flags, countries, bloodbaths. It started as a fort, built by the French before they massacred the Natchez Indians, who were the descendants of earlier Indians who'd been living there on the bluffs since prehistory. In close succession in the eighteenth century, Natchez was under French, British, Spanish, and finally, in 1798, American rule. So one way to look at the Natchez story is that trouble and blood on its hands were birthrights from the beginning of its recorded history, in the same way that slaveholding by high-minded and eloquent founding fathers is part of America's deceitful birthright, and thus the legacy and shame and paradox of our seemingly insoluble dilemma these two centuries later. But that sounds too highfalutin in a story about the Ferrells, who always lived close to the ground, whose blood was never blue.

O ut of this soupy mix, the steamy jambalaya known as Natchez, in the early 1920s, came the Ferrell progenitor who'd one day bristle his bat in the middle of Charles Moore's photograph. If you had to describe Billy Ferrell's origins in one line, the line might be: townie, up from almost nothing, who made eventual good in the society of bluebloods. "Sounds like we moved every time the rent come due" is the way Billy once explained his earliest years. That must not have been far off. He was born in a back room in his grandparents' house, which was where his mother and father lived. His father, who'd been raised across the river, in Concordia Parish, Louisiana, was a river man (and part-time lawman on both sides of the river). His mother was a Natchezean of modest culture but no means. There must have been some sense of Catholicity and propriety in the family, for Billy attended the local parochial school, where he was instructed in his euclid and catechism by both nuns and the Brothers of the Sacred Heart. (There's always been a strong Catholic minority presence in Natchez, as well as a Jewish one. One of the bigoted jokes a visitor soon hears—three slurs for the price of one—is that "In Natchez, the kikes owned it, the Catholics ran it, the niggers enjoyed it.")

When school was done—he dropped out in eleventh grade—the war was upon him. He worked for a while out of the state. He got his draft papers on December 26, 1942. Two days later, he was wed to redheaded Hazel Hampton. In the service, he quickly rose through the low ranks to warrant officer, which is an intermediate rank between commissioned officers and noncoms. "You was an officer," he once explained. "You wore an officer's uniform. You rated a salute." They sent him overseas on the HMS *Arundel Castle*—where they tried to feed him cod catfish for breakfast on that blimey boat. No thanks. The native son subsisted on Hershey bars until the ship docked. In England, he served in the Ninth Army and was awarded three bronze stars. Also in England, he got the news that William Albert Ferrell, Jr., his father, had died in a gothic river accident. Billy was in three campaigns in the European Theater. He was part of the D-Day invasion, although he wasn't in the early and bloody waves. (His group went in several weeks afterward.) He came home from the victory overseas on another boat, into New York harbor, where pretty little Red Cross women, as he later put it, waved at him with flags and wanted to hand him "a quart of milk or something or a Coca-Cola or just anything that we hadn't had in a long time." There was this new invention called television. He and a buddy got off the boat and saw a guy with black dots all over his face talking in a box in a store window. The buddy said to Billy, "How in the hell did they get that guy in that thing there?" They went around back of it and looked for a camera or a projector.

Then home to sweet Natchez, having ridden down the spine of the country on a troop train like a conquering warrior, so hungry to see Hazel and his little girl, Sherry. He drove trucks and dug ditches for Brown & Root Construction Company. The following isn't the whole list of his employers, but it can be said that he drove a pipe truck for Tom Hicks Transfer; he drove a Navy reconditioned 361-International truck for fifty cents an hour for the Stallman Lumber Company; he drove a Gulf Refining Company diesel for thirty dollars a week. He took the exam for the post office. He passed. For the next eight years, he carried the mail. His face got well known in town, not a bad thing for a guy with no funds who wishes to be elected a head lawman. For a while, before that dream fastened onto him like a lamprey, the mail carrier and Hazel lived in a kind of glorified chicken coop at 523 Union Street, behind Sheriff Conner's house. That's where his second child, Tommy, was born, on June 7, 1947. (Sherry Ferrell, Tommy's big sister, was born during the war, in 1944, just before Billy went overseas.) With secure civil service employment, Billy and Hazel were able to plunk down enough down payment to get their first home, at 817 Washington Street. It was just around the corner from where the old cancer-ridden and heart-gone depressive and wasting man would die five decades later, age seventy-five, on Martin Luther King Street, originally Pine Street. It was a nifty house, 817 Washington, and in its own way, a very large reach. It was Victorian, painted white, with a porch, with gingerbread trim. Up and down that street were other nice homes, and at dusk on summer evenings, their porches would get trimmed with lamps, which were resting on tables, beside wicker, beneath lazily curling ceiling fans. Some of the homes offered side gardens, where people gathered in the evening under bowered trellises while bumblebees fumbled atop the roses. Billy and Hazel lived at 817 Washington for thirty-odd years, never gentry, but quite respectable. It's the house that all the grandkids came to know and love, including the one whom Billy nicknamed Waddle.

By 1953, Billy had begun to figure out that "working for the post office department you didn't have to have anything but a strong back and a weak mind anyhow." That's when he went to sheriffing, as he called it—deputy-sheriffing, first for Conner and then for others in succession, with some odd-jobbing and squabbles in between. In 1959, he put his hat in for the top-cop job in the county—and got it, in the runoff with Morris Doughty. It was a dirty election, with bribes on all sides, but that is not front-page news in either Mississippi or Natchez.

The lawman did his first term, 1960–1964, the nadir or high-water mark of which—depends on your perspective—was the business up at Ole Miss with James Howard Meredith. It's a fact that he cleaned out numerous slot-machine and back-room casino operations, not to say moonshiners. He had campaigned on a pledge to get rid of the gamblers and bootleggers. He filed taxes for that first year on what he said was personal income of $3,600. When the four years were over, he laid out for the next term, because of that Mississippi law that a sheriff couldn't succeed himself.

There's little question that he was at loose ends during his interregnum. Many things were tried for gainful employment. One was the purchase of a Gulf filling station. (Down on the dock in 1997, Billy remembered that by the time all the overhead was paid he was making 6 cents on the gallon, meaning that he had to sell 6,000 gallons just to make $600 a month, and there was no damn way that was going to happen in Natchez.) He tried employment with the Sovereignty Commission. (This was not remembered—or at least mentioned—down on the dock.) On June 15, 1964, the outset of Freedom Summer, the sheriff-in-exile wrote a letter of application to the Sov-Com. He listed his credentials and then closed with this: "I feel that my experience and contacts made in law enforcement over the last 12 years in this area would be beneficial to the Sovereignty Commission, the State of Mississippi and the residents of Southwest Mississippi, if assigned to this area as a resident investigater [*sic*], particularly at this time." He didn't get that job, for whatever reason. Still another thing he tried, not happily, was a stint as a town policeman, serving under the man who'd once been his chief deputy at the sheriff's department, J. T. Robinson. They'd been boyhood friends, and now J. T. was top dog at the police station, and Billy was out of office at the sheriff's department, just another guy in a patrolman's blue uniform. That was a comedown. But he needed a paycheck. Still another thing that was tried was a small investigative service for the oil fields of Adams County. Billy and his old boyhood friend George Gunter ran the service. Gunter was still an FBI agent; he was moonlighting.

And yet still another thing that was tried, among at least half a dozen more that could be mentioned during his four-year interregnum, was the Ku Klux Klan—or so goes the legend. To this day, nobody really knows for sure if Billy actually joined, or just flirted around the edges. You hear it both ways. You hear an awful lot of such talk, even now, forty years afterward. Nobody seems to have any real proof one way or the other. The documents that are available in the post-totalitarian society wouldn't prove it—they'd just suggest it. Certainly, his family denies he was ever in the Klan. As noted earlier, it's a fact, however, and his family wouldn't deny it, that the name Ferrell showed up on several Klan lists compiled by investigators and civil rights groups in the sixties. (Billy's brother, Robert Earl Ferrell, who served as a town policeman in the sixties, was also on at least one such list as having formerly been a Klansman.) But again, what does a name on a list really prove? The Klan was a secret organization, and rumor swirled constantly around it. The town was full of accusations as to who was wearing a hood and who wasn't. I have talked to Natchezeans who can remember coming on little Klan cells in the middle of nowhere—out in the woods—and being terrified out of their minds. A Natchez native named Arlen Coyle, who works now as a clerk in the U.S. District Court at Oxford, remembers going swimming as a kid naked in the ponds and sliding down clay banks. This was in the late fifties. Suddenly, there before Coyle and his pals was a little cabin with Klan flags in the windows. Yes, the Klan in Natchez and the rest of Mississippi had its renaissance after Meredith, but it had never truly died out in the forties and fifties.

Besides George Gunter and other agents, there was an FBI investigator living and working in Natchez in the mid-sixties named C. G. Prospere. Allegedly, he was going around saying that Billy was a Klansman, along with some of those who'd served under him in his first term. Even Billy's family doesn't deny that this story and many others were afloat in a town that has always seemed to thrive on its gossip and rumor. Billy and Prospere had never gotten on in the first place. One day, Billy confronted him out front of Top's Grill, on Main Street. (Top's Grill had a jaunty little top hat glowing atop its front.) It looked like they'd slug it out. "You're full of shit, I ain't Klan," he said to Prospere. To which Prospere grunted and reputedly said he knew what he knew from his informants and that Billy had better watch his backside.

Forty years later, when I contacted him, Prospere, an old man going deaf, who lived out of town in a community called Church Hill, declined to talk about it or to see me. He did acknowledge that some kind of confrontation on a downtown street did take place. As for Billy actually being in the Klan, as opposed to only sympathizing with it, Prospere said: "I'm not going to comment one way or another on any of it." He said that there'd been "too much stuff misreported already." When I asked Billy's son, Tommy, about Prospere's reputed claims (Billy had been in his grave for five months), the sheriff of Natchez said, "The thing is, those informants were derelicts and urchins and miscreants, no-counts." Tommy didn't seem upset in the least.

The man who succeeded Billy as sheriff in 1964, Odell Anders, appears to have been a Klansman. He served one term and is dead now. In the late nineties, when a prizewinning investigative reporter for the *Clarion-Ledger* named Jerry Mitchell confronted Anders with the fact that his name was on old Klan lists, the old sheriff said, no, he'd only attended a few meetings back then. Most people who outlived the Klan's heyday and have survived into modern times as esteemed Mississippians have professed to reporters that they "only attended a few meetings." Mitchell—whose reporting has broken open many old civil rights cases and led the way to convictions in the courts— called up Sheriff Tommy Ferrell in November 1999 and talked to him about still-unsolved crimes from the ugly era. To which Tommy replied, "Hell, I'd like to put 'em all away." His father had been dead for nine months.

On September 29, 1964, in the middle of a series of Klan bombings and other terrorist acts in Adams County, Billy Ferrell and two of his former deputies were stopped on a rural road outside town by the Mississippi Highway Patrol. Governor Paul Johnson had recently sent a special detachment of highway patrolmen to the city to try to calm things. Billy had been out of office for nine months and was at loose ends. The previous month, the United Klans of America (headed by E. L. McDaniel in its Mississippi divisions) had established a Klavern in Natchez under the cover name of the Adams County Civic and Betterment Association. Most of its members had previously belonged to the White Knights of the KKK, the most violent of Klan factions operating in the state. It was nine o'clock at night when Billy and his two cronies were pulled over about five and a half miles beyond the city limits on Liberty Road. In the days immediately proceeding, the Klan had bombed two Jitney-Jungle grocery stores, a Cadillac car agency, the home of a prominent black contractor, and the home of the mayor, John Nosser. Liberty Road is a winding two-lane, unlighted. The road goes past the Johns Manville plant, out into a black community. What were three men, former cops, doing on that road that night?

The highway patrolmen said they wanted to search the car. Billy refused.

One of the patrolman said he was going to take a look in the trunk. Billy again refused and demanded to know if the cop had a warrant. Billy was ordered to get out of the car. He asked if he was under arrest. From a news story two days later in the *McComb Enterprise-Journal,* under the headline "Former Adams Sheriff Ired by Patrol Search": "Former Adams County Sheriff W. T. Ferrell asked the FBI today about the possibility of filing civil rights violation charges against the Mississippi Highway Patrol. . . . The former sheriff said he and two others were riding down Liberty Road when they were stopped by Patrolmen A. L. Rutland and B. J. Ray. Ferrell said they were told to get out of the car and show a driver's license, which they did. . . . Ferrell said he was told he was under arrest, but no specific charge was given. He said that he, Mario Hernandez, his former chief criminal deputy, and Layton Wingate, had to stand by while the car was searched. Ferrell said they were then released and told to drive on."

In an account published the day after the incident in the *Natchez Democrat* ("Ex-Sheriff Ferrell Tells of Car Search"), Billy described the treatment as inexcusable and shameful. He said it was harassment. He called his former deputies "both reputable citizens." Nothing illegal or unlawful was found—no hidden explosives, no rifles hidden under blankets. The riled ex-sheriff, who felt his civil rights had been violated, didn't explain—and maybe the reporter didn't ask—why he was out riding around with two former deputies on a dark road in the vicinity of a black settlement in the time of intense troubles in the county.

One theory is that they were on their way to a UKA meeting. Another is that they were acting as sentries for a bombing about to take place. And still another is that they were just riding around, taking the night autumn air.

One of the highway patrolmen who stopped Billy's car that night is dead. The other, B. J. Ray, is long retired. He lives in the center of the state, in McCool, Mississippi. He said he couldn't recall the incident except in the vaguest terms. He remembered the general time context of the many bombings and beatings in Natchez. He remembered the recalcitrance of the man who was told to get out of the car. No incident report was ever filed by either officer.

"Must have been something that made you suspicious," I said to Ray.

"Bound to have been," he said. "If we stopped them, there must have been something. Bound to have been. We would have had some kind of report or rumor we were trying to check out. There was something going on that night, or that was about to go on, even if we never found it."

When I asked Tommy Ferrell about this incident, he was not in the least disturbed. "Well, you gotta remember. This is almost before television, and guys in the South in a place like Natchez, that's what they did. Cops and ex-cops were known to ride around. They were agitating." The sheriff repeated it: "They were out agitating." He used the word in an innocent context. Those guys were just seeing what was going on.

In 1967, with a powerful thirst to have that thing again, the "thing" being the office of sheriff, the top dog, Billy put almost everything he and Hazel owned in hock. He needed campaign funds—for posters and handbills. He needed money so he could take time off from work to do the stumping. He hocked the family car to two different banks, he took out a second mortgage. Hazel went to Billy's closest friend, Premo Stallone—who'd given Billy a foreman's job during the interregnum. "He's hocked all the furniture," Hazel wailed to Premo. Billy had done this the first time he'd run, too, in 1959. Some folks around town heard him remark that the first time he was sheriff he'd "gone in poor and come out poor, too," but by damn if he was going to have that thing again, he'd sheriff "according to local custom," meaning, of course, payoffs.

In any case, he won. The hocking of the furniture and car was worth it. Good thing he never got that job with the Sov-Com.

During the campaign for his reelection (there were the usual rumors of bribes), he was led one night to a backwoods meeting of "the bedsheets," as Billy called them. This, too, is a well-known Natchez story. Billy himself told it many times over the years. (He told it in his 1997 sessions with the oral historian from the University of Southern Mississippi, and he told a somewhat different version to me on the dock.) Supposedly, a fellow police officer (who almost assuredly was in the Klan) said to the candidate one morning at a breakfast joint that a secret group of local men would like to hear what he had to say. "Do they vote in Adams County?" Billy asked the brother officer. "Yes, every one of them," the officer said. "Fine," Billy said. "I'll make a speech before them, a political speech, but I want to set two stipulations. I'll be armed. I won't come to a Klan meeting without my gun. Number two, I'll have somebody else with me." The somebody else was once again Mario Hernandez, who'd served as his chief criminal deputy for several years in his first term. Billy sometimes liked to refer to him as "the Cuban." He was a crude and tough individual. He is dead now. His name has shown up on various old Klan lists.

Billy and Mario met the messenger at night on U.S. 61, south of town, out front of what everybody in Natchez knows as Black Mammy. Black Mammy was a restaurant in the shape of an igloo, crowned by a twenty-eight-foot-high Aunt Jemima. (On the other side of apartheid, the structure is still there, beside the highway, recalcitrant, out of time, like Bryant's Grocery & Meat Market in deserted Money. Now, it's called Mammy's Cupboard, and you can go inside and get lunch, buy jams and jellies.) The messenger led them to the meeting. From Billy's oral history with USM: "And we pulled up in this little old lane into the woods and there's a cattle gap across the road. Well, when we got to the cattle gap, a bedsheet got up . . . from out of the bushes. Had a long shotgun with him. He walked over to the car and looked in at me, and I said, 'Good evening.' He looked at Mario and Mario says, 'Hi.' . . . The meeting was held under a big pecan tree that had four of those gas lamps hanging around the bushes. There was fifteen men in the group." About a week later, according to Billy, two FBI agents stopped him on a downtown street and said they knew he'd been at a Klan meeting. "I says, 'How'd you bastards know that?' He says, 'Well,' says, 'you want me to tell you how many people was in the field?' I says, 'I'll tell you. There was fourteen or fifteen people there.' He said, 'Yeah, and five of them was ours.' "

He won the election and took office again at the start of 1968. "That thing" would be his for the next twenty years, until he'd had enough. A handful of times, the FBI investigated the sheriff for alleged financial improprieties and physical abuse and intimidation. Complaints were filed against Billy for reputed bootlegging, taking kickbacks from gamblers, being involved in prostitution. Nothing much came of any of the charges, and some of the accusations—as can be determined from available documents—seem to have been concocted by those who despised the Ferrell family. In any event, there were no criminal indictments, and the cases died. Almost all of the names in the documents have been blacked out by government censors. A complaint to the FBI, filed August 28, 1976, stated: "A male, who declined to identify himself, telephoned the Jackson Office and related information to the effect that the above captioned subject [William Ferrell, Adams County Sheriff] is involved in the receipt of kickbacks from gamblers and prostitution activities in the Natchez, Miss., area. The complainant advised that a black female [blacked-out name and description] operates a well known house of prostitution on [blacked out] in Natchez. The prostitutes employed at this house come from varying locations around the United States and this house of prostitution is allowed to exist with the consent of Sheriff FERRELL, who is completely aware of this activity. . . . Gambling activities with high stakes games occur in Natchez and FERRELL purportedly receives kickbacks" from local businesses.

The whorehouse was almost certainly Miss Nellie Jackson's. The FBI supervising agent wrote on the bottom of the case file in his own hand: "She has too much on the town to have to pay off." The case died.

Two years later, another case judged by the FBI to be without merit, or at least not worth pursuing, involved an Adams County black man who charged (quoting now from the declassified document itself, the names blacked out) "that he has been harrassed [sic] by the sheriff of Adams County, Mississippi, since he made allegations to the FBI in Alexandria, Louisiana, indicating the sheriff was involved in bootleg liquor. He advised that when he returned to Natchez, Mississippi, 'hit men' are after him at the sheriff's request. He advised the sheriff was keeping him from drawing unemployment and that he needed protection from the FBI." The investigation was dropped when the complainant was determined to have mental problems, which may have been precisely the case.

In January 1968, when Billy came back into office, his boy, Tommy, who would eventually succeed him, was twenty and in night school. Billy liked to call him *his boy,* in the way Tommy would eventually speak of his own son as *his boy.* It's a term of endearment. Tommy had not had a success in college, first time around. After finishing public high school in 1965, he put in a year at Mississippi State University in Starkville. When his dad was reelected, Tommy was living in Natchez, working as a dispatcher for the Arkansas Freight Company. (In the KKK story, Billy reputedly borrowed Tommy's little VW beetle to go give his political speech—he didn't want to tip anybody off by showing up at Black Mammy in his own sedan.) Tommy, who had a damn fine head but was never meant to be a rocket scientist—this was Billy's own estimation of his boy years later, down on the dock—"had overbooked himself that first term in college with high technical courses." There was another complication, in that Tommy had gotten married in 1966, at nineteen, to the former Carole Anne Christina of Camden, Texas. He needed money to support his new family. As they say in the South, "a bun was soon in the oven." That was William T. Ferrell III, born in the first year of Billy's new administration. Tommy, more earnest about the books the second time around, earned his bachelor's degree in business administration in 1969 at the University of Southern Mississippi in Hattiesburg. He and Carole and little Ty went to Houston, where Tommy took a job at a subsidiary of Texas Instruments. Houston proved to be a horrid experience: a hot, swarming city; cramped up all day in a little box of an office with no window. It was as if he was fighting his own nature. He lasted three months. This was the first and last time that Tommy would try to stave off the family profession. One morning, he called his father and begged to come home to Mississippi and work for him as a deputy. Practically his whole life, the son had been around the sheriff's department without an issued gun or formal badge. "They tease me that as a child I teethed on a six-point star," Tommy liked to say. As a teenager, he had loved riding with the sheriff on Saturday night, helping clean out slot machines from the back rooms of the juke joints. "Toting slots—that was me in high school," Tommy would tell interviewers after he had that thing himself.

Tommy came back to Natchez to start working for his father for real in 1969 as a sheriff's deputy in the tax department of the Adams County sheriff's office. (By at least 1971, Mario Hernandez was the head of the tax division in the office—then he went to work for H&R Block. Hazel Ferrell also worked for the county in the tax office and knew Mario well. For a time, Hazel also served without pay as a sheriff's deputy.) When he returned home, Tommy had a wife and a one-year-old, and a renewed zeal to make good, and thus began the start of his own amazing climb in law enforcement. There weren't any drug problems in Natchez in 1969 for a lawman to combat, other than controlling the moonshine bootleggers. The son sheriffed for his father for almost nineteen years, the last nine as his chief criminal deputy. "Deputy Ferrell, go do this," the sheriff would bark at his boy, not cutting him any slack, and people in the office would grin. They knew Tommy was the sheriff-in-waiting. By the late eighties, the succession and transformation were complete. Billy felt old, felt tired. Tommy felt ready. On December 30, 1987, the eve of the takeover, there was William T. Ferrell the younger in the *Democrat,* with his own incisored, tough-guy, top-dog grin. "Like Father, Like Son" was in the headline. The story said: "The chief deputy will replace his father, retiring Adams County sheriff of twenty-four years, William T. 'Billy' Ferrell, for whom he's worked for the last eighteen years." The story quoted the sheriff-elect as saying that the only real difference between father and son "is age difference. The sheriff who is retiring was sheriff in an era that was not as complicated as today. The only way I'll be different is in the technology of changes that have come along." Tommy said that he intended to combat the stereotype of the tobacco-chewing, cola-drinking, potbellied, bigoted, bribe-taking, illiterate Southern sheriff. "I've got to fight that image," he said. He was going to promote a modern image, a righteous image, of an educated, "well-groomed sheriff's department." The old ways were the old ways, he said.

The elder's dreams had been confined largely to Mississippi. Like a character in Faulkner, Billy had striven to rise above his low origins. He could have been out of the Snopes clan. He'd achieved a certain bourgeois respectability. The next in this line had far larger ambitions. It's how families in America are supposed to up themselves. When Billy sat down and wrote a letter of application to the Sovereignty Commission in 1964, he composed it in his imperfect grammar and got his résumé onto one page. To see a copy of Tommy's professionally done résumé almost four decades later, in the late nineties, after he'd been in office a decade and enjoyed national stature among lawmen, was to understand a lot about generational improvement. Tommy's curriculum vitae ran to more than seven pages of qualifications and awards and organizations. He listed everything, from his membership in Ducks Unlimited to appointment as vice chairman of the nominating committee of the National Sheriffs' Association in 1993 (just one more rung on the ladder of his climb to the eventual presidency of the NSA). But, really, it was the same Ferrell hubris and hunger to improve oneself, just more technologically enhanced and sophisticated. If Tommy had the ego and arrogance of the man in the middle of Charles Moore's photograph—and then some—he also had the kind of polish and political acumen, not to say higher education, his father never had. Tommy presented himself in office as the leading practitioner of law enforcement on a county level in his home state. He felt himself the equal of any sheriff anywhere, applying business school techniques and computer technology to run criminals to ground—and the presentation was difficult to argue with. But for all the modern ways, he was a Ferrell, his father's son, and a large part of being a Ferrell was loyalty to one's own and devotion to history. At certain moments, it came back, in hard bites.

In late 1987, when Tommy, at forty, with a growing paunch, with an extremely loud voice, was assuming the office of head lawman, the third in this line of WTFs was nineteen and screwing up in college. It was as if a swerve had come in the family fortunes and destinies. This inheritor was a law enforcer in his soul, as all the Ferrells were, but in his father's view he was also a confused and rather soft and disappointing child-man who'd zigged and zagged too much. Tommy loved his son, there wasn't any question of that, even if he had a hard time showing it, just as he had a hard time showing it to his younger child, Cricket, the brainy one. But had his own father ever showed it directly to him? Billy had transmitted his love by indirection, through pride of work and other things. It's what Tommy tried to do, too. It was as if his boy, Ty, didn't really know what he wanted from life. It was as if he'd somehow gotten all these feminine genes inside him. No one in the family had any idea then, but a decade hence, Ty would be doing the family work in the racially complex American Southwest. Doing it very well, doing it with what seemed like existential torment, as if he were meant to be a roiling repository for so many unnamed, unclaimed Ferrell family shames.

R esponding to a question, he's once more choking back the tears: "I think he is. I think he might be. I'm the only son he's got. If I was washing dishes at Burger King, he'd still have to be proud of me in some ways because I'm his son. I'm the only one he's ever going to have." The choking back came on the last few words. The question I asked him was: Is it possible your father is prouder of you than he's able to let on?

It came up just now because last night, over dinner, Ty had said, "It relieved me, having a daughter instead of a son. I don't want to say I had Mallory as an experience, but I somehow think it's easier, you know?" He said it searchingly—and, again, almost tearfully. Because the moment had been strained, the conversation shifted. Perhaps the tears didn't come because both

Mallory and Carla Ferrell were in the restaurant booth with him. Later, Ty said he had been worried during Carla's pregnancy that if the baby "had come out a son, I wouldn't know how to do it. You know what I mean? I don't want to say I didn't have a dad, growing up. That's not accurate. But I guess I worried that I might not have anything to fall back on." The honesty seemed coupled to the lack of bitterness in it.

Also at the Golden Corral last night, Ty had said that "the only time in my whole life I've ever seen the man break down was at the funeral—and that was for maybe twenty seconds." He was talking about Tommy, at Billy's funeral.

"Can you imagine living with a tyrant like that?" he'd said a moment later about his father, in a slightly different context. But again, it wasn't condemnatory.

Still later in the evening, talking of the things that pass invisibly down in families, he'd said: "I think it's a learned behavior. Basically, we're going to become our parents. They were teaching us to be parents all along."

Carla Ferrell has her own disarming honesty, and in this and in other ways, she seems a match for her husband. She's a mile-a-minute talker. She likes to give Ty lists of things to attend to at home, and this seems fine by him. She's something of a Southern pistol, not quite a belle, who loves to doll herself up in stylish clothes and cosmetics and go out to eat. She gets along wonderfully with her father-in-law—she and Tommy talk straight at each other. When Tommy calls from Mississippi, he'll say, after a few minutes of difficult conversation with his son, "Listen, put Carla on, will you?" Then he'll get all the news. They'll talk for half an hour. Carla and Tommy send emails back and forth. She knows she's the bridge in the fragile relationship.

At the steakhouse last night, Carla said: "Here's the thing with my husband you gotta know. He was doing all that for his father, and he's doing this out here for himself. That's why he loves this job. He's free of Tommy." Like her husband, she said it with no discernible judgment. By "all that," she meant the various things that Ty tried, in Mississippi, in and out of law enforcement, before entering the Border Patrol Academy and coming out to the Southwest, where he soon found himself in love with the work and sick for home.

There was something off about the waiter at the restaurant last night. He seemed eager to please to the point of being sycophantic. Was the guy just trying to build his tip? When this theory was proposed to Ty, he shook his head. "No, it's something else. He's an ex-jailbird. He's got a crude tattoo on the top of his hand. He probably put it on himself, with a needle and ink from a pen. He could have gotten an ink pen in the joint because they made him a trusty. The way he's running around this restaurant, doing anything to please us and everybody else, tells me he's almost not even aware of what he's doing. It's a learned behavior from prison. You'll do anything to stay on their good side, as a manipulative way of getting what you really want. Which is more freedom. See, a guy in prison is always trying to get something over on the people who run it. He wants something more specific—more privileges. That's the psychology of what's going on here, and this guy doesn't even realize he's giving himself away."

Carla said, "That's a Ferrell talking."

Her husband grinned. "It's normal life to me. I wouldn't know how to react any other way. You're always observing, sizing it up."

Today the inheritor, without his wife and child, is sitting in the café of a Barnes & Noble bookstore in the suburbs of El Paso, around the corner from the small apartment where he and Carla and Mallory live. He's had his eye on a panhandler working the bookstore's customers for cigarettes and change. "He was in the parking lot when we pulled up," Ty says. "I noticed him right off."

It was his suggestion that we come here to talk. He likes bookstores, likes taking his daughter to them. In college, he'd thought briefly of becoming an English major. That was at the University of Southern Mississippi, which everybody in the state seems to refer to as "Southern." He put in about three semesters at Southern. "After second semester, when I again didn't make grades, my parents refused to support me." What was he studying? "Business," he says, his palms turned upward. "How vague can that be? I never knew what I wanted to be, what I was doing there. I had no idea what I was doing there." He had this notion of restaurant management, but, really, he sees now that he was just trying to avoid the family profession.

He left Southern and came back to Natchez and worked for a while as a waiter at the Cock of the Walk—which is not a restaurant named for the first and second generations of Ferrells. He also took courses at the local community college. He moved to Jackson and worked for an upscale restaurant. For two years (1992–94), he worked in drug enforcement support on the Gulf Coast. For the next three years (1994–97), he was a deputy sheriff in Gulfport under Sheriff Joe Price, who was a good friend of his father. In this same period, he was training to be an officer in the National Guard. He felt that perhaps a life in the military might take him away from family tensions. "The commitment was three weekends out of every four. I'd work all week on the Gulf Coast and then drive up to Camp Shelby in Hattiesburg for OCS on the weekend. It was terrible. I'd get knots in my stomach, couldn't sleep, get constipated." It would start happening to him on Wednesday, before the Friday night sign-in. "By Thursday, no sleep at all. Just overcome with anxiety."

Why was it so stressful?

"I'm not sure. I think because of the way the officers and instructors drove us. Finally, I dropped out. I dropped out in the December drill." He would have been commissioned a second lieutenant the following June. His father couldn't understand the decision to quit. Tommy had gotten his officer's commission in the U.S. Army back in 1976. He's a lieutenant colonel in the Mississippi National Guard, military police branch.

Did he tell his parents about the weekly knots in his stomach? A quick and almost violent shake of his head. "And show my weak side? Show my weakness? No, obviously not."

Then: "When I was in high school, I'd be terrified to come home after I'd done something wrong—staying out late or whatever. No matter what I did, and I never really did much wrong in the first place, I was always getting caught. He'd get all over me. You don't know what it's like to have to face him. My little sister, Cricket, would give it right back to him. He'd be following her down the hall to her room, just right on her neck, yelling at her, and she wouldn't say a word, just slam that door right in his face. Which of course would drive him crazy." (Some months later, when Tommy Ferrell was asked about the knots in his son's stomach, he said: "No, I didn't know about that. But my response to that would be, 'Well, why not triumph over it?' ")

When he was in the guard, Ty trained to be an air traffic controller at Fort Rucker, Alabama. He has always liked aviation and he had this idea he'd finish his military commitments and join the Federal Aviation Administration as a civilian controller. He also had wondered about a career in aerospace. He did very well in his air-traffic-control training courses, and he even did some instructing on his own. But he didn't pass the FAA exam. He was apparently too knotted up.

Once, on the Gulf Coast, working as a lawman, he saw something that knotted him emotionally for weeks. In a way, it was the obverse of the incident with the cop who'd brutalized the squirmy Asian teenager. A much older man named Roy had gotten a job in law enforcement. He was a sympathetic character, not cut out for the work. He'd gotten the job as a kind of favor owed to him. One day, he was given an assignment to escort a funeral cortege. He got caught in an intersection on his motorcycle, after the line of cars had gone through. He was hit broadside by a car that wasn't part of the funeral, and the force of it sent him sailing off the cycle. Ty, who was in the vicinity and who liked the old man a lot, heard the 1099 emergency call. He tore to the scene and saw the officer on his back, with his teeth out and his hair all bloody. The paramedics were working on him. Ty started to break down. He felt people were looking. He walked away. It's one of the only times he can recall breaking down on the job.

The idea of going to work for the Border Patrol came about inadvertently. Ty was working as a transport officer in the sheriff's department of Harrison County on the Gulf Coast, and one day he drove over to Baton Rouge, Louisiana, to pick up a prisoner from the Border Patrol. He asked the agents about their work. They talked it up. "You'll probably have to leave Mississippi," they told him. He didn't really act on the idea for another two years. When his father heard that his son was thinking about entering the Border Patrol, he blew up. Goddamn security guard job, was Tommy's approximate reaction. A few years later, Tommy would tell a Natchez reporter, "They didn't get the bug for the badge and the gun." He was talking of his children—one in law, the other in the Border Patrol.

What about going home to succeed his father as sheriff when Tommy has had enough—has he thought of it?

Immediately: "I want to do that. I've always wanted it. I'd want to go back and take over his job, succeed him, just as he did his father. I think I could be good at it. It's different now, though. You can't work as a deputy to your father anymore because of the nepotism laws in the state. Even my dad had to get some kind of exemption for it. I'd have to do it totally on my own, just go back there and establish my name in some kind of job, maybe not even law enforcement, and then when the time came, run for sheriff, using the Ferrell name."

What's keeping him from trying?

The palms upward, the ruddy-faced grin: "Fear."

I first met Ty Ferrell's fear-inspiring father on October 1, 1997, in the afternoon of the same day I first met Ty's grandfather. This was two years before I went to the Southwest to meet Ty. When I pulled up to the lake house on Ferrell Lane that morning, Paw-Paw and Mimsy were just getting ready to bat off to Baton Rouge for the imminent birth of their granddaughter's twins. After the Ferrells departed for Baton Rouge in the white Lincoln, I drove back across the river and into town and parked opposite the sheriff's office. It was still early in the day, and I thought I would just take my chances and see if I could get a few minutes with the current sheriff of Adams County, who was also the rising fifth vice president of the National Sheriffs' Association. In the next five years, Tommy was slated to proceed through the four vice presidential chairs ahead of him before reaching the top-dog slot, in the early summer of 2002. Tommy and I had spoken briefly on the phone from Jackson the day before I arrived in Natchez.

Tommy's squad car, with his name across the side of it, was parked out front of the sheriff's department, which also serves as the jail, and is directly across from the courthouse. It's a handsome, modern, redbrick building. A secretary sitting in an outer office seemed immediately to know who I was. She talked of how wonderful it was that Paw-Paw and Mimsy were about to be great-grandparents, and how they are all just family in the Adams County sheriff's department, and how deer season for bow and arrows had just opened, and how she and her husband preferred hunting deer with rifles. "Next up'll be the rifles," she said. On the wall, floor to ceiling, were pictures of Tommy, standing next to officials from across the state and the nation. There were certificates and awards and citations. There were pictures from his high school reunion; pictures of himself with Trent Lott, with the then–attorney general of the United States, Janet Reno; pictures of himself and his fifty-odd-person agency—a museum of Tommyville.

An inner door opened and the sheriff appeared, his voice preceding him. It was very loud and deep. Everything seemed large—stomach, greeting, attire. He was extremely cordial. He had on a silver rodeo belt buckle that looked the size of a tennis shoe. He had on handsome and soft-leather cowboy boots. He had on a big gold watch. His hair was prematurely white and made him look less a law enforcer than a florid Southern politician. Running diagonally down the collars of his brown uniform shirt were two gold bars, the kind military officers wear. The bars said SHERIFF. He looked and didn't look like his father.

The CEO of law and order led the way down the hall to his office. He closed the door. He didn't go around and sit behind his desk but instead took a seat on a little red leather settee. Behind his head were beautiful prints of Stonewall Jackson and Robert E. Lee and Nathan Bedford Forrest, the last being a cofounder of the KKK, but also a romantic and ruthless ex–cavalry general in the Confederacy's western armies. In *The Mind of the South*, W. J. Cash wrote of the Lost Cause and the cult of the Confederate general as it affected grandsons and great-grandsons in the twentieth century: "Every boy growing up in this land now had continually before his eyes the vision, and he heard always in his ears the clamorous hoofbeats, of a glorious swashbuckler, compounded of Jeb Stuart, the golden-locked Pickett, and the sudden and terrible Forrest . . . forever charging the cannon's mouth with the Southern battle flag."

No sooner had he sat down than the sheriff of the county stood up and took the gun off his hip and placed it on his desk. Tommy went around behind the desk and took the receivers from two phones off their hooks and placed them on his desk. (The two phones were side by side, next to two computers.) He came back to the settee and sat down again and crossed his legs. There was a ballpoint in his shirt pocket. He took it out and began clicking it on his boot top. His glasses were suspended by a lanyard around his neck. The office, not huge, was full of photos, awards, recognitions. There was a bumper sticker that said TRENT LOTT FOR PRESIDENT. Lott is his very good friend, he said.

He was blunt, arrogant, likable, candid, almost comically full of himself. It was as if he was so far out there into egospace that the fact of it did a strange turn in your head. It was like a brilliant theater piece, except that it wasn't acting, apparently. It was Tommy. After a while, you could take the performance on its own terms, be almost perversely charmed by the cocksureness.

He called his domain "a li'l ol' redneck sheriff's office down here in Mississippi," giving a big grin to the big lie of it. He said (he was tabbing on his fingers) that a successful sheriff, in order to be successful, "has to be, in my opinion, one, arrogant; two, egotistical; three, straightforward blunt; and, number four, in an all-assuming position of leadership."

"By arrogant, Sheriff, do you mean confident?"

"No, I pretty much mean arrogant as arrogant," he said.

"I'm a very regimented individual," he said. "I have a calendar in my drawer here so that I can tell you who I was with, who I was talking with, every minute of the last twenty-eight years."

"Really?"

"Exactly," he said.

On the stereotype of Mississippi sheriffs: "It's frustrating, it's embarrassing, it makes me mad. When I go to my national sheriff meetings, guys from New England or California or somewhere will come up and give me the business about Mississippi. Not only is it embarrassing to me personally, it is unfair to Mississippi. It's part of my mission to enhance the image of law enforcement in our state at the same time I am improving it nationally. I love it out of every pore to be a Mississippian. I was born and raised here. I'm a seventh-generation Mississippian. I hate that 'Ghosts of Mississippi' and 'Mississippi Burning' crap that Hollywood puts out about our state. I hope you won't be doing that in your report." I told him I would do my best not to fall into traps of stereotype. "Good, that's mighty fine," he said in the public-address-announcer's voice.

We talked for nearly two hours—he just made the time. "I made the Little League games, the dance recitals, the tryouts," he said. "Okay, maybe a little distracted, and then, too, you walk in with a firearm at your side and that stops everything." He said that he was a "proactive sheriff—meaning that I fight the crime." He said that the job was 50 percent political, 50 percent professional law enforcement, and "soon as you tip it one way more than the other, your troubles begin." He said that 85 percent of the crime in the county these days was drug-related. He said he felt himself damn lucky not to have remortgaged his house or lost his marriage due to some damn crack-cocaine habit of his own. "I know lots around here who are like that. Providence of God. By the way, I've been successfully married thirty-two years."

I asked about Billy, whom I'd only briefly met. He said his father "was a fair father, not a good one." He said that Billy "couldn't do it now. It passed him by. He's a dinosaur. He stayed four years too long as it was. If he'd have stayed four more as sheriff, he would have been in a federal penitentiary." This topic was pushed a little, but the politician-lawman wasn't buying. "The rules changed, is all," he answered.

He said they were mainly Southern Baptists in his family, although a few Ferrells, like his father, had grown up Roman Catholic, not fervidly.

He said that his daughter, Cricket, was up at Ole Miss Law. She'd done her undergraduate work out of the state. She could have had a scholarship to college if she had stayed in Mississippi and gone to school, but, no, she had to do it her own way, go to LSU in Baton Rouge. He said, "She's a good student. She's not a brilliant student, because she's a cop's kid." He said that when Cricket was in high school, she went out for sergeant major of the drill team at the public high, and of course she got it, because she had put her mind to it, just as she had to get into the homecoming court, and just as she had to get the top dance spot, "the chief ballet thing for the Audubon legend. Now, I don't know why every girl in the South has to take ballet, but they do, it's just one of the rules." He and Cricket pass John Grisham's novels back and forth, he said. One of the things he loves about Grisham is that Grisham's "got this stuff in there about the passage of time, how things get handed down in families." For a while, he said, it looked like Cricket was going to study literature in school. " 'What the hell we gonna have now, an English teacher?' I said to her one day after I heard that. Well, it looks like it won't work out that way now." He grinned the toothy Ferrell grin.

He said that his son, whom everybody called Ty, had recently gone out to Santa Teresa, New Mexico, as a federal agent, and "that my little granddaughter, Mallory, is out there, too, and it's just too damn far away." He had Mallory's picture, framed, sitting on his desk. In another corner of the office was the portrait of Billy, Tommy, and Ty looking heavenward with their guns. The conversation moved on.

Natchez was about as layered and stratified a place as you could get, he said. That very night, he could, if he wanted, get himself into a monkey suit and go off to some reception at the civic center for actors Kurt Russell and Goldie Hawn and that guy who runs the Disney studios. (He was referring to Michael Eisner.) Only he didn't want to. "And tomorrow I could just as easily fit into a barbecue in a gravel parking lot in my jeans, and the next day after that I might appear at some function at Mt. Zion Baptist Church. Which is black. But my point is, this is what I mean by stratified."

He talked of the number of blacks on his force and in his support staff. He said that the ratio of blacks to whites in Adams County was about 60 percent to 40 percent, and that was the approximate ratio he tried to keep in his agency. (According to the 2000 census, the ratio is 46 percent white, 52 percent black, two percent "other.") He said that in every civic election the blacks were about 3,000 votes behind the white community, and that always tipped the scales in favor of the whites. There were two blacks on the county board of supervisors—out of five. He said it irked him to have to go "prostitute myself annually before a bunch of incompetents called a board of supervisors" in order to settle his department's budget. He said it was important that I talk to some of the black deputies who served him. "You'll need that perspective."

In the middle of this, the door opened and an elderly woman shambled in. She was mumbling and looked disoriented. The sheriff stood up. Suddenly, he seemed out of character. "Uh, can I help you, ma'am?" he said. There was a deputy right behind her, and he quickly got her by the arm and led her out. "I must apologize to you for this woman in my office," Tommy said with an odd, comic formalism that I would experience again the next day, when Tommy's father, down on the dock, suddenly spoke of Bobby Kennedy as a pissant featherweight and a snively-nosed little sonofabitch. A few minutes after the woman was led away, the deputy returned to make his own elaborate apology to the sheriff. The woman had been on a bus to Hattiesburg, but had gotten off and come to the sheriff's department. Before anybody could stop her, she was in Tommy's office. "Okay, okay, you explained it, now get the hell out of my office," Tommy said to the deputy. And the deputy did, grinning through his anxiety.

Occasionally, there was banging above our heads. There were about a hundred prisoners upstairs, he said. Some were awaiting trial, others were serving their term. "Mostly drugs, robbery, driving under the influence," he said. The greater percentage of the prisoners were black males, he said. "So you're gonna get accused of it, racism, by what I call radicals. I get accused of racism by the radicals because of the disproportionate number of black arrests." He paused. "I'm color-blind when I make the arrests. I don't care who the violator is. I arrest criminals. I process twenty-five hundred people a year through this jail. In a ten-year period, that's twenty-five thousand people. What we do here in Mississippi is successfully enforce the law."

He said he "gets sued all the time by his inmates—frivolous jail suits. My lawyers love me. Never lost one yet."

Over the next couple of years, there were several more lengthy talks with Billy's son. For instance, he made himself available for two such extended conversations in the summer and early fall of 1999. (I still hadn't met Ty yet.) The sheriff of the county was up for reelection for his fourth term, and even though the outcome wasn't really in doubt, Tommy wasn't taking chances. He chose not to campaign—that would be unseemly—but he was apparently talking up his achievements every chance he got in every unsubtle way that he knew, so I was informed. ABC-TV correspondent Connie Chung was scheduled to come to town in a few weeks to interview him for a 20/20 segment about modern law enforcement and about old unrequited civil rights crimes in Mississippi. (After the interview, which took place in August, Tommy updated his résumé with the fact. For a long time afterward, he kept snapshots of himself and Chung on his desktop, to show visitors. The segment itself on 20/20, which aired in the late fall, generally annoyed him. A lot of it was playing on the standard old Mississippi stereotype crap, he told me on a later visit. But he still loved the fact that Connie Chung came to town to interview him.)

The sheriff had arranged that I be given a tour of the department and the jail. There was much to be impressed by, at least in the way the CEO had things locked down. The menus for the week were posted on heavy doors and walls in the jail. ("Lunch: 1 cup Irish stew. 1 cup string beans. 1 piece cornbread. Two tabs butter. Koolaid or coffee.") There were windows up there, but you couldn't see out of them. They were covered over and were tinted. The reason for this, Tommy later explained, was because the prisoners "were up there making such clatter—they'd beat on the windows and yell down to people on the street. They were yelling through the vents and disturbing the public. Judges across the street would complain that they were disrupting their courtroom."

There had been a riot in one cell block of the jail in 1998. There were both blacks and whites in the block. It went on all day. Camera crews from around the state showed up on his doorstep. It all defused when a special crisis intrusion unit from the highway patrol went into the block and broke the riot's back.

I had also talked by this time to some cops in a special drug-unit task force that Tommy had organized with fellow law enforcers and federal agents from other counties and nearby states. Again, there was much to be impressed by. The drug enforcement officers were using the latest digital cameras and recording devices. They communicated to each other by computer: "CENTER INTELLIGENCE SUMMARY. Davidson County, Tennessee—58 pounds marijuana, 1 vehicle, 2 arrests . . . at 1843 hours, Tennessee 20th Judicial District Drug Task Force Agent Mike Garbo stopped a 1992 Mercury Grand Marquis, Texas registration . . . at mile marker 196 eastbound on Interstate 40, for a traffic violation."

I had also spoken to half a dozen deputies who worked directly for the sheriff, several of whom were black. In the main, they had good things to say, and this included the ones who were offered the opportunity to speak anonymously. I also talked to some secretaries and support staff (they, too, generally had good things to say), who opened some of the departmental bookkeeping and recordkeeping. Under Tommy's directive, the sheriff's department was storing all of its old available case files—reaching back to 1953—on permanent computer disks. The only trouble was that some of those case files, especially from the movement years, were extremely sketchy. When he left office the first time, in 1964, Tommy's father had taken with him all of his old records. This surprising fact had come to light when Billy's successor in office, Odell Anders, appeared before the United States Commission on Civil Rights at hearings in Jackson in February 1965. Anders said he couldn't find his predecessor's records, they didn't seem to be anywhere about. Another sheriff, John D. Purvis, was asked about this disappearance later in the hearings. Purvis was a sheriff up in the Delta. "Do you know of any practice in Mississippi by which some sheriffs, at least, take away all the records and turn nothing over to their successors?" a commissioner asked. Purvis replied from the witness stand: "I have heard of it, but I can't say I know of it, because I don't."

When Billy returned to office, he brought his case files back, at least portions of them. And his son was putting them on disks now, for history's sake. According to Tommy, what his father had done was perfectly legal in Mississippi statutes. And he could have gotten away with bringing nothing back. "I could do it, too, if I wanted. Nobody could stop me. But I won't."

I had also talked in the interim to several dozen other people around town who weren't in Tommy's employ. Some were involved in local politics, others were ordinary citizens. By and large, people on both sides of the color line seemed to think of him as a fair and straight lawman. Certainly, it was easy enough to find Natchezeans who hated the Ferrells, who hated Tommy for his infernal ego, just as they had hated Billy for his. But relatively few Natchez blacks with whom I spoke seemed ready to accuse Billy's son of being bigoted, and those who did seemed to be nursing personal grudges not related to specific examples of racism per se. Almost everyone spoke of Tommy as an astute politician, always a couple of jumps ahead on the checkerboard of wherever you thought you were. If you could get past the ego, they said, you could get along with the guy. He was effective and efficient. That seemed the consensus.

The wisest perspective on the Ferrells, father and son, first and second generation, came from Judge Mary Toles, a lifelong Natchezean. She is black and upper-middle-aged. For nearly two decades, she had served as a justice court judge, which is a low-level court in the Mississippi judicial system. I sat one early morning in her home, in a black neighborhood, near the old tire-and-rubber factory, where there had once been so much Klan activity. She was in a wheelchair and had her leg in a cast. She propped it up on a red sofa in a semidarkened room. The light, clean and cooling at that hour, was trying to work its way in under the pulled blinds. Several years before, one of Toles's children had died of AIDS, having contracted it in Washington, D.C., and the sadness in her was palpable. She had come up as a young person through the sixties and civil rights and said she knew where all the bodies were buried, literally and figuratively. She'd won election to the bench in 1982. When she decided to run for the office, she sought Sheriff Billy Ferrell's support—and got it. He about owned the town by then, she said.

"But by 1983, 1984, it became apparent to me that he wanted me to do exactly what he wanted. I understood then that this is why he and his son supported me. He was used to having people in town do exactly as he wanted." But she remembered this: After deputies in the sheriff's department began addressing her as "Mary" in her courtroom, not as "Judge Toles," she went across the street and complained to Billy. "And he took care of that disrespect right away. He said, 'This isn't right, Judge. This will be corrected.' And it was. I'll give him that."

Five years later, in the summer of 1987, when she had grown more confident in her legal authority, Toles got into a bitter dispute with Billy. It played itself out in the papers. She called him "racist and uncooperative." The dispute arose over the sheriff's unwillingness to have his deputies deliver subpoenas for her court. Toles charged that the Ferrells had refused to serve subpoenas for the justice court because they believed the duty beneath them. Serving subpoenas for a justice court judge was the work of a constable, not a sheriff's deputy. Toles saw it as disguised bigotry—the Ferrells didn't wish to assist the work of a black woman on the justice court bench. Toles hauled the sheriff's chief criminal deputy (Tommy) into court and ruled that both Ferrells had until the following Thursday to show why they should not be held in contempt. The judge also scissored out the photograph from *Life* and sent it to Billy in the mail. She said that she intended to print up five or six thousand copies and distribute the pictures in the black churches if need be. "He knew when he got that picture in the mail I wasn't kidding. I wasn't going to be on the end of that billy. He knew I was going to do whatever was necessary *not* to be hit with that billy. He knew I was prepared to say, See this picture? This is who he really is. This is who they really are. We can never forget."

The public argument over the serving of subpoenas for her courtroom was resolved mostly in her favor. "He avoided me like the plague after that. I don't remember ever having one conversation with him after that," Toles said. She paused. "What I believe is that he accommodated to the times because it was politically expedient, not morally necessary. It was tolerance in terms of race. It wasn't something in his heart. But if you could somehow divorce the color issues, I'd still say he was a pretty good sheriff, a pretty good lawman. I'll have to say that. He cleaned up the town. Again, I'll give him that." She paused again. "People really don't change in their prejudice, not underneath, in their true character. It's the rarest exception, when someone really converts. You have to have education, you have to have maybe something religious happen to you. I went to Catholic school. A sister told me, 'If you throw enough mud up on the wall, some of it's going to stick.' "

What were her feelings now about Tommy? She answered without hesitating: "A good lawman. He's got the respect of the citizenry, and that includes a lot of the black citizenry. Tell you the truth, Tommy's kind of caught, and in that you can sympathize. He has to be fiercely loyal to his father, and he knows he can't defend all that stuff that went on in the sixties. But there's a very stubborn streak in him, too. He will do what he wants."

We looked at the photograph. I asked her what she thought its central message was. "Here's the message: James Meredith wants into this school. I'm Billy Ferrell, I'm the high sheriff, and I'll do whatever I have to to keep him out. But, listen, he was just doing what all of them were thinking. I don't want to lay this on Billy Ferrell. You got to lay it on the entire South. The whole community thought that way. He got caught with that camera on him. You see, the names change, but the game is always the game."

And the game is? "And the game is, black people are still subservient. Black people should not be given a chance."

I asked if there was any way to think of Billy as a victim of his own culturally dunned and ill-educated origins. "No," she said. "Too smart a man. Too devious. Not a victim. No." Justice Court Judge Mary Toles and I talked on in her shaded living room on Bluebird Drive in north Natchez. I said that my goal was to make my way down the family rungs, and that the family was allowing me to keep on with it, to my continual surprise. I said that it wasn't beyond the realm of possibility that some distant relative of Billy could be married to a professor of African-American studies at, say, Vanderbilt or Emory or even Ole Miss. She clacked into laughter. "Yes, it's theoretically possible, isn't it?" she said. "At a minimum, it would have to be once removed from Tommy."

One day I showed the photograph to a woman named Mamie Lee Mazique. She is a black Natchezean, famous for her work in the movement. She laughed, and there seemed a certain forgiveness in it. "Yep, that's him, bristling his nightstick," she said.

I showed the photograph to Louis Baroni, a white liberal in his late seventies who had worked at the tire plant for thirty-eight years. He was the widower of perhaps the town's most visible female white activist, Marge Baroni. She had grown up Baptist and had converted to Catholicism in the forties. She became a friend of Catholic activist Dorothy Day, who had founded the Catholic Worker movement in the Bowery of New York City. During the troubles, the Baronis would get hate calls in the middle of the night. Lou would get shunned at work—or else called "nigger-lover" to his face. He worked in the curing room at Armstrong Tire & Rubber, which had about 1,100 employees. Klansmen were everywhere around him. He feared for his life, for Marge's life, for their six kids' lives. In the summer of 1965 (when Elizabeth Proby and hundreds more were arrested and taken to Parchman prison), a Klansman fired shotgun pellets into the Baroni living room on Monroe Street in downtown Natchez. "Did you call the police?" I asked. "That's a joke," he said. "You mean, you'd be reporting it to the Klan?" He answered, "Of course." Then he said, "Well, I didn't approve of their inhumanity to people, I guess. I'm talking about the whole town. You see, Marjorie was classified as a 'nigger-lover' and all that, but the truth is, it wasn't a black and white thing. She was for people. It was people. If she could help them, she would. She didn't believe in humiliating people. I suppose I thought the same way. She had feelings for people, is what I'm trying to say."

In July 1999, Ty Ferrell's father granted a long interview in the sheriff's office with the door closed. Once again, the sheriff of the county gave a powerful impression of having not a thing to hide about himself or his family's past. He took the twin phones off their hooks again. He had a toothpick in his mouth. He again sat on the little sofa beside his desk, choosing not to sit behind his desk, where he might enjoy a psychological power advantage. He was balancing his glasses in his fingertips. He wasn't in a sheriff's uniform—he had on a sport coat and wing tips and a dark blue dress shirt with a gold tie. I told him about the mostly good things that people were saying about him as a law enforcer. "And you were surprised, weren't you?" he said.

He told of a reception in Washington he'd attended that winter. The sheriff of Boston, a pal, had pulled him over to meet Ted Kennedy. "I stuck out my hand, put it right there, got right in his face with it. I said, in the biggest and proudest Southern voice I could summon, 'Senator, I'm Sheriff Tommy Ferrell, from the great state of Mississippi.' He had his hand out. You could see his face change instantly. I won't say he jerked his hand away. But it surprised the shit out of him. I enjoyed hell out of it."

I had brought along a stack of documents relating to his father. They were from the Sovereignty Commission and from other civil rights archives in and out of the state. He said he didn't wish to look at them, didn't need to look at any of them. "Maybe later I'd like to take you up on your offer to see them. I think you can appreciate what I mean," he said with something that sounded almost like doubt. But he recovered and said that he knew what he knew about his father.

I persisted anyway and asked him about Billy and the Klan. "Has anyone ever found any actual proof?" he said. I mentioned lists. "I've seen that list," he said. He didn't give a damn about any list. He believed with all his heart that it just wasn't true. For one thing, his father was Catholic, "and it's a known fact that the Klan hated Catholics." He asked if I had ever found an FBI document spelling out in any hard way that Billy had belonged to the Klan—or had even attended meetings? I said I had not ever found such an FBI document.

We talked about his father's letter of application to the Sov-Com in 1964. Tommy glanced at a copy of the letter, then said: "Well, again, that was in that era when men like my father would sort of see the Sovereignty Commission as just another branch of Mississippi law enforcement."

We talked about the question of alleged payoffs and other financial impro-prieties. None of the documents I had obtained proved anything conclu-sively—only inconclusively suggested it. Again, the son was having none of this. He said he would have known if his father was on the take. "I was there," meaning that he had worked in the sheriff's tax office before switching to the department's criminal and investigative side. He said he would have seen the difference in how his parents lived. And then he went into a story that I had not heard before and was surprised by: In the 1970s, the IRS came after his parents and put liens on the family property for something like $30,000 in back payments. It was all pretty innocent and mistaken, the son said. His chief tax deputy, Mario Hernandez (formerly the chief criminal deputy), had inad-vertently screwed things up and not made a proper reporting. "My parents lost everything they had," Tommy said. "They had to start over." He said that the feds attached a little farm that his father had bought out of town, trying to get a cattle business started, which was futile anyway, because Billy knew nothing about farming and didn't have the time in any case. "That farm was mort-gaged to its eyeballs, and what wasn't mortgaged, the feds took," Billy said. They also took his parents' first lake house over in Louisiana, he said.

I wanted to move the conversation in the direction of Tommy's own tenure, more than a decade old, growing yearly in its national esteem. I asked about Jerry and Bill McDaniel, brothers of the ex–Grand Dragon. Jerry had retired from Tommy's staff two years earlier; Bill was at work in an outer office as we spoke. "Well, I was leery of the name, of course," Tommy said, knowing exactly where the topic was going. "But, you see, you got to realize a few things that you don't understand about the South and about the Ferrells. First, there is the loyalty factor. Very loyal man, Jerry. Just like his brother Bill, who I have out there working for me now. And then a very good deputy, Jerry. Very good at his work. For a long time. Then he sort of topped out. We all reach a burn-out stage, and he reached his, but he was good for a very long time." He hesitated. "I don't let the attitude of other people influence me one way or the other."

But wasn't it politically risky, just in terms of the name and sibling identi-fication, resurrecting all those old sixties ghosts, the more so in terms of Tommy's own growing visibility on the national stage of law enforcement?

His answer: "I had many people telling me I shouldn't have the McDaniel brothers working for me. It pisses me off, these smart guys in suits or whatever coming by my office to say, 'Now, Tommy, don't you do that; that guy Jerry's going to cause you trouble, just with his name, do you harm, you've got to think of your national reputation.' These politicians and lawyers are coming into my office and sitting in my chairs and they're saying this shit and I'm looking at them and I'm saying right back, 'Who the hell are you to tell me how to be a sheriff?' I'll run my sheriff's department as I see fit. I measure an individual on his individuality. I don't believe in guilt by association."

At the end of the visit, we walked down the hall and looked at some old framed photographs from his father's time. At least two of the seven policemen lined up with Sheriff Billy Ferrell in one of the photographs had been identified as Klansmen in sixties government documents.

Two months later, the sheriff again made himself available for several hours, and this time the talk was even blunter. He wore a blazer with gold buttons and had on expensive-looking half-frames. The candidate for reelection looked like a prosperous small-town bank president. Connie Chung of ABC-TV had recently been in Natchez to do her interview with him. While the tapes had rolled, Chung had asked whether it was racially sensitive for the sheriff of the county to keep a framed picture in his office of a cofounder of the KKK.

I asked the same question now. "I'll be damned if I'll take it down," he said. "For you or Connie."

But what would he say if a black woman in the community came into his office to tell the sheriff her troubles and suddenly looked up and saw Nathan Bedford Forrest's picture above her head or on the other side of the room? "I'd tell her what I just told you," Tommy said. "I admire the man's military tactics. I'm a student of the Civil War."

I asked him if it was awkward discussing race with non-Southerners. "I think we're more open about it than in other parts of the country," he said. "I think we're more honest in saying what we really feel. I've been around blacks my whole life. I live in a predominately white neighborhood. There are some blacks there. They don't bother me."

He went on. "Remember the O. J. Simpson trial? What's his name, that cop who said he'd never used the n-word?"

Mark Fuhrman.

"Yeah, you'd never catch me saying that on a witness stand. Ask me that question on the witness stand and I might look at my watch and say, 'Let's see, it's three o'clock. Well, I may have used it an hour ago.' I'd never try to tell somebody I don't use it. I don't use it in the context you're asking about. I don't use it to just say it. Or to insult somebody. Hey, I've had blacks call me 'Nigger.' And you know they call themselves that, don't you?"

"Yes, but in a sense they're allowed to."

"Why? Where is that written down?"

He was exercised. "I could use the word 'spic' or 'wop.' We don't have to limit it to 'nigger' in this conversation. First of all, you have to think about the street talk of cops. They have bad mouths. They'll say, 'Lock that motherfucker up.' That may offend some people. Law enforcement people have the trashiest mouths around. It's because we're always dealing with that lower element."

Has he tried hard over the years to try to avoid saying the n-word?

"Of course. Time I was twenty-one years old, I may have used it every other word. That's in the past." Does he still slip and say it? "Shit, yes. You've heard me use it couple times in here in the last few minutes. But I wasn't using it just to use it. I won't allow that. I'm not in the game to offend anyone. And here's another problem. I can remember having the name problem when I was a young deputy. The whole thing of what to call blacks went in a sense from 'nigger' to 'colored person' to 'African-American.' You'd be out there on the radio and you might hear somebody from the highway patrol saying, 'Look out for a a nigger male.' Or 'Look out for a nigger female.' Well, hell, every cop in the state was talking like that. I'm not saying it was right. I'm saying that's just the way it was. We had to learn to change here in the South. I won't allow that talk on my staff now. It isn't right."

We talked of police corruption, of cops on the take. He said that he prayed every day "not to succumb to the temptation to go over to the other side. If I do, it'll be for something big—big money. You can put that down."

That evening, the sheriff of Natchez spoke before a mostly white audience at a Candidates' Forum at the Lady Luck Hotel on Canal Street. The forum was sponsored by the Adams County Chamber of Commerce. Candidates for coroner, constable, supervisor in the Fifth District, circuit clerk, sheriff of the county presented their credentials. Billy Ferrell's son stood against a wall and awaited his turn, not patiently. He was due to appear in the middle of the bill. He talked to a crony in a loud whisper. He kept creeping further down the wall, closer to the front of the room. When his time did come, Tommy went to the lectern and pushed aside the microphone. "You elected me your sheriff in November 1987 for the first time," he said. "I have been honored and humbled to serve and would like to be able to continue doing so. I succeeded my father, the late Billy Ferrell. I have a dedicated staff of fifty-five." He went on for another ten or fifteen minutes. He was effective and confident and polished. His wife, Carole Anne, and his mother, Hazel, applauded him, along with everyone else. Carole Ferrell is attractive and petite and vivacious. Over the years, she has sold Mary Kay cosmetics to Natchez homemakers. I told her that I had met their daughter, Cricket, up at Oxford, and that I thought I could see some Ferrell cop genes in her. (Through the years she has considered work in some legal aspect of law enforcement.) I told Carole what I imagined her son, Ty, might be like. Carole said I was mostly right. "He's just kindhearted," she said. "Ty will go right up and hug and kiss people in the family if he hasn't seen them in a while. Cricket would never do that. He's too good to be a cop, really. So many things tear him up. You'll see when you go out there."

At the reception for Tommy and the other candidates, Hazel Ferrell introduced me to some of her widowed friends. Her red hair was beautifully coifed. She had on a lovely dress. There was a great sense of refinement about her. "The old sheriff told him some stories before he died," she said.

When Billy Ferrell was an old used-up lawman, out of office, he used to go downtown and work as a security guard in a parking lot at the Natchez Little Theater. It was just for something to do. "You'll never catch me doing that when the game is over," Tommy Ferrell has said to me several times.

Six weeks after the Candidates' Forum, the old sheriff's son drew almost 9,500 votes out of about 11,100 cast, a landslide victory by any measurement except Tommy's. "Eighty-nine percent of the electorate and I'm still mad because I didn't know I had eleven percent enemy." (According to the paper, the percentage was 84.89.) "I owe my victory to the professionalism of my office and the employees that I have," Tommy was quoted as saying. Ten days later, on November 13, there was another story in the *Democrat*. The two-column headline on page 1: "Bondsman Says Sheriff's Policy Racist." Two bail bond agents, both black, had accused the sheriff of preventing them from writing bonds at his jail. The sheriff denied to the reporter that he was acting out of any racial bias. "I don't know what the color of the bondsmen are that we're using now," he said. "It doesn't matter what color they are." But it was a public embarrassment for Tommy, the more so coming on the heels of his smash victory.

(A good while later, I talked to one of the bondsmen who accused Tommy of racism. Joe Martin, a native of McComb, Mississippi, where so many civil rights battles were fought, told me he was an old movement person. "I was in SNCC," he said. He'd marched with Bob Moses as early as 1961. He was once thrown in jail by Billy Ferrell. Martin and others had come to Natchez to protest. "Nothing's changed," Martin said. "He's still got the same policy. He's discriminating against me. He would never interview me [for writing bonds]. He let us put our names up there on the list at the jail, but he still refuses to let us write bonds. In my mind, the son falls right in behind the old segregationist dad." I asked Martin if his civil rights past could have anything to do with his troubles in securing licensing for bond approval at the Adams County jail. "I couldn't tell you," he said. "But they could pull up my file in a second if they wanted to.")

About a week and a half after Tommy Ferrell got nearly 85 percent of all votes cast for sheriff, his conflicted and honest son, out on the New Mexico border, within the first half hour of conversation, said, "Oh, I hate him for his pride."

Near the beginning of W. J. Cash's *Mind of the South,* there are these lines about Southern men: "In every rank, they exhibited a striking tendency to build up legends about themselves and to translate these legends into explosive action—to perform with a high, histrionic flourish, and to strive for celebrity as the dashing blade."

O pponents of United States immigration policies claim that the border patrol doesn't so much stop illegal entry as move it around, that it merely shifts the problem, like desert sand, from one community to the other. The border between Mexico and the United States is 2,000 miles long. The United States spends roughly $2 billion a year to control this line—ineffectually. It is estimated that there are now about twice as many illegal immigrants in the United States as there were a decade ago. Recent census figures suggest that the undocumented population of the country is somewhere between 6 million and 9 million, the highest since the Immigration and Naturalization Service started keeping records. Mexico is the source of about half of all illegal immigrants in the country. Critics of America's border policies say that Washington lacks the guts to send in the Marines or the National Guard or the Army. If America really wanted to cut off the flow from the south, the country could post a sentry every ten feet along the 2,000 miles of shared border—and lock it all down. Ty Ferrell agrees. No matter how much he likes his work, there is some sense in which he feels he is just part of a hypocritical show between nations. Sometimes it seems to him that he's not so much a cop as a pretend cop, caught in the middle of political expediencies. And here is another predicament that grows greater in him the longer he stays on the border: How do you keep seeing them as individuals? There are so many to apprehend, every shift. No matter your best intentions, after a while they're like faceless forms.

(If you were just counting numbers, especially in the wake of the September 11, 2001, terrorist attacks on America, the illegal entry problem would seem to have gotten better. In 2000, more than 1.6 million people were caught on the U.S.-Mexican border, the highest number ever recorded. In 2001, the figure dropped to 1.2 million. In 2002, it fell again. Apprehension figures are a key indicator for gauging the number of migrants trying to get across. Why the drop over the last few years? Fewer jobs in the United States, as well as increased patrols following the September 11 attacks, are almost certainly factors. Some observers also point to television commercials broadcast in Mexico warning that one migrant per day dies while attempting to get across.)

On the first visit, after we'd had lunch, we drove out to the line. We rutted around on broken roads in the green Suburban. He was a man in his element, a tracker, a cowboy, a cop. Even though Ty wasn't on duty, he kept his Border Patrol radio on and listened in as he pointed out things about the landscape. A loud squawking interrupted him. "They've caught two over by the 489 Port One," he said. He drove over to the vicinity of that sensor. He saw the other vehicle and pulled the Suburban alongside the van of his fellow agent, driver's side to driver's side, as if they were two ship captains at sea who've jibed their crafts close together for a little visit.

"They were hiding," the fellow agent said. "This one right here we've caught before." He jerked his head to one of the two faces behind him. The two faces were behind a wire grate. You couldn't make out the age of the two who had just been caught. They didn't seem old. Their clothes looked dirty. They were hunched forward, leaning over the seats, their faces pressed up against the grate. They seemed to be listening to the conversation—which they almost certainly did not understand. The grate separated the front seat of the van from the seats in the back. The two detainees didn't seem particularly unhappy. One waved to Ty, as if he knew him.

"I think one's got a fake leg or something," the agent said to Ty, which lit something in Ty.

"Yeah, I think I caught him once before," Ty said.

They continued talking over the top of the prisoners for another few minutes and then the agent drove off to headquarters. The two citizens of Mexico in the back of the van could have been bagged animals. This was suggested to Ty. "I think I still feel about them the way I did when I started this job. I think I still have that basic understanding for their situation. But it's hard. It's what happens to cops."

More than a year later, on another visit, Ty and I sat in the living room of his newly purchased home in Santa Teresa and talked of the hard subject of race and of Mississippi and of his own family's attitudes. "Racism is alive and well in my home state, and always will be," he had said the first time we had met, but neither of us had pursued the topic directly. It wasn't the right time. This visit was in May 2001. A month earlier, in a statewide referendum, Mississippi had voted overwhelmingly, after more than a year of public and national teeth gnashing, to retain the Confederate battle symbol on its state flag. Governor Ronnie Musgrove and other moderates had favored a banner with twenty white stars on a blue square. The moderates and liberals had been voted down, two to one. "Our people have spoken," the governor said. "It is important that we accept the majority vote and move forward."

Ty and his wife had just moved into the first home they'd been able to buy as a married couple. They were very proud. The day they moved the furniture in, Ty and Carla found they couldn't get the sofa up the stairs—the stairs were too narrow. "The observant cop who checks everything out beforehand," he said.

Just before this visit, Ty's father sent an email, in response to an email I had sent to him regarding the next trip to Mississippi. "Looks as if you might be having a tough time with Ty's schedule. Good luck. We don't hear from them that often either. He is very independent and secretive as such. . . . I will be out of town next week on Monday afternoon and Tuesday morning. I have a Blue Lighting Operation's Center Steering Committee meeting in Orange Beach, Ala. on Tuesday morning. I am flying down Monday afternoon on a private plane (Civil Air Patrol) and back Tuesday afternoon. Range qualifications at our new range is Thursday. Yes, even old Sheriffs have to qualify and be proficient." Tommy, a man in motion.

Yesterday, first day of this visit, we went out riding on the line again. We stopped at a stable and looked at the two horses Ty rides on his patrols. Today, Ty is due to go to work at 3 P.M., but his daughter has come down sick, and so he has agreed to be Mr. Mom so that Carla can go to her job. Ty likes staying home with Mallory. He's very good at taking care of her. He has traveled with her to Mississippi without Carla. Once, Ty and his young daughter rode to Natchez in the cab of an eighteen-wheeler. Carla's brother is a long-distance truck driver, and he was coming back from California. He stopped in El Paso to pick up his brother-in-law and his niece. Ty sang to his child and told her stories on the way across. The father and his little girl were together for several weeks.

There is tension in his voice and face and body—we're talking of race. Two cats are meowing and making an annoyance of themselves beneath our feet, and he sweeps them up almost roughly and puts them in the next room and closes the door.

"How have you escaped it, or largely escaped it, racism?"

"I don't know that I have. I can't explain or put words to it why I'm not a racist person per se. But I do know how to be racist. Maybe it's my age or generation, to think about always trying to treat somebody with more dignity."

I ask his feelings about affirmative action. "I'm against it. Of course," he says. Affirmative action "has kept friends of mine from getting the job they deserved. They're victims of affirmative action. Why do you think I would be for that?"

What does he think about the vote over the Confederate flag?

"It embarrasses me. It embarrasses me to hear what people living out here in New Mexico think of Mississippi. You know what the Confederate flag means to me? It means rednecks drinking beer. It means magnolias and girls in hoop skirts. I remember parades in Gulfport when I was a deputy sheriff. These redneck hippies would be riding on flatbed trucks waving the Confederate flag. It was just an excuse to get drunk. That's all it meant to them to be waving that flag."

It's not a coded emblem of support for racism?

"Not to me it isn't."

Then: "If anything, *I've* been a victim of reverse racism. That's the racism I've seen. That's the racism *I've* experienced in my lifetime." His voice has gotten hard. Several times, his hand has shot out toward an old magazine on the table between us. The magazine is opened to a photograph of his grandfather.

"Does it come back, not just the n-word, but everything about racism, when you go home to Mississippi?"

"Yes. But I don't go home, get off the plane, and say, 'Hey, let's go shoot some niggers' and put on my KKK hat just because I'm home, if that's what you're asking."

"Do you slip and use the n-word?"

"Yes. When I go home and people are saying it, it's such a shock to my ears—at first. Then I can almost find myself saying it. I know it's not right. I don't want to say it. It's all around me. That's what I'm saying."

Does the photograph from *Life* embarrass him?

Quickly, defiantly, with his hand shooting out toward the magazine: "No. I asked for it, the copy that's laminated on the board. I've had it on the wall of several places where I've lived. I had it for a while in college. I had it hanging in a house in Jackson for six months when I was managing a restaurant. It doesn't embarrass me at all. 'That's my grandfather.' That's the way I look at it. I wish I had it now. 'That's my grandfather in *Life* magazine.' That's exactly what I'd tell friends of mine when they asked. 'See that? That's my grandfather, center of the picture, with that bat in his hand. All the law enforcement of the state is there. James Meredith is trying to get in the University of Mississippi. My grandfather is there. He's part of that show.' "

He's resting his hand on Billy's face. "I think anybody in the United States could look at this and understand what this moment is." He's looking at me hard.

Has he ever wondered if his grandfather was a Klansman?

He softens a little. "Honestly, I love my grandfather to death, but it wouldn't surprise me if he was in the Klan back then. An elected official in a little Mississippi community? I can almost *not* imagine him not being in the Klan." (A few minutes later, he'll change his mind and say he guesses that Billy never did join.)

Did his grandfather ever talk to him about the photograph and the events surrounding it?

"He never said, 'I was trying to keep James Meredith out of Ole Miss,' if that's what you mean. I think he just might have said, 'Hey, Waddle, look here, boy, that's your grandpop in *Life* magazine.' "

The talk drifts to Billy's funeral, two years previous. At 2 P.M. on that early spring day in Natchez, when many things were already in bloom, there'd been a solemn procession from Laird Funeral Home to St. Mary's Basilica. "It's real hard to talk about," he says. "If I do, I'll start crying." And a moment later, he does.

Nothing changes in Mississippi. And everything changes. Two days later, about 9 A.M., the door of a little brick rambler in Natchez opens. A woman is smiling, beckoning inward. A green garden hose is coiled on the front step. This is a modest subdivision north of town; this is the home of anybody who ever worked for hard wages in America. You've knocked here many times in the past few years, but no one was ever home, or at least didn't answer, until now.

"Yes, he's home. You can go in there and talk to him," she says. She stands aside, with a curve of smile. She's in late middle age, in a blue dress, thin, with glasses, momish. Is this his wife?

He's sitting in a wheelchair at the end of a dining room table, eating breakfast cereal. He's in a white T-shirt, pajama bottoms, slippers. He's angular and has on wire glasses. He's nearly bald. He's spooning in the cereal with his right hand. His other arm is limp. His left hand is resting like a fleshy knob on the table.

"Take a seat," says the former Grand Dragon of the United Klans of America.

He's in his late sixties. He suffered his stroke on August 29, 1999. He has five grown kids and has been married to the same woman for forty-odd years. He has never really been convicted of anything, unless you wish to count that time in 1959 when Eddie McDaniel, not yet the Dragon, was axed from his job at the Johns Manville plant for stealing coins from a milk-vending machine. His name and shrouded story are in almost any book or civil rights archive or government report you can find relating to the sixties and the Klan and Mississippi. To quote from John Dittmer's book *Local People,* in its sections on Natchez and the revival of the Klan: "Its leader in Adams County was twenty-nine-year-old Edward Lenox McDaniel, a Natchez native with a tenth-grade education. . . . Under E. L. McDaniel's leadership, the Klan struck quickly in Natchez, terrorizing the black community as the local police looked the other way." In early 1966, at the HUAC hearings in Washington, E. L. McDaniel was identified as one of a core group of Natchezeans who "advocate violence and are extremely strong segregationists." He was subpoenaed to those hearings. Over and over, the witness took the Fifth.

And here he is, in Natchez, this morning, spooning cereal, in his pajamas, out of time and memory, like Emmett Till's grocery store in Money, like Black

Mammy on the south side of town. His useless left hand is curled in a half fist. There is such a disconnect.

Directly behind him is a double-door closet. The closet doors are open, so that you can see several dozen uniform shirts and pants on hangars. They're not Klan robes, but that's all you can imagine. The shirts and pants are bunched together—maybe thirty or forty densely packed, identical-looking uniform shirts with their dark trousers. Small American flags are sewn on the sleeves of the shirts. There is lettering on each shirt: ALL STATES SECURITY. Eddie McDaniel owns a security-guard company. The company provides guards for schools, hospitals, corporations. These days, because of the stroke, one of his sons takes care of the business.

He's being friendly as pie, regular as tap water. He's open, intelligent, courteous, just some old retired guy with a disability. "No, I have no regrets about anything I did," he says. "I am not embarrassed about any of it, and if I had to do everything again, I'd do exactly the same—unless I had some different information."

Over the years, he has participated in oral histories—such is a supremacist's notoriety on the far side of apartheid. He did a lengthy and valuable oral history with a scholar at the University of Southern Mississippi, relating how his grandpa got him started with the dream of the Klan. According to Eddie, the forebear spoke to the oldest of the seven McDaniel children in an alley behind the family home: "Son, I'm going to give you a little advice. I don't want you to say this to anybody else, but if you ever have a chance to join the Klan, join the Klan."

In the early sixties, having come back to the South after another failed try in business in California, he joined the Original Knights of the KKK. They recruited him from their Klaverns across the river in Louisiana. His job was to begin establishing cells in Mississippi. The Originals expelled him for alleged misappropriation of funds (which he denies). Next, he helped form the White Knights of the KKK of Mississippi, which soon emerged as the most dangerous Klan faction in the state. In their judgment, violence was a justified response to the federal government's intrusion in the affairs of Mississippi, most notably in the case of Meredith at Ole Miss. From the ex-Dragon's oral history with the scholars of USM: "Then the Meredith deal hit on September 30, 1962. . . . There's no doubt in my mind that he would eventually enter. But the way they did it, it showed me that something had to be done. And I got very bitter toward the federal government. I saw that my kids were going to suffer in the years to come." After he was expelled from the White Knights, the Klansman threw in his luck with the United Klans of America. In September 1964, at the Imperial Klonvokation of the UKA in Birmingham, Robert Shelton, the Imperial Wizard himself, announced the new Grand Dragon for

Mississippi: Eddie McDaniel. This was just before the former sheriff of the county and two ex-deputies got stopped on Liberty Road after dark and then suffered the search of their car.

"Shelton paid me the grand sum of a hundred thirteen dollars a week when I quit my job to go full-time on the UKA," he says. "Couldn't get rich on that, no sir." When the call came, he'd been driving a truck for the Red Ball Motor Freight Company.

Does it bother him having his name in the history books as a hater of blacks?

"Nope." He puts down the spoon. He slaps the useless knob of his left hand. It's sitting there like Play-Doh.

Joan McDaniel has both hands up in the air and is making quotation marks with her fingers. "Take 'hatred of blacks' out of the quotes, please," she says. "His thing was government encroachment. That's what it was really about." She's originally from Idaho. She met her husband in California in the early sixties, before he went bankrupt, before he listed debts of $4,522 against assets of $200.

During the troubles, her husband used to tell reporters that the UKA was "100 percent Pro-American." He was leading "non-violent soldiers of Christian civilization." At cross-burning rallies in Natchez parks, he vowed that the Klan would "fight to our last breath" to defend the Southern way of life.

He flew to the HUAC hearings in Washington with Shelton. They left from Birmingham on a big airliner. A couple of Klan speedsters drove the Dragon's car from Natchez to Washington, so that Eddie could have wheels in the nation's capital. Only thing, the damn redneck speedsters burned up his damn automobile. Still gets his goat to think about it. "Just overspeeding the damn thing," he says. "Practically brand-new car." But he's laughing. It's okay, an old memory, and the deep burn of it is gone.

"Cold up there at those hearings," says Joan. "Snow. Ice. Ugh. Remember, honey?" She shivers.

Joan "was one, too," her husband says. "I'll tell you this, she was a good old Klanswoman herself. Yessir." He reaches over and gives her an affectionate pat. The fourth finger of his good hand has a huge ring on it. There are six diamonds set in a square gold band. The diamonds flash in the fluorescent light.

His wife had her own robes? Joan's nodding, smiling. "Sure did. Marched in those parades."

Does he worry, in his advancing age and infirmity, that the government will come after him for unpunished offenses?

"Doesn't bother me a bit to think of it. They could indict me tomorrow and I wouldn't worry for a minute. Because I know I didn't do any of that violent stuff."

It isn't fair, he adds, "the way they get all these black juries and convict people. Just like that guy over in Birmingham—what's his name?" He means Thomas Blanton, Jr., convicted (on May 1, 2001) for his role in the bombing of the Sixteenth Street Baptist Church. "Well, if he done that, if he blowed up those little girls, sure, he should go to prison. But my point is, they should've done it at the time, not wait all these years later." Besides which, he says, they know how to stack the juries.

He quit the Klan altogether in 1966, he says. (Other accounts have him quitting much later.) "Too much violence, out of control." He says that the biggest years for the Klan in Mississippi, in terms of membership recruitment, were in late 1962, after Meredith at Ole Miss, and continuing through all of 1963 and 1964, especially during Freedom Summer.

How many Mississippi Klansmen were there at the height of Freedom Summer—10,000?

"Way over ten thousand. But I never paid any attention to numbers. But I know way over ten thousand. Oh, I'd hate to say how many." (Historians have doubted many of his claims, not least his claims about numbers. He is famous for telling different versions of different stories to different people.)

"When it was all said and done," he ended up being good friends "with one of my sworn enemies, Charles Evers. I got to know Charles personally." After Medgar Evers was murdered in Jackson in 1963, his brother Charles—a far more controversial and self-promoting figure—took up a self-proclaimed leadership role in the movement. He became state NAACP field secretary. In the late summer of 1965, Evers came to Natchez to lead protests.

Did the eventual change in his feelings about his sworn enemy, Evers, have anything to do with religion?

"Nope. Just change in attitudes, getting to know more things about some of them."

What do his kids think of his role in civil rights history?

"Just proud of me as they can be."

Was Billy Ferrell ever in the Klan?

He shakes his head in a no—emphatically.

Without warning, he instructs Joan to leave the room. There is command in his voice. "I don't let her in on all this stuff," he says. This seems to surprise her. She gets up. She understands what is happening. Her husband is going to start his crying again. She goes around to the other side of the wheelchair. She's on his right side, the side that the stroke didn't touch. He's struggling to control his emotions. He looks up and hugs her. She bends down to the wheelchair and hugs him, kisses him sweetly on his forehead.

"Damn good woman I got here," he says.

"If you got a good man, hang on to him," she says. She's crying now.

Joan leaves the room. The man bound to his steel wheels can't hold it back. He's crying copiously. His face has deeply reddened. He takes off his glasses, wipes his eyes with a tissue. "I'm sorry," he says. "You'll have to pardon me. It's because of my stroke. It just comes on like this. I can't control it. I never know when it's about to happen."

I ask: "You say that you never know when the crying is about to happen, so is it possible that the way it comes over you is related to what you did back then?"

He's already shaking his head. "No. I don't have any guilt. It ain't that at all. It's my stroke."

Having recovered, he permits a few more minutes of talk. He says that he knew Billy Ferrell very well over many decades. "Helluva good sheriff, no question."

And Tommy Ferrell? "Better than his father even as a sheriff. Smarter, more educated." He says it again: Neither Ferrell was ever in the UKA or any other Klan that he knows of. "I'll say it categorically."

Would he call Tommy a friend? "I think so. I know I feel I am certainly a friend of his. I hope he thinks he's my friend. I'd like to know."

That afternoon, at the sheriff's office, Tommy Ferrell is told of the impromptu meeting with Eddie, and of some of the things the ex-Dragon had said. Tommy is asked if he thinks of him as a friend. There is only momentary hesitation. "Yes, I am a friend. I consider him a friend in need. I think he's been in anguish, maybe not enough. I think he's still in denial. He needs a friend. I've been to his home. I would be a pallbearer at his funeral. You see, in the South we're into forgiveness, when death comes."

The same day, on the editorial page of the *Jackson Clarion-Ledger,* there are the usual back-and-forth arguments about where Mississippi is in its race relations. One female letter writer from Vicksburg opines: "Regarding the recent flag vote: The boat sank—get over it! All of the wailing and teeth gnashing is getting really old. The voters turned out and the people spoke, loudly and unequivocally."

In Mississippi, nothing ever changes, and everything always changes, and sometimes it seems as if God put Mississippi on earth purely for our moral and confounding contemplation.

A nd still there is the land. "In Africa," the British novelist Doris Lessing once wrote, "when the sun goes down, the stars spring up, all of them in their expected places, glittering and moving." It is like that in Mississippi, too. "To me," James Meredith once wrote, "Mississippi is the most beautiful country in the world, during all seasons. In the spring, all is green and fresh, the air is clean and sweet, and everything is healthy. As a boy I knew that any running stream of water was fit to drink. I feel love because I have always felt that Mississippi belonged to me and one must love what is his."

In the Family of Meredith: Loving What Is Theirs

> The conflict between the will to deny horrible events and the will to proclaim them aloud is the central dialectic of psychological trauma.
>
> —Judith Herman, *Trauma and Recovery*

When Cricket Ferrell was a law student at Ole Miss, she bopped around Oxford in a black Ford Explorer with a sheriff's star on the license plate. This was a nod to her father. Tommy and his wife Carole were picking up the monthly payments on "my truck note," to use Cricket's phrase. Cricket was as secretly proud of her father as she was sometimes openly disdainful of him. Her parents, who were 250 miles away, down in Natchez, in the southwest corner of the state, weren't putting her through law school—Cricket paid her own way with loans. She said she wished to try to be free of Tommy's control. Ty Ferrell's little sister was in her mid-twenties (she hadn't gone straight to law school after college at LSU, but instead had worked for a casino in Natchez) and, unlike Ty, gave every impression of knowing exactly what she wanted from the world. Among her goals were a husband and a nice house and a job that paid good money. Cricket wasn't long out of Ole Miss Law (she got her degree in May 2000) when she secured all three. The big traditional August wedding was held at the First Baptist

Church of Natchez, and the evening reception was at an antebellum mansion on the Natchez Trace Parkway. She seemed so in command of her life, possessed of all the alpha-male Ferrell characteristics. At the same time, there was a very feminine quality about her—she was slender and attractive. It made for a potent combination. But it was clear that when push came to shove, Tommy's daughter was always going to act much more like Tommy than like her soft-spoken mother. Maybe this explains in part why Cricket had had such battles with her father when she was a teenager living under his roof: They're too much alike. One summer during law school, Cricket interned for a corporation in Nashville that staffed and built prisons. For a while she considered going into the family business after graduation. She joked that she could picture herself as some kind of white-collar pistol-packing mama, perhaps doing behavioral studies of the criminal mind for the FBI. (Tommy and Carole weren't thrilled to hear that.) In the end, the intellectual of the family chose a more conventional law job, at a firm in Nashville. The man Cricket chose for a husband was a certified public accountant, mild in personality.

She and I met a couple of times when she lived in Oxford. Right off, you could see the masculine qualities—but also a kind of residual Southern belleness. "I'm waiting for my ring," she said, holding up the fourth finger of her left hand and flashing both the toothy Ferrell smile and the bright enamel of her painted nails. (She got her engagement ring a month or so later.) This was a good while before I traveled to the Southwest to meet her brother. Once Cricket and I sat in the grill at Alumni House, which is directly across Grove Loop, maybe forty yards distant from where her grandfather swung a club in an old photograph. The photograph itself didn't come up in the conversation, although James Meredith did—indirectly. I asked her if she knew that Meredith's son Joe Meredith was also a grad student on campus. In fact, they didn't live far from each other. Cricket looked across the table. The expression on her face said, *What's that have to do with my life?* I didn't try to arrange an introduction.

It would have been a flop from the other end as well. Joe Meredith graduated magna cum laude in economics from Harvard. He prep-schooled at Phillips Academy at Andover and finished with honors. He has an MBA from Millsaps College in Jackson. He has worked for a large Jackson bank and as an oil-and-gas-industry analyst for a large consulting company. And yet he has long had terrible difficulty meeting and talking to strangers, the more so if they're female and confident. In his tortured, nervous, slow-to-answer-anything way, Joe would have probably impressed Billy Ferrell's granddaughter as an ignoramus. She wouldn't have been able to appreciate his extremely alert mind; she would have experienced only the socially stricken man.

"I realize at least I don't like this about myself. I want to meet people. But I always use the shyness and inability to talk as an excuse to just . . . do nothing," Joe said one night over dinner. This was in the summer of 2001. We'd known each other for not quite three years. He'd been at Ole Miss since September 1998. And very few people, relatively speaking, either on or off campus, knew he was there. Fewer still had ever made the connection between his name and that of the man who'd made such a dent in history on that campus and in that town forty years before. It's exactly as Joe wanted it.

"No, almost no one knows it. They don't understand it. It doesn't come up," he'd said—not that evening over dinner, but the very first time we met, at a bookstore and café called Square Books. This was in the spring of 1999, two and a half years earlier. It was clear how inwardly turned he was, but the fact of his anonymity in tiny Oxford didn't make any sense: Why don't they know he's here? Why isn't the university, no matter Joe's introvertedness, seeking to employ him in some crucial way to reflect on the past? Ole Miss could hold a piece of its own past right in its hand, explore it, honor it, as a way of trying to move forward.

Here was one reaction to the news that a son of Meredith was working on a Ph.D. in finance at the university: "What? I am shocked. I don't know this. This is an incredible story. I just can't think we lost this story. I am baffled and ashamed. How did this blood son of James Meredith get on this campus, and we didn't know? That's a story in and of itself, isn't it?" Those words are historian's David Sansing's, and he said them after Joe had been on campus for a full academic year. Sansing is the author of the authorized and respected book *The University of Mississippi: A Sesquicentennial History.* It had recently been published. After the emeritus professor recovered from his shock (I had called him on the phone, suspecting he didn't know), Sansing said that the only thing he could think was that there must have been some kind of unofficial and secret deal to keep things quiet that was hatched at the outset between the Meredith family and the chancellor's office. He was wrong, though. There was no deal. The grad student's presence in town was a virtual secret because Joe was Joe and because the University of Mississippi—for all of its progress racially and academically in the previous four decades—was still capable of being retrograde and blind, fixed in a pre-sixties, frat-school, football amber. Not that Sansing saw it this way when we next spoke about it. By then, he'd come to believe that the obliviousness only proved how far his university had come in its race relations. "You see, the irony of the fact that Meredith's son is getting a doctorate here is just not important to us anymore. We can just leave him be to do his work. We don't need to connect his name with James Meredith's name at all. We don't see it as irony. We've gone right past that." Sansing added, "There is no university in America that's had more

racial trouble than this one. But we've been open and honest about it, in trying to solve that trouble."

The first time we met, Joe said, in his coded way, "We get along, but we
don't talk." He meant his father. He had paused. "I inherited all his personality traits. More than anyone else in the family, I'm like him."

Almost everyone in Oxford who has any connection with the university
goes to Square Books—it's probably the best-known meeting place in the
immensely livable and attractive college town. The café and bookstore are on
the square, opposite the courthouse that figures in so much of Faulkner's fic-
tion. It's a short walk from the campus. Joe had never heard of Square Books,
didn't know where it was. We sat on the upstairs veranda. It was an afternoon
in late April, and there was a soft breeze. The muscled, blocky man in the blue
polo shirt and Tommy Hilfiger jeans kept looking down at his athletic shoes,
kept moving his head and shoulders in a rocking motion, side to side, almost
as if he were blind. There were names and numbers written in blue ballpoint
ink across the back of his hands. The word "fat" was spelled in capital letters.
Not far away was a bookcase devoted to works on race and Southern literature. There was a new one by Constance Baker Motley titled *Equal Justice
Under Law*. His father's picture was on the cover. There was another recent
one, by Nadine Cohodas, entitled *The Band Played Dixie: Race and the Liberal Conscience at Ole Miss*. His father's face was on that one, too.

"The student newspaper called me up once," Joe said. "They wanted to
do a story. I said, 'Give me a year and call me back.' They won't. I put them off
on purpose." He said that by his estimates about 40 percent of the students at
Ole Miss "are just numbskulls, and the rest aren't doing the work."

"They're partying?"

"Well, whatever. But I wouldn't want my daughter to come here."

Two and a half years later, in the summer of 2001, when we agreed to
meet at the bookstore again (we'd met elsewhere in the interim), Joe had
turned thirty-three and was finishing his studies. (He was born in March
1968, the same year as Ty Ferrell, the same year that Joe's dad got his law
degree from Columbia and the same year that Billy Ferrell came back into
office after his four-year interregnum.) Joe had not been back to Square Books
since the spring of 1999, although he said he had gone out once or twice to eat
at inexpensive Oxford restaurants. He was the father of a five-year-old daughter named Jasmine Victoria, who was living in Austin, Texas, with her mother.
Joe's talk could still lapse into a "That's hard to say" or an "I don't know" or
just silence itself. And yet there seemed a willingness in him to try to say the
truths of his life, if in code. He'd swing open the door to things—and then
close it. "As you know, our family is plagued by a lack of normalness," he said.
He told several awkward and painful family stories—and yet there was a pro-

tectiveness there for his father and his family. It was clear that he would tolerate no disdain about his family from other people; if there was any disdaining, it would be his. Later, he asked quietly if some of the personal stories he had told about the family could be kept out of whatever I was writing. But he didn't demand it.

The divorced father was spending days and evenings in his small, cluttered apartment on Riverside Place, running figures and spreadsheets on a computer, while the TV played behind him. He would have it on all day, liked it for its white noise, the sense of company it gave. He said he had no real friends in town, although there were a few friends down in Jackson with whom he could still go out and have a beer now and then when he was visiting his father and stepmother. He didn't appear to feel sorry for himself. Indeed, there seemed a lack of bitterness in him about anything—even though, it was true, he could flash with momentary anger about things that had happened to him in his life. Mostly, he seemed amused at how insane the world was. This was a few weeks before the September 11 terrorist attacks on America.

His pattern was to rise about 9:30 A.M. His computer was against a wall in the dining room. He always made sure to tape *Fox Morning News*. He'd find out what was going on in the world and eat his breakfast and then get going on his keyboard. At 11 A.M., he'd pause in his calculations and spreadsheets to watch *The Young and the Restless*. Jerry Springer's talk show came on at midday, and Joe would again turn around to watch "the part near the end when the Springer trailer trash starts yelling at each other. I always enjoy that."

What he missed was being able to exercise. It was the ongoing struggle with lupus, he said. Lupus is a disease that affects the skin and inflames the joints and often attacks other systems in the body. The illness causes a breakdown of the body's immune system. "Your body thinks something's inside. You never know. It ebbs and flows. It's a chronic, invisible illness," Joe said. His lupus had been diagnosed in his senior year at Harvard. He'd come down with a 104-degree temperature and had landed in the university hospital. A dozen years later, in Mississippi, he was still taking heavy doses of steroids to fight it. The old prep school and collegiate wrestler could no longer lift weights or go running. Even to jog half a mile through the streets of Oxford brought pain to his insteps. His stomach was getting large, and he hated that, because his athleticism had long been a part of who he was. As long as he got proper rest and didn't overstress himself, the disease could be controlled, he said.

In John Ed Bradley's 1992 *Esquire* piece, published two years after Joe had finished Harvard, Joe had been quoted as saying: "I am fighting a fungal infection. Lupus destroys your organs, and there are immune implications. I always thought I'd make it, but the chances that I won't are good. I did some research on the subject when others wouldn't give me the truth." He had paused and looked away and then said to the author, "I learned that only two of ten people who are treated with this infection live. The mortality rate is eighty percent." Joe was living then in a garage apartment behind his father's house in Jackson. He was working toward his MBA at Millsaps. His father had recently driven to Metairie, Louisiana, to spend a day with David Duke. They'd gotten their pictures taken together. The subject of the photo op had come up in the *Esquire* piece.

"Yes, but only sitting down. I never would've had my picture made standing up with David Duke," James Meredith said.

"What's the difference?" Bradley asked.

"Authority, power, who's in charge."

Later, when Duke was making his scorned bid for the Republican presidential nomination, Meredith suggested that he should run as Duke's vice president.

After he got his MBA, in the mid-nineties, Joe took a job at Deposit Guaranty National Bank. He got sick again. Was it the stress of the workplace, the stress of living at home? "Stress? I can't really say. Was it stress? Mmm, that's an interesting question," Joe told me at dinner in Oxford, dragging out each word, sighing, head bopping.

In the summer of 2001, the finance student at Ole Miss, older than most of his fellow grad students, impecunious, about to start his fourth year in town, said: "I have a high tolerance for pain." It didn't seem as if he was talking about lupus. That evening, as we ate, he said, "I have an on-off personality." He was trying to explain how he'd once found the wherewithal to ask someone to marry him. He took three packets of sugar and placed them on the table in a diagonal. The first packet was real sugar. "Now this little white packet is the ultimate situation for Joe Meredith. It's the highest spot in the grid. I've got a social life, I've even got a girlfriend. I've clicked it on."

The second packet was a blue packet of artificial sugar. "This Equal, this one's in the middle. I opt for the work. The TV. It's safe. I don't go out, I don't like it this way, but it's okay. It's a life."

The third packet was a pink packet of Sweet'n Low. "This is the bottom of the barrel," he said. "You get up your nerve and go to a bar and say hi to somebody and get rejected. They look at you and say, 'Who's this loser?' " He laughed very loudly. A minute later: "You know, most people who've ever known me for years feel they're lucky to get just a yes or no out of me."

He talked about a literature seminar in college. Every student was required to give a five-minute presentation about a short story. "What happened was that the teacher was so uncomfortable that I was so uncomfortable that he never called on me once. I went the whole term without presenting or speaking. He kept going around the room, skipping me. He knew. I read the material and never talked about it once. We had the exam. I got an A or an A-minus for the course."

He had lived in Eliot House at Harvard, which is one of the beautiful old residential dorms down by the river. What were his weekends like? "Kind of wandering around Cambridge by yourself. You could crash a party, but that's terrible because then you're just sitting by yourself."

After we had ordered and were waiting for our food (there had been the awful silence while he tried to pick something from the menu and while the waitress stood by with her pad), Joe spoke about a civil rights documentary he'd caught a few nights earlier on cable. He'd been channel surfing. It was late. There was his father on the screen. One part of the film concerned Meredith's 1966 March Against Fear through Mississippi. Meredith had started out the march from the Peabody Hotel in Memphis on June 5. The first day, he walked twelve miles to the state border dividing Mississippi and Tennessee. The following day, he got sixteen miles into Mississippi before he was shot by a white man. A semireclusive Ole Miss grad student with a resonant name stood in the middle of his Oxford apartment and watched some grainy footage taken before he was born "where the police grab the guy out of the bushes. They ask if he did it to my father. The guy says no. The cops say, 'Okay, why don't you get in the car.' I mean, they don't cuff him or anything. They just ask him if he'd mind getting in the car. That's what got me. Fair, huh? That's America." Joe guffawed.

He said of his father, "He always has to start off by saying something like, 'The truth is this.' He's driven by this overwhelming need to be ahead of Jesse Jackson or Martin Luther King or whoever, and the only way he thinks he can do it is by saying absolutely what 'the truth is.' " The words were tough, but the tone wasn't. A few minutes later, in a similar vein: "My father has an overwhelming need to be famous and so will do whatever he thinks will provide that and get him attention—Jesse Helms, David Duke, you name it, even if it's only for a day."

In the *Esquire* piece, Joe had been quoted as saying of his father's effect on the family: "Silent, almost telepathic. He has had a great influence on me without being overbearing. He has never told me what to do. Everything I've ever done is because of his strength."

Joe said he was hoping to have the bulk of the research and writing done on his dissertation by the following spring. He wanted to leave Oxford and to win a tenure-track position on a business school faculty at a good university, preferably in Texas or Oklahoma, so that he could be close to his child. His dissertation had something to do with the corporate uses of derivatives to hedge energy price risk. It involved lots of math equations and a concept called "regression." He had earned all A's except for two B's in grad school, he said, "and here's a guy who never presents in a conference, never talks in class." He said that the business school held graduate mixers in the Grove, but that he had almost never been able to go. "I want to go. It comes time, I just can't leave my apartment."

On our way out of the restaurant that evening, Joe stopped to look at some mounted black-and-white photographs. One was of a rural lane, lined with trees and shrouded in fog. "It looks like Andover," he said. He said he had been back to his Massachusetts boarding school just once since he graduated in 1986, to teach a summer course in precalculus. During our dinner he had talked—briefly—of how lonely he'd been at boarding school, even though his twin brother was also there. "Packages come, for a holiday or whatever, the other kids are opening them, and you got nothing."

Did his father and stepmother come to the graduation?

"Yes."

How about Harvard?

"No." Then: "Maybe forty percent them, sixty percent me. I kept it from happening, basically. You could say I preempted it. Because I didn't want to be hurt."

He had also talked—again, elliptically—of his real mom, Mary, who'd died when he and his twin were eleven.

"What was she like?" I'd prompted.

"Monster. Harsh," he said, declining to go on.

When we shook hands goodbye, I said I really couldn't see much resemblance in personality between his father and him. Well, it might be the same pain, he said, "just expressing itself a different way."

By the summer of 2001, having come to like and respect him a lot, there was an equation in my head. It was an emotional, not a math, equation: What *they* did to his father, *he* had to carry, more than his siblings. Why? Possibly because it was the last fate on earth James Meredith would have wished for his most inwardly turned child.

There were something like 100 minority students—blacks and Hispanics—out of an enrollment of about 1,200 when the Meredith twins, Joe and James Jr., boarded at one of the most affluent secondary institutions in America. (No one seems to be able to say now how the tuition was afforded, other than the fact that there seems to have been substantial scholarship help.) Both are remembered as highly intelligent. James is remembered as the far more outgoing. Joe is remembered as the athlete: varsity wrestler and defensive back on the football team. (James ran some track.) In the small world of New England prep school sports, Joe stood out. His wrestling coach was Jim

Stephens, who teaches and coaches now at an academy in Ohio. Stephens said he had no visual memory of Joe. "Quiet is maybe all I can remember," he said. "I remember nothing about him in class. He must have been very smart. I am trying to see his face." But in the next phone conversation, the coach remembered something: "Of all the wrestlers I've worked with, he was one of the only kids who could do the arm drag well." In an arm drag, Stephens said, "you're trying to get yourself set up for a takedown. You're trying to take advantage of the other wrestler's reaction." The opponents face each other. "You're going to try to get in on me, and I'm not going to let you. Here's how it works. I am controlling your right wrist with my left hand. While I do that, I reach across with my other hand, grab your tricep. Then I pull you across in front of me. Basically, I'm exposing your side. And then I go into the takedown." The move, the coach said, is all about protecting yourself, a defensive idea, by initiating a sudden offensive move.

Half a dozen teachers from the Andover years were queried about Joe. The consensus was that both brothers were "pretty normal if quiet kids running around just being the usual teenagers," as a longtime history teacher, Tom Lyons, put it. But this, too, was remembered after a little while by most of the faculty members who were asked about Joe: In 1982, when his sons were ninth-graders, James Meredith came to Andover to speak. It was a disaster, beginning with the drive from the airport to the school. Two faculty members picked him up. Meredith was arrogant and angry. His much-anticipated address was full of condescension and impenetrable statements.

I n 1997, a year and a half before Joe matriculated at Ole Miss, his father announced that he was going to give his personal papers to the university. This made headlines in Mississippi. There had been delicate backstage maneuvering to get the papers, which amount to 250 linear feet of clippings and printed material. It was thought for a long while that Meredith was going to donate his papers to Jackson State University. The university archivist at Ole Miss and the provost and a history professor, Charles Eagles, made trips to Meadowbrook Lane. They convinced Meredith that his papers belonged at Ole Miss. On the other hand, it might have reasonably been asked by an outsider, what had Ole Miss ever done to earn the gift? As a seminal figure in the university's history, Meredith was out of view. A man named Ed Meek—a former assistant vice chancellor for public relations and marketing—taught at the school for years. "Every year I'd bring up James Meredith," he said. "Those classes of mine, including blacks, had no idea who James Meredith was." In 1992, three decades after the riot, the university put up a small plaque in Baxter Hall, the redbrick dormitory where he had lived. The plaque reads: "Baxter

Hall was the home of some distinguished Mississippians—one of them being James Meredith, the first black student to enroll at the University of Mississippi in 1962."

"This was the first time Ole Miss even acknowledged that there was a James Meredith," Meredith was quoted as saying by the *Daily Mississippian* at the time of the 1997 donation of his papers. But he also said, "America is still a free society, people can do what they want, Ole Miss is still number one, it is the Harvard of the South."

The formal handing-over ceremony was held in March 1997 at the beautiful new John D. Williams Library, named for the man who'd been chancellor when the 1962 riot broke out, when Ole Miss became—for about twenty-four hours—the most famous university in the world. According to news reports, the transporting of the papers to Oxford from Meredith's house had required three van loads and an additional moving truck. Meredith attended the ceremony with some friends and family. (Joe wasn't there.) There is reported to have been deep collective relief on the part of the administration that the donor didn't flip out. It was a smallish crowd. In his introduction, Chancellor Robert Khayat called him "Dr. James Meredith." He spoke of the prominence of the state's oldest institution of higher learning and of the importance of being able to accommodate future generations of Meredith scholars. He only touched on the events of late September 1962 and said that "although much tragedy and pain are associated with that event," it was also true that there'd been a very positive outcome. The provost, Gerald Walton, also could only seem to dance on the skin of the riot. "A classic civil rights battle," he noted.

Meredith got up. "They limited me to three minutes," he said. His huge eyes counted the room. He licked his lips. He twisted his head. "I've written eighteen books. I've sold a lot of them." There were ten of them waiting outside the door to be purchased, he said. He began introducing old friends and family. The introductions went on and on. There was some looniness in his delivery and explosive laughter at wrong places, but mostly it was all okay, and, really, he looked smashing that day. "She bought this suit I got on," he said, wagging his arm at his sister, Hazel. He had paid twenty bucks for a shave and a haircut—"never paid anything like that in my life." After ten or twelve minutes had passed, the guest said, "Now I'm going to give my two-minute talk." Individual sentences and phrases were eloquent. "Mississippi from now on will live the impossible dream in reality," he said. He remembered what his long-deceased father, Cap Meredith, had said, sitting in the Grove on graduation day, 1963: "These people can be decent." Beat. "I want to report to my father that today in Mississippi, these people are decent."

Soon the grandiosity came back. His personal goal was to make Mississippi "number one." He ranted a little about black English. He also said, "Today, I want to launch my campaign to become mayor of the city of Jackson." He said, "So, uh, I'm finished." He lurched to his chair and then the chancellor got up. Uh, um, it was great to know that Dr. Meredith was running for mayor, but of course the university could take no official position on that, Khayat said.

Afterward, there was a reception. The room where it was held wasn't very far in linear feet from the area on the second floor where the library shelves its old bound periodicals—*Time* and *Newsweek* and *Life* and the *Saturday Evening Post,* and all the others. If a researcher or pesky out-of-town visitor had gone through the aisles looking for stories about what had happened at Ole Miss in late September and early October 1962, he would have discovered that most of the stories weren't there. The periodicals themselves exist—but almost all of the stories have been scissored or ripped out. Whole issues are missing from the shelves, including the issue of *Life* containing Charles Moore's photograph.

Eighteen months after that ceremony, on September 21, 1998, Meredith came back to the library to give a talk, and this time Joe was in the audience. He'd just begun his graduate work. Joe's father had on the same handsome suit, only this time he wore an Ole Miss baseball cap. "Play the tape," he ordered his son, who was sitting in the front row, on the far left, next to a boom box. Joe was hunched over. He punched a button. Blues music came on. "Turn it louder," commanded Joe's father, who began to move around at the front of the room. He had some moves—crazy, inspired, sixty-five-year-old moves. "Play it louder," he called out. The hunched son, who had on an Ole Miss ball cap, too, turned it louder. "Believe me, this is the most important part of the speech," Meredith shouted to the audience, sashaying, finger-popping, shoulder-bobbing. A few minutes earlier, the provost had introduced him, but Gerald Walton now looked like a deer caught in headlights. "That was Elmore James," Meredith said when he allowed the music to be turned off. He looked joyous. Joe was still looking at his feet.

The speaker got onto the royal Choctaw thing and wouldn't leave it alone. "I was a selected one," he said. He made some impolitic and sexist claims. He took questions. Two black women in the audience were visibly angry. One got up and said, "I've heard several people [before today] call him crazy, and quite frankly, listening to him, I can understand that." She and Meredith began to interrupt each other loudly. Suddenly, he seemed very afraid, very old, bewildered. Listen, he said, I know I've made some folks mad here today, okay, enough of this, "we're gonna talk about *football.*"

That was in the fall of 1998, and in the following spring, on the veranda of Square Books, our first meeting, Joe sighed heavily and said: "That's a hard question, because it integrates what he did with what he's done in the family. Am I proud of my father? This is what you're asking. Okay, I guess very proud of the event of history you're talking about. But then you've got to look at everything else. For instance, you could say because of my father, I went to Harvard. Okay, there's that. And the other way to look at it is that he pushed me too hard."

The subject of Jesse Helms came up. "You take that," Joe said. "You start thinking, okay, what effect did that have in your family. For the next five years, you have to answer that question. 'Hey, why did your father go to work for Jesse Helms?' I can tell you what he says about it. He says he wanted to do research at the Library of Congress."

Come again?

"That's what he said. He said he wrote all these letters, and Helms and maybe one other senator were the only ones who answered. I don't know if it's true. I can tell you it was a financial disaster. You don't make much money working for a congressman. We were living in California—my stepmom had gone there to take a job—and so we were paying two rents."

"Did what happened to your father at Ole Miss wreck his life, and in a way the family's?"

"It's a contributing factor. It's not causal. When he does something, it's because he thinks it's right, even if he can't explain it to anybody. He goes to work for Jesse Helms, and it makes sense to him. I've heard people say, 'Oh, if he hadn't integrated Ole Miss, he wouldn't have done all these crazy things.' I don't think that's it. I think it's something else. I'll call it his eccentric philosophy. This is my theory. He does these things—almost as a kind of offensive strike to throw you off—so that he can find the energy to do whatever else he wants to do. For instance, supporting David Duke. Why in hell would you ever support a racist like David Duke if you're James Meredith? Well, maybe he knows he's going to get all these articles and letters about that, condemning him. And that somehow gives him the energy to do what he wants to do next."

Joe talked about the wrestling team at Harvard. He had participated in the sport for three years and had earned his letter. The next year, the lupus came, and in a way it might have been a relief. He was never a star on the team—the step-up in class from prep school to the collegiate level was too great. Harvard had turned into a national wrestling power in those years. Of his teammates, Joe said, flashing the bitterness: "I was outcasted. Whenever there was a breakout in groups of two, I was the only one without a partner. You swallow your pride and go up to somebody after practice and say, 'Hey, you want to wrestle?' 'No, I'm tired.' After a while, it makes you very bitter. Same thing with the wrestle-offs, to see who's going to be starting for the team that week. You could feel them rooting against you."

Joe sat silent. "So you think of my father forty years ago at this school. First day of class, every student in his class wants to leave the classroom. Every day, you go into the cafeteria at lunch, and you hear the taunting. They start banging their trays on the table. What I mean is, sometimes I think I know what my father felt."

F or something like the last fifteen years, a lawyer and public servant in Cincinnati named Tyrone Yates has been trying to write the authorized Meredith biography. A young adult biography exists, less than 10,000 words, but there has never been a full biography of Meredith. Yates is African-American. He was once vice mayor of Cincinnati. He has served on the city council. He has law-clerked in the White House. Currently, he does trial work for the public defender's office in his hometown. He says that many of his fellow blacks, some of whom are nationally prominent, have tried to dissuade him from writing Meredith's story. "They feel he is not worthy. They're embarrassed by him. They'd rather just have people forget about Jay Meredith. Well, to me he's a hero. I think of James H. Meredith as my hero." Yates, who nearly always speaks of Meredith as "Jay," as family members do, is certainly not blind to the difficulties of Meredith's personality. He has suffered at the hands of it. That doesn't matter to him. He sees Meredith as "a genius who was trapped in the constraints of poverty and racism." Yates: "You see, in a flash, he was one of the most famous people on earth, as Jay himself would say. I think it's a natural situation that one does strive for that kind of thing again. I think he expected that level of fame would keep up."

The two came to know each other not long after Meredith and some of his family had relocated to Ohio in the mid-eighties. Yates asked Meredith if he would present a talk to a local group. Meredith replied that he didn't talk to anyone for free. Yates presented him with a $20 bill. Meredith laughed and said, "Okay, I am indebted to you now." They became close friends, and when Meredith lost control of the students in his constitutional law course at the university (Yates had originally been slated to teach the course), the attorney stepped in. Yates has many convictions about Meredith, and a central one is how "extraordinary a father he is, despite what anybody thinks from the outside. He is absolutely committed to the welfare of his children. Can you imagine how hard that is for him, given his tortured mind? I've actually seen very few fathers, or mothers for that matter, keep such a focused eye on the welfare of his children. I know he would do anything for his kids." Yates hesitated and said that the pity is that it all gets screwed up. The law of unintended consequences, perhaps.

In late summer 1987, Meredith called Yates. James Jr. had just been involved in that car accident in Maine and two people were dead. James Jr. was eighteen and had been driving. Yates: "He called and told me. He was absolutely terrified. Stricken. He said, 'Tyrone, I need you to do something for me. I need you to do it right now.' " He asked Yates to call former presidential assistant Richard Goodwin, still very close to the Kennedy family. Goodwin would be able to help secure the best defense attorney in New England, Meredith said. Yates called Goodwin and was then directed to other influential people in Washington, D.C. Yates: "Jay raised twenty thousand dollars on the spot for the defense. That was the least of his bolting into action to save one of his children." Two years after the accident, on August 22, 1989, the son was sentenced to a year of house arrest, which essentially allowed him to continue his undergraduate studies at Penn without interruption. He was given a $350 fine. He lost his driver's license for five years.

Yates says he will see his Meredith biography through to completion and publication, even if he has to sell it himself. "Anybody who did what he did deserves the thanks of this country. But we don't want to give it to him."

Jim Peckham was Joe's old wrestling coach at Harvard. He is retired but is still nationally known in collegiate wrestling circles. He was told about Joe's feeling of ostracism by his teammates. Peckham said he had no idea. "That's terrible. That's terrible. I must have let him down. We all must have let him down. In the sport of wrestling, it's almost impossible not to bind with someone. It's so intimate and involved." Joe's former teammates seemed less stressed in trying to recall Joe. They said they could remember an athlete with solid if unexceptional skills, but who didn't seem willing to work hard enough to secure his place. The fire in his belly wasn't there. Not one team member (of the six who were asked) could remember taking a class with him, or seeing him around Harvard Square, or ever sitting across from him in a dining hall. They said they could recall him only at the gym, working out. Almost always, he kept to himself, whether getting into or out of wrestling togs or walking to the shower or back to the college houses. Scott Merriner, a classmate and average-skilled wrestler, now a minister at a church in Alaska, remembers reading the newspaper stories about Joe's father going to work for Helms. This was in the fall of senior year, 1989. Merriner: "I remember trying to kind of dig at that, the Helms story. I was really curious why Joe's father would have done that. But I couldn't connect with him on it. . . . I was pretty conservative myself, especially in a place like Cambridge. I certainly wasn't a liberal. I just wanted to talk to him about it. He wouldn't do it. You always got the feeling that Joe perceived his father as someone he could not be unreservedly proud of." Merriner added, "I don't ever remember him speaking against his father, though." Tim Kierstead, another classmate on the team: "Nice guy. . . . Couldn't know him. . . . I vaguely remember something about his twin brother getting in that automobile accident. I vaguely remember somebody telling me that his father went to work for Jesse Helms. It wasn't something you would have ever asked him about. He was closed off to conversation in general but that kind of conversation for sure. I think these kinds of things might have piled up on him."

*N*ewsweek, October 22, 1962, beneath the headline "What Manner of Man Is This?": "He is small (about 5 feet 6 inches), with delicate bones and features. His eyes are brown, large, and luminous. He has a pencil-line mustache. He dresses neatly and, almost invariably, in a dark suit, white shirt, with a handkerchief folded square in his breast pocket. When he is self-conscious, he issues a tiny, tentative laugh. But he gestures passionately with his left hand when he becomes indignant about what he regards as an insult or ill treatment of Negroes."

James Meredith has three sons and one daughter. His oldest son, John, is in his early forties. He is eight years older than the twins and works as a congressional lobbyist in Washington, D.C. He is single and a self-described loner. In August 1963, he was the child sitting on Cap Meredith's lap during graduation ceremonies in the Grove at Ole Miss. John Meredith carries himself very well and is polished in conversation and looks almost eerily like the man being described in that old article from *Newsweek*. John says he rarely goes home to Mississippi to see the members of his family. "Not a particularly sit-around-the-fire-talking family," he says.

He's in a hotel restaurant on K Street in Washington. It's the first of two meetings, and this one will last for more than two hours. In both, little emotion will slip through cracks, and very little evidence of sibling love will manifest itself. The eldest son has on a yellow tie and a white shirt and a dark suit. His eyes are brown, large, and luminous. He's just come from a round of meetings on Capitol Hill. He is dining on bay scallops and his table manners are exquisite. He places his left hand on Moore's photograph (he has not seen it before), holds aloft the fork in his right hand. "First thought that hits me looking at this is: This is why black people don't trust cops," he says.

Once, he approaches anger. "Oxford, Mississippi," he says. "They have a Martin Luther King, Jr. Street there. Why? King was never there. Why isn't there a James Meredith street in Oxford?" At another point, he recounts a racist incident during a job interview at an employment agency in Jackson a few years ago. "The white guy in the next cubicle was being offered fifteen dollars an hour for something I was more qualified for. I could hear it. In my cubicle, the guy looks over my résumé and says, 'Well, we've got one here for seven an hour. But you're probably overqualified.' " Pause. "I don't care about the beauty of the land in Mississippi. You can have it."

He tells of a recent altercation he got into in New Jersey recently with a white woman who wouldn't let him have a parking space. He blocked her car in. She called the cops on her cell phone. They surrounded his car and told him to get out. "And of course they believed her story, not mine."

He is asked about the fact that there has never been a biography of his father. "It's simple. Black publishing doesn't want it. Because they don't want a divided electorate. A bio would create problems. It could move some blacks off the Democratic rolls." He listens when encounters with his younger brother in Oxford are described. "I guess I haven't spoken with Joe in a while," he says. "Sorry to hear he struck you like that."

On the traumas in the family caused by James Jr.'s auto accident. "Yes, a rough time, a rough time."

Do people he meets in the course of his lobbying work on Capitol Hill connect his name with that of his father? "Very little name recognition now," he replies. "Especially since what my father did at Ole Miss is not something taught very much in schools. I would never want to use the name for advantage anyway."

Has his father been an influence on his own conservative political views?

"Indirectly," he says.

"Telepathically?" he is asked.

"Maybe you could say that."

The eldest son has contributed opinion pieces to the newsletter of the Leadership Institute, an archconservative, nonprofit educational organization headquartered in suburban Washington. According to its Web site, the prime mission of the Leadership Institute is to identify, recruit, train, and place political conservatives in public policy jobs. From one of John's published pieces: "The liberal media of today don't want you to hear James Meredith: He doesn't fit their mold of a proper black American. The civil rights 'leaders' of today hope you won't listen to James Meredith: he won't submit to their entitlement mentality. These plantation owners of elite opinion can't stand the sight of an uppity James Meredith, not content with the place they've assigned him." From another piece: "While James followed the road less traveled, the anointed black leaders veered increasingly left, roaring down the dead-end, weed-infested lanes of Marxism, radical separatism, preferential treatment and violent struggle. James's ostracism reached its nadir in 1989, when he accepted a position in the office of conservative North Carolina Senator Jesse Helms. For exposing the long-cultivated myth that black leaders must be liberal, James was excoriated by the media and his former colleagues. Despite the unceasing vilification, my father remains uncowed. His vision is keen. And he still stands tall."

One morning during his second year at Ole Miss, Joe and I met at a McDonald's near his apartment. Jasmine was living with him. He had just dropped off his daughter at day care. He came into the restaurant in a Hilfiger jacket and an Ole Miss baseball cap pulled low. He smiled and shook hands. He stood at the counter, shifting his weight, bobbing his head. He studied the menu posted over his head. The young black clerk on the other side of the counter cleared her throat. Did she have any idea who he was? Probably not. Three or four people in line behind Joe began to fidget. Joe sighed and said without making eye contact that he guessed he'd have the eggs and a stack of pancakes and potatoes. What did he want to drink? He didn't seem to hear the question. She asked again. "Lemonade," he finally said, sighing.

In the booth, he said he was still having great difficulty communicating with his father. "We almost never talk. But maybe things are a little better. A couple of years ago, he was in a period of wanting to die. But he's recovered from that. He wants to write his autobiography. He's still in precarious health. Sleeps a lot. Basically, I've given up that we'll ever really communicate."

When Joe and his brothers were young, their father would drive them to school in the morning. He'd pick them up in the afternoon. There was almost never any talking in the car.

One of Joe's classes started at 4 P.M. and was finished at 5:15, which meant he had to jog to his car before Jasmine's day care closed at 5:30. They charged him a dollar for every minute he was late. The university was paying him a stipend of $800 a month, Joe said, and late fees didn't figure into his budget.

He said he had a little more respect for the math that was involved in getting a doctorate in finance. Had he changed his mind about the overall caliber of the university? He laughed. "Still a bunch of party numbskulls, you ask me." He was worried that an Ole Miss doctorate wouldn't count much in landing him a job. A lot of it was perception, he figured.

In the *Esquire* story about his father, Joe was asked what goes through his mind when James Meredith refers to himself as a king. After a minute of silence, Joe uttered softly, "I haven't interpreted it yet."

A Harvard story that has been interpreted in various ways over the years: Joe Meredith once refused to get off his stool during the final minute of a wrestle-off. His opponent was a teammate named David George, known to be a horse of an athlete. Peckham was officiating the match, which was tied. After the final time-out, the coach nodded to both of his men to come at each other again. Joe sat on his metal folding chair at the edge of the mat. His head was down and he was shaking it from side to side. Peckham: "He wouldn't get off the stool. It was unheard of. I still don't know what it means. Was he afraid? Was he disappointed in how he'd performed? Did he just want to shut it all out? You couldn't know." The following week, as the squad was getting set to board a bus for a road trip, the captain, Kelly Flynn, a big, likable kid from Iowa who liked to fool around, showed up with a gym bag under one arm and a metal folding chair under the other. In a telepathic instant, everybody knew, everybody laughed, everybody but Joe, who climbed on the bus and took a seat alone and stared out the window.

Several months after I heard this story, Joe and I had dinner in a restaurant on the Oxford square. It was Christmastime and the town was trimmed in lights. Joe hadn't been downtown since our last dinner. He kept turning his head to look at how pretty the square was. The day before, his father had been in town. A documentary crew from New Orleans had convinced James Meredith to come to Ole Miss. Joe went over to the university library, where some of the shooting was taking place. The meeting between father and son had the usual awkwardness about it. Joe was pretty sure his dad stayed only one night in town and was gone by the time we met.

"So you found out about throwing it in," Joe said, when the conversation drifted to Harvard and wrestling.

Why didn't he get off the stool?

"Because that's the one match I most felt they were rooting against me. I just said the hell with it. I wouldn't even look at them."

A few days earlier, Joe had taught his last class of the fall 2001 term in an undergraduate course in finance. (While working on his dissertation, he helped earn his keep at the graduate school by teaching low-level courses and by doing tutoring.) A student named Kimberly, to whom he had given private tutoring, was in the restaurant. She saw him and passed by the table with some of her sorority sisters. It was very warm between the black teaching assistant and the white coed from Atlanta. He gave Kimberly a small hug. He bopped his head and shoulders from side to side and smiled broadly. "I know you want that A," he kidded. He didn't seem antisocial in the least, not then.

After his student was gone, we talked of his twin brother, an investment counselor in California. They're not often in touch, Joe said. Pause. "You have to understand, he's the happy one. He's the one with friends." Again, the loud laugh.

Later that evening, I went out to the Ramada Inn on the west side of town and introduced myself to the night clerk, Vondaris Gordon, an undergraduate and past president of the Black Student Union. Gordon, affable, handsome, interested in politics and history, a native of the Delta, was studying for an American history final. He was reading a book about the admission of James Meredith to Ole Miss. I said that I had just been to dinner on the square with Meredith's son. I asked if he knew that Joe Meredith had been living in town for more than three years and was close to finishing a doctorate. The past president of the BSU said he could hardly believe that. "Is he just like his dad?" he asked.

In Vicksburg, at Shoney's, late at night, in the last month of last century, an interracial couple came in and took a booth. He had tattoos, she had nose piercings. They both seemed about twenty. They sat beside each other and passed a smoke back and forth. When the food came, they ate from each other's plates, from each other's forks. They knew the taboos they were breaking—it seemed to be the point. In Pascagoula, a few days earlier, in the dining room of the city's finest motel, a young and fit black man in a well-tailored suit sat across the table from an attractive blonde. Both looked to be in their early thirties. They talked quietly over breakfast, heads bent toward each other. Had they spent the night together, or was this an early-morning business meeting? Their presence didn't seem to be causing any stir. In north Jackson, seven months later, in an upscale shopping center, an elderly white woman brought two little girls out of a restaurant and stood on the curb while an elderly man fetched the car. One of the little girls was white, the other black. The woman, who must have been the white child's grandmother, held each by the hand: black child on her right side, white child on her left. While they waited, the three swung their arms and sang a nursery ditty. It was a July evening, still early, the air lambent, not stifling, and it was easy to imagine that these genteel and morally upstanding grandparents, native Mississippians, having taken two best friends of different color out to eat, were accompanying them back home now, where the black child would be invited to stay and watch a rental movie and to sleep over with her white chum in a big frilly poster bed. And yet the next morning, in the Clarion-Ledger, were all of the old reminders, travails, intractable ghosts. The lead editorial was about the recent suspicious hanging death of a black teenager from Kokomo named Raynard Johnson. He'd been found in his front yard, under a pecan tree, hanged with his own belt. Was it a suicide or a lynching? The editorial urged a full investigation, inasmuch as the word "lynching" had so resonant a history in the state. A column over, the letters to the editor were about the ongoing "flag flap": whether to keep the old state flag, with its Confederate battle emblem, or to come up with some new design that would embrace all of the citizenry and not serve as a reminder of slavery to blacks. One or two of the letters were reasonable, although most were knee-jerk, warning of "the final demise of Mississippi" should the left-wingers and do-gooders and outsiders get their way. On page 1, the leader of a neo-Confederate hate group called League of the South was quoted: "If you stand up and defend the Confederate flag, you're a racist. It's false. It makes me angry. It's frustrating to have to put up with this." John Thomas Cripps of Wiggins wasn't interested in applying the salve of reconciliation. The head of the League of the South said he planned to run for governor in 2003, and he had votes.

Confederate Shadows: Good Son

> The shadow of dark hangs over them, making whatever narra-
> tives we construct around them seem sentimental and beside
> the point.
>
> —Mark Strand on Edward Hopper

S
o many stories, mysteries, interconnected lives, curling outward from
some faces under trees. This story, for instance, which can only be out-
lined at this point. It concerns Jim Scott Middleton, who lives in
Clarksdale, Mississippi. Scott's dad, Sheriff Jimmy Middleton of Claiborne
County, three over from the right in the photo, was much loved by Scott.

The inheritor is a churchgoer and a devoted family man in his middle
fifties. The inheritor is a golfer, with a membership in the local country club.
He's a duck hunter, proud to own his own "duck hole," whatever that is. He
drives a big sedan with a phone in it. He's an old self-described Pi Kappa
Alpha boy out of the University of Southern Mississippi (he was on the six-
year plan, he jokes), who doesn't seem fretful about cholesterol or calorie
intake. What he most seems, however, is a man comfortable in his upper-
middle-class white skin. Scott Middleton is the only direct male heir of Jimmy
Middleton. The father—who passed on his big-boned frame to his only son,
and who got only as far as eighth grade—isn't remembered as an outgoing or
comfortable man. But neither does he seem to be remembered, by blacks in
the county over which he presided, as a hateful seg. What his son's life sug-

gests, perhaps, is that it *isn't* all just ineluctable; that sometimes the story line—the through-line in the script, as moviemakers say—seems to shift greatly just one generation down. The gene mutates for the better. The blades of hope are discernibly there.

Jimmy Middleton was the head lawman of Port Gibson and Claiborne County, which are about two hours south of Clarksdale. (By Mississippi standards, Clarksdale, which is about an hour below metropolitan Memphis, is a city and is one of the larger industrial places in the Delta.) As noted earlier, Claiborne County and Port Gibson were never known—not even in the late nineteenth century, when lynchings were a commonplace—as the region of the cudgel and the rope, of the fagots burning in a pyre beneath the figure dangling on a noose. The county's indecency to its fellow man was then and seems now a far more deceptive thing. Port Gibson's bigotry has always sought to mask itself behind a kind of noblesse oblige. The head lawman of the county in the early sixties—and for some of the fifties, too—was pretty much an extension of his jurisdiction: a paternalistic supremacist working to keep a bitter system in place.

Consider him in the photograph, and how once more form seems uncannily to follow function. He's part of the group, and yet in another way not. He's standing off. Is he leaking doubt? Does he think that this is something of a bad idea? Who can tell? But the shadow of that suggestion is there.

Scott Middleton, Green Bay Packer fan, has a lovely Lebanese-American wife named Lynn and a slightly indulged but entirely charming young daughter named Marlene. (It's his second marriage, second family.) Scott and Lynn worship at the Catholic church in Clarksdale. They're not practicing Catholics, but Marlene is being educated at the parish school, and so her parents feel that they should worship there as a family on Sundays. Scott has enjoyed coaching in his daughter's integrated T-ball league. On most weekends from March to November, the gregarious man loves going to his segregated country club. In the late fall, when the Delta is sodden and gray, he loves sitting before daylight in his duck hole. Afterward, he'll get cleaned up and go to work.

To get to work, he climbs into his Buick or SUV and drives north from Clarksdale on Highway 61 (which is the old famous blues highway that used to deliver gifted Delta black musicians to Memphis and points north) before turning off onto a side road. This two-lane takes him through the fields into a village called Jonestown, in the middle of which is a manufacturing and cotton-processing firm called Delta Oil Mill. Scott is its general manager. His office is behind a glass-enclosed door in a wooden cottage on the grounds of the plant. The warehouses and processing barns of Delta Oil Mill tower over tiny Jonestown in more ways than one. At noon the GM gets back into his car and goes home to eat with his spouse, because Clarksdale is only about a twenty-minute drive from his office and because you wouldn't want to try to get a bite to eat in Jonestown. Before he can get out onto the highway, where he'll gun the car, Scott first must drive through the heart of Jonestown.

In a state full of towns of an almost mind-beggaring poverty, Jonestown, predominately black, is in a league by itself. It's as if everything about it is idle and crumbling and full of despair. That isn't literally true, because some black Jonestowners—hardly enough—are employed at the oil mill and are able to earn livable wages. (Others are fetched up to Tunica County by bus, where they hold better-paying jobs at the casinos, which are supported by metropolitan Memphis.) I have been in the big sedan with the windows rolled up as the GM passed down the main street, past Mississippians who seemed to possess nothing except the rags on their backs. One evening early in December, Scott drove me through Jonestown while a Christmas "parade" was in progress. Neither of us said anything, because it was the saddest Christmas parade imaginable. Scott maneuvered the car out onto the highway and we went on to dinner in his tastefully decorated home on Second Street in Clarksdale. Second Street is one of those avenues in the South that look like a photograph from *Architectural Digest*. Jim Middleton's son spoke that evening about the welfare system in America, and of how in his view it is ruinous. It wasn't said with anger.

"I don't think Daddy was," he said. We were discussing the question of whether his father had belonged to the Klan.

On another day, in his office, he said, just as evenly: "Daddy had a good reputation as a law enforcement officer, even with the blacks—I think you'll find that. I'm not going to say he wasn't tough with them, strict with them, and back then it would've been pretty easy to do almost whatever you wanted to do. But I think local blacks would say he treated them fair, in business and whatnot." Scott was dressed casually for work: a polo shirt with an Illinois Central logo on it. He looked like about a sixteen handicap, a Republican, a bank board member (he keeps his connection to Port Gibson by sitting on the local bank board there), a cotton man, a Missisippian, a well-fed Deltan, who gets on airplanes and goes to trade shows and conventions now and then in big cities like Washington, D.C.

A cotton man and Mississippian and Deltan who told me he didn't know the name Emmett Till.

One night, we dined at a place called Katherine's, on Moon Lake. We were eating big steaks. There were other Delta cotton men at nearby tables and the GM went over and glad-handed them, laughed with them. He came back to his seat and asked what I had been discovering on my own about his father.

"Pretty much what you've said," I answered.

On my most recent visit to Port Gibson, I had sat on a smooth cement slab outside a co-op grocery called Our Mart. The store had been started during the time of the troubles, when Claiborne County blacks launched an economic boycott against the white merchants. An elderly man named Nathan Jones, who'd helped found Our Mart in the mid-sixties, said: "Jimmy Middleton bought posts from me. We shared farming in common. We'd talk about cattle. You knew exactly who he was, but he wasn't going to harm you, like some around here." Next door to the grocery was the county administration building. Inside was a permanent exhibit entitled "No Easy Journey," which described Claiborne County's civil rights movement in photographs, text, and other materials. There was a wonderful sepia photograph of a handsome and strong and young Nate Jones, just home from World War II.

The deceased sheriff's son said that evening at Katherine's on Moon Lake, "If it proves to be otherwise as you go on, however, or even if you come on something big about Daddy, I think I can live with it."

Employees at Delta Oil Mill have told me that Jim Middleton's son is a very fair boss. It could reasonably be asked what they would have to gain by talking badly about their employer to an out-of-stater carrying a notebook. Even though they seemed to appreciate their boss, I do not think they were trying to suggest that he was free of racial feelings.

In the summer of 2001, the golf club to which Scott belongs gained statewide attention when two married black physicians were denied membership. Scott said he wasn't present when the all-white membership of the Clarksdale Country Club voted down the applications. He said he wasn't precisely clear on how he would have voted—he felt himself caught in a wedge between friends and business relationships and his own heart. He said he was still struggling with the morality of it. "A private club is a private club," he said, "and the membership can rightfully set its own policies. That isn't unique to Mississippi." He said he had gotten to know one of the turned-down physicians through his daughter's T-ball league. "Fine, decent, sophisticated people," he said. He cleared his throat. "But the club belongs to its members."

Earlier in the same year, Scott had voted in the statewide referendum of whether or not to adopt a new Mississippi flag. He voted, distinctly in the minority, for a new flag. "My heart was clear on that one," he said.

Did he think that the country club—where almost all of of the social and leisure life of white Clarksdale takes place—might ever change its policies?

"Forever is a long time," he said. "I don't think it'll be soon. This is Mississippi."

"But isn't it somehow wrong?"

"I can't really sit here and say that it is."

He said he struggles to think right and to act right and to fight the things in himself that are automatic. One day in his office, talking of the cotton mill, Scott said, "We work blacks here." The air wasn't dry on the sentence when he said, "I didn't mean it to come out that way. I'll apologize for that. Sounds like plantation stuff." Another day he described a job interview, which had taken place two decades before. The man interviewing him for the position said, "Son, how do you feel about blacks?" Scott answered, "Sir, I've lived around them all my life." Another day, after we had eaten lunch and had taken a brief tour in his car through nearby fields blossoming with cotton, Scott spoke of a black employee for whom the mill provides housing and payment of utilities. He's an extremely good worker and has many years in. His father was there before him.

"How is the condition of his house?"

"Well, we have to get on him about that," he said.

Again, there was a look of pain, a seeming wish to stuff the words back into his mouth. "Well, we don't get on him about that, it's not what I meant to say. That sounds like I'm a damn overseer or something. We're not trying to be paternalistic. But we do have to sort of say to him every once in a while, 'Ricky, you're letting the condition of your house slip a little.' And then he spruces it up."

Imagine: A Mississippi backcountry farm family had traveled in one generation from a father who didn't get beyond grammar school and defended a system that was an extension of slavery to a college-educated son who sits behind a desk and seeks to be fair to his black workforce while he makes his own handsome living, one token of which is membership in a country club that won't admit blacks. In some ways, that seems about the right metaphor for Mississippi in a new century: all the shadows of the overhanging Confederate past, along with the new shoots so susceptible to quick loss, trampling.

"So have you broken the chain?"

"I have. I have. I'm proud to say I have," Scott said. He wasn't talking specifically of race but of how the prior generation of American fathers often seemed incapable of communicating with their children. Scott has three grown children from his first marriage—two daughters and a son. "Breaking the chain" sounded so freighted.

All theories and hypotheses and suppositions about other human beings are suspect. And in another sense, maybe all theories and hypotheses and suppositions about other lives are equally true. How do we ever really know what the other is thinking, feeling, imagining, dreaming? We got up and shook hands and I drove through the utter flatness of fields, toward Memphis.

Epilogue
Hope and History Rhyming

Every blade of grass has its angel that bends over it and whispers, "Grow, grow."

—From the Talmud

We had the experience but missed the meaning,
And approach to the meaning restores the experience

—T. S. Eliot, *Four Quartets*

Half a mile back, a dog with mottled fur slunk up out of a culvert full of water from the early winter rains. The animal's appearance in the middle of the two-lane, forcing a swerve, only adds to the edginess of returning to an all-but-empty town for another look at the falling-down building by the side of the road that was once an unremarkable country store called Bryant's Grocery & Meat Market.

Money is still as a church.

When Emmett Till took the overnight coach of the Illinois Central railroad from Chicago to visit his Southern kin, Money was a more going idea. The trains would make whistle stops for alighting and embarking passengers. Money was said to have a population of about 200 in 1955, but that must have included all those who lived in the shotgun cabins out in the cotton fields. The town still appears on the list of towns on the official highway map of Mississippi—but there's no population given. A decent guess might be that a hundred live scattered hereabout now, counting cats.

The building, stoving in on itself, functioned as a grocery and dry goods store until sometime late in the 1980s. It changed names and hands several times after the murder—which is one reason why the green lettering on the white tin sign above the front door makes no sense. What's visible is the YOU of what once was YOUNG'S, partially obscuring the OLFE'S of what once must have been WOLFE'S.

Nobody seems alive here.

A green van pulls up and makes a left turn. A man in a great hurry bounds out. He is delivering flowers. It turns out there's going to be a wedding tomorrow at the small Baptist church in Money. The church, which serves a white congregation, is down a side street from the store about a hundred yards.

The delivery man is opening the back of his van.

"Hello."

You're trying not to startle a white Mississippian with his back turned. You tell him you've been standing out front of the grocery store for about forty-five minutes, and he's the first person to come by.

"Emmett Till, huh?"

"Yep."

"You sure you got the right building? I think it may have been one over there that got torn down. Folks like you want to make history sometimes when you ain't got no history to make." He says it with utter friendliness.

He's headed up the steps of the church with two large vases; you are falling in behind. "Let me tell you something else," he says over his shoulder. "I was a year out of high school. I was walking past my grandmama's bridge game. I just overheard one of the women say to the others that when Emmett Till's mama—I think her name was Mamie—went into the mortuary for the first time to look at the body, she started screaming before she even got inside the door, 'That's my baby! That's my baby!' Now, I know that's true. The undertaker himself told that story. You see, the body was so decomposed, you couldn't tell it was him or not. But that didn't stop her."

In Chicago, on September 3, 1955, which was the first day that the pine casket with its shockingly un-made-up contents were open for viewing, 10,000 people were said to have clogged the streets outside the funeral home.

"But what about the ring he was wearing? They found it on the body and that helped identify him."

"Ring?" he says, half turning.

"It had the initials L. T. It had a date on it: May 25, 1943. It belonged to

Emmett Till's father, Louis Till. It had a flat crown. Emmett had been wearing it when he left Chicago. There were pictures of the ring in the Memphis papers. It had been taken right off the body when it came from the river. An undertaker took it off. The sheriff who was at the scene is still alive. He lives in Moorhead. When Emmett was murdered, he was the deputy sheriff of Greenwood. He showed the ring to Emmett's uncle, who said it was Emmett's ring. There are pictures of him holding the ring up for newspaper photographers. Here, I'll show you. His name's John Ed—"

"Don't know about a ring," he cuts in. "Never heard about a ring. You sure that came out at the time?"

"Positive, sir."

But this is a man who's unconvinced. Who's got flowers to arrange inside for tomorrow's wedding. Who's got to get on to his other deliveries and then back into Greenwood. Whose turned back seems suddenly stiffer now, or is that something imagined? Who may believe deep in his white Southern glands that the past is nothing but the past and why stir it up and get folks thinking again about things that can't be undone.

"Write us a good one now," he warns with all the prior pleasantness.

About a year and a half after I first got to know him, John Ed Cothran's grandson and namesake—who said in the first conversation that he didn't know who Emmett Till was, but that he did know about James Meredith—lost his double-wide mobile home to bankruptcy proceedings. This was in December 2000, not many months after John Cothran had made the first payment on his $68,000 dream in the all-white community of Strayhorn. He'd had so many improvement plans for that place in the countryside. But even though he lost his home almost as soon as he had bought it, and even though his work schedule remained crazy (often doing back-to-back shifts at two jobs), other things in his life seemed to perk up. On Thanksgiving Day 2000, stocking shelves at Kroger while other folks ate turkey and watched football games, John started making time with a cashier named Bobbie. She was five years older and maybe three inches taller, but they went home together that night and enjoyed their own leftovers and turned out the lights. He moved into her place a few days later. Bobbie lived a few miles from the strip mall in Southaven, just below the Tennessee state line, where she and John worked. She grew up in suburban Washington, D.C., and was a mother of two and had a thirteen-year-old son living with her. She had moved to the Memphis area a few years before with a husband, who had become an ex-husband. The son who lived with her was named Michael, and John tried to fill in as a kind of surrogate friend and instant authority figure, taking the boy for rides in his truck, but also threatening to take off his belt and go after him for his sass. Once, he threw water in Michael's face when the teen failed to rouse himself for school after two calls from his mom.

After the first of the year, John told his superiors at the Home Depot that he didn't want to run the kitchen and bath department anymore. This time, they listened. He transferred to plumbing, working nights. He decided to quit Kroger—the measly paycheck wasn't worth his time, he said. He and Bobbie were making ends meet with their semipooled paychecks—sort of. At the Depot, he put in a request to work the overnight shift, handling incoming freight, unloading pallets. This way, he wouldn't have to deal with the public anymore, wouldn't have to supervise anybody. The new work and hours suited him fine.

On weekends, he saw his twins, who were down in Senatobia with their mom, about forty minutes away. The twins loved going to Burger King, so that's where their dad took them when he came to visit. Often he just watched while they ate, because there wasn't enough money in his pocket for him to eat, too. One summer evening, with a few hours to kill before clocking in, he drove down to Senatobia to try to find a ball field. The twins were in a T-ball league and he wanted to see them play. He couldn't find the field. He drove around for an hour, cursing, then got back on the highway and drove back to Southaven and went into work. "My life," he said.

One winter night, returning to Southaven from a visit with his kids, John's vehicle broke down. He got out and started walking northward into the sleet. Three black guys in a pickup, going the other way on the interstate, did a U-turn and picked him up. He squeezed in beside them and couldn't stop trembling. "You all right, man?" they said. They wanted to pull off somewhere and buy him coffee, but he said, no, he'd be fine. His teeth chattered all the way to Bobbie's place. He went inside and got twenty-five bucks from her and brought it back out to them. "I swear I'll make this up to you someday," he said. "You already have, man," one of them said. They awkwardly embraced.

The following August, John brought the twins' stepsister, Ashley Nicole, from Tupelo to live with him. His daughter was an overweight teenager, a sweet child of his third marriage, who'd been left back in school a couple of times and was talking of quitting. Her father wasn't going to let that happen. He said he'd damn well see to it that she'd have a chance at a better life than his. When he told her he'd screwed up so many things—had been a drunk and a doper at sixteen—Ashley said, "Don't worry, I ain't going there, Daddy." She didn't have a lot of things to pack when she left Tupelo and moved in with her father and his girlfriend and his girlfriend's son. She brought her diary and dolls and scrapbooks and clothes. One page of her diary had a drawing of a Confederate flag, and the words "It's a Rebel thang" written beside it. Another had a drawing of crosses and a Bible, and beside the Bible and the crosses there was a poem that she'd composed. It was entitled "Thank You Jesus." Its last lines: "When I get to Heaven, I will see you / We will begin anew / I want to say: / Thank you for dying for me / and taking my sin / and setting me free. / When I get there I'll be glad / because I won't have to worry / about being sad." She signed it, with little hearts: "By Ashley N. Cothran." John's daughter barely knew her great-grandfather on her paternal side—she said she knew he had been a Mississippi lawman in a bad time. "I'd like to know more about all that someday," she said. "We've heard some of it in school."

After the attacks on the World Trade Center and the Pentagon, John put a flag on the front license plate of his Chevy Silverado pickup. He pasted a LET FREEDOM RING decal on his back bumper. How goddamn dare they do that to my country were the words that often seemed to be in his head. Despite the general anxiety in America, John said he felt more stability in his own life than he'd known in years. He seemed to get along with black employees at the store better than with the white workers. He and Bobbie were trying to buy a new house together—maybe the banks would float a loan despite the recent bankruptcy filing. On the night shift, there were twelve employees, plus a supervisor, and they'd have to hump anywhere from 100 to 180 pallets of freight. By that October, John had held his job at the Depot for four years, something he was quite proud of. He'd moved from lumber to plumbing to the head of kitchen and bath, back to plumbing and then to overnight freight. The head of overnights was a woman named Dawn. "John knows how to work," she said of him early one morning several weeks before Christmas 2001. John was clocking out, putting his gear away. He and I were going to breakfast, and we had agreed to meet at the store. John lugged out to his pickup a twelve-inch miter saw that he'd just bought for his dad as a Christmas present, and while he was gone, Dawn said: "He's a very hard guy not to like, really. I do think he's carrying a lot inside. You can always sense that anger. I don't know what it's about." John's left arm was in a soft cast; he'd injured it while helping a buddy move a water heater on a day off. All the lifting on the overnight shift was aggravating the injury, but what could he do about it?

He was even more buoyant than usual at breakfast that dawn, pushing his sunny-side-up eggs into his hash browns and sausage patties and then churning it into a soupy mix. He and Bobbie were renting a new place in an adjoining town called Horn Lake, corner of Grace and Cliffwood. It was just a coincidence that his parents lived on a road called Grace.

What could he do about the bubbles of rage that still dizzied him when he least expected? One night he flared so suddenly at Bobbie's boy that he whispered prayers of gratitude afterward that something irreversible hadn't happened. He'd picked up a baseball bat and gone to Michael's room. "I won't have this sass and disrespect," he said. His hands and voice were shaking. When it was over, he told Bobbie that he wouldn't have hit her son with the bat, although in another minute he might have gone out and smashed the shit out of her car or his car or anything else that was handy. A few months later, he did smash the bejesus out of her car—not with a bat, but with his fist. He and Bobbie had had an argument, and Bobbie had stalked off to her Hyundai and sat inside it with the windows rolled up and the doors locked. John followed her out to the carport and kept yelling at her through the glass. She wouldn't look at him. He was standing in the narrow space between the side of the house and the windshield. There was no room to rare back and swing, so it's still a mystery to him how he ended up breaking her windshield. "My intention was to hit the window to get her attention—not break the damn window," he said. "It was just contained aggression, I guess. I splintered it. Sometimes I wonder if this anger stuff will ever leave me alone."

John's life continued to seem a study in extremes. He totaled his pickup early one morning after work. He was so wound up from the shift that he couldn't go home to sleep, so he decided to drive around for a while. He dozed off at the wheel and awoke to find the truck out of control. He wasn't hurt, "only pissed." So now he was back to driving—barely—a beat-up sedan.

He spoke with affection of his new neighbors, a black husband and wife, who lived directly across the street from where he and Bobbie were now renting. He would nod to them and wave when he saw them bringing in groceries from the carport. One day John was standing in his own driveway, trying to carry on a conversation with "the Mrs.," whose name he didn't yet know. "She and I were calling to each other, and she said, just easy as anything, 'Well, why don't you come on over, so we don't have to shout at each other. Let me show you what I'm planting in the back.' " John went over. He went inside and was invited to sit down in their living room.

Not long afterward, John gave Bobbie a ring. "I told her, 'We've done about everything but hit each other with frying pans—but I hope to marry you,' " said John the next time I saw him.

As for John's dad, Billy Cothran, who lived with his deeply faithed wife, Alice, in the backcountry village of Gore Springs, well, he had changed his business card. He wasn't a car salesman any longer; he was running the whole department at Grenada Nissan. The new card read: "The Car & Truck Store. W. T. (Billy) Cothran. Sales Manager." Billy didn't have that job very long, though: In early 2002, the owners let him know they had someone else in mind for the job. In his mid-sixties, Billy retired to his Shangri-la in the woods to take up full-time fishing and wood carving and lawn tending and of course churchgoing. "This retirement thing'll kill you," he said on the day I stopped in to see him. He'd been out in the yard for hours, fussing with tools, just as his own father, a couple of counties over, closing in on ninety, was trying to do the same.

In June 2002, the high sheriff of Adams County realized the most powerful dream of his life and saw himself installed as president of all the sheriffs of the United States. Tommy Ferrell's "inauguration" (as his late father once called it), with Tommy's mother and his wife and children and granddaughter and other family members in attendance, occurred on the concluding night of the annual convention of the National Sheriffs' Association in Tulsa, Oklahoma. The NSA represents nearly 3,100 sheriffs in America; the full membership of the organization is over 20,000. Approximately 3,500 conventioneers came to Oklahoma for the sixty-second meeting. During the cocktail hour, before the big installation banquet, Tommy had said he was "scared as hell—but, hell, scared is good, right?" Did he have his inaugural address ready? "Been working on it for weeks." Several weeks before the convention, I had asked him on the phone if his hometown paper, the *Democrat,* had been devoting the proper amount of coverage to its local son and his big moment. "Not in my opinion," he had said immediately.

The high executives of the association were brought into the convention hall in ascending order of rank. Spotlights flooded each vice president and his spouse. The lawmen wore white dinner jackets; the ladies were in formal evening wear. Tommy and Carole Ferrell came in waving, with music playing. They took their places at the two-tiered head table. That day, in California, a three-judge panel of the U.S. Court of Appeals for the Ninth Circuit had ruled that the words "under God" in the Pledge of Allegiance were unconstitutional. The convention hall stood to recite the pledge. At the disputed words, Tommy leaned into the mike and said in his basso profundo, "UNDER GOD!"

The outgoing president was presented with a sword and a commemorative pistol. Many speeches were made. Tommy introduced his mother, who got up and waved. He introduced his son, "a federal agent for the Department of Justice." Ty stood, looking very uncomfortable. The new president spoke of his long climb to the top, which had taken fourteen years. "Twenty-seven committee assignments later and various vice presidencies, and here I am." He paraphrased Robert Frost—"miles to go before we sleep." He told the audience it was his "greatest sadness" that his father—legendary Mississippi lawman and a good, good man—wasn't present. He spoke of what a righteous and wonderful place his native state was. He talked of how the nation more than ever, in the wake of what had happened nine months before, on September 11, must gather behind and trust in its law enforcers. Through all of it, he seemed a peace officer in total control.

Afterward, I spoke briefly to Ty. He said the big news was that he and his wife and daughter were going to be transferred back to Mississippi, not to Natchez, but to the Gulf Coast. He didn't have a precise date but hoped the transfer would take effect in the early months of 2003. "Going home," the inheritor said.

Joe Meredith, for whom Mississippi has never really been home, received his doctorate in business administration at Ole Miss in May 2002. He spent most of his last year in Oxford looking for a teaching position. The more he sent out résumés, the more discouraged he became. On March 27, 2002, I received this email: "I know as a good writer I shouldn't use worthless modifiers but this is how I feel: utterly disappointed, absolutely devastated. I'm not even close to getting a job. I'll get trying. May 11 is the big day. I'll be crowned the best PHD graduate student to come to olemiss and like the weakest link I LEAVE WITH NOTHING."

It turned out not to be true. The following month, Joe flew up to North Carolina for an interview at a small liberal arts school, Elon University. It offered him a job on the business faculty for good money, and he accepted. Right after he got back to Mississippi, we had dinner. I had been in Oxford for a few days, waiting for his return. Joe was more buoyant than I'd ever experienced him. We drove to a catfish joint out in the country. "I sent letters to Texas schools and got no interest whatever," he said. "I wanted to be near my daughter. I was giving up all hope." At Abbeville Catfish, we heaped our plates twice and went back for dessert. Joe said offhandedly that he had received the 2002 Outstanding Doctoral Student Achievement Award in the school of business. He said just as offhandedly, "In the morning I'm supposed to do an interview with my father on CNN. The university is promoting me big-time. They've caught onto this story, me getting my Ph.D. in the fortieth anniversary year of my father integrating the school. They've discovered me. Ha. I'm supposed to show up at 7 o'clock at a TV studio on campus. Bishop Hall."

"Your dad will be here in the morning?"

"I guess," Joe said.

"He'll be coming up from Jackson?"

"I assume."

"Where's he staying?"

"No idea. He hasn't communicated with me."

Early the next morning, Joe's white Nissan Maxima was parked outside of Bishop Hall. By then, I had in my possession a university press release, written as a feature story: "Civil Rights Activist's Son Named Outstanding Student." There was a nice picture of Joe with a caption describing him as the "son of the man who integrated higher education." The release said: "History has come full circle at the University of Mississippi. Forty years after James Meredith integrated the campus, his son has been named a distinguished graduate student at the same university. Joseph Howard Meredith, thirty-four, receives his doctorate in business administration during commencement ceremonies May 11, just 200 yards from the spot where federal marshals and troops fought an angry mob. . . . Unlike his father, Joseph Meredith maintained a low profile during his studies. Many of his classmates remained unaware of his relationship to the man who broke the color barrier at the university. The younger Meredith says his independence began to blossom during his younger days in private boarding schools. 'Independent thinking comes from being different,' he said. 'It also comes from being in boarding school for years and not having anyone to rely on but myself.' " The press release ended with this quote from Joe: "My idea of success is not living on the east coast making $300,000 a year and appearing on 'Larry King Live' wearing a bow tie. Success for me is looking at my daughter as she peacefully sleeps."

In the campus TV studio, Joe sat on a stool, wired for sound, staring into a monitor. He looked elegant in a sport coat and loafers and red tie and neatly laundered shirt. He was perspiring.

"Uh, my dad's not coming," he said. "I found out he's doing it from down there."

Now he was on the air. These words showed up on the screen: "A Father's Footsteps. History Comes Full Circle." A CNN anchor in Atlanta said hello to the audience and to the two Merediths. The screen cut to a full picture of a wispy man in a white beard and dark suit. That man, approaching seventy, seated in a studio in Jackson, was licking his lips, darting his eyes, hunching forward.

"James, do you hear me all right?" the anchor said.

Silence. "I can't distinguish too much. I want to say . . ."

"Can you hear me, James?"

They got the sound wired correctly. The anchor asked Meredith how he felt about his son's Ph.D.

"It's the vindication of my entire life." Adding quickly: "You called me an African-American. I'm a Native American." You could tell that the Choctaw thing was rising up in him.

The anchor tried to cut in. "Joseph, I can tell your dad is a tough guy," she said. She tried to get Joe to talk. Joe's dad was still talking. "You gotta remember I was fighting a war. My goal was the total destruction of white supremacy."

Joe found himself. He said that in his own way he was still fighting his dad's war. He talked of his difficulty in finding a job, and he cited statistics he had dug up on the still shamefully low percentage of black professors on college faculties. "A very covert system in place now." He spoke slowly, convincingly, and it was as if the deliberateness had a clearing effect on the terrible mind of the bearded man in the other studio 160 miles away. "You see, it's more vicious now because it's largely unseen," James Meredith said at the end, with sudden force and beauty.

Ole Miss itself can be a place of such sudden force and beauty. All you have to do is drive down Fraternity Row on a sunlit morning in spring—those stunning houses with their pillars and dewy white rockers out front. There's something so redolent of the old customs, acceptances, dispensations, symbols, encoded in the shorthand name for the University of Mississippi. Will that name, with its more-than-faint racist overtones, ever be formally abandoned? It seems improbable. The name is too cherished, entrenched. There isn't any doubt that the University of Mississippi has made progress in its race relations, nor any doubt that there is much ground still to be gained. For almost all of the forty years after Meredith's admission, there were still only two civil rights memorials on the campus, and both were very modest. One was the plaque in the lobby of Baxter Hall (which is now the high-tech telecommunications building) noting that Meredith had once lived there. The other was a maple tree in front of the Lyceum, in the Circle, with a small stone at its base noting that the tree was dedicated to the memory of Mae Bertha Carter, mother of seven black Ole Miss grads.

Almost 13 percent of Ole Miss students are black. In the first year of the new century, Ole Miss elected its first black student body president. Nick Lott ran as a conservative Republican. There exist now at the university courses and curriculums in Afro-American history. (About 5.5 percent of the faculty is black.) There exists now the Institute for Racial Reconciliation, and its early guiding light was a white native Southerner (from Georgia) named Susan Glisson, who has a way of bearing strange gifts to authority. "What often happens in Mississippi is progress that's in an absence of information," says Glisson. "But I still believe that Mississippi in general and Ole Miss in particular can be a leader and impetus for healing in the nation, because of all that happened here." Several years ago, under Glisson's prodding and leadership, the university began planning a civil rights monument. The site chosen for the memorial, intended from the start to be large and prominent, was the plaza between the Lyceum and the new library, in the heart of the campus.

The name given the memorial was "Open Doors." It was designed by an artist from Brooklyn, New York, and featured a pair of archways and etched glass doors, with bronze bells resting atop the words "Freedom Henceforth— Justice Forevermore." Forty years after the riot and Meredith's forced integration of the university, on the last weekend in September 2002, a model of the work was officially presented to Oxford and the university community. (The monument itself wasn't scheduled to be completed until April 2003.) Many dignitaries and players from the old drama came for the fortieth anniversary: Meredith; long-retired U.S. marshals; Senior Judge Constance Baker Motley of the U.S. District Court for the Southern District of New York; Charles Moore, who drove himself over from his home in Alabama with a new digital camera. It was Moore's first time back in Oxford and on the campus since 1962. He had only half deliberately stayed away all these years. He barely slept at all the night before he drove to Mississippi.

All weekend, the weather was dry and sunny and full of good piney smells. Autumn wasn't quite in the air. Football was, although Ole Miss didn't have a game scheduled that weekend. Sorority and fraternity rush was on, and that seemed to consume the real energy of much of the student body, along with campuswide election campaigns for Colonel Reb and Miss Ole Miss. Still, there was a lovely quiet; at moments the Grove and the Circle felt almost churchlike. University officials had constructed a self-guided walking tour for "Remembering the Events of 1962."

In the week leading up, Meredith had said his usual strange things. "It was an embarrassment for me to be there, and for somebody to celebrate it, oh my God," he told a wire-service reporter for the AP. "I want to go down in history, and have a bunch of things named after me, but believe me that ain't it." Of the civil rights movement: "It was of no concern to me basically. Nothing could be more insulting to me than the concept of civil rights. It means perpetual second-class citizenship for me and my kind." He was sixty-nine and in the used-car rental business now. He had taken over a two-story brick garage near the railroad tracks west of downtown Jackson, and he was spending his days sitting in an almost empty room, answering his own phone, using a big white board on the wall to keep track of his fleet of ten-year-old Fords, Pontiacs, and Hondas. "I really consider this of equal if not greater significance than what I started forty years ago," he told a reporter for the *Memphis Commercial Appeal*. "I've got a used-car-dealer license, but it's not really about that."

On Sunday evening, before Meredith arrived, there was an outdoor movie on the square in downtown Oxford—two movies, really, both old documentaries made by movement people. People were invited to bring lawn chairs; the police had cordoned off the streets. The lights from the black-and-white films flickered eerily against the east side of Mr. Faulkner's stone white courthouse, even as forty years before, on the same Sunday night, other lights— from guns and gas and Molotov cocktails—had illuminated the community. Four decades of September Sundays had come and gone. There weren't two dozen people watching the films.

An hour before, as it was growing dark on campus, Moore and I walked through the Grove toward the Lyceum. A still-wiry photographer in his seven-ties—recently back from a photojournalism conference in France, where he had been honored for his life's work—Moore said, "I risked my life here, it's true." He kept turning around, looking to the left, to the right, as if trying to get his bearings, his balance. "This wasn't here," he said of a new stone walk. We walked over to the approximate spot where he had taken the photograph of Billy Ferrell and his cohorts on the early afternoon of September 27, 1962. "You see something, it's there, and you shoot it," he said. Later that evening, after the movies on the square, Moore and I sat out front of his hotel. He spoke of maybe moving on from Florence, Alabama—maybe back to Asheville, North Carolina, maybe somewhere else. He told a story about flying many years ago as a young newspaper photographer in the private plane of the governor of Alabama, John Patterson. He was a staffer at the *Montgomery Advertiser*. This was before Oxford and 1962. The governor of his state got hold of Moore's arm and said, "Listen, Charles, you get a lot of that nigger pussy, right? You really love it, right, Charles?"

On Tuesday evening, October 1, Anniversary Day (of Meredith's registra-tion as an Ole Miss student), Ole Miss hosted a three-dollar-a-head commu-nity dinner in the Grove. There was gospel singing. Twenty-seven hundred people came. Meredith joined in a candlelight symbolic walk through the Lyceum, to the spot where the monument would be erected. Members of his family were present. Not his son Joe, however. Joe stayed away. He was up in North Carolina at his new teaching job at Elon University. (Later, we exchanged emails. "No, I didn't make it," he wrote. "I'm not enthused with the university right now. . . . From what I read, blacks didn't care enough to attend events." He mentioned the newspaper piece about his dad in the Mem-phis paper. "The usual stuff.")

Things had been arranged so that Meredith didn't formally speak. Myrlie Evers-Williams, widow of Medgar Evers, who was also being honored on cam-pus that weekend, gave the address. Meredith sat on the dais behind her. He was quiet, dignified. He seemed to understand. You could believe everything about the South really had changed. Not least James H. Meredith. Not least the University of Mississippi.

And still the retreats to the past. You'll just come on them. They can be so jolting. If you go out to the Beacon Restaurant on North Lamar early on a Sat-urday morning, you'll probably have to wait in line for one of the best breakfasts in the South. The hostess may stick you in the Red Room, which is aptly named, because the Red Room features a blindingly red wall of Ole Miss Rebel symbols.

"The problem with Mississippi, you see, is that it's essentially premod-ern," Ole Miss professor of history Charles Eagles once said, early in my trav-els in the state, and the truth of that remark has only seemed to grow greater. (In the spring of 2002, the controversy in Jackson, debated on talk radio and editorial pages, was "yard parking." The city council had put in an ordinance to ban parking in yards, and much of the citizenry felt it an infringement of personal rights.) Eagles is writing the definitive story of race at his university. His book is a couple of years off; it will be worth waiting for.

On the campus, so pastoral, so architecturally beautiful, so fragrant, so *white*, the collective visual memory of the Confederacy and the lost cause and sixties apartheid seems never very far away. The reminders are there in the Rebel mascot at all athletic events, in the Confederate statue guarding the school's entrance, in the James O. Eastland Room on the third floor of the Law Center. The room, which is generally kept locked, is a replica of Eastland's Senate office in Washington. Some while ago, archivists carted down from the Capitol the great racist's red leather sofa and matching chair and immense desk and his nameplate and seal, not to say boxes and boxes of photographs of the great man with other great Washington men. On May 27, 1954, a week after the Supreme Court's ruling on *Brown v. Board of Education of Topeka*, Eastland rose in the Senate and spoke floridly for close to an hour. "Mr. President, a court cannot enforce its will in these fields. Racial instincts are normal, natural, human instincts. . . . The southern institution of racial segregation or racial separation was the correct, self-evident truth which arose from the chaos and confusion of the reconstruction period. Separation promotes racial harmony. . . . Mr. President, it is the law of nature, it is the law of God, that every race has both the right and the duty to perpetuate itself. . . . Segregated schools will be maintained by the proper and legitimate use of the police power inherent in every State, regardless of what the Supreme Court says. . . . The future greatness of America depends upon racial purity and the maintenance of Anglo-Saxon institutions."

Fallbacks. Retreats. A year before the fortieth anniversary, at Halloween 2001, Auburn University in Alabama made ugly national headlines when two fraternities hosted parties with racially offensive Halloween costumes. The same thing happened that year at Ole Miss, although for some reason the Auburn story seemed to have greater legs in the press. In Oxford, two members of the Alpha Tau Omega fraternity posed for a picture that went out on the Internet, on the Party Pics Web site. The photograph showed a brother, clad as a police officer, holding a gun to the head of a fellow brother who was in blackface and a straw hat. He was kneeling at the feet of this cop with a bucket of cotton. The fraternity was suspended for a year. The *Daily Mississippian* led the calls for punishment.

In 1962, the *Daily Mississippian*'s editor was a senior named Sidna Brower. She was a lone student journalistic voice seeking calm in that terrifying autumn. In a special edition on October 1, 1962, the morning after the riot, she wrote a signed editorial in which she accused some fellow students of bringing "dishonor and shame." The following day, she wrote: "Banners stretch across the street in front of the Student Union Building to solicit the votes for Homecoming Queen. But what is there to come home to?" Three days later, she wrote: "Homecoming for the University of Mississippi would be the regaining of personal dignity and continuation of the integrity and quality of a fine old institution of higher learning." Five days after that, she wrote: "I have received comments from students on campus and from letters in the mail that I have been brainwashed by the federal government. I most certainly have not been brainwashed nor have I received pressure from anyone. I simply, but firmly, believe in writing what I feel is right." For such courage, the Scripps-Howard newspaper chain immediately offered Sidna Brower an internship up north for the following summer. She took it. Today, a native of Memphis, who found she couldn't go home again, lives near Princeton, New Jersey.

Vondaris Gordon, from a small town in the Delta, has come home again, and again. He's a former president of the Black Student Union. He has served on the sensitivity and respect committee, investigating campus racial incidents. He graduated from the university in 2002 but has found ways to stay close. One night several years ago, working the front desk in his part-time job at the Ramada Inn, he said: "I'm delighted to be a student here. I've lived out of Mississippi—in Montreal, in Detroit. I have family members up there. I've lived in Jackson. But there's something about this town and this university. I love it so much. It always brings you back. If we can just tease apart the prejudice from the history, that's the key." Many nights, going to work, Gordon would find himself driving down Fraternity Row. "You go slow, you'll see it," he said. He meant the Confederate battle flag. "You'll see it. It's up in a little window or thumbtacked on a wall. You look in those windows, the beautiful windows of those beautiful fraternity houses, where all those frat boys live, and you'll see the flag. The lights are on and you can see through the yellow windows and there it is. There's a part of me that's not even sure I want the flag to disappear. It's just part of our history, like Meredith, like Emmett Till."

The small Delta town that Vondaris Gordon is from is Moorhead. As a kid, he used to ride his bike around Moorhead, although never to the other side, across the railroad tracks, where the Southern crosses the Yellow Dog. Out that way, on West Washington, currently lives an old enfeebled sixties lawman going deaf, whose life has touched two overriding Mississippi myths: Meredith and Till. The second is far greater than the first.

Perhaps it's remarkable only to an outsider, one who'll never be a Southerner, that the ghosts of Emmett Till seem everywhere in Mississippi. It's as if a fourteen-year-old Chicagoan, and what happened to him in 1955, haunts the air, the water of Mississippi. Roy Bryant, one of the acquitted killers, died nine years ago at Mississippi Baptist Medical Center in Jackson—but his kin and in-laws and cousins various times removed are said to be all over Mississippi. One of his three blood sons is up in the Carolinas, and another is reported to be in Texas, but there is a third son who lives in the state, as well as a daughter, as well as stepchildren, as well as sisters, as well as a half brother with the resonant name of Milam, as well as grandchildren and great-grandchildren. These family members and relations by marriage are said to live in towns named Ruleville and Sidon and Drew and Minter City and Eupora and Pontotoc. Bryant's obituary in 1994 listed fourteen grandchildren and a great-grandchild: Many were in the Delta. His ex-wife, Carolyn Bryant, is said to be around that country yet. But if she is, she's a hidden woman, with a different name, certainly hidden from anyone with a notebook and prying eyes. She is protected by those who love her. The former Mrs. Bryant must look nothing like that twenty-one-year-old rural beauty queen with the coils of coal-dark hair who used to live with her shrimp-hauling husband and small children in the back and upstairs of a Delta grocery. She'd be close to seventy now, if indeed she's alive. In so many ways, she must have died decades ago.

Ghosts. Touchstones. Breathing witnesses. I'll close with three. In the Delta town of Tutwiler, five miles north of Sumner, where the trial was held, there's a black mortician named Woodrow Jackson. He's lost track of his age, but the good Catholic nuns who run the small medical clinic in that Tallahatchie County town estimate him to be on the other side of ninety. In 1955, Woodrow Jackson worked for Tutwiler Funeral Home. He embalmed Emmett Till.

"Oh, Lord, look what I got here," he said to himself, studying the bloated corpse. He had just driven down to Greenwood in a hearse to pick up the body from a Negro mortician named Chester A. Miller at the Century Funeral Home at East Gibbs and Walthall Streets. Woodrow Jackson loaded up his cargo and drove back to Tutwiler and went to work at four o'clock in the afternoon and didn't finish up until five the next morning.

"Did it make you sick?" I wonder.

"No. 'Cause I took a few drinks," he says. Jackson's got on gold-framed glasses, black wing-tip loafers, white socks, a blue uniform shirt with blue serge pants. "See, it's hard to do a body wet. Emmett, he was decomposed, 'cause he laid in that water so long. It was rough. I took that first look at him down in Greenwood, I said, 'That's it, all right. I guess they done it to him, all right.' " He remembers that he drove Emmett back to Tutwiler, worked on the body through the night, put the body into a wooden casket, loaded the contents into his hearse, then drove to the depot in Clarksdale in time to get the coffin on the afternoon train to Chicago. "And that's all there was," he says.

Although he must have been at least eighty-nine or ninety on the day when we met, Woodrow Jackson was still an embalmer. He worked for Delta Burial, in Marks, Mississippi. "I been doing it since I was thirteen, working on the bodies," he said. "Emmett was just one of them." He said he had gotten up at 2:30 A.M. on the morning we met to get ready to go to work at 6:30.

And then there is this touchstone to a story that keeps rising from the dead. The witness's name is Ernest C. Withers. He lives in Memphis and was born in 1922, which would make him past eighty as you're reading this. "Pictures Tell the Story," it says on his fuchsia-colored business card. In sixty years of photography, he has shot Elvis Presley and B. B. King and Martin Luther King, Jr., and Howlin' Wolf and Johnny Cochran, too. For years, he drove around his bluesy hometown with this advertisement painted on the side panel of his 1941 woody: ERNEST C. WITHERS. 519 VANCE. PRESS & PUBLIC PHOTOGRAPHERS. HOME PHOTOS. "A Shutter That Clicks to a Blues Rhythm" is the way the *New York Times* headlined its feature on the man a year or so ago.

And this morning the man is here, a monument on the other side of time, reminiscing, taking his breakfast in a thumpy little joint called Java, Juice & Jazz on Elvis Presley Boulevard. He's got two freelance jobs today; can't waste time. He's ordered ham and eggs over easy, grits, stacks of toast. His red Park Avenue Buick is parked outside with a bumper sticker that says SOULSVILLE USA. He's been married to his sweetheart, Dorothy, for six decades. "Same wife," he says. They raised seven boys and a girl.

"My mother was a seamstress," he says. "She gave me a finite eye."

In 1955, Withers went to Sumner to record the Till trial. He was sent by Defender Publications, a national chain of black newspapers, and in particular he was sent by the *Memphis Tri-State Defender,* and it paid him thirty-five dollars for that scary week. The *Tri-State Defender* has been publishing Withers's pictures since the end of World War II: Memphis nightclubs, Negro League baseball, churches, fish fries, proms, the more-than-occasional city homicide. And of course the civil rights struggle.

In the Sumner courtroom, the photographer made pictures of the defendants and their lawyers, including John W. Whitten. After the acquittal, he made pictures of Roy Bryant and J. W. Milam leaving the courthouse in their open-collared white shirts, with their big grins and little boys saddled in their arms. A full record of Withers's work from the Till murder appeared in a little booklet that Withers printed up and sold for a buck apiece across black America, by mail order and direct outlet: *Complete Photo Story of Till Murder Case. Authentic Pictures Taken on the Spot. Designed to Meet Public Demand.*

"Your subject has to be true to the view in the viewfinder. It's not a tape measure, it's a visual measure," he says.

"Well, it took stamina. In the craft, stamina is required," he says.

"I went down there with L. Alexis Wilson," he says. "Alex was the top black civil rights reporter in the nation for Defender Publications. He later got promoted to editor of the *Chicago Daily Defender*. But he died too soon. Anyway, Alex and I went down to Sumner and Tallahatchie County. Naturally, we were a little worried about where we might sleep. We thought we might get killed if we stayed overnight in Tallahatchie County. So we stayed up in Clarksdale, which was a bigger place, closer to Memphis, and even had streetlights. We stayed with some black folks. There was only one bed in the room. I told them folks, 'I don't sleep with no man.' Well, they dragged a couch in. I got the couch."

"What is it about the Till story that bumps up past all the others?"

"I don't know. I've thought a lot about that. I guess because he was so young and from someplace else. And then the way they came for him, in the middle of the night."

"Were you worried that someone might come for you that way?"

An old man, finishing a killer breakfast, chuckles. "We were calm enough not to give away our true purposes in Mississippi. Which was to picture them exactly as they were."

T he last time I saw him, he'd been reading Revelation that morning, one of his favorite books in the Good Book. As usual, he'd been up since five, sitting in the La-Z-Boy in the front room while Maudine slept in till seven. The arthritis in his legs was so debilitating now that he'd been able to put in only a shadow of a garden: three little durn rows of corn, greens, onions. "Been spending a lotta time with ol' Arthur," he said, rising slowly from the rocker. "I reckon I know all them Ritis boys. Yessir. Especially ol' Arthur Ritis." That oozy curve of smile, that red meaty hand poking out from the stolid body for a shake. He could still grasp surprisingly strong. It was clear, though, that John Ed Cothran was going down, in both body and spirit.

We went out and looked at the diminished garden. We stood over the new growth. "Used to grow bushels of this stuff for the widow women. Now there ain't many widow women left."

His hearing was worse. "Can't even hear m'self poot anymore," he said. A cancer had returned to the tip of his ear, and they were going to slice off some more of that ear before long, he said. He said that the doctor man he'd been seeing for his arthritis had given him a little black box to put in his pocket that was attached to a wire that was supposed to shoot electronic impulses into his spine—but he didn't like its jolt and had said the hell with it. A couple of weeks before, he'd been in the hospital for three days for a fierce bellyache. "Diverticulitis," he said, drawing out all six syllables.

It was clear that Maudine Cothran's health was declining, too. Her eyesight was all but gone: macular degeneration. "I can't see your face," she said, standing three feet away, after we'd returned from the garden to the house. "I got great-grandbabies and I can't see their faces." She, too, had had emergency stays in the hospital. A gallbladder attack had come on Mother's Day. "Now if you get sick on Sunday, it's too wet to plow," she said. "There's nobody going to help you that day."

We went out to the screened porch. John Ed sank into a metal porch chair. The sun hadn't come to noon yet, so there was something of a breeze. He sat with his hands folded, staring. Sweat formed on his upper lip. Behind him was the little handsome pecan grove that he loved to keep tidy. He'd mowed it just the day before on his Murry riding mower. He'd also run over one of Maudine's mock orange trees and felt awful about it. "Don't know how I missed seeing the durn thing."

He told a joke or two, an old story or two. Once he used the term "colored women." Another time, in another story, he said "nigger," as I've often heard him say the word, with no seeming malice, making me wince once again.

Mostly, Maudine and I talked that day. "I don't think he'll ever go to a nursing home," she said in a loud whisper. "I'd like to sell out here and just go. The two of us could go into this retirement home they have in Greenwood. You don't have much room in a place like that. John Ed says he'd blow his brains out first. He wouldn't do that. I don't think he would."

Maybe her husband had heard some of this. "I reckon the thugs that shot little Emmett's head off are sure enough dead now, ain't they?" he said.

"Milam and Bryant," I said loudly. "Milam died twenty years ago. Bryant died in 1994." But it was as if these dates weren't registering. Or maybe he just couldn't hear. Or maybe he was wandering in a biblical dream.

The book of Revelation is the last book in the New Testament. It's only a few pages. It's apocalyptic and eschatological, meaning that it's about final accountings and ultimate destinies and other worlds to come. It speaks of the alpha and omega. It talks of the seven seals and of the last plagues and of the wild tormenting beast that comes up from the abyss. Bible scholars have long remarked that the language of apocalyptic writing is deeply symbolic, and that the true significance of the visions described is not to be found in their literal meaning. I drove away from Moorhead, from an old man who once had his back turned in a photograph, with a vision: On judgment day, all the slain bodies from all the fevered and silted Mississippi waters will rise as one.

A Bibliographical Essay

Henry James once said that a good story is both a picture and an idea, and that the picture and the idea should try to be "interfused." The idea for this book came on February 19, 1995, while I was standing in Black Oak Books in Berkeley, California, paging through an outsized text of black-and-white images entitled *Powerful Days: The Civil Rights Photography of Charles Moore.* I'd never heard of Charles Moore, although I love black-and-white photography and although I was familiar with some of the images in *Powerful Days,* especially those the photographer had taken in Birmingham, Alabama, in 1963, of fire hoses and dogs baring their fangs on their choke chains. I kept turning the pages of the book, thinking anew about that parting line in late-twentieth-century history known as the sixties. Then I saw page 55, and the photograph there stopped me in my tracks. It was a good while before I understood that the book I set out to write, as I stood there, wasn't about the photograph so much as it was about what came down from those seven Mississippi faces. I didn't begin to get that part until after my editor of two decades, Jonathan Segal of Knopf, had studied the image and had then told me in a single word where the true direction of the story lay: "legacies."

The material for *Sons of Mississippi* has been gathered in three ways: First, it has come from my own interviewing—breathing sources, whether intimately or tangentially related to Moore's photograph and to the history of civil rights in Mississippi. The interviewing process has spread over nearly seven years, beginning with the initial exploratory reporting trip to Mississippi in June 1996. It concluded when the work was in galley form, when I was somewhere on the other side of thirty-five reporting trips to Mississippi—some lasting three or four days, but most lasting a week or more.

The most important interviews were with the principals themselves, and their family members; they were the chief source of my information, which I then verified, double-checked, and supplemented in every way I could. I am referring especially to the long chapter-portraits of sons and grandsons in Part Three, but also to portraits elsewhere in the book, notably of James Meredith and Charles Moore in Part Two, and, not least, to two chapter-portraits in Part One: Billy Ferrell and John Ed Cothran. In each instance, extended conversation with the principal himself made the difference. As is clear from the text, Ferrell and Cothran were the only lawmen from the picture who were alive when I started the project in earnest in 1997; I feel lucky to have had a chance to interview them both, to spend time with both. My time with Cothran—running over nearly five years, from mid-1998 to late 2002, as his health and memory slowly declined—was obviously far more extensive than the brief window of time I had with Ferrell, in 1997 and 1998, before the onset of heart disease and cancer and his fairly quick death the following year. And yet, in many ways, Billy Ferrell, in the center of the frame, resides in the center of my imagination, in the center of the story, in terms of what was passed down, good and bad: to his namesake known as Tommy, sheriff of Natchez and Adams County and president of the National Sheriffs' Association (now finishing up his year-long reign in the latter); to his namesake known as Ty, the federal lawman out on the border with the large, conflicted heart and propensity to tears. If I had never been able to meet the flesh-and-blood Billy, the entire work might have aborted, no matter how intriguing the two men down the generational ladder from Billy turned out to be.

A book seeking to derive its storytelling impetus from figures in a forty-year-old photograph—and all that flows outward from their histories—would have been impossible to do without many other interviews: with historians and social scientists and informal observers of the South, with ex–movement people (both black and white), with old cops and state troopers, with clergymen, with lawmakers and public officials, with civil rights lawyers and journalists who were on the scary soil back then, with journalists who are on the deceptively quieter ground now, as the struggle for justice continues in a new century. If most of the legal, political, and judicial battles of racism have long since been won in Mississippi, the human battles of race, its immense social conflicts, are still being waged. That is a sadness and unfairness hardly unique to Mississippi.

The second way of gathering information was from documents and other primary materials, whether stored in personal files or—more commonly—in public archives and repositories: national, state, local. These ranged from public libraries and courthouses in the towns where the lawmen once lived to repositories and archives far from Mississippi—such as the extensive civil rights collection at the State Historical Society of Wisconsin Library on the University of Wisconsin campus, or the even more vast civil rights collection at the Library of Congress in Washington (LOC). At the LOC, on microfilm, are the papers of CORE (Congress of Racial Equality), of SNCC (Student Nonviolent Coordinating Committee), of the NAACP (National Association for the Advancement of Colored People), and of other organizations relevant to race and civil rights. Further afield, papers of the VEP (Voter Education Project) and the SRC (Southern Regional Council) are at the Woodruff Library on the campus of Clark Atlanta University in Atlanta. The Archives of the Martin Luther King, Jr. Center in Atlanta has many papers, some of which are also on microfilm at the LOC and elsewhere. I made use of a good civil rights collection at the Department of Special Collections, University Research Library, UCLA, and more so at the Amistad Research Center at Tulane University in New Orleans. The biggest private cache of papers came from an old civil rights attorney in the Justice Department, John M. Rosenberg, now in eastern Kentucky, still fighting on the side of the oppressed. Rosenberg worked in Mississippi in the sixties, largely in Greenwood and Leflore County, fortunately for my project. He has hundreds of pages of documents in his possession relating to Leflore and Greenwood and the Delta, and he generously made them available: affidavits; government-compiled statistical reports; histories of the Delta; copies of lawsuits by the federal government against officials in Mississippi; news clips.

Oral histories in various libraries and archives—at Howard University in Washington, D.C.; the University of Memphis; the University of Southern Mississippi; the University of Mississippi; Tulane University; and elsewhere—were extremely useful. At Tulane, the Dent Collection (its formal name is the Mississippi Civil Rights Oral History Project) contains audiotaped oral histories that are especially relevant to the story of Greenwood; the tapes are not transcribed. A quasi-public civil rights archive in Jackson—the Freedom Information Service Archives—has been maintained all these years by Jan Hillegas, an old movement person, mostly at her own expense. She made copies of things for me free of charge, and I am grateful. Just to have her clippings file from the major news outlets of the day, in and out of Mississippi, felt like a gift bequeathed from heaven. Regarding U.S. government documents: As noted in several places in the text, previously classified papers from the Justice Department and the FBI were obtained through the Freedom of Information/Privacy Acts (FOIPA). In some cases, I had to wait many months, but the wait was worth it, no matter that the material came with blank pages or pages heavily blacked out. As for the declassified files of the Mississippi State Sovereignty Commission, they were officially opened in Jackson on March 17, 1998, after much litigation on the part of plaintiffs and civil liberties groups. I had nothing to do with their opening; I was just a beneficiary of timing and luck that the closed society was, against its will, unlatching itself—somewhat. In those files, as I pointed out in the text, are 300,000 personal names and 87,000 separate indexed names (although not 87,000 individuals, because each variation on the same name constitutes an entry), seven of which are the names of my sheriffs, with a long paper trail.

The third way I gathered material was from the literature, published and unpublished, on civil rights in Mississippi and in the South: in books, monographs, theses, and dissertations; in newspaper, magazine, and journal articles; in the transcripts of government hearings. While I am now familiar with much of this literature, I hardly know it all. I doubt any one researcher could ever know it all—it is galactic. As I go along, I will cite some of the core works I consulted for specific sections and chapters.

These notes are not meant to be all-inclusive or line-by-line citations. Rather, they are a bibliographical guide to identifying the key sites and the key people interviewed. If a book and its author appear by name in the text, I do *not*, in most cases, repeat them in these notes. When I do repeat that book here, with the full citation, it's because I wish to signal the work's importance to my overall research.

In another way, these notes are an opportunity to be grateful publicly for having been *allowed in*. I was the researcher at the door, the stranger at the door, and the door opened, in most cases. In a less important way, these notes are also an opportunity to tell a story or include an anecdote or add a postscript that I couldn't fit into the text itself.

All of the events and facts and stories in this book are true, to the best of my ability to know them and to report them. In Part Three, in the chapter "Sometimes Trashy, Sometimes Luminous," the reader will have noted that I changed the names of two people. The names I used are Buddy Harris and Ariel Jeffords. I did so for reasons of privacy and at the request of the two people in question. These people, who appear only briefly, are relevant to the telling, but their real names aren't crucial to know, or so I have judged. All other names are the real ones. Finally, there is a small number of sources—about a dozen people—with whom I spoke between 1996 and 2003 who agreed to talk only on the condition of anonymity. Thus their names do not appear anywhere in the text and do not appear in these notes. At the end of this essay is an alphabetical list of the names of everyone else to whom I spoke who was helpful on the project, whether in the form of a substantive telephone conversation or a long sit-down at their home or office. Often, I interviewed people multiple times. This is self-evidently true for the major characters in the story—John Ed Cothran, John Cothran, Tommy and Ty Ferrell, and Joe Meredith. I remain grateful for their willingness to let me keep coming back as the years piled up.

Prologue: Nothing Is Ever Escaped

The precede, opposite the photograph, is from my first conversation with James Meredith, in May 1997.

Emmett Till. His story seems to override everything in Mississippi connected with race, and that quickly became apparent, which is why I've stood many times—waiting, imagining, wondering—in front of a building that may soon flutter away with the wind, unless the preservationists begin to act. So many myths are connected with that grocery and with the myth of Till. For instance, how exactly did Roy Bryant, who was out of town, and his brother-in-law, Big Milam, find out about the alleged wolf whistle and reputed inappropriate talk? There has long been a belief that Bryant heard the story from one or several of the black youth who were with Emmett outside the store that evening. In other words, the naive-cum-cocky Chicagoan was Judased by one of his own—willingly or inadvertently; in either case, a chilling thought.

In my own brief retelling of the story, I consulted journalistic accounts from Memphis, Jackson, and New Orleans dailies, from the *Greenwood Commonwealth,* and from the *New York Times. Jet* magazine had good coverage of both the murder and the trial. Stephen J. Whitfield's *A Death in the Delta: The Story of Emmett Till* (Baltimore: Johns Hopkins University Press, 1988); Clenora Hudson-Weems's *Emmett Till: Sacrificial Lamb of the Civil Rights Movement* (Troy, Mich.: Bedford Publishers, 1994); and Juan Williams's *Eyes on the Prize: America's Civil Rights Years, 1954–65* (New York: Viking Press, 1987) were very helpful. David A. Shostak's "Crosby Smith: Forgotten Witness to a Mississippi Nightmare," in *Negro History Bulletin,* vol. 38 (December 1974), was important. Murray Kempton's courtroom dispatch, filed for the *New York Post* on September 22, 1955, is collected in *America Comes of Middle Age* (Boston: Little, Brown, 1963).

Bill Minor, a still-active Mississippi journalist, eighty and counting, of whom I will speak at greater length in my acknowledgments, covered the trial for the *New Orleans Times-Picayune,* and remembered for me the courtroom atmosphere. Because there are no extant trial transcripts, or at least none anyone can locate, a master's thesis done at Florida State University, in 1963, by Hugh Stephen Whitaker has become an important document. Whitaker had access to the transcripts before they were lost or deliberately destroyed, and he used portions of them throughout his work, which is titled "A Case Study in Southern Justice: The Emmett Till Case." Whitaker graciously duplicated and sent to me all 205 pages of his work. In addition, Whitaker's 1965 Florida State doctoral dissertation, "A New Day: The Effects of Negro Enfranchisement in Selected Mississippi Counties," was a helpful document, though not specifically for the Till case. Another thesis, done at the University of Texas at Dallas in 1996 by Charles R. Ealy, Jr., was helpful: "The Emmett Till Case: A Comparative Analysis of Newspaper Coverage." My interview with eighty-year-old John C. Whitten, Jr., was in December 1999 in his office. Across the street, in the Sumner courthouse, the circuit clerk showed me the big red bound books under the counter, and there, in blue ink, on page 45 of a volume entitled "General Docket and Fees and Subpoenas No. 4, State Cases, 2nd District, Tallahatchie County, Circuit Court, September 1955," were all the names of history in a case styled *State of Mississippi v. J. W. Milam & Roy Bryant.* John Ed Cothran's name was penned there, as a subpoenaed witness for the plaintiff. Seeing the name made the myth of Till more goose-bumping— although not nearly as goose-bumping as a letter that was sent to me after I had published an article about the murder and the trial in the *Washington Post.* The *Post* piece forms the basis for the prologue and the start of the epilogue of this book. That piece ran on February 27, 2000, which is the day that John Herbers, whom I will acknowledge at greater length later in these pages, sent me that letter. Herbers is the distinguished and retired *New York Times*man whom I mention in Part Two, now living quietly in suburban Maryland, but who, in 1955, was a shoe-leather reporter for United Press International, always on call, based for the wire service on his home ground of Mississippi. He was sent to cover the Till case, a big break and something that Herbers instantly understood, though he had no idea of what the case would truly become. Here is what Herbers wrote in his letter dated February 27, 2000, forty-five years after he experienced the trial with his own eyes.

UP sent me, a virtual beginner, from Jackson to cover it alone while the big papers were staffing it with their stars, INS [International News Service] with their famous trial reporter, James Kilgallen I think his name was, who had covered the Lindbergh kidnapping trial, and AP with two or more experienced reporters. . . . We had a telephone installed in the hallway of the first floor, the closest they would let us have to the courtroom. As the trial got underway and became a big story both nationally and abroad, the demand for last-minute developments increased dramatically. The wires would move five or six new leads every cycle. With every new development, I would have to leave the courtroom, run downstairs and phone it to Atlanta while the locals who could not get in the courtroom crowded round me to hear what I was dictating, then run back upstairs to the courtroom and get a fill on what I had missed from a reporter not under deadline pressure. In addition to that I was besieged by Atlanta with queries from around the globe—Paris and Tokyo and multiple American papers I remember quite well—saying something like their competition had an angle more sensational than we did and demanding we match it. . . . I did not know anyone there who thought the verdict would be any different than it was. The white attitudes we had surveyed before the trial told the story. I dropped by the Greenwood *Morning Star* (long since set) where I had had my first newspaper job to ask the publisher's opinion. He thought too much was being made of Till's tender age. "He may have been only 14 but I'm told he had a dong on him like this," elevating his forearm and dismissing any suggestion that the lynching was wrong. . . . I doubt Milam and Bryant could have continued to live in the Delta if they had not resorted to murder. Anyway by the end of the trial I had developed impressive leg muscles from running up and down the stairs. Exhausted and angry after the clean-up reporting I drank a beer, got in my car and headed for Jackson. A little ways out of Sumner I had a terrible feeling in the pit of my stomach. I wouldn't stop. All I could do was cry and I did for many miles.

Part One: Deeds of the Fathers

DYING BILLY

There are two extended portraits of Billy Ferrell—this one, and the one folded into Ty Ferrell's story in Part Three. An oral history—conducted by interviewer Vincent Clark, of the Center for Oral History and Cultural Heritage at the University of Southern Mississippi, on August 1 and August 12, 1997—was very helpful. In addition to members of Billy's extended family, and in addition to those whose names appear in the text, key interviews for understanding him and/or Natchez, past and present, were Tony Byrne, Premo Stallone, Alma Carpenter, Bob Dearing, Thomas Boo Campbell, Mamie Lee Mazique, Jerry McDaniel, Rev. Leon Howard, Rev. D. W. Howard, Justice Court Judge Mary Lee Toles, Lou Baroni, Don Simonton, and Cynthia Jardon. (Some of these appear by name and voice in the second portrait of Billy, in Part Three; some of their names will be repeated there.) Three old Mississippi highway patrolmen were helpful: Gwin Cole, J. D. Gardner, and Sonny Speight. The Teletype of July 5, 1961, to authorities in Jackson about nosy visiting collegians from New York, was found, as I note in the text, in the Sovereignty Commission Files, and the Teletype should be read in conjunction with a second document, written by a Sov-Com investigator, A. L. Hopkins, on July 18, 1961. Adams County Criminal Case Report 7074, eleven pages long, on the shootout at Lake Mary, including the closure order on the death of DeWayne Sampson Russell by County Judge Robert A. Bonds, was found in the files of the Adams County sheriff. As for Billy Ferrell's name on alleged Klan lists, see Archives and Special Collections, J. D. Williams Library, University of Mississippi—Box 13, Folder 7, Baroni Collection, under "Segregationist Material." (The citation in the finder guide is "List of Natchez individuals suspected of belonging to Klan.") In the Paul B. Johnson files at the University of Southern Mississippi, in the William D. McCain Library and Archives, there are several FBI lists of law enforcement officials suspected of belonging to the Klan. Billy's name is not on these. But in this same file is an undated list of names of cops and others, county by county, said to be in the Klan. This undated list of "Members" of the "Adams County Klavern" is placed after a 9/23/65 FBI list. Toward the bottom of the first column are the words "Ferrell, FNU."

LOST BOY

The portrait is drawn almost entirely from my own interviewing, essentially with members of Jim Garrison's family in Oxford, and with those who either worked with him at the fast-food restaurant in Corinth or knew him there. In addition to those whose names appear in the text, Larry Brinkley was especially helpful. His friend Jim's obituary ran July 9, 1986, in the *Oxford Eagle*.

GRIMSLEY

The most important sources for the portrait appear in the text. Their memories and voices were crucial, since Grimsley was long dead, as was Jim Garrison. However, in Grimsley's case, as opposed to Garrison's, there was a large paper trail. In addition to those who are in the text, Don Broadus, Frank Ely, Regina Hines, Jack Maples, Harry McDonald, Robert Oswald, and Robert A. Wilson were important sources for understanding either Grimsley or his saltwater town at the bottom of the state. Wilson is a retired FBI agent who was once a resident agent on the Gulf Coast, and who, as a private investigator, helped protect newspaperman Ira Harkey when Harkey felt his life was in jeopardy from Grimsley's henchmen. (He didn't really know Grimsley so much as he knew everything about him, in an investigative sense.) Wilson still lives on the Gulf Coast.

As for the redoubtable Harkey: I first came on Ira B. Harkey, Jr.'s *The Smell of Burning Crosses: An Autobiography of a Mississippi Newspaperman* (Jacksonville, Ill.: Harris-Wolfe Publishers, 1967) in the endnotes of John Dittmer's *Local People: The Struggle for Civil Rights in Mississippi* (Urbana: University of Illinois Press, 1994). The former work was crucial, and so was a weekend of hospitality and talk in Kerrville, Texas, in April 1998, with Harkey himself. (Harkey had some personal papers, which he provided, but he quickly directed me to the State Historical Society of Wisconsin; see below.) As I have suggested in the text itself, the latter work, *Local People*, was a biblical talisman for me throughout the entire project, helping me to grasp the story of civil rights in Mississippi in an almost geographical way: from Pascagoula in the south to Oxford in the north to points and regions in between. I spoke to Dittmer a couple of times on the phone during the project—he lived outside of Greencastle, Indiana, retired from the faculty of DePauw University—and am grateful for his direction and insights. Years ago, in Mississippi, Dittmer taught history at historic Tougaloo College in Jackson.

For the origin and history of the office of sheriff in America and in Mississippi, I consulted: Robert B. Highsaw, *Guidebook of the County Sheriff* (Oxford: Bureau of Public Administration, University of Mississippi Press, 1948); Robert B. Highsaw and Charles N. Fortenberry, *The Government and Administration of Mississippi* (New York: Thomas Y. Crowell, 1954); Henry C. Pepper, *Sheriff's Handbook* (Atlanta: School of Business Administration, University of Georgia, 1953); Walter H. Anderson, *A Treatise on the Law of Sheriffs, Coroners, and Constables* (Buffalo: Dennis & Co., 1941); The Brookings Institution, *State and County Government in Mississippi* (Washington, D.C.: The Brookings Institution, 1932). Critic Benjamin Schwarz's quote about sheriffs was in the *Los Angeles Times,* August 23, 1998. Mark Strand's quote on Hopper is taken from his *Hopper* (Hopewell, N.J.: Ecco Press, 1994), as are the other Strand quotes on Hopper that appear elsewhere in the book. John Szarkowski's statement about Eudora Welty's photographs was made March 23, 1992, and accompanies an exhibit of Welty's work on permanent display at the college library on the campus of Millsaps College in Jackson.

The bound transcripts of the February 1965 hearings of the United States Commission on Civil Rights are in the USCCR headquarters in Washington, along with bound volumes of various reports published later in the year, including the one titled *Law Enforcement: A Report on Equal Protection in the South.* (The commission also produced a forty-minute film on the hearings.) As noted, Ira Harkey's personal papers are in the State Historical Society of Wisconsin Library in Madison, a treasure trove on Harkey himself, on Grimsley, on Pascagoula, and on the Jackson County Citizens Emergency Unit. Regarding declassified documents from the FBI and the Civil Rights Division of the Department of Justice obtained through the provisions of the Freedom of Information/Privacy Acts: On December 8, 1999, the DOJ released to me a preliminary batch of papers on Grimsley and the JCCEU. On October 6, 1999, and again on February 29, 2000, the FBI in Washington released several hundred pages on Grimsley and the JCCEU. On June 21, 2000, the special agent in charge of the Jackson FBI released further pages. All of this material, with its many redactions and page omissions, is in my possession.

Finally, four books were of great importance to me not just for understanding the man in the center of this chapter but for a way of thinking about the whole narrative: C. Vann Woodward, *The Strange Career of Jim Crow,* 3rd rev. ed. (New York: Oxford University Press, 1974); James W. Silver, *Mississippi: The Closed Society* (New York: Harcourt, Brace & World, 1964); Robert Penn Warren, *Who Speaks for the Negro?* (New York: Vintage, 1966); and David J. Garrow, *Bearing the Cross: Martin Luther King, Jr., and the Southern Christian Leadership Conference* (New York: William Morrow, 1986).

JOHN HENRY, JIMMY, BOB

Key interviews for John Henry Spencer were John Burt, Sonny Clanton, Rev. Jim Vance, and Annie Lois Spencer. The Sov-Com documents relating to Taylor Ford are dated April 25, 1961, and May 2, 1961.

For Jimmy Middleton: Jim Scott Middleton, the sheriff's son, was the most important. In addition, six Claiborne County African-Americans—who either worked for Middleton directly or knew him before, during, or after the time he was sheriff—were helpful: Rev. James Dorsey, Hezekiah Ellis, James Gray, Nathan Jones, Elonzo McClorine, and John L. Moore. In addition, the following four people shed light on Claiborne County: Emma Crisler and David, Emilye, and Patty Crosby. Emilye, the daughter of David and Patty, is a history professor at the State University of New York, Geneseo. She wrote her doctoral dissertation on the civil rights movement in her home county, and that work is astute. There were also several important telephone conversations with her in 1999 about Claiborne County, and I am indebted as well to a piece that she wrote about her hometown in the journal *Southern Exposure:* "White Only on Main Street" (Winter 1990). Crosby's dissertation is "Common Courtesy: The Civil Rights Movement in Claiborne County, Mississippi," Indiana University, 1995. David and Patty still live in Port Gibson and fight the liberal cause in a town that has grudgingly come to terms with life after apartheid. The dates of the three Sov-Com documents relating to Middleton quoted or referred to in the text are, in order: January 30, 1961; September 18, 1961; and June 27, 1960.

For Bob Waller, his two living deputies, Willie Oubre and Gene Walters, were core interviews. (Walters, a gregarious and longtime Forrest County sheriff, who served after Waller, was hugely knowledgable on the history of Hattiesburg cops; he has his own small museum of law enforcement behind his house, including a whip from Parchman penitentiary made out of "a bull's dick," or so Walters said, with a gleam.) Others who either remembered Waller or were able to help with the flavor of Hattiesburg were Chip Edmonson, Francis Farmer, Sara Gillespie, Bud Gray, Sally McInniss, Robert Miller, and Bill Smith. Gray is an aged and gigantic and esteemed highway patrolman who held many head jobs in state law enforcement and also in Forrest County. He was at Oxford during the Meredith troubles. He pulled from an old yellowed envelope an even more yellowed newspaper clip from the *New York Times.* The clip was preserved in cellophane. Trooper Bud Gray's picture was on page 1 of the *Times,* September 27, 1962: a brush with immortality. "They came from all over the state to go up there, those sheriffs," he said, wrapping the paper back into its cellophane. "And when they got up there, they just laid under the shade. I don't know what they thought they was doing, going up there. Didn't do nothin'.'" Two Forrest County residents and professors at the University of Southern Mississippi—Neil McMillen, history; Noel Polk, literature—were helpful in numerous ways, although not specifically on Sheriff Bob Waller. I'm indebted to their scholarly writings and also to their hospitable conversation. (I will cite their work elsewhere.)

THE MAN WITH HIS BACK TURNED

The literature on Greenwood, Mississippi, is extensive—but you have to know where to look, since the Greenwood story is almost always tucked into larger stories of Mississippi during the struggle over civil rights. The following works, whether scholarly or popular, were important to my understanding of Greenwood and of the Greenwood movement and/or of the character of the Mississippi Delta itself: V. O. Key, Jr., *Southern Politics in State and Nation* (New York: Knopf, 1950); John Dollard, *Caste and Class in a Southern Town* (Garden City, N.Y.: Doubleday, 1957); Taylor Branch, *Parting the Waters: America in the King Years, 1954–1963* (New York: Touchstone Books, 1988); Branch, *Pillar of Fire* (New York: Simon & Schuster, 1998); Charles M. Payne, *I've Got the Light of Freedom: The Organizing Tradition and the Mississippi Freedom Struggle* (Berkeley: University of California Press, 1995); Sally Belfrage, *Freedom Summer* (Charlottesville: University Press of Virginia, 1965); James Forman, *The Making of Black Revolutionaries* (Seattle: University of Washington Press, 1997); Howell Zinn, SNCC: *The New Abolitionists* (Boston: Beacon Press, 1965); James C. Cobb, *The Most Southern Place on Earth: The Mississippi Delta and the Roots of Regional Identity* (New York: Oxford University Press, 1992); Tony Dunbar, *Delta Time: A Journey Through Mississippi* (New York: Pantheon, 1990); Howell Raines, *My Soul Is Rested: Movement Days in the Deep South Remembered* (New York: Putnam, 1977); Pat Watters and Reese Cleghorn, *Climbing Jacob's Ladder: The Arrival of Negroes in Southern Politics* (Harcourt, Brace & World, 1967); Clayborne Carson, *In Struggle: SNCC and the Black Awakening of the 1960s* (Cambridge, Mass.: Harvard University Press, 1981); Endesha Ida Mae Holland, *From the Mississippi Delta: A Memoir* (New York: Simon & Schuster, 1997); Townsend Davis, *Weary Feet, Rested Souls* (New York: Norton, 1998); Dittmer, *Local People;* Penn Warren, *Who Speaks for the Negro.*

Of dozens of other secondary sources I consulted for the chapter, I wish to cite three that were very important: The first is *Mississippi Black Paper: Fifty-seven Negro and White Citizens' Testimony of Police Brutality, the Breakdown of Law and Order, and the Corruption of Justice in Mississippi*, with a foreword by Reinhold Niebuhr and an introduction by Hodding Carter III (New York: Random House, 1965); second, Joseph Sinsheimer's interview with Sam Block in the journal *Southern Exposure*, vol. 25, no. 2 (Summer 1987), entitled "Never Turn Back: An Interview with Sam Block"; third, a long-playing audio recording entitled *Story of Greenwood, Mississippi*, Folkways Record FD5593. A twenty-three-minute black-and-white documentary, "The Streets of Greenwood," produced in 1963 by movement people Jack Willis, John Reavis, Jr., and Jack Wardenberg, was also helpful in terms of evoking the mood of that time and place. Crudely made, and all the better for it, the film intercuts interviews and SNCC personnel with footage of demonstrations in front of the courthouse. Greenwood cops, with their World War II helmets and riot sticks, are putting people into the back seats of squad cars. John Ed Cothran manages to stay out of the camera's eye, as was his way, but he is surely there. Regarding archival documents, the SNCC papers have the richest

Greenwood material, although they are only slightly ahead of John Rosenberg's private cache of old government documents. As I said above, almost all of these documents in Rosenberg's personal files concern Greenwood and Leflore County: affidavits, statistical portraits, lawsuit testimony, maps, pamphlets, field reports, sworn statements, newspaper clippings.

As for breathing sources: The wheel to make it all turn was John Ed, of course, but the smaller wheel within the bigger wheel was those who have known him in one capacity or another through the decades, directly or indirectly, in his family or out of it. Many of their names and voices appear in the text. The following, not in the text, were also important to an understanding either of Cothran or of Greenwood, past and present: Sara Criss, Lawrence Guyot, Jim Frazier, Rev. Aaron Johnson, June Johnson, Tim Kalich, Boyce Little, Gordon Lackey, Bud McGee, John Rosenberg, and Bob Salveson. Each was helpful in unexpected ways, and it is my regret that I couldn't find a way to tell some of their own stories within the text itself. For instance, William Bud McGee was one of fifty-eight blacks arrested by Sheriff Cothran in Itta Bena, right outside Greenwood, on June 18, 1963. Itta Bena is visible from U.S. 82 as a dust of trees and water tower. McGee lived on West Henry Street in Greenwood when he offered to show me around Itta Bena, which is where he'd been assigned during the movement. He took me through an impoverished little black section known locally as Balance Due—unconscious poetic expression for the cultural and spiritual dunning blacks have always suffered in Mississippi. McGee was a gospel deejay and a tax accountant; he'd once been a pin boy at the Greenwood bowling lanes—that is, before he came under the wing of organizer Sam Block. When I met him, so many years later, he had a kind of heh-heh, caving-in-on-himself chuckle. He was close to sixty and had lived in Leflore County all his life. After visiting Itta Bena, we drove out to the county work farm on the other side of Greenwood. He started laughing and recalled: "You'd say to the Shot, who's watching you with the gun, 'Gotta go to the bathroom here, Shot. Bumblebee here, Shot.' Shot says, 'You bigger than they are, boy. Finish your business.' Sometimes you have a good Shot, sometimes bad. You stay too long in the bushes, Shot would say, 'You better bring something back on a stick, boy.' " Gordon Lackey, from the list above, is a white man, and he was also helpful in forming indelible pictures of sixties Greenwood. In old AP wire stories, Gordon Mims Lackey had been identified as an alleged "kleagle," or organizer of the Mississippi White Knights of the KKK. In 1966, he was subpoenaed to come to Washington as a witness before the House Un-American Activities Committee. He took the Fifth on all questions related to alleged Klan activities or involvement. When I contacted him, he lived in a redbrick rancher on the "other side," on East Barton Avenue. He had me in, put on the coffee. He sat on a stool in his breakfast nook. He was coughing and hacking and wheezing. All he was back then, he said, was "politically active." His best Greenwood friend for many years had been Byron De La Beckwith, convicted slayer of Medgar Evers. I had old FBI reports in my possession in which Lackey allegedly had told a source for the Jackson bureau of the FBI that he, Lackey, had been involved in the shooting of Evers. All bull, Lackey told me, his voice growing menacing. He leaned close to my face, dragging on his cigarette, swilling black coffee, coughing. "I never asked Delay if he killed that damn nigger. And he never told me, neither." I asked him about John Ed. He broke into a grin. The sun was out suddenly. "Can't say too much bad about him as a lawman. Sorta kept outta sight. Buzzard arrested me one time for speeding when I was just a young punk. He called my damn daddy on me."

Some specifics: The war-diary tally of violence against SNCC was in a SNCC press release, March 20, 1964. Mayor Sampson's "nigger civic league" quote was in the *New York Times* on April 6, 1963. (The piece was by Claude Sitton, one of the most esteemed civil rights reporters in the country.) *Newsweek*'s "theater of war" piece was on April 8, 1963, by Karl Fleming (another heroic and early-on-the-scene civil rights reporter). Mayor Sampson's public statement about "agitators" was on March 29, 1963. The quote about Chief Lary is in Rev. William Wallace's oral history at the Moorland-Spingarn Oral History Collection, Howard University. The KKK Hate Sheet regarding Martin Luther King, Jr., is in the Race Relations Collection, "A Delta Discussion—Issue 2 of a Series," J. D. Williams Library, University of Mississippi. Paul Klein's affidavit is in Belfrage's *Freedom Summer,* among other books. For more on Mac Cotton's trial lasting five minutes and John Ed's refusal to answer questions, see Cotton's affidavit in *Mississippi Black Paper.* The information on Cotton suffering drip from his penis and a guard shouting, "You goddamn niggers shut up . . . ," comes from "Statement from Hollis Watkins in Parchman State Penitentiary," SNCC files. (This statement is titled, inaccurately, "Report: Greenville, Mississippi," dated October 5, 1963.) The dates of newspaperman Thatcher Walt's editorials quoted here are August 17, 1962, and March 2, 1963, both in the *Greenwood Commonwealth.* Sam Block and "the sheriff" and the spitting episode was in James Wechsler's *New York Post* column on March 19, 1963. John Ed's quote in *Newsweek,* "white people around here feel pretty mad" about Emmett Till's murder, ran on September 12, 1955. His supposed "disagreeing" with Clarence Strider appeared in *Jet,* September 15, 1955.

Photographs generally proved a fine catalyst for triggering John Ed Cothran's memory. That memory, as it edged toward ninety, could be startlingly precise, and also deliberately or undeliberately foggy, obscuring, misdirecting, and withholding. I didn't show him the copy of *Life* right away, although I had it in the car the first time I drove up. Eventually, I brought to his home reproduced copies of various photographs of John Ed relating to his days as a Greenwood lawman. We'd peer at them together, and stories would unlodge. I had collected numerous pictures from newspapers and magazines regarding the Emmett Till case and his role in it. (The first time I met him, he asked me if I could get him a "copy of that *Jet* book," with his picture in it.) The first time I showed him the picture in *Life,* he squinted at it and said, "Guess that's *shore* enough me, standing there with my back turned looking at Billy Ferrell." He asked what the white armband was for—I told him for identification. "Guess I forgot that part." He asked how I had found out the names. I told him that Ferrell, at our first meeting in 1997, had provided the names, and had shown me an old letter he'd sent to a Southern historian, who was doing his own research and had asked for the names. There was a slow curve of a smile from Cothran. "Didn't even know they took my picture that day. Don't even think I saw the durn photographer." He seemed to have forgotten that the image had appeared in *Life.* He seemed to think it was out of a newspaper.

Part Two: Filling Up the Frame

AMERICAN HAUNTING

The following are the core works I consulted for my own retelling of what happened when James Meredith integrated Ole Miss: Branch's *Parting the Waters* (his chapter "The Fall of Ole Miss" makes for brilliant, condensed reading); Silver's *Mississippi: The Closed Society;* Walter Lord's *The Past That Would Not Die* (New York: Harper & Row, 1965); David G. Sansing's *The University of Mississippi: A Sesquicentennial History* (Jackson: University Press of Mississippi, 1999); William Doyle's *An American Insurrection* (New York: Doubleday, 2001); James Meredith's *Three Years in Mississippi* (Bloomington: Indiana University Press, 1966); David J. Garrow's *Bearing the Cross: Martin Luther King, Jr., and the Southern Christian Leadership Conference* (New York: William Morrow, 1986); Constance Baker Motley's *Equal Justice Under Law* (New York: Farrar, Straus & Giroux, 1998); Victor Navasky's *Kennedy Justice* (New York: Atheneum, 1977); Nadine Cohodas's *The Band Played Dixie* (New York: Free Press, 1997); Russell H. Barrett's *Integration at Ole Miss* (Chicago: Quadrangle Books, 1965); Carl Brauer's *John F. Kennedy and the Second Reconstruction* (New York: Columbia University Press, 1977); William Manchester's *The Glory and the Dream: A Narrative History of America, 1932–1972* (New York: Bantam, 1975); Frederick S. Calhoun's *The Lawmen: United States Marshals and Their Deputies, 1789–1980* (Washington, D.C.: Smithsonian Institution Press, 1990); and Will D. Campbell's *And Also with You: Duncan Gray and the American Dilemma* (Franklin, Tenn.: Providence House, 1997).

A documentary film, *U.S. Marshals: The Real Story,* by Andrew Solt Productions, Los Angeles, was extremely helpful, especially hour one of the series, "Mission in Mississippi." It contains much newsreel and documentary footage. The Mississippi Department of Archives and History has 8-millimeter footage and audiotapes, as well as the papers of Ross Barnett and a good vertical file on the University of Mississippi. The John F. Kennedy Presidential Library in Boston, in Presidential Papers, President's Office Files, has audiotapes of conversations between JFK and Barnett, and RFK and Barnett. In the archives at Ole Miss, I consulted written transcripts as well as audio recordings under Presidential Recordings Transcripts, "Integration of the University of Mississippi." Navasky's *Kennedy Justice* makes expert, storytelling use of transcripts between RFK and Barnett, and I compared these to the actual declassified transcripts from the U.S. Marshals' Service that were obtained by Ole Miss professor of history Charles Eagles under the provisions of FOIPA. Also among the declassified papers released to Professor Eagles were voluminous shift reports, daily and weekly, filed by the men who guarded Meredith during his enrollment and in the months after, while he attended classes.

Regarding the history of lynching in the South and of the general mind-set of white male Southerners in postwar America, leading up to civil rights, I consulted: Dittmer's *Local People;* Cash's *The Mind of the South;* Lewis M. Killian's *White Southerners* (New York: Random House, 1970); Numan V. Bartley's *The Rise of Massive Resistance: Race and Politics in the South During the 1950s* (Baton Rouge: Louisiana State University Press, 1969); Dewey W. Grantham's *The South in Modern America: A Region at Odds* (New York: HarperCollins, 1994); Meredith's *Three Years;* Whitfield's *A Death in the Delta* (as with Branch's chapter on Ole Miss in *Parting the Waters,* Whitfield's lynching chapter, titled "The Ideology of Lynching," is essential reading); Neil R. McMillen's *Dark Journey: Black Mississippians in the Age of Jim Crow* (Urbana: University of Illinois Press, 1989); Grace Elizabeth Hale's *Making Whiteness: The Culture of Segregation in the South, 1890–1940* (New York: Pantheon, 1989); Leon F. Litwack's *Trouble in Mind: Black Southerners in the Age of Jim Crow* (New York: Knopf,

1998); Philip Dray's *At the Hands of Persons Unknown: The Lynching of Black America* (New York: Random House, 2002); James Allen, Hilton Als, John Lewis, and Leon F. Litwack's *Without Sanctuary: Lynching Photography in America* (Santa Fe, N.M.: Twin Palms Publishing, 2000); Stewart E. Tolnay and E. M. Beck's *A Festival of Violence* (Urbana: University of Illinois Press, 1995). For James Meredith's life in the unfathomable years after Oxford, my principal sources were newspapers in Jackson, Cincinnati, New York, Washington, D.C., and elsewhere; John Ed Bradley's 1992 Meredith profile in *Esquire;* Henry Hampton's 1987 PBS documentary series, *Eyes on the Prize*. Also at the Mississippi Department of Archives and History, I made use of an excellent vertical file on Meredith. My portrait of the man who took the picture, Charles Moore, derives both from original reporting and from a first-rate biographical essay that accompanies Moore's civil rights photo anthology, *Powerful Days*. The essay, in that long-overdue celebration of a documentarian whose work hasn't gotten nearly the attention it deserves, is by former *Life* correspondent Michael Durham, who knew and worked with Moore when they were both at risk in the South in the sixties.

As for interviews for this chapter, in addition to those whose names are in the text, I need mention these five for their overview insights about Mississippi: Charles Eagles, Neil McMillen, Bill Minor, Charles Sallis, David Sansing. Minor is a journalist; the others are historians of America but specialists in and even advocates, until they die, for the complexities of Mississippi. Finally, this note: One of the first lawmen in Mississippi I interviewed was Gwin Cole. He'd worked as an investigator for the highway patrol and was there at Oxford in his Raymond Chandler fedora and Telly Savalas bulk. He showed me a picture of himself, on page 186 of a chamber-of-commerce sort of tome called *Mississippi: Portrait of an American State*. We were sitting in a booth in a restaurant in Clinton, Mississippi. The old retired trooper lit up with a memory: "There was a fellow up there in a tree with a carbine that we never could get to. We couldn't find him that night. He'd let loose on the Lyceum building: *zattattatatat*. All that smoke and gas from that damn riot. I was three months getting that stuff out of my car."

Part Three: Hopes of the Sons

SOMETIMES TRASHY, SOMETIMES LUMINOUS

This chapter is the product of my own interviewing.

Of the people in this book, I feel I have come to know John Cothran the best. After I had been talking to him for three years, and after I knew his parents pretty well, too, I wrote to John's father: "Yesterday, Sunday, while you were in Moorhead with John Ed and Maudine, I was in Horn Lake with Johnny. We visited two hours. I brought him up to date. He said casually, without making a big deal of it, that his friend from work, Charles Hawkins, a black man, was coming over for a barbecue. They were having T-bones. I had met this Mr. Hawkins at the store myself. But that is a down-through-the-generations kind of parable, isn't it? Thick steaks in the backyard with a buddy from work who happens to be black. John is a terribly fascinating person for me—much screw-up in his life, no money, many mistakes. And yet a story like that."

THE DISTANCE FROM NATCHEZ, MISSISSIPPI, TO SANTA TERESA, NEW MEXICO

As with Greenwood, the literature on Natchez is extensive, but, again, that literature is often folded into larger treatments. Although I was bent primarily on achieving a narrative in the story of three generations of Ferrells—from Billy to Tommy to Ty—I recognized that that narrative had to be built in some way on the lush *external* history of the alluring river town in the southwest corner of the state. Professor Dittmer's *Local People* was important. A much more vertical and specific treatment is Jack E. Davis's *Race Against Time: Culture and Separation in Natchez Since 1930* (Baton Rouge: Louisiana State University Press, 2001). Professor Davis made manuscript pages of his book available before publication, for which I remain grateful. A long series of newspaper articles on the civil rights legacy of Natchez, in 1998, by journalist Stephanie Saul of *Newsday,* was helpful, and so was a scholarly historical piece by William Banks Taylor, "Southern Yankees: Wealth, High Society, and Political Economy in the Late Antebellum Natchez Region," in the *Journal of Mississippi History,* Summer 1997. The Sov-Com files are overflowing on Natchez and on Billy Ferrell. Billy's 1997 oral history with the University of Southern Mississippi was extremely useful. On August 31, 2000, Billy's FBI file (with its frustrating blackouts) was released to me through the provisions of FOIPA. The papers of SNCC, CORE, and the NAACP at the LOC have oceans of material on Natchez, including first-rate "background reports" on the town that had been prepared for the voter registration activists who went to work there in the sixties. Various reports by the United States Commission on Civil Rights relating to Adams County and Natchez were helpful, as they were elsewhere in this book, especially Chapter 2 of "Law Enforcement: A Report on Equal Protection in the South." I also profited from a publication entitled *The Present-Day Ku Klux Klan Movement,* a 1967 report stemming from 1966 hearings of the House Un-American Activities Committee. In this HUAC report are overviews of Natchez, its background, its Klan history. The transcripts of the HUAC hearings themselves, "Activities of the Ku Klux Klan in the U.S.," which are available in the LOC, produced a trove of Natchez material, just as they produced much Greenwood material. The hearings were held in Washington, D.C., on January 4–7 and 11–14, 1966. E. L. McDaniel's 1977 oral history with the University of Southern Mississippi was an important document. Jan Hillegas made available a document entitled "Adams County People Associated with Right-Wing Activities." Anthony Walton's *Mississippi: An American Journey* (New York: Knopf, 1996) has eloquent Natchez passages. Lastly, the archives of the *Natchez Democrat* were invaluable. The following people among those I interviewed shed particular light on the Ferrells or on Natchez, past and present: Lou Baroni, Tony Byrne, Thomas Boo Campbell, Alma Carpenter, Arlen Coyle, Bob Dearing, George Greene, Rev. D. W. Howard, Rev. Leon Howard, Jim Ingram, Dorie Ladner, Mark LeFrancis, Lewis Lord, Mamie Lee Mazique, E. L. McDaniel, Jerry McDaniel, Jerry Mitchell, Bruce Payne, Elizabeth Proby, J. T. Robinson, Don Simonton, Premo Stallone, William H. Terrell, Judge Mary Lee Toles.

IN THE FAMILY OF MEREDITH: LOVING WHAT IS THEIRS

This chapter is the product of my own interviewing, although, as should be obvious from the text, I am indebted to John Ed Bradley's December 1992 *Esquire* profile of James Meredith.

CONFEDERATE SHADOWS: GOOD SON

This chapter is the product of my own interviewing.

Epilogue: Hope and History Rhyming

James and Joe Meredith's interview with CNN, concerning Joe's graduation from Ole Miss, was on April 28, 2002. The story on James Meredith in the *Commercial Appeal* during the forthieth anniversary weekend was on September 29, 2002.

Interviews

Ronnie Agnew, Lou Baroni, Richard Barrett, Sherry Bernhard, Albert B. Britton, Jr., Sam Block, Larry Brinkley, Don Broadus, Anne Brooks, John Burt, Tony Byrne, Thomas Boo Campbell, Will Campbell, Alma Carpenter, Lindsay Carter, Sonny Clanton, Gwin Cole, Alice Cothran, Billy Cothran, John Cothran, John Ed Cothran, Maudine Cothran, MacArthur Cotton, Arlen Coyle, Emma Crisler, Sara Criss, David Crosby, Emilye Crosby, Patty Crosby, Bettie Dahmer, Ellie Dahmer, Vernon Dahmer, Jr., Charles Davis, Hiram Davis, Bob Dearing, Bill Dillon, John Dittmer, Nell Dogan, Rev. James Dorsey, Brad Dye, Charles Eagles, Chip Edmonson, Hezekiah Ellis, Frank Ely, Gray Evans, Francis Farmer, Christina Ferrell, Hazel Ferrell, William T. Ferrell, William T. Ferrell, Jr., William T. Ferrell III, Bill Ferris, Tyler Fletcher, Kelly Flynn, James Forman, Jim Frazier, J. D. Gardner, Sara Gillespie, Jim Gilliland, Susan Glisson, Vondaris Gordon, Rich Gorham, Bud Gray, James Gray, Jimmy Green, George Greene, Tony Greer, Lawrence Guyot, Dale Harkey, Ira B. Harkey, Jr., Evans Harrington, Barclay Harris, Bob Helfrich, Mary Katharine Hemphill, John Herbers, Regina Hines, Rev. D. W. Howard, Rev. Leon Howard, Dave Ingebretsen, Jim Ingram, Woodrow Jackson, Pat James, Cynthia Jardon, Rev. Aaron Johnson, June Johnson, Nathan Jones, David Jordan, Tim Kalich, Tim Kierstead, Nick Kip, Gordon Lackey, Dorie Ladner, Leon Lambert, Tanya Lambert, Ginger Lancaster, Joe Lee III, Mark LeFrancis, Boyce Little, Lewis Lord, Ella Jean Lucas, Tom Lyons, Jack Maples, Chuck Mayfield, Mamie Lee Mazique, Elonzo McClorine, E. L. McDaniel, Jerry McDaniel, Harry McDonald, Bud McGee, Kathleen McIlwain, Sally McInniss, Carolyn McLean, Joan McLemore, Leslie McLemore, Neil McMillen, Ed Meek, James Meredith, John Meredith, Joseph Meredith, Scott Merriner, Scott Middleton, Robert Miller, Bill Minor, Jerry Mitchell, Charles Moore, John L. Moore, Mike Moore, Willie Morris, Audine Stutts Nix, Willie Oubre, Bruce Payne, Wazir Peacock, Jim Peckham, Susan Plunk, Noel Polk, Pete Pope, Elizabeth Proby, Donald Quave, Bessie Randall, B. J. Ray, J. T. Robinson, John Rosenberg, Charles Sallis, Bob Salveson, David Sansing, Dub Shoemaker, Bill Simmons, Don Simonton, Bill Smith, Jerry Smith, Sonny Speight, Annie Lois Spencer, Premo Stallone, Jim Stephens, Alton Strider, William H. Terrell, Mary Lee Toles, Jimmy Travis, Rev. Jim Vance, Thelma Walt, Gene Walters, Hugh Stephen Whitaker, Ronnie White, John W. Whitten, Robert Wilson, William Winter, Ernest C. Withers, Tyrone Yates.

Acknowledgments

I have said at the end of other books that there is a real sense in which each one is only a record of those who have believed in it. Above, I have tried to name as many individuals as I can who were crucial in helping me gather material for a particular section. Here I would like to speak of those friends and family and colleagues who were there with their belief and support in a transcending way.

My spouse and two sons—Ceil, Matt, John—once again, they put up with the years of anxiety. Only occasionally would they ask about it. Usually, they just let the book-in-progress be, and in that silence I could hear the eloquence of their love and their trust that it would one day get done.

My former associates at the *Washington Post*—I worked happily on staff for twenty-three years and was always allowed to go off on book projects. On this project, I went off and didn't return. So, again, I wish to pay particular and final respect to these *Post* people: Ben Bradlee, Donald Graham, Leonard Downie, Robert Kaiser, Mary Hadar, David Von Drehle, Deborah Heard, Bobbye Pratt, Pam Kendrick, Robin Groom.

I want to thank friends and associates, old and new: Lysa Bennett, Carol Boston, Douglas Brinkley, Shelby Coffey, Greg Djanikian, Bill Gildea, Wil Haygood, Richard and Lisa Howarth, Howard Kohn, Denny May, Howell Raines, Elaine Rubin, Wendy Steiner, Kevin Willey, Mike Woyahn; my wonderful agent, Kathy Robbins, and her equally wonderful right arm at the Robbins Office, Inc., David Halpern; the Washington Theological Union, in Washington, D.C., a place of peace and justice that provided a book-writing office for three years—and, in particular there, Jim Coriden, Vincent Cushing, Rita Gibbons, Joe LaGressa, Dan McClellan.

There were Mississippi mentors, whether in Mississippi or not, and above all there were two: John Herbers and Bill Minor. They are brothers in a reporting fraternity that is as nearly select now as the brotherhood of ex-presidents: uncommonly courageous men who were present, writing it down in newspapers, from the dawn of the civil rights movement onward. Not only that, but both Herbers and Minor, who are also brothers in their generosity, have accomplished that nearly impossible thing: growing old gracefully in the hard and often dirty business of journalism. It's nearly inconceivable that I could have finished the project without their friendship and counsel. I want to single out two others, the first being the premier investigative journalist in the state, the second being a superb professor of American history at Ole Miss: Jerry Mitchell and Charles Eagles. Finally, there is David Halberstam, author of something like eighteen books, whose first reporting job out of college, almost five decades ago, was in West Point, Mississippi. He went on to fame for his work as a *New York Times* reporter in Vietnam and other places—but I think much of his life as a chronicler of our culture must have been formed as a kid from New York City who'd wound up in Mississippi. He remains a personal inspiration.

At Alfred A. Knopf I am grateful to Sonny Mehta, Carole Devine Carson, Iris Weinstein, Ida Giragossian, Paul Bogaards, Michelle Somers, and Ellen Feldman, but above all to my editor, Jonathan Segal. For Jon and myself, it's four books, twenty-three years, and counting. I have run out of ways to thank him for his friendship, his belief, his wit, his spare bedroom, his credit card at our favorite Manhattan restaurant, his astounding way with both a pencil and an idea. It has been a privilege.

Index

A Note on the Type

This book was set in a typeface called Primer, designed by Rudolph Ruzicka (1883–1978). Mr. Ruzicka was earlier responsible for the design of Fairfield and Fairfield Medium, Linotype faces whose virtues have for some time been accorded wide recognition.

The complete range of sizes of Primer was first made available in 1954, although the pilot size of 12-point was ready as early as 1951. The design of the face makes general reference to Linotype Century—long a serviceable type, totally lacking in manner and frills of any kind— but brilliantly corrects its characterless quality.

Composed by North Market Street Graphics, Lancaster, Pennsylvania

Printed and bound by R. R. Donnelley & Sons, Harrisonburg, Virginia

Designed by Iris Weinstein

Map by George Ward